MY ISRAEL QUESTION

ANTONY LOEWENSTEIN

MELBOURNE
UNIVERSITY
PRESS

MELBOURNE UNIVERSITY PRESS
An imprint of Melbourne University Publishing Ltd
187 Grattan Street, Carlton, Victoria 3053, Australia
mup-info@unimelb.edu.au
www.mup.com.au

First published 2006
Reprinted 2006 (twice)
Text © Antony Loewenstein 2006
Design and typography © Melbourne University Publishing Ltd 2006

Cover design by Andrew Budge, Designland
Text design by Phil Campbell
Typeset in Baskerville by TypeSkill
Index by Kerry Biram
Printed in Australia by Griffin Press, SA

National Library of Australia Cataloguing-in-Publication data:
Loewenstein, Antony.
    My Israel question.

    Bibliography.
    Includes index.
    ISBN 978 0 52285 268 4.

    ISBN 0 522 85268 8.

1. Arab–Israeli conflict. 2. Zionism. I. Title.

956.054

*To my parents, Violet and Jeffrey, who have
taken the bravest journey of all.*

CONTENTS

ACKNOWLEDGEMENTS

Writing a book of this scope is a collaborative affair. The idea of the lone writer issuing pages of perfect copy may be romantic, but it's hopelessly inaccurate.

Over the last two years, I've spoken to any number of people in Australia, the USA, Israel and Lebanon, all keen to challenge the accepted narrative of the Israel–Palestine conflict. Thank you especially to the following people for graciously giving their time and enthusiasm: Mohammed Alawi, Tariq Ali, Uri Avnery, David Bernstein, Barbara Bloch, Gidon Bromberg, Scott Burchill, the late Richard Carleton, Matthew Carney, Chantal Chalier, Noam Chomsky, Fadia and Said Daibes-Murad, Shraga Elam, Dror Etkes, Norman Finkelstein, Amira Hass, Jonathan Holmes, Jane Hutcheon, Gideon Levy, Robert Manne, David Marr, Chris McGreal, Alex Mitchell, Ed O'Loughlin, Jon Henley, Matan Kaminer, Ali Kazak, Randa Kattan, Ron Pundak, Stuart Rees, Tanya Reinhart, Craig Roberts, Mumammed Rodaina, Peter Rodgers, Amin Saikal, Chris Sidoti, Guy Spiegelman, Rod Webb, and Mara and Sam Wisel.

There are some whose names I am unable to mention—subject to personal and professional threats—but I thank them for standing up and being heard when it is much easier to remain silent.

Robert Fisk has been a constant source of inspiration, and his personal and public encouragement has given me much-needed strength.

John Pilger and Phillip Knightley have both supported my work from the beginning and continue to believe in the importance of dissent. I thank them for their wise words.

Margo Kingston took me under her wing and showed me the possibilities of courageous and campaigning journalism. If only more journalists shared her belief.

Cath James was my invaluable transcriber and part-time researcher. I thank her for her patience and word-perfect skills.

Macquarie University's Andrew Vincent bravely offered me a position on the board of Macquarie University's Centre for Middle East and North African Studies. Andrew knows a thing or two about not accepting the dominant narrative of history.

Any number of friends have offered words of advice, encouragement, criticism and challenges, and I dearly hope they never stop. I would like especially to thank Tanveer Ahmed, Rory Buck, Marni Cordell, Peter Cronau, Sharon De Silva, Clinton Fernandes, Iain Giblin,

Edwina Hanlon, Emily Howie, Mark Jeanes, Karen Middleton, Mariesa Nicholas, Rachel Nicolson, Emma Oshlack, Jack Robertson, Selena Papps, Peter Slezak and Helga Svendsen.

Israel's finest historian, Ilan Pappe, agreed to read the history of Zionism chapter and offered expert advice.

Thanks to the various experts, readers and advisers who have provided invaluable assistance on the manuscript, ironing out bugs and improving clarity.

My agent Lyn Tranter has been with me since (nearly) the beginning and always provides a no-nonsense approach. I thank her for standing by me in recent years.

Melbourne University Publishing director Louise Adler has been a strong supporter since the very beginning. I knew she would 'get' the material. She has provided that, and more. Publishing a dissenting book on the Israel–Palestine conflict guarantees an abusive and vitriolic response, so I thank Louise for understanding the importance of doing so.

My invaluable editor, Sybil Nolan, helped to reshape and restructure the book in your hands. Her patience and insights have been nothing short of extraordinary.

Thanks to copy editor Lucy Davison and project coordinator Wendy Skilbeck for their care during the vitally important last stages of the book. The MUP team have also been invaluable in ensuring a smooth birth.

My partner, Liz, has often suffered an absent boyfriend over the last years. Her seemingly endless support, honesty and love have guided me through many dark days. I've never met a woman like her. To the Wise family and Ibolya Stark: thank you for your generosity and encouragement.

My parents, Violet and Jeffrey, have given more than any only child could ever hope for. Their strength, in the face of irrational personal setbacks, has shown me that there is a price to pay for speaking uncomfortable truths. Their personal journeys have taken them further than anyone else I know. I couldn't have done this book without them.

Finally, to the hundreds of people who have written to me in recent years, read my articles and blog, and challenged and provoked me, I hope this conversation is only just beginning.

ISRAEL AND THE OCCUPIED TERRITORIES

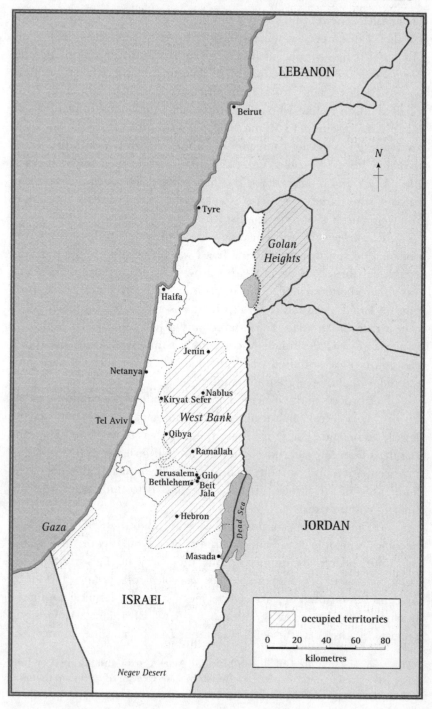

LEBANON

Beirut

Tyre

Golan
Heights

Haifa

Jenin

Netanya

Nablus
Kiryat Sefer

Tel Aviv

West Bank

Qibya

Ramallah

Jerusalem Gilo
Bethlehem Beit
Jala

Gaza

Hebron

Dead Sea

JORDAN

Masada

ISRAEL

occupied territories

0   20   40   60   80
kilometres

Negev Desert

INTRODUCTION

From the moment I first entered public debate over the Israel–Palestine conflict, I discovered it wasn't possible to tread carefully—people still got upset. I had simply suggested, in an article in the *Sydney Morning Herald*, that the Israeli occupation of Palestinian land must end if there was to be any chance of a comprehensive peace. In response, I was accused, often by Jews who chose to remain anonymous, of being a self-hater and antisemite. In March 2006, a few months before the book you are reading was released, a reader of online magazine *New Matilda* wrote that they hoped it would 'lie in the tip alongside such other works as *Mein Kampf* and the *Protocols of the Elders of Zion*'. The message was clear. Anyone who dared to criticise Israel would receive threats and abuse. You were either with us or against us.

My Israel question reframes the Israel–Palestine conflict from a very personal perspective. As a liberal Jew, I was brought up to question the established historical narrative, but it wasn't until my late teens that I was able to better articulate my opposition to the accepted Jewish position on Israel. I wanted to know why it was almost treasonous to advocate a Palestinian state. I wondered why a Jew couldn't be both pro-Israeli and pro-Palestinian. And I couldn't understand why dissenting viewpoints were shunned and ridiculed. It almost seemed as if Jews wanted to maintain a ghetto mentality.

This process of discovery led me to a broader understanding of the historical, political, financial and psychological connection to the Jewish homeland. The more I saw, the further removed I felt from the standard line. After all, how could the long-suffering Jewish people justify occupation and brutality against the indigenous inhabitants of the land? One of the things this book attempts is to understand this disturbing conundrum.

My Israel question examines the ways in which the Palestinians have become 'unpeople',* seemingly unworthy of sympathy or understanding. 'Our' people are important, but 'they' are not. This narrative has been constructed through a complex web of media, politics and lobbying, and has resulted in a skewed perspective on the defining conflict of our time. I spoke to Arabs, Palestinians, Jews, Christians, Muslims and atheists in Australia, the USA, Lebanon, Israel, Palestine, France, the

---

*This term was first used by British historian Mark Curtis, and adopted by John Pilger, as a word to describe victims of Western state-sponsored terrorism that is all but ignored in the West.

United Kingdom and Switzerland to hear alternative voices, possible solutions and legitimate grievances. Some will be familiar; many will not. Many of these individuals risk ostracism from their own communities for speaking out.

As I delved deeper into the Jewish community in Australia—and received growing amounts of hate mail—I became aware that the current Israeli path was unsustainable. How could a democratic state maintain a brutal occupation over another people for nearly 40 years? But I was heartened by the amount of support I received from concerned citizens, Jews and non-Jews, who saw the conflict through the paradigm of colonialism, and I had little choice but to agree.

My Israel question is a plea for mutual respect and understanding. One of the most powerful messages I heard over and over again during my travels around Israel and Palestine was that neither side thought the other cared about its stories or suffering. This made reconciliation next to impossible. In an age of political unilateralism—an arrogant concept, deliberately designed to subjugate one people to another—we must move past using dehumanisation and delegitimisation as weapons to be wielded against the Palestinians.

I support the state of Israel and believe in its existence. This book examines how much Zionism—the ideology of Jewish nationalism—is to blame for this intractable conflict. There must be a way for Israel to exist securely while allowing justice for the Palestinian people. A sustainable future for Israel and the Palestinians is my central concern.

I am often accused of being anti-Israel and hostile towards the Jewish people. Nothing could be further from the truth. I support the rights of Israelis to live in peace and security, but not at the expense of the Palestinians. Why do we constantly hear about Israel's need for 'security', as though that justifies erecting walls, checkpoints and barriers? Why is the world told to believe that the Palestinians should only accept peace on Israel's terms? I've come to the sad realisation that many in the West simply don't like Arabs or Palestinians very much and therefore believe that we have the right to treat them as we wish.

In all of this, the news media play a crucial role since they are the major conduit for the debate. This book is as much about the media and their role as it is about the Zionist lobby.

It is time for a radical rethinking of the conflict.

GETTING PERSONAL ABOUT ISRAEL

THE ASHRAWI SCANDAL

*Remember the solidarity here and everywhere in Latin America,
Africa, Europe, Asia and Australia, and remember that there is
a cause to which many people have committed themselves,
difficulties and terrible obstacles notwithstanding. Why?
Because it is a just cause, a noble ideal, a moral quest for
equality and human rights.*

Edward Said, 2003[1]

HANAN ASHRAWI IS A Palestinian and an advocate of the Palestinian cause, an intellectual and a moderate who once served in Yasser Arafat's Palestinian Cabinet, but resigned complaining of corruption in its ranks. A resident of the West Bank city of Ramallah, Ashrawi is Christian and a feminist activist, and has worked for more than 30 years for the establishment of an independent Palestinian state. Like another prominent Arab intellectual, the late Edward Said, she is able to address Western audiences on their own terms.

In 2003, Ashrawi was named as the sixth recipient of the Sydney Peace Prize, and a noisy controversy broke out in Australia. Opponents of her selection fought a battle both in the news media and behind the scenes to stop Bob Carr, the Premier of New South Wales, from presenting the Palestinian with her award. When Ashrawi finally arrived in Sydney to accept her award, she commented that she had never before faced such a barrage of abuse, distortions and slander from the Zionist lobby.[2]

Serious questions remain about the lobbying that occurred during the Ashrawi affair, and the role of this kind of behaviour in Australian democracy. At the heart of the controversy was the political and military situation in Israel–Palestine, and the way in which this fraught conflict is represented in the West. The saga of the 2003 Sydney Peace Prize is a fascinating case study of the operation of the Zionist lobby in this country. For me, it also represented the start of a journey into personal controversy, which led me to question the way the debate about Israel is presented in Australia, and ultimately to write this book. Looking deeper into the Ashrawi scandal, I became determined to challenge the Zionist reading of the conflict and to present an alternative perspective. I also felt obliged to defend a moderate Palestinian from politically motivated slurs.

The prize

Established in 1997, the Sydney Peace Prize aims to honour people who have made an outstanding contribution to advancing human rights, including contributions 'to building democracies within organisations and government' and 'support for the philosophy and practice of non-violence'. The prize is worth A$50 000 and in 2003 was financially supported by the City of Sydney, mining giant Rio Tinto, finance corporation Citigroup, legal firm Gilbert & Tobin, and Kerry Packer's publicly listed company PBL. An executive committee selects the winner, and other recipients include Archbishop Desmond Tutu, Xanana Gusmao, Sir William Deane, Mary Robinson and Arundhati Roy.

Announcing Hanan Ashrawi's award in August 2003, the director of the Sydney Peace Foundation, Emeritus Professor Stuart Rees AM, director of the Centre for Peace and Conflict Studies at the University of Sydney and author of several books on peace and conflict resolution, wrote that Ashrawi had been 'a leader in dialogue with Israelis, with Americans, Europeans and within Palestinian communities. Her life and work are distinguished by her courage and the spiritual strength required to negotiate just outcomes to personal, national and international conflicts'. The *Sydney Morning Herald* (*SMH*), announcing her selection,[3] featured messages of support for Ashrawi from Mary Robinson and Desmond Tutu. 'No one could be more deserving of this prestigious award', Tutu said. The newspaper's story also presented a number of dissenting views, including one from Jeremy Jones,[4] president of Executive Council of Australian Jewry (ECAJ), which hinted at the trouble that lay ahead. Jones said the Sydney Peace Foundation had been 'blinded by celebrity', and he accused the Palestinian of being 'an old style propagandist'.

It was not long before the *Australian Jewish News* (*AJN*), Australia's mainstream Jewish weekly newspaper, entered the debate. On 5 September, the paper reported that the New South Wales Jewish Board of Deputies (NSW JBD)—the official umbrella body of that state's Jewish community—would consult with various Jewish groups to determine an appropriate response. President of the NSW JBD, Stephen Rothman, argued that Ashrawi was an unsuitable recipient of the award, and suggested that the Sydney Peace Foundation 'has sought to be provocative in order to engender greater publicity than would otherwise be the case, and we are mindful that anything we do ought not to encourage such an approach'.

On 23 September, *AJN* journalist Allon Lee contacted Bob Carr's director of communications, Walt Secord, questioning the premier's attitude to the award. Lee's email read like a prepared script and included false claims such as 'Ashrawi doesn't support a two-state solution' and 'she rarely condemns violence against Israelis'. This email signalled the start of a concerted campaign to convince Carr not to present the award to Ashrawi. It concluded:

> Question: Does Premier Bob Carr feel comfortable presenting a peace prize awarded to an individual who, it is claimed, has expressed sentiments and supported actions of a violent nature up until the present time, especially in light of Premier Carr's comments that 'until you [the Palestinians] chase out the murderers in your midst, and people who detonate bombs who take innocent lives, then there won't be a peace process'?

Within weeks virtually every mainstream Jewish organisation was expressing its opposition to the award. The Australia/Israel and Jewish Affairs Council (AIJAC) shouted the loudest. A staunchly Zionist lobby group with strong ties to the Liberal Party and Australian Labor Party (ALP), the Melbourne-based organisation is arguably the most effective Australian lobby group against Palestinian advocacy of any kind. Executive director Colin Rubenstein and national chairman Mark Leibler are both close to the Howard government. In the years since the attacks on September 11 2001, they have strongly advocated strengthening anti-terror laws, invading Iraq and warned Iran, all policies shared by John Howard and his senior ministers.

Almost from the outset of the Ashrawi affair, the most extreme objections to the award originated in Melbourne's Jewish community, with Sydney providing a more conciliatory tone. The Jewish leadership in both cities shared a similar goal, but their strategies differed. Melbourne (and AIJAC in particular) favoured a more direct, even aggressive, approach, apparently hoping to shame Ashrawi supporters into changing their views. They sought to bully Rees, the Sydney Peace Foundation, politicians, journalists and the broader Jewish community. Attempting to convince Bob Carr to withdraw from the presentation, Mark Leibler commented bluntly in *AJN* in late September: '[Carr] is a friend of Israel and the Jewish community. It is a mistake of judgement. I wonder to what extent he was properly briefed'.

Ashrawi's record: the allegations and the facts

Opponents of Ashrawi's award repeatedly described her selection as ill informed. Yet the same criticism could be levelled at them, for few of the combatants in the controversy seem to have seriously investigated the public record to assess her worthiness for the prize.

In early October, Sam Lipski, a prominent former *AJN* editor, used his regular column space in the paper to attack Ashrawi's record, accusing her of being an 'absolutist and rejectionist' in relation to the conflict, and someone who ultimately believes that Israel has no place in the Middle East. This is demonstrably untrue. He claimed that Ashrawi's stance is little different from that of Hamas and the Islamists because she believes 'Israel itself—not the occupation, not the settlers, not the borders—is the problem'. In fact, she has principally campaigned against the occupation since 1967, forming Miftah, a Palestinian group pushing for human rights, in 1998.[5] Lipski also suggested that Ashrawi had described the Holocaust as a 'deceitful myth', a claim that he retracted in the following issue: 'I have subsequently been advised that [she] did not make the statement'.[6] Lipski's stature in the community gave Ashrawi's enemies traction they didn't deserve. After all, the false allegation that she denies six million Jewish deaths in the Holocaust and the right of Israel to exist struck at the very heart of Australian Jewish belief.

Ashrawi has long believed in peaceful coexistence between Jews and Palestinians.[7] She identifies Israel's continued occupation of most of the territories it seized in the 1967 Six Day War as the main source of Palestinian angst, and believes that legitimate resistance is both acceptable and just. She has described Palestinian demands for only a fraction of mandate Palestine as a 'historic compromise',[8] and calls for Israel to cease building settlements and to return stolen land. Her critics refuse to accept Ashrawi's central claim: that Israel must acknowledge its role in Palestinian dispossession.[9] While she served in Yasser Arafat's Palestinian Liberation Organisation (PLO) Cabinet in a variety of roles, she has remained independent and has won a seat for the 'Third Way' Party in the 2006 Palestinian elections.

Ashrawi is also critical of most US-led peace initiatives. 'The Palestinian people feel victimised by this "peace process"', she said in 2000. 'The "process" is reinvented all the time to suit Israel. And America thinks as long as there is a "process", God is in his heaven. Now the Americans are indulging in crisis management and individual legacies— the people in Washington have come to the end of their careers'.[10] She once observed—accurately, as it turned out—that the Oslo Accords 'could lead to a disaster or a state. It's not an agreement, remember. It says specifically that it is a "declaration of principles"'.

Her public statements are those of a passionate defender of the Palestinian cause, and reveal her fierce anger towards a Western media that often blame the victims for the region's troubles and for Israel's belligerence. Her critics have used her anger against her, citing it as evidence that she hates Israel. She has even been labelled an 'Arab apologist for terrorism'.[11] Ashrawi refuses to accept the 'myth of the generous offer, with a typical patronising mentality of the occupier against the occupied: You have to be grateful for whatever we dish out'.[12] Such proud Palestinian nationalism strikes at the heart of Zionist myths and presumptions.

Yet Yasser Arafat's death in November 2004 cast an interesting light on the nuances of Ashrawi's attitude, and on her role as a voice of caution and moderation in the political, diplomatic and military conduct of the Palestinian cause. In an interview with the eminent Middle East correspondent Robert Fisk, Ashrawi reveals her willingness to stand up and question the status quo:

'I was the only one who would call him up and say he was wrong,' she told me. 'I would say, "Mr. Chairman, this is wrong, this will not work." And after, his advisers would come to me and say, "How can you speak to the Chairman like that? How dare you criticize him." But someone had to.'[13]

It was clear that Ashrawi sees herself as someone who will not blindly follow the Palestinian program.

Nevertheless, she was publicly loyal to the elected Palestinian leader. In the days before Arafat's death, Ashrawi spoke to the ABC's *Lateline* program and praised Arafat in the face of US and Israeli isolation. She highlighted the Israeli and US mistake of blaming the failed peace process on Arafat alone. 'The Americans took their cue from Sharon and decided to ostracise Arafat', she said, 'even though they claim to be democratic, but they refuse to accept the democratic choice of the people who freely elected President Arafat'.[14]

The controversy erupts

Within weeks, the row over Ashrawi's award was being reported in the national press and in Sydney and Melbourne's daily papers.[15] On 13 October, in his weekly column in the *Australian*, political commentator Glenn Milne reiterated the Jewish community's deep misgivings in relation to Ashrawi.[16] Taking his cue from a recent AIJAC press release—even copying significant quotes—Milne warned Bob Carr of the consequences if he presided at the awards ceremony, namely Jewish community displeasure with the ALP. Carr has said since that former ALP powerbroker Laurie Brereton advised him to stand firm in the face of this lobbying. 'It's very important that you don't be seen to pull out of this', Brereton reportedly told Carr. Brereton claimed that AIJAC's Colin Rubenstein had his 'hand all over this'.[17]

But AIJAC wasn't the only part of the Zionist lobby getting busy. On 22 October, Sydney's Mayor, Lucy Turnbull, withdrew the City of Sydney's support for the Peace Prize, arguing that Ashrawi was an unsuitable choice. In a letter sent to Professor Stuart Rees, Turnbull cited many problems with Ashrawi, including her 'opposition to the "Road Map to Peace"' and her voting 'against the Oslo Peace Accord and a two-state solution in the Middle East'. The *SMH* reported rumours that Lucy Turnbull's decision was influenced by her husband Malcolm Turnbull's bid for Liberal preselection in Wentworth, a federal seat in Sydney, which reportedly has the second highest percentage of Jews in the country. Professor Rees claimed that 'the row was being used against [Turnbull's] campaign to win ... preselection'. The *SMH* also reported that the other corporate sponsors continued to support the award.

However, over the following weeks all the sponsors were targeted, and Rees himself soon received a barrage of abuse. Hundred of letters were sent to his office, and the ferocity of some calls and emails suggested a coordinated campaign to stifle any views that were opposed to the dominant Zionist line. Photographs of dead babies, presumably killed by suicide bombers, landed on his desk with the message 'Are you a party to this?' Some emails asked how Rees could live with his conscience.

The most revealing piece of journalism published during the affair was by *SMH* columnist Alan Ramsey. On 25 October, he exposed an alleged campaign, orchestrated by unnamed powerful figures, which had targeted Lucy Turnbull, the University of Sydney, Stuart Rees and the prize's corporate sponsors. Kathryn Greiner, wife of former Liberal premier Nick Greiner, was chairwoman of the Sydney Peace Foundation. Ramsey's column featured a transcript of a phone conversation between her and Rees,[18] which included discussion of the possible ramifications if the foundation continued its support of Ashrawi:

Kathryn Greiner: 'I have to speak logically. It is either Hanan Ashrawi or the Peace Foundation. That's our choice, Stuart. My distinct impression is that if you persist in having her here, they'll destroy you.'

Stuart Rees: 'You must be joking. We've been over this a hundred times. We consulted widely. We agreed the jury's decision, made over a year ago, was not only unanimous but that we would support it, together.'

KG: 'But listen, I'm trying to present the logic of this. They'll destroy what you've worked for. They are determined to show we made a bad choice. I think it's [billionaire businessman] Frank Lowy's money.'

SR: 'I won't be subject to bullying and intimidation. We are being threatened by members of a powerful group who think they have an entitlement to tell others what to do. This opposition is orchestrated. The arguments are all the same.'

Ramsey's column exposed the threats and intimidation that occur when a Palestinian gains international credibility and presents an alternative reading of the conflict. After the column appeared, Greiner refused to comment.[19] Lowy did likewise, until the end of November, when he admitted to calling Carr to ask why he had supported Ashrawi.[20] He said he'd disagreed with Carr on his stance and refused to speculate whether he would act differently if 'another Palestinian advocate' were awarded a similar prize.

This would not be the last time that Frank Lowy's name would come up in relation to lobbying around the prize. Lowy, a billionaire Jewish businessman who arrived penniless in Australia from Israel—where he had fought in the Jewish underground in Palestine, the Haganah—is chairman and co-founder of the global shopping giant Westfield. He was a board member of the Reserve Bank of Australia (1995–2005), heads the Football Federation Australia Limited and is a strong advocate for Israel. He founded the Lowy Institute for International Policy in 2002 as a gift to his 'adopted country'.[21] Carr has described him as Australia's most successful immigrant.[22]

Two days after Ramsey's column appeared, Malcolm Turnbull indignantly denied the suggestion that his own political battles had influenced his wife's decision to withdraw the city's support for the Sydney Peace Prize. 'Lucy's critics do not countenance for a second that she's exercised independent judgement or independent intellect or conscience', he told the *SMH*. 'She's either a pawn of her husband or the pawn of the Jewish lobby. And that is both misogynistic and anti-Semitic, and it's sickening.' (In a letter to the editor, a reader asked, 'How can Malcolm Turnbull brand comments by Professor Stuart Rees as "misogynistic and anti-Semitic", when this year's winner is a woman and a Semite?'[23])

The paper reported that Lucy Turnbull denied experiencing pressure from Zionist groups, but acknowledged that Frank Lowy had congratulated her on her stance: 'He said, "thank you for being so brave and supporting us. We're very worried about Hanan Ashrawi winning the Peace Prize." Well, I did a lot of work on this, Frank, and thought it was the right thing to do'. She went on: 'What became very clear to me is that she [Ashrawi] is a very strong proponent and polemicist for the Palestinian cause'.

Malcolm Turnbull went on to win his preselection battle (and the seat). Months later, when he began his election campaign in Wentworth, he spoke at the Jewish National Fund in Melbourne, an organisation dedicated to providing infrastructure and trees for Israel. While accepting and defending Israeli government tactics, he continued to defend his wife's actions over Ashrawi: 'Lucy is not anti-Palestinian. But Lucy, like many others (Jews and gentiles) who considered the matter objectively, recognised Dr Ashrawi as an effective but often savage spokesperson for one side in an increasingly bitter struggle'.[24]

On 28 October, the federal Minister for Health, Tony Abbott, entered the Ashrawi debate by suggesting she was an unsuitable recipient because 'she has not been active in promoting the road map [for peace]'.[25] He argued for stronger ties between Israel and Western democracies as 'September 11 demonstrated that Israel and the West not only have common values but also share vulnerability to similar enemies'. Responding to Ashrawi's supporters in Australia and to critics of Israeli actions in the occupied territories, Abbott pushed for a black and white reading of the situation: 'What is it, then, to proclaim moral equivalence between an Israeli leadership striving to preserve a liberal, pluralist democracy and a Palestinian leadership running a one-party statelet dedicated to destroying its neighbour?'

Although the Prime Minister, John Howard, and the Minister for Foreign Affairs, Alexander Downer, also publicly expressed their reservations about the award, Abbott offered one of the strongest repudiations of Ashrawi by a member of the federal government. His position on Israel is similar to the views of many of his Liberal colleagues. Although he has rarely commented on the subject publicly, he sympathises with Israel and with its post–September 11 fight against 'terrorism'. 'When the passenger jets tore into the World Trade Center and the bombs ripped through Bali night clubs', he told the Victorian Zionist Council, 'the rest of the Western world began to experience what it has long meant to be an Israeli. Far from demonstrating the dire consequences of supporting Israel, these atrocities reveal the extent to which Westerners are all Israelis now'.[26]

Online political magazine *Crikey* reported that, after making this speech, Abbott joked that Colin Rubenstein had vetted it, asking, 'Did I get anything wrong? Colin, you better correct it so I get the script right'.[27] The *Australian* asked Abbott why he had consulted Rubenstein and he said he had 'asked Colin to have a look at the speech on the Middle East because he's an expert in a way I'm not'. Abbott surely knew what suggestions Rubenstein would make.

ABC Radio's *Religion Report* weighed into the debate on 29 October, when presenter Stephen Crittenden spoke to Yael Dayan, member of the left-wing Meretz Party in the Israeli Knesset and daughter of the famous Israeli general Moshe Dayan. Dayan defended Ashrawi, saying that it was 'more difficult to be a Palestinian peacemaker than an Israeli peacemaker':

> The fact is that Israel is also doing some immoral things, and we are doing selected shooting, targeted shooting, and none of that's denounced. It's a war, and the question is whether we advance the dialogue towards peace. And this Hanan Ashrawi ... she has some obstacles which we have to understand: being a woman in a patriarchal society, and being a Christian in a

Muslim society, I think she's very courageous, and she contributes quite a lot to the peace process.

Dayan's statement of support was one of the few offered by a prominent Jew during the controversy—the media simply ignored other Israeli supporters of Ashrawi. Since the main debate within the local Jewish community was over tactics, Dayan's comments are of special significance. Her desire not to demonise a Palestinian woman simply because of her background stands in stark contrast to the tenor of the local debate, in which the leading local Jewish organisations have demonstrated their unease with the prospect of any Palestinian winning a prize or being elevated to a position of influence.

The *Religion Report* also featured a statement on Ashrawi by the Committee for Accuracy in Middle East Reporting in America (CAMERA), a Jewish media-monitoring organisation based in the USA. Echoing the tone and attitude of many Australian critics of Ashrawi, the statement suggests actions to counter the media's supposed love affair with the Palestinian advocate:

> Action items: Whenever Hanan Ashrawi levels her usual charges, be ready to counter them. If a newspaper has published an op-ed by Ashrawi, write a brief letter to the editor, countering her main point. Also, let the op-ed editor know that Ashrawi brazenly distorts and misrepresents so many facts that *it's a disservice to readers to publish her* [my italics]. If Ashrawi is on a broadcast that takes calls, phone in and factually challenge her assertions. Be sure to ask at the outset that she respond to your question, rather than launching into one of her patented filibusters.

The AIJAC also published a 'fact sheet' about Ashrawi, which includes claims that she frequently engages in anti-Israel rhetoric and is 'not a moderate in any Western sense of the word'.[28] The publication suggests that she is at 'best ambiguous about a two-state solution' and that her criticism of violence against Israelis is pragmatic rather than ethically motivated. In fact, she has questioned the validity of the US-imposed 'peace-process' because, as she told Robert Fisk in 2000,[29]

> we are all being fed well-worn phrases: 'peace process', 'back on track', 'ceasefire', 'time-out', 'put an end to violence', 'Arafat to

restrain/control his people', 'do we have the right peace partner?' This is a racist way of looking at the Palestinians and it obscures the fact that we've suffered an Israeli occupation all along.

She also told Fisk that, while she was against suicide bombing, Palestinians nevertheless 'want the right to resist occupation and injustice'. For the AIJAC, such statements prove her support for 'terrorism'.

November brought a bizarre development. Splashed across the front page of the *Australian* was a story about a senior Australian army officer serving in Baghdad, Colonel Mike Kelly, who had written to Bob Carr arguing that the premier's support of the award 'encouraged the kind of terrorism that I and my colleagues in the Coalition Forces are engaged in fighting'. The email had been received by Carr's office on 9 October. Kelly, a senior adviser to the forces in Iraq, wrote that, while he was a long-standing member of the ALP and a

> staunch ALP voter ... I find your action at the least naïve and misguided but in my opinion it amounts to a betrayal of the service personnel in the field, negating the sacrifices that are being made by them ... It would be hard to explain to a solider here who has just lost both legs in a terrorist attack why an Australian State Premier (supposedly an ally in this war) has been in effect comforting the enemy.

Bob Carr responded tartly in the *SMH* on 3 November:

> Mike Kelly ought to understand the mission. The Australian mission in Iraq is not to engage in a war with the Arab world or the Palestinians but to remove Saddam Hussein and find and destroy weapons of mass destruction ... If he's clanking around in colonel's regalia [and] not understanding the mission of the Australian Government in Iraq, then he ought to read the Prime Minister's speeches.[30]

Carr by this stage was certain that public opinion favoured even-handed treatment of Ashrawi. During an interview in November 2003, the premier told me that he had never before received such over-whelming public support on any issue: 'Nobody has raised an issue with me as they raise the Ashrawi affair, in my entire premiership, or going back further, as leader of the Opposition. Forest controversies, urban planning controversies, tax rises for poker machines, electric privatisation or workers' comp reform. This has been extraordinary'.

Certainly the letters-to-the-editor columns contained some of the most complex and thoughtful comments in the debate. On 27 October, Tony Cutcliffe, director of the independent think tank the Eureka Project, offered *SMH* readers this analysis of how the Israel–Palestine conflict played in the West:

> The Palestinian people represented in Australia do not have the resources to be influential in the funding of political campaigns. Nor are they lucrative clients of law firms, banks and other big business. Nor do they have a voice ... As a consequence, one half of the Middle East conflict remains unrepresented, and any clinical assessment of Israeli politics immediately becomes politically incorrect.

In the same issue, Peter Thomas called for calm to prevail:

> While prejudice and bigotry are perpetuated, there will be no end to the misery and suffering [in Israel–Palestine]. I met many people [on a recent trip to Israel] who understand that neither side has a monopoly on the truth, that the problems are profoundly complex and that goodwill is essential. And so to return to Sydney to witness the Hanan Ashrawi debate against a background of petty local politics, grubby pressure groups and financial blackmail is a shaming experience.

Lowy again

On 1 November, Andrew Clark reported in the *Australian Financial Review* that Frank Lowy had called Bob Carr urging him to reconsider presenting the peace prize to Ashrawi. Carr denied that Lowy had requested him not to present the award, telling Channel 9's *Sunday* that Lowy had 'asked me why I was presenting the prize, why I'd reached the decision, but it was an absolutely courteous call. It was not a request for me not to do it'.[31]

Lowy later provided details of this private conversation on ABC Radio,[32] and he confirmed Carr's version of events, saying that he respected the difference of opinion with the New South Wales premier. He also wrote a letter to the *SMH* confirming that he was a 'passionate' supporter of Israel but denying the suggestion that his money or power was behind any intimidating tactics: 'My money has nothing to do with the issue and I resent the suggestion that it has'.

On 2 November, *Sunday* aired a robust interview with Carr. Reporter Helen Dalley asked who had lobbied him to withdraw from the peace prize. When he refused to name anyone, Dalley pushed him: 'Why does that have to be confidential? Someone who has private access to you that the rest of the community can't know about, they can put a private view to you'. Carr said it didn't matter, but Dalley persisted: 'Well, it does matter, Mr Carr, doesn't it, because that's what's become the controversy, about how ferocious the lobbying has been and who's done it?' Carr responded that the calls 'weren't demanding. It's nothing unfair. We're a robust democracy, people are entitled to have views'.

Channel 9, owned by PBL, was not afraid to investigate the source of the lobbying and the way in which Carr reacted to it. Despite Zionist groups putting some pressure on PBL management, the network's flagship current affairs program seemed to be unaffected and was one of the few outlets that asked the right questions of Carr. A senior PBL executive and Sydney Peace Foundation Executive Committee member, James McLachlan, told me in December 2003 that the media organisation supported the prize and Ashrawi because it believed 'Palestinian voices were marginalised in the media' and because 'most Australians see Palestinians as terrorists'. He told me that senior executives at PBL received calls of complaint from leading Zionist groups—he wouldn't name them—demanding that the organisation condemn Ashrawi. PBL never hesitated in its support for the Peace Prize, he told me. Many of the allegations made against Ashrawi, McLachlan said, were 'fabrications', including the claim that she was a Holocaust denier.[33]

The other sponsors of the Sydney Peace Prize have also confirmed to me that they were put under pressure over the Ashrawi award, including receiving threatening emails and phone calls. Rio Tinto and Gilbert & Tobin received minimal protest, consisting of some emails and terse phone calls to management. Citigroup's New York office was pressured by Jewish groups in an attempt to change its Australian counterpart's decision, but this failed.

Although every sponsor except the City of Sydney stayed the course in 2003, since then all of them, except the City of Sydney, have withdrawn their support for the foundation. Stuart Rees told me that the organisations were told their 'client base' would be affected if they continued their support. He says there were 'miscellaneous reasons' for the sponsors' departures but 'the controversy surrounding the award to a Palestinian such as

Hanan Ashrawi probably acted like a catalyst to any anxiety those companies may have had about being associated with "peace with justice".[34]

Former Federal Court judge Marcus Einfeld, a consultant for Rio Tinto, says that Rio Tinto asked him how to approach the issue. 'I told them to tell the interveners that they had nothing to do with the fixing of the prize, they merely supported what they thought was a worthy cause and I agree with the cause'. Einfeld was strongly against Ashrawi receiving the peace prize but argued that the campaign against Carr would be counterproductive. Einfeld has shown a lifelong commitment to human rights issues yet, like so many liberal figures in the Jewish community, could not support a moderate Palestinian voice. He even suggested in an interview with me that the reason Bob Carr had received so much support for his pro-Ashrawi stance was because of 'anti-Jewish' sentiment within the community, rather than, as Carr sees it, people's desire for an even-handed approach to the conflict.

Carr, nevertheless, is a lifelong Zionist. His comments at the launch of *Jews and Australian politics*[35] in May 2005 revealed his sympathy for the Zionist perspective: 'The reason I supported Ashrawi [in 2003]', he said, 'is that I felt, especially since the 1990s, the Palestinians deserved support for finally ending their commitment to destroy Israel and talk peace. If a Palestinian like Ashrawi, a moderate, is talking peace, she should be supported'. Carr talked about his long-term commitment to Israel and his love of the Jewish people. His language suggested that support for Israel should be unconditional rather having to be earned. His comments implied that Israel is constantly engaged in peace-making; the Palestinians, on the other hand, have to show they are behaving before they can be praised.

The last week of the debate

Although the *SMH* editorialised on 3 November that the award ceremony should go ahead with Ashrawi and Carr, the vast majority of the paper's columnists were content to rehash negative rumours about Ashrawi and push a reactionary Zionist perspective. The most telling example was Gerard Henderson. On 28 October, Henderson, the executive director of the privately funded Sydney Institute, wrote that when he first met Ashrawi in 1999 in Adelaide, he had commented on her opposition to the armed struggle in the Middle East. Yet he was now suggesting that she 'was no committed peace activist'. Henderson complained of her 'virulent verbal attacks on Israel' at the World Conference against Racism in Durban in August 2001, arguing that they had contained 'not one skerrick of self-criticism from the Palestinian side'. Henderson labelled Ashrawi a 'polemicist'—would he have called an equivalent Israeli the same?—and questioned her credentials as an activist for peace. He falsely stated that she had not often worked with the Israeli peace movement, despite the fact that Ashrawi had been a prominent participant in Palestinian negotiation teams since the early 1990s. The AIJAC called Ashrawi an 'activist', implying that her work was more about politics than human rights.[36] Presumably the lobbyists never called Ariel Sharon an Israeli 'activist'.

Meanwhile the *Australian* had softened its stance. On 23 October, the paper had editorialised that Bob Carr had made a tactical error in agreeing to present Ashrawi with the peace prize. 'About the strongest thing that can be said for Mrs Ashrawi', said the leader, 'is that as Palestinians go, they come a lot worse, but even her commitment to the Road Map and a two-state solution to the Israeli–Palestinian conflict remains debatable.' The Murdoch flagship suggested that Carr would alienate the ALP's Jewish supporters, who were 'already wondering how deeply the party has been infected by the knee-jerk Israel bashing of the Left'. By 5 November its tone had changed decidedly. While still calling Ashrawi's selection a bad choice, the paper argued for 'free expression by an influential Palestinian voice, so long as it is a moderate voice that brings people closer together'. Now describing Ashrawi as 'a relatively moderate face of Palestinian politics', the paper editorialised that the Jewish community 'looks to have scored an own goal' and Bob Carr had 'emerged looking decisive after consistently asserting he would not back down'.

The *Australian*'s Elisabeth Wynhausen produced the most comprehensive analysis of the Ashrawi affair,[37] focusing on the influence of the Zionist lobby. Her article was headlined 'A powerful minority of Jews stifles debate'. It was the first time a mainstream Australian paper had attempted to portray the issue in all its intricacy. The article painted a picture of elite individuals with direct access to the corridors of power. Wynhausen was honest enough to suggest that 'money or political donations' could buy you influence, though to say so publicly would get you 'labelled anti-Semitic'. Tellingly, she included a comment from the Zionist Federation of Australia (ZFA), which had recently said there was 'a longstanding understanding within the Jewish community' that responsible leaders in the Diaspora did not make statements on Israeli internal security matters. 'Those who do so', wrote Wynhausen, 'may be subject to a frenzy of emails, letters and phone calls. This brutalising use of free speech to inhibit free speech is a tactic perfected by the Christian Right in the US'. Moderate Jewish leaders and citizens were afraid to speak their minds because of the likely backlash: personal attacks and accusations of disloyalty to the cause. And that was it for media investigation of the harassment of those who awarded Ashrawi the Sydney Peace Prize.

Ashrawi arrived in Sydney on 5 November to accept her award. ABC Radio's *World Today* featured extracts from Ashrawi's first press conference in Sydney.[38] When asked about the campaign against her, she responded by saying she had never experienced anything like it anywhere in the world: 'I was amazed at the degree of not just negativism on this, but a certain degree of hatred, which I don't find even in my discussions with Israelis, because they know the situation better, probably, and they wouldn't dare use the language and invective that was used here'.

'I will not be broken or silenced'

Ashrawi's Sydney Peace Prize lecture was a characteristically passionate detailing of Palestinian aspirations and grievances. In the first of many swipes at her critics, she praised Stuart Rees and Bob Carr for choosing courageously 'to take sides in the struggle against injustice as opposed to the refuge of so-called neutrality or the self-interest of power'.

The lecture's central argument revolved around mutual recognition of suffering. She highlighted what so few of her opponents want to acknowledge: pain and suffering has occurred on both sides, and both Jews and Palestinians need to understand the other's narrative before they can ever truly find peace. 'I will not be a broken or silenced Palestinian', she said, 'especially when it comes to the cause of peace and I will continue to speak out against injustice and oppression everywhere and I will continue to relay my people's message because I don't believe peace is made by defeated people'.

The 2003 Sydney Peace Prize was awarded on 6 November at the New South Wales Parliament. Bob Carr's speech was heartfelt and highly sympathetic to the Palestinian cause: 'You've seen Palestinian children born without a citizenship, growing up without nationality'. Hanan Ashrawi's response articulated the challenges faced by the Palestinian cause, including the need for Israel to realise its occupation is immoral ('we have to provide accountability for people who refuse to acknowledge that there is such a thing as a global rule of law and parity and equality for all peoples'), and she launched a pointed attack on her critics in the Zionist movement in Australia: 'I would say the collective spirit ... has defeated that attitude of hate and resentment and exclusion and fear. They must have been tremendously insecure to feel threatened by one voice. And I think they have come to the realisation of the folly of their ways'. She closed with her vision for Palestine and the future of the two peoples: 'There can be no legitimacy for Israel without the Palestinians. And there can be no legitimate Palestinian state without sharing the land of Palestine and recognising the legitimacy of the State of Israel'. She had stated her belief in a two-state solution, but not simply on US or Israeli terms. Her acceptance and understanding of the state of Israel was far more ideologically advanced than many in the Zionist camp, some of whom are still resistant to Palestinian independence.

A couple of days later Alan Ramsey wrote a final wash-up of the debate,[39] which revealed the contents of an email sent by the Vice-Chancellor of the University of Sydney to his staff, explaining why the university was unable to give the Sydney Peace Foundation the use of their Great Hall. Vice-Chancellor Kim Santow wrote of dates clashing with other events, but also admitted that in February 2003 a member of the Jewish community had approached him and had highlighted concerns with the choice of Ashrawi.[40] 'That approach brought home the importance of dispelling any suggestion the university was thereby taking sides', he wrote, 'particularly if the ceremony were to take place in the Great Hall'. In this world view, hosting a Palestinian speaker was 'taking sides', while presumably an Israeli or Jewish speaker would present no such problems. 'The whole thing stinks like a dead rat under the floorboards', an employee of the university remarked.

Ramsey had little patience for these explanations and suggested that the university had backed out under pressure from elements of the Zionist lobby. Stuart Rees now says that the University of Sydney acted with cowardice. Simply put, they were worried about losing future funding and bowed to threats. The university was never fully questioned about its role and still refuses to discuss the matter.

The lobby backfires

The real problem with Ashrawi's prize, for much of the Jewish community, was the legitimacy it bestowed on the Palestinian narrative of occupation and oppression. The ALP's multicultural affairs spokesman Laurie Ferguson recognised this in an article for the *Australian*, arguing that for many Jews 'unless a Palestinian totally surrenders then they are by imputation terrorist aligned'.[41]

The AIJAC's Colin Rubenstein commented in December that 'The "Palestinianisation" of this year's Sydney Peace Prize was the source of profound and widespread dismay not only among Australian Jewry, but also among other knowledgeable friends of Israel who hope for a secure peace'.[42] Throughout the debate, the *AJN* was mostly content to condemn Ashrawi rather than analyse her record. It endorsed insinuations about her previous association with the PLO. Arafat was seen as a terrorist and obstacle to peace, so Ashrawi was tarred with the same brush.

The *AJN* ran many articles by Jewish leaders who argued among themselves over the most appropriate method of isolating Ashrawi and of keeping the wider non-Jewish community on side. There was concern that images of an overbearing Jewish lobby had reinforced existing negative stereotypes. While the letters page featured the occasional pro-Ashrawi opinion, the paper remained largely obsessed with internal wrangling. 'The Jewish community has become the focus of this issue', said *AJN* editor Vic Alhadeff,[43] 'rather than whether or not Dr Ashrawi is a worthy recipient. It looks like the Jewish community is anti-free speech when the reverse is true'.

Even ALP MP and staunch Zionist Michael Danby thought that some people had overdone it. Though suspicious of Ashrawi and her motives, he argued in the US Jewish newspaper *Forward* that much of the lobbying, including the pressure put on corporate sponsors, had been counterproductive.[44] In a rare demonstration of public disagreement, Danby broke ranks with the AIJAC in arguing that the Jewish community should at least engage with people like Ashrawi: 'It is in Israel's interests to maintain lines of communication with those who will be a part of that [future Palestinian] leadership, whatever they may have said in the past'.[45]

The *AJN* continued to report the profound impact the Ashrawi affair had had, but its angle was factionalism in the Jewish community. The 7 November edition editorialised under the headline 'Ashrawi: Who speaks for the community?' Acutely aware of the damage certain lobbying had done to the reputation of Jews in Australia, the editorial argued that the community had not spoken with one voice, instead sending out mixed messages to Bob Carr and the mainstream media, and giving the impression that they were not united against Hanan Ashrawi: 'The issue should have been about Dr Ashrawi. It should have been about the Sydney Peace Foundation and its questionable process. There needs to be a co-ordinated community strategy on such issues—and it needs to be handled by those elected to represent the community'.

Its view merely highlighted the divisions between the rightest pro-Likud viewpoint of AIJAC and the slightly more moderate NSW JBD. AIJAC advocated aggressive tactics, practically harassing Carr to withdraw his support and briefing willing, mainstream journalists on Ashrawi's allegedly suspect past. Carr told me that Rubenstein initially informed him that Ashrawi was a Holocaust denier and should be shunned. Carr said that he was sick of being harassed by the likes of AIJAC and Rubenstein and advised them to be a 'little more selective about their fights with journalists'.

Even the ALP's Michael Danby argued that 'once [Carr] had decided to present the prize, there was no point in criticising him publicly'.[46] He felt confident that after hearing Carr's 'unalloyed truth' on the conflict, Ashrawi would be better equipped to make peace with Israel. It was patronising beyond belief. Danby was caught in the middle, however, being an avowed Zionist and sympathetic to the AIJAC agenda, but also a Labor man and Carr comrade. He was attacked by AIJAC for not issuing a complete condemnation of Ashrawi and slammed as 'ludicrous' for his belief that she may 'have become a genuine partner for peace if the Jewish community had kept quiet'. Anything other than demonisation of Ashrawi was 'appeasement', according to Rubenstein.[47]

The *AJN* labelled AIJAC's actions as 'counterproductive'. Although the positions of the major Jewish groups on Ashrawi were virtually identical, AIJAC's methods caused deep disquiet within the Jewish community and NSW JBD head Stephen Rothman accused AIJAC of not representing the interests of the Jewish community, and of placing their own political interests first.[48]

As a reader of *AJN*, I found this editorial particularly jarring. Focusing on the Jewish community's response is one thing, but what about the litany of false charges levelled at Ashrawi? The paper preferred to ignore the larger questions. Moreover, the kind of Palestinian who would have been more acceptable as a recipient of the prize was never discussed. An op-ed piece in the *AJN* by Middle East affairs analyst David Langsam reinforced this perspective. For the first time in living memory, a high-profile organisation, AIJAC, was heavily criticised for its bellicose stance. 'The public perception is that AIJAC uses bullying tactics to stop debate', he wrote.[49] 'AIJAC appears not only to want to decide the Sydney Peace Prize, it also apparently believes it has the right to choose which Palestinians are acceptable for Jewish contact. In the process, it intimidates opponents.'

The affair opened up fault lines in the Australian Jewish community, and in the space created, new voices were heard, both Jewish and non-Jewish. Ian Cohen, a Jewish New South Wales Green MP, saw the Ashrawi affair as a breakthrough for Jewish community politics, invaluable 'in opening up the ability of people in or around the Jewish community to have a view that was only tolerated before'. His view was shared by Barbara Bloch, a member of Sydney-based Jews against the Occupation, formed in 2003 to counter the established Jewish orthodoxy on issues related to Israel–Palestine: 'There's been a sense in the past that we keep it all inside, and don't air our dirty linen in public. Things have been leaking out this time'.

The Ashrawi affair was a seminal event in the Australian Jewish community. The mainstream community was given a rare insight into the players and tactics of the Zionist lobby and its belief that bullying tactics are an acceptable means of promoting its agenda. The media, unimpressed by AIJAC's arrogance and aggressive attitude, focused on the story, though not comprehensively. AIJAC's Mark Leibler claimed his group's aim was simply to ensure that the 'media emphasis was on whether Ashrawi had unequivocally condemned terrorism'[50] and that she didn't defame Israel. In fact, AIJAC's activities were specifically designed to slander Ashrawi because she was Palestinian.

By the time Ashrawi had received her prize, media across the country and overseas had reported the machinations. Yet the Jewish community has learnt little from the controversy. There has been no discernable progress in listening to, and understanding, the Palestinian point of view, and similar attitudes would probably be displayed again if another prominent Palestinian arrived in Australia to receive an award. The tactics employed may differ, but that is missing the point. What will it take for Zionist insecurity to abate? And how long before a Palestinian is as respected as an Israeli or Jew?

The Ashrawi debate has exposed the Australian Jewish community's obedience to Israel and its government. Where did their loyalty lie? If a moderate such as Ashrawi can be defamed and vilified by almost every Jewish commentator, the obvious conclusion is that any recognised Palestinian will be automatically silenced and smeared. Two competing narratives should be able to coexist within the one debate. Does listening to a differing viewpoint somehow make Jews feel they are betraying their heritage and homeland? Diaspora Jewry is too often content to mouth Zionist platitudes without knowing all the facts. As Stuart Rees wrote in a final article published on the *SMH Webdiary* on 19 November: 'It is as though the debate in Australia should be conducted along the same lines as violence in the Middle East. One side must win, the other must not only lose but must be taught a lesson from which they may never recover'.

2

HOW HANAN ASHRAWI CHANGED MY LIFE

Reporters who criticise Israel are to blame for inciting anti-Semites to burn synagogues. Thus it is not Israel's brutality and occupation that provokes the sick and cruel people who attack Jewish institutions, synagogues and cemeteries. We journalists are to blame ... If we want a quiet life, we will just have to toe the line, stop criticising Israel or America. Or just stop writing altogether.

Robert Fisk, 2002[1]

IN JULY 2003 the *SMH* published my first article. I was a trainee journalist for Fairfax Online, writing on the newspaper's website, and it took a lot of lobbying, but eventually I persuaded the *SMH*'s opinion editor to publish the piece. It appeared under the headline 'Defiant Israel blind to what it has become' and outlined the brutality of the ongoing occupation, the suffering of the Palestinians and the apparent Jewish acceptance of the situation. I argued:

> The ability of so many in the Jewish world to dismiss the obvious facts of the occupation is due, in no small part, to ignoring the facts in the Middle East. From the time Israel was established most Jews appeared unaware or unwilling to hear

the stories of thousands of displaced Arabs, the violence against them by the early settlers and the lack of redress for their grievances.

I had no idea of the vitriolic response this statement would provoke—looking back I can see how naïve I was! It shocked me that the most vicious comments were made by Jews keen to tutor me in the 'correct' reading of the Israel–Palestine conflict and to highlight my perceived ignorance. I was telephoned and hassled at work, and emailed by people I'd never met or spoken to. I was informed that I was part of the problem, not the solution. One reader wrote that my piece was 'historically inaccurate and riddled with errors ... Why don't you take your self-hating somewhere else? Just remember, that you would have been carted off to the gas chambers as well'. Another long email suggested that it was only because I was a 'self-hating Jew' that the SMH had printed my article.

More distressingly, members of my extended family got stuck in too. A cousin in San Francisco wrote: 'do you not understand that your liberal leanings that speak so maliciously of Israel just help create and sustain anti-Semitism?' Another relative in the USA sent a six-page email. He claimed that he was 'one of the most left people I know concerning Israel' but went on to say that he felt so much 'shock and outrage that I blocked your email address and cursed your name'. He was incapable of finding any fault with Israel's treatment of the Palestinians and its conduct during the occupation, arguing that anti-Zionism is antisemitism and that 'Israel's record on human rights is among the best in the world'. I had a 'fixation' with Israel and was counselled to write about 'more pressing world issues'—none of which should involve Israel. I was simply 'promoting my career as a very chic and marketable anti-Zionist Jew'. I have had no contact with this cousin since this letter, except being asked by him after a group email in mid-2005 to 'remove me from your list and never write to me again'.

This barrage of vitriol was marked by a blind devotion to the state of Israel and a desperate need to justify its actions: it seemed to me that nationalism had become something beyond religion for too many Jews. Devotion to the state of Israel, sacred and beyond criticism, had become central to contemporary Jewish thought.

A few months later, I entered the debate on the Sydney Peace Prize, publishing a piece that supported Ashrawi and questioning the motives of her accusers on the US website ZNet.[2] Again, I received emails that expressed personal contempt: the problem was me, not the controversy.

The personal backlash I experienced during the Ashrawi controversy changed my life: it made me realise that rational debate was extremely difficult in such an emotive environment and that personal abuse had become the preferred mode of communication for many who wished to engage on this issue. I became even more determined to continue examining the conflict, despite the growing number of people ridiculing me.

How I became a 'chic anti-Zionist'

I was brought up in a liberal Jewish family in Melbourne. My grandparents had fled Austria and Germany in 1939, but their relatives had remained trapped in Europe, unable to escape their fate. Travelling in Eastern Europe in my mid-twenties, I was profoundly moved by my heritage, not least when I visited Auschwitz with a close friend of mine. For an entire day, we barely spoke: I was experiencing a revulsion many others have felt before and since. Something about that day changed me. Seeing the results of blind hatred and unchallenged devotion slowly led me to be more questioning on a range of matters, including my heritage and the state of Israel.

As a child, I was sent to a private Anglican school, attended regular Sunday school Jewish education and completed my bar mitzvah at the age of 13. So far, so normal. My parents said they wanted to send me to a non-Jewish school because of their concern that a Jewish education would be too narrow. There were very few Jews at the school, and petty antisemitism was rife. I was teased from a young age, and by the time I completed high school, I was used to occasional taunting, especially the accusation that I was 'a tight arse' with money. This was life in a predominantly WASP environment. The growing ranks of Asian students were also the target of racist gibes.

I saw my parents as observant liberal Jews who expected my attendance at synagogue on major Jewish holidays and at Sabbath dinners. They were both born in Melbourne during the final stages of World War II, and their parents had instilled in them a strong sense of community, perhaps in memory of what they had lost after fleeing Nazi Europe. My parents encouraged me to have both Jewish and non-Jewish friends, but seemed to believe that I would somehow feel closer to the Jewish ones. It was expected that I would only have Jewish girlfriends. After all, they would often say, we Jews have to stick together after everything we've been through. There's something different about Jews, they argued, and only we understand that. I never felt comfortable with what I saw as a racially superior mentality. It seemed disturbingly close to racism. When challenged on this, they vehemently denied it was racism, but rather a case of 'sticking to your own'.

My parents were unthinking Zionists. As my father told me recently, we may have rarely talked about the Jewish state, but he knew 'that Israel could provide a sanctuary if antisemitism became rife and intolerable'. As a young man, my father even considered becoming a rabbi. This was partly because both my parents had been immersed in the life of the local synagogue from a young age, and my father felt that he could contribute something to the community. I recall raising criticisms of Israel in my teens and receiving unqualified defences of the country's actions. I now know my parents, like so many other Jews, were uninformed, relying on the Jewish and mainstream press for their news.

Living in a secular country and attending a non-Jewish school always suggested to me that I would live and mix predominantly with Australians who were not Jewish. Isn't that what a truly integrated, multicultural society is all about? My young cousins enthusiastically embraced Jewish youth groups, essentially forums aimed at fostering a lifelong love of Israel. I went to a few meetings, mainly to please my parents, and felt isolated. I didn't love Israel. Why would I? I'd never been there. In my teens, I attended regular get-togethers with friends I had met during my Sunday school years. We were all liberal Jews, led by a progressive rabbi. We discussed a variety of issues, many not related to Judaism. I vividly recall enjoying these events, probably because we were not being indoctrinated with a staunchly Zionist viewpoint. Most of us were more interested in talking about love, death, sex and other teenage obsessions. Back then, being a good Jew didn't mean falling in love with the Jewish state (though some in the group have subsequently done just that).

By my late teens, my enthusiasm for Judaism was waning. It was if my parents expected their strong beliefs to imbue me with a sense of feeling and acting Jewish. Alas, this was not how it worked out. I attended Melbourne's Monash University, not because of the high percentage of Jewish students (as perhaps my family saw it) but because of its proximity to my home. When I started my first serious relationship with another student, a Polish girl, I soon encountered my parents' disapproval. I found their reasoning illogical and paranoid. Poles were notorious anti-semites, they said, so who knew what her parents really thought, let alone her own views. The girl was born in Melbourne and had never uttered anything even vaguely resembling racial intolerance to me. I recall her parents acting similarly. It mattered little, though; she was never accepted in my family home, and neither were later girlfriends, most of whom were also non-Jewish. The few Jewish girlfriends were more warmly embraced, and this rankled with me. It seemed as if a girlfriend's religion was more important than her personality or background.

This kind of behaviour led me to a serious reappraisal of my views on Judaism and its virtually indistinguishable relationship with Israel. If this was the face of Diaspora Jewry, I didn't want a bar of it. Today, I have a wonderful partner, Liz, who is Jewish—her views on political matters are similar to mine—and my parents treat her like family. I couldn't ask for a warmer welcome, but I suspect I've mellowed in recent years. Whereas once I might have resented my parents for treating her better than non-Jewish girlfriends, now I'm just relieved to have a supportive relationship.

Looking back on my Sunday school lessons, I felt that I had been hoodwinked. Indeed, it was a remarkably similar history to the one I learnt at school about Australia's colonial past and its treatment of Aborigines. In both cases, inconvenient facts were whitewashed. I was taught about the creation of Israel, but not about the indigenous Palestinian inhabitants. We discussed Arab terrorism but never what may have caused it. Zionist pioneers were praised for their ability to turn an empty land into a fertile Jewish homeland. Perhaps most disturbingly, though, we were told constantly that the only believable reason anyone might hate Israel is antisemitism. The morality, or otherwise, of Israeli actions was never questioned, let alone given context. In the eyes of this dominant Zionism, Jews have always been and remain blameless victims and visionary pioneers.

I cannot remember the first time I felt uneasy with the default Jewish attitude towards Israel, but it soon became clear to me that any criticism of Israeli government policy was regarded as completely inappropriate and was silenced, or simply given no platform. Jews who expressed such criticism were tarred with the 'self-hating Jew' tag. Non-Jewish critics were labelled as antisemitic, and who, after all, wants to be known as that? It took me many years to understand these brutally effective tactics, which would explain why, until I consciously sought it out, I rarely heard serious debate on the effects of the occupation, house demolitions, checkpoints and the ever-expanding settler movement. The Jewish press was usually mute and content to provide space for the official line and for zealots who almost religiously campaigned against perceived anti-Israeli bias in the media. I soon learnt that this 'bias' was attributed to any chastising of Israel or its supporters.

It was as if all Jews were expected to express an almost limitless faith in the Jewish state. By my early twenties, this position became untenable, largely because of my self-education on the plight of the Palestinian people and the ongoing efforts of the Zionist enterprise to deprive them of a homeland. The more I studied the question of Zionism, the more I realised that it was anything but un-Jewish to question its basic tenets. Albert Einstein, a Jew from Germany who fled to the USA in 1933, gave a speech in 1938 to the National Labor Committee for Palestine in New York in which he opposed the creation of a Jewish state because he was afraid 'of the inner damage Judaism will sustain—especially from the development of a narrow nationalism within our own ranks'.

While at university, I started reading Palestinian academic Edward Said, and discovered the generations of Palestinians dispossessed by the establishment of the Jewish state and the post-1967 occupation. Australian journalist John Pilger's writings were perhaps more incendiary because they were written by a countryman and highlighted the brave Israelis who fought for justice and human rights in their religious state. I read Noam Chomsky on the incestuous relationship between the USA and Israel, and Norman Finkelstein and Ilan Pappe along with the work of other moderate Israeli intellectuals.

I agreed with Judith Butler, a lecturer at the University of California, who has written that although antisemitism is undoubtedly on the rise, and that care should be taken to distinguish between legitimate criticism of Israel and outright hatred of Jews, a mature Jewish community needs to be able to discuss matters of vast importance to the Jewish state in open forums. No topic should be deemed off-limits. 'For a criticism of Israel to be taken as a challenge to the survival of the Jews', Butler says, 'we would have to assume not only that Israel cannot change in response to legitimate criticism, but that a more radically democratic Israel would be bad for Jews'.[3]

I started feeling increasingly uncomfortable with the association of the word 'Jew' with 'Israel'. They are not the same thing, nor should they be. Surely the ever-increasing number of Jews within Israel and the Diaspora who are fighting for a just resolution to the conflict, and who vehemently disagree with current government policy, are struggling for a more egalitarian Jewish state? Zionism is not Judaism. Deliberately associating the two is a dishonest method of silencing anyone who may disagree with either. Moreover, to suggest that any issues one may have with, say, Israeli violence against civilians is best discussed covertly, if at all, struck me as dishonest. Butler rightly compares this kind of censorship to an American being called a 'traitor' for opposing US imperial ambitions in the Middle East. It was these reflections that led me to become a vocal critic of Israel's current incarnation. I believe that the Jewish state should be a viable, democratic and equal society, where one people are not given privileges refused to others; the current Israel is not the kind of country of which I could ever be proud.

In discussions with various members of my extended family during my twenties, I sensed a distinct dislike of Arabs, and of Palestinians in particular. This sense was rarely based on anything greater than a rehashing of anti-Arafat diatribes and noble Zionist history. My Jewish friendships dwindled. I knew I was being more dogmatic, and perhaps I bored my friends. But there was little that could be done to calm me down once I wanted to debate an issue. My Jewish friends were probably puzzled by this ideologue whose background and life experience didn't explain his increased antipathy towards Israel. I was aware of their frustration but enjoyed challenging their prejudices and my own preconceptions. Soon enough, however, I realised that we weren't enjoying each other's company, and I drifted apart from many of them. My non-Jewish friends cared less, and for this I was thankful.

Then my parents began to question the default setting. The true reasons for this still baffle me, but I think it was at least partly because they began to read material that revealed the realities of contemporary Israel. It was a remarkable transformation. Both my mother and father today share my unease with Israel's behaviour. Their relationships with many Jewish friends have been affected to the point where international matters are routinely ignored and my work completely shunned. 'Sometimes', my father told me recently, 'I realise that your mother and I are alone'.

How could one still have blind faith in a country that enacts citizenship laws to prevent Palestinians who marry Israelis from living in Israel with full rights?[4] How could one idealise a nation with an army that, despite Sharon calling it 'the most moral in the world', frequently engages in war crimes in the occupied territories, collectively punishes the Palestinian people, and destroys and steals Arab land for expansion of settlements? My parents and I drew closer. Now we may not always agree, but we can all see that the future of Israel is too important to be left to the self-appointed and self-important guardians of the Zionist cause.

Not happy!

After my first article appeared in the *SMH*, I decided that I would no longer allow my secular Judaism to cloud my judgement about Israel. I had learnt by this time that there were many others who felt the same way as me and were making their own strong stands. Sara Roy, whose parents are Holocaust survivors, is a senior research scholar at Harvard University's Center for Middle Eastern Studies. She delivered a passionate Holocaust Remembrance Lecture in April 2002 at Baylor University, telling her American audience not to forget the Holocaust, and asking them to question the morality of the Jewish state:

> Within the Jewish community it has always been considered a form of heresy to compare Israeli actions or policies with those of the Nazis, and certainly one must be very careful in doing so. But what does it mean when Israeli soldiers paint identification numbers on Palestinian arms; when young Palestinian men and boys of a certain age are told through Israeli loudspeakers to gather in the town square; when Israeli soldiers openly admit to shooting Palestinian children for sport; when some of the Palestinian dead must be buried in mass graves while the bodies of others are left in city streets and camp alleyways because the army will not allow proper burial; when certain Israeli officials and Jewish intellectuals publicly call for the destruction of Palestinian villages in retaliation for suicide bombings, or for the transfer of the Palestinian population out of the West Bank and Gaza; when 46 percent of the Israeli public favors such transfers and when transfer or expulsion becomes a legitimate part of popular discourse; when government officials speak of the 'cleansing of the refugee camps'; and when a leading Israeli intellectual calls for hermetic separation between Israelis and Palestinians in the form of a Berlin Wall, caring not whether the Palestinians on the other side of the wall may starve to death as a result.[5]

Many of my family members were killed in the Nazi concentration camps during World War II, so I was particularly struck by her analysis that, as Jews, we often characterise 'our' suffering as being worse than the Palestinians':

> In the post-Holocaust world, Jewish memory has faltered—even failed—in one critical respect: it has excluded the reality of Palestinian suffering and Jewish culpability therein. As a people, we have been unable to link the creation of Israel with the displacement of the Palestinians. We have been unwilling to see, let alone remember, that finding our place meant the loss of theirs. Perhaps one reason for the ferocity of the conflict today

is that Palestinians are insisting on their voice despite our continued and desperate efforts to subdue it.[6]

The sentiment that Roy identifies is one I recognised in much of the response to my first opinion piece, and in the response to articles I wrote on the Ashrawi affair. I never expected to be thrust so deep into the debate, but my easy access to the mainstream media meant I was able to play a small but significant role. I had reported Ashrawi's only public speaking engagement in Sydney for the *SMH Online*[7]—my sole official reporting job during her visit—and noted her conciliatory tone. This was a woman who could negotiate with Israel and Jews, if only they could accept a nationalistic Palestinian. I started to receive abusive emails telling me that I was siding with terrorism.

On 4 November 2003, the Ashrawi affair reached millions of readers around the world, when Robert Fisk, Middle East correspondent for the United Kingdom's *Independent* newspaper, wrote a column about the smearing of Palestinians throughout the world media.[8] Ashrawi and the late Edward Said were his two examples. He wrote of the campaign by the Zionist lobby in Australia to 'prevent the Palestinian scholar Hanan Ashrawi—of all people—from receiving the 2003 Sydney Peace Prize this week'. Fisk also commended my essay on *ZNet*: 'A Jewish writer in Sydney has bravely defended her—not least because the local Israeli lobby appears to have deliberately misquoted an interview she gave me two years ago, distorting her words to imply that she is in favour of suicide bombings'.

Margo Kingston, then a journalist for the *SMH*, decided to reprint my original *ZNet* column and the Fisk piece on her *Webdiary* on 5 November. The response was immediate, and the following day she ran a sample. The messages were mixed: some supportive, but many outraged that such views were published at all. Edward Baral was incensed: 'This is not about Israeli/Palestinian balance but a direct attack on the Jewish people. I ask that you withdraw this article, publish an apology and advise what steps you will take to ensure that vilifying material such as this is not published in the future'. Duane Kelly was more supportive: 'Excellent work publishing the Antony Loewenstein piece. It was the first time I had seen any media space given to the Palestinian point of view and it does not surprise me one bit that it had to have come from a member of the Jewish community. After all, if anyone else had said it, they would have immediately been labelled anti-Semitic and dismissed'.

Kingston asked me to contribute a chapter to her book on the government of John Howard, *Not happy, John!*[9] What fascinated us both during the Ashrawi debate was the emergence of previously unheard voices on the Israel–Palestine conflict and the ways in which political and economic power was wielded in Howard's Australia. I wanted to articulate Ashrawi's moderation and the urgent need for debate on 'unspeakable' topics. My chapter detailed the Zionist lobby's pressure on then New South Wales premier Bob Carr to withdraw his support for Ashrawi as well as the financial threats made to the Sydney Peace Prize sponsors. I examined the wrangling inside the Jewish community, its rejection of a Palestinian moderate and the wider community's realisation that there were many readings of the conflict, not just the usual Zionist perspective. Perhaps most importantly, calmer Jewish and Arab voices were heard, albeit briefly.

We were acutely aware of the hornet's nest into which we were descending. I interviewed many of the players in the controversy, including New South Wales Jewish Greens MP Ian Cohen, who had publicly supported Ashrawi. Something he said perfectly articulated why I felt so strongly about this debate and why complacency in the Jewish community sounded hollow to me. Cohen told me: 'I remember a Jewish academic at a semi-public meeting at Sydney University who said, "it doesn't matter what Israel does, I'll complain about them internally, but I will never make public statements against Israel". I found that rather appalling from a person with education'.[10] I also found the situation revealed by this statement to be completely contradictory to the Jewish tradition of questioning and debate. Was the Jewish community so fragile that it couldn't handle dissent?

When *Not happy, John!* was released in June 2004 and soon became a bestseller, the media response, especially within the Jewish community, provided ample evidence of Sara Roy's 'failed memory' thesis. The *AJN*'s performance was shamefully inadequate. Rather than seriously engaging in debate, the paper took the easy way out, publishing numerous letters and opinion pieces hammering the same message: Kingston and I were anti-Israel and antisemites. I knew they were suppressing letter-writers who not only supported a more questioning position but also wanted a more honest debate. For the most part, the mainstream media ignored the issue altogether.

The *AJN* interviewed Kingston and me in mid-June.[11] The published story conveniently omitted one of the central contributions the chapter made to the Ashrawi debate: Bob Carr's chastising of the Zionist lobby over its aggressive tactics during the Ashrawi affair. Up until then, Carr had acknowledged that he had been lobbied, but publicly had characterised it as a form of acceptable dialogue. In *Not happy, John!* he advised Zionist lobbyists to be 'much more relaxed about the fact that, in a pluralist media, there will be criticisms of Israel appearing'. He cautioned them to be more selective in their fights with journalists because aggressive lobbying tactics do 'a great disservice to the Israeli cause in Australia and the Jewish community'.

Instead, *AJN* journalist Peter Kohn provided a superficial outline of my claims, made a number of factual errors, which suggested to me that he hadn't actually read my work, and featured four long paragraphs of denial by AIJAC executive director Colin Rubenstein. I had written 'an intellectually weak polemic', Rubenstein claimed, '[that] merely sets out a self-aggrandising fantasy'. Rubenstein ignored the allegations against AIJAC in the chapter and preferred to engage in personal put-downs.

Online political newsletter *Crikey*, in one of the few public affirmations, wrote in late June that the book was condemned in the *AJN* by Rubenstein ('a feisty advocate if ever there was one'), and praised me for exposing the connections between billionaire Jewish businessman Frank Lowy, AIJAC chairman Mark Leibler and the Howard government. 'Brave stuff from Loewenstein', *Crikey* said, 'given the Westfield faction of Lowy mates who sit on the Fairfax board'.[12] The Fairfax board of directors included Dean Wills and David Gonski, both directors of the shopping centre giant.

In early July, Rubenstein was given close to a full page in the *AJN* to defend AIJAC's tactics, slander Kingston and me and yet still comprehensively fail to engage with any of the claims made in my chapter.[13] I belonged, according to this self-appointed spokesman of the Zionist cause, 'to an ignoble tradition of Jewish individuals being used to legitimise attacks on consensus Jewish community positions'. Furthermore, my investigations were 'a self-aggrandising morality tale', and although I was 'entitled to base [my] Judaism on whatever [I] like, even fighting the supposed evil Jewish establishment on behalf of anti-Zionism', I represented 'a dangerous trend of political vilification in Australia and around the world—that any Jewish expression of opinion on political issues is tantamount to illegitimate lobbying, abuse of financial power and intimidation'. His final piece of rhetoric: 'If Jews in Australia are going to continue to be equal citizens with full rights of political participation, we need to fight this calumny. AIJAC will be making this a priority. I ask other community organisations to do likewise'.

Rubenstein was following a predictable routine: smear your accusers, ignore the charges, and claim that you are defending the democratic right to lobby and defend, without question, all Israeli government policy in the name of dutiful Zionism. His bombastic article elicited many responses in the *AJN*. I was most affected by a letter that the paper refused to publish by Melbourne Jew Mannie De Saxe (he emailed me his letter):

> There are approximately 100 000 Jews in Australia. Not all are Zionists, not all accept the 'facts' as presented to them by self-styled, so-called representatives of the 'mainstream' Jewish/Zionist organisations.
>
> Strangely enough, there are still large numbers of Jews in Australia who interpret the 'facts' differently, and come to different conclusions, and I and many others are sick and tired of having 'their facts' quoted at us as being the mainstream, and the only acceptable answers to the Israel/Palestine problem.
>
> After Rubenstein and others of his ilk have registered to have votes cast for these bodies by the Australian Electoral Commission and ensured that 100% of the Australian Jewish population have cast their votes should he dare to make his presumptuous assumptions, and draw his equally presumptuous—and outrageously arrogant—conclusions.[14]

I demanded that the *AJN* print my right of reply, and the following week I explained what the Ashrawi affair really said about the Australian Jewish community. I called for an opening of the debate on the conflict and hoped that Palestinian voices, rather than the usual Jewish ones, might start being heard in Australia:

> Perhaps there is change in the air. In Britain in late June [2004] more than 347 Jews signed an open letter to the British Board of Deputies demanding it acknowledges and represents the many British Jews critical of Israeli Government actions. Prominent rabbis, professors and MPs contributed signatures, including Eric Hobsbawm and Alexei Sayle. Being a true humanist means speaking out when oppression occurs.[15]

I expected a barrage of abuse, and the *AJN* did not disappoint. For over a month, the paper printed letters denigrating my views and my right to express them, and warning against the danger that I posed to the Jewish 'cause'. Not one letter of support was printed, though I was personally sent a number by Jews who were appalled at my treatment in the Jewish press and agreed with my calls for a more honest discussion. One letter-writer accused me of inflicting 'a hatchet job on the Jewish community and Israel'. Furthermore, 'the leaders of AIJAC are too busy promoting the pro-Israel views espoused by the majority of Australian Jewry to waste their time lending a patina of respectability to the anti-Zionist views held by a fringe of Israel-bashing zealots'. Another wrote that my 'naïve narrative ... provides camouflage cover for anti-Semitic propagandists'.

The most transparent attempt at character assassination was that of the Jewish Labor MP for Melbourne Ports, Michael Danby. His letter reflected the desperation of a man fighting a concerted campaign against a Liberal competitor, David Southwick. It was, after all, the height of the 2004 election campaign. Southwick wrote an opinion piece in the *AJN* some weeks later.[16] He said of Danby: 'Sure, he is quick to rush to Israel's defence when it doesn't cost him anything, as evidenced by his castigation of Fairfax journalist Antony Loewenstein for his take on the Ashrawi affair in Margo Kingston's new book—but he did not attack his own Labor colleague [health spokeswoman Julia Gillard] for launching that very same book!'. Southwick spent his entire campaign trying, unsuccessfully as it turned out, to convince voters that he would be even more dedicated to the Zionist cause than Danby and wouldn't have to deal with the ALP's 'anti-Israel elements which exert a powerful influence on the party's agenda'. It was as if Danby wanted to prove to his constituents that he was more loyal to the Zionist cause and would tolerate nothing less than a complete silencing of dissenting views (even writing in mid-August in the *AJN* that he had 'volunteered as a kibbutz worker to replace Israeli soldiers who were at the front' during the 1973 Yom Kippur war):

> Antony Loewenstein is a non-entity who represents a telephone-box group of Jewish Australians. He was deliberately chosen by Margo Kingston for his unrepresentative views. Appropriately he is promoting Palestinian non-entity Dr Hanan Ashrawi. Of course these fringe players here and in the Israel–Palestinian conflict are entitled to their views.
>
> Yes, it is unfortunately true that AIJAC made a tactical mistake in being perceived to be in conflict with NSW Premier Bob Carr after he had made the decision to award Ashrawi her worthless prize.
>
> I have these questions for Loewenstein, Kingston *et al.* Do you support Ariel Sharon's disengagement plan or not? Do you support the withdrawal from Gaza? Do you support the UN

secretary general's alarm at the recent worldwide upsurge in violent anti-Semitism?[17]

Weeks later, the letter writers to the *AJN* were still seething. One woman wrote that 'Hanan Ashrawi getting a peace prize was like a known pedophile becoming Father of the Year' and 'it seems that free speech and the right [for Jews] to protest is limited to people whose political views are acceptable to Margo, Antony *et al.*'.

I was pleased with the coverage but disappointed with the narrowness of the debate. I had naïvely hoped the *AJN* would allow dissenting voices to be heard but they were virtually absent from the paper. My parents were proud of my work but equally frustrated with a Jewish community from which they felt increasingly alienated. I wished that other young, Jewish voices had been heard in support of my stance. I soon discovered the personal price of my outspokenness.

I was at a family wedding in Melbourne in early November, when a distant cousin approached me in the men's toilets. 'Your views and works are a disgrace and disgusting', he spat. 'You're a Jewish antisemite.' He started to rant:

> Your work is influential and read by many people and I just think you should think about what you're writing and the effect that it has. If there is trouble for your parents, you'll know why. After all we've been through. You write well but your work is ignorant. I know many Jews and non-Jews who find your work appalling. It's discussed and that's what many people think.

I responded that cornering me in the male toilets was a sign of real bravery and suggested that there were multiple interpretations of this issue and perhaps he should discover some of them. He stormed off. I was taken aback, and my parents were incensed. I suspected his position was shared by others in my family, yet only he felt the need to tell me to my face.

The mainstream media coverage of *Not happy, John!* was initially muted, perhaps because of the book's harsh criticisms of the increasing commercialism of news and current affairs. Only the *Canberra Times* review mentioned the Ashrawi chapter explicitly, and positively. The *Wentworth Courier*, a local Sydney newspaper serving the area in which Malcolm Turnbull ran his successful campaign for federal parliament, wrote a sympathetic profile of me in early July.

By the time the heat finally died down several months later, I was exhausted and disappointed. I was frustrated not so much by the media's failure to engage with the issues raised in a bestselling book, as by the predictable response to my attempt at opening new lines of dialogue. The Australian Jewish community simply wasn't ready to engage.

Guilty as charged

When I began the research for this book in 2004, the late *60 Minutes* reporter Richard Carleton told me that he had been warned off speaking to me by a senior member of the Jewish community in Sydney. He had asked Carleton not to return my calls or be interviewed by me, because I was a 'young rebel'.

Well, guilty as charged—when I began writing about Israel I was 28 and had been a journalist for only a few years. I was not a veteran reporter with a Filofax full of contacts and an established reputation as a heavy hitter. I was simply a young Jewish Australian who thought it was time to allow some fresh voices to be heard in the debate about Israel–Palestine. That is still my position.

By dismissing me as a young rebel, the community leader seemed to imply that I was not entitled to speak and had not yet earned the right to be listened to in debates about Zionism and the Israeli occupation of Palestine. Self-appointed Zionist leaders claim that experience and knowledge bring credibility to this debate, but experience and knowledge are only attributed to those who agree with their position. The charge of youthful naïvety is levelled against me, but it seems solely because I challenge and threaten the accepted dogma. Although I majored in history at university, my knowledge of the Middle East is predominantly the result of extensive reading, and of spending time in the region, speaking to Israelis, Arabs and Palestinians. Fear of being intellectually outgunned keeps many young people in line, though I soon discovered that the likes of Colin Rubenstein are better at bluster and bullying than bare facts. Being a 'young rebel' isn't enough to ensure longevity in this debate, but my confidence is boosted by the realisation that many Zionists are extremely insecure.

In 2003 the American playwright Tony Kushner parodied the rejectionism of the Zionists:

> The Palestinians cannot be mentioned for they do not exist. There are no such people. They are an invention of the Arabs to provide a pretext for destroying Israel, a pretext for 'a second Holocaust.' They are Hashemite Jordanians; let Jordan take them. They are an invention of anti-Semites; they are the latest

fad of the left. There were not 1.2 million of them living in British Mandate Palestine before 1946. There were only 600 000; there were 250 000, there were fewer than that. They sold their land, and they stole the land. They have no culture and no history; they are death-obsessed; their children are crazy with hate; they have refused great kindness from the enemies; for their own suffering they have only themselves to blame. Accounts of Israeli attacks on them are propaganda, the result of falsified, unbalanced information, a lack of sympathy for sufferings of Israelis, and anti-Semitism. And modern Israel is the Jewish patrimony; it was given to us by God.[18]

I have heard this rationale all my life. Denying Palestinians their dignity and humanity is one of the great failings of contemporary Judaism, and no historical calamity justifies it. My reading has led me to embrace a view that sees beyond simple nationalistic slogans and religious obligations. Many other people think the same way, both here and overseas, though reading and listening and watching the Australian media you'd be hard pressed to find evidence. Indiscriminate violence against any people should be condemned, and even more so when it is committed by a people as persecuted throughout their history as the Jews. As long as Israel continues being an aggressor state, we have a moral duty to speak out.

3

JOURNEY INTO ISRAEL

Zionism has exhausted itself ... If the Zionism of today isn't a success story, it's the fault of the Zionists. It's because of the religiosation and Likudisation of Zionism and because what was supposed to be a state of the Jews has become a Jewish state.

Amos Elon, *Haaretz*, 24 December 2004[1]

The Jews' long history as the victims of murderous persecution must not cause us to wrap ourselves in a cult of self-pity, but, on the contrary, should encourage us to take the lead in the world-wide struggle against racism, prejudice and stereotypes that begin with incitement by vile demagogues and can end up in genocide.

Uri Avnery, March 2005[2]

IN EARLY 2005, I spent more than a month in the Middle East and the USA, researching this book. It was the first time I had visited Israel and Palestine, and I had two aims: I wanted to see the situation for myself and talk to ordinary Israelis and Palestinians; I also wanted to hear some of the alternative voices in the debate first hand. Many—such as the grandfather of Israel's peace movement, Uri Avnery—are established journalists, authors and activists in Israel and Palestine, and their views are derived from their lived experience of the Israel–Palestine conflict, but their work receives little attention in Australia.

I had been warned that at Tel Aviv's Ben-Gurion Airport, zealous immigration officials would probably grill me about my plans and intended destinations. A number of pro-Palestinian activists had been barred from entering the country. Ironically, as it turned out, I was questioned for over an hour by a security official apparently obsessed with why a Jew such as me had not made it my business to visit Israel before now. Eventually I persuaded him that the time had never previously been right.[3] I was a Jew in a Jewish country and I was made to feel unwelcome.

The timing of my visit was fortuitous: since Yasser Arafat's death in late 2004, there had been a lull in violence between Israelis and Palestinians—partly because of the Hamas ceasefire negotiated by Palestinian President Abu Mazen—as both sides waited to see what the new Palestinian leadership would bring, though Israeli incursions and settlement construction continued unabated. This relative calm would enable me to travel around much more easily than at other times. During the cab ride into Tel Aviv, I asked the driver whether he thought the situation would continue to improve. 'The death of Arafat, the super terrorist, was a good thing', he told me. 'I hope things will improve. We've given them [the Palestinians] a lot already'. The driver clearly felt that Israel had made enough concessions towards the Palestinians and received little in return. Such misguided views of Israel's supposed generosity appeared constantly throughout my trip.

The centre of Tel Aviv brought to mind the cities of Eastern Europe before the fall of communism, but with more colour and life. The buildings were almost all uniformly grey but interspersed with pleasant green spaces. By arrangement I met a former Australian citizen, Guy Spiegelman, near Rabin Square, the site of the assassination of former Israeli prime minister Yitzhak Rabin in 1995. Spiegelman, a bespectacled 34-year-old, was running for the Israeli Knesset as a member of the Labor Party.[4] Born and raised in Sydney, and a former head of the socialist Zionist youth movement Habonim Dror, he has lived in Israel since 1994.

He told me he is driven to fix Israel's myriad social and economic problems. 'We've spent 60 billion dollars in the territories, and the fastest growing business in Israel today is soup kitchens', he said. 'Our education system in the 1970s was the best in the world and now we're number 25'. The cost of holding on to the territories is simply excessive, he said.[5]

Spiegelman, a progressive, argued that Zionism needs to change and adapt its mission. He talked about the need to evolve a 'new Zionism, sustainable Zionism or post-establishment Zionism', a concept that I will hear other Israeli intellectuals discuss on my visit. What this means is not always well defined, but in Spiegelman's case it seems to mean finding a footing that will provide security and prosperity for Israel, while recognising the validity of Palestinian demands for their own state. Spiegelman told me that he supports in principle the return of half of Jerusalem and the evacuation of the settlements in West Bank and Gaza. He would also back it in practice 'if I could be convinced that they [the Palestinians] weren't going to keep on shooting rockets and sending over suicide bombers'.

He has pushed for Jewish leaders to accommodate left-wing viewpoints because the Left is 'attempting to do the tough work of engaging those who are expressing anti-Israel views. It is a lot more difficult than speaking to the pro-Israel Christian right'.[6]

He derides former Likud minister Natan Sharansky for complaining about the rise of antisemitism and anti-Zionism on US campuses. To Spiegelman, the answer to building a sustainable Israel is greater tolerance:

If you want the future leaders of the Jewish community to stop being silent, to stop feeling like they are in Soviet Russia, encourage criticism and all streams of Jewish thought, left, right and in between to get out and make their many voices heard. Let them speak about Israel for good and for bad, warts and all. You may not like some of what they say—but if you don't let them say it, you may alienate them forever and be left with no footsoldiers in the battle for public opinion, especially amongst academics, unions and left-wing politicians—who used to be Israel's greatest supporters.[7]

Playing pool in Ramallah

From Tel Aviv, I travelled on to Jerusalem. My first priority was to visit the nearby town of Ramallah. A short bus ride took me to the Qalandia checkpoint. Signs of the occupation didn't exist for most Jews living in Jerusalem. Travel down the road, however, and Israel's elaborate occupation was apparent. The 'security' fence snaked around the horizon. The high, imposing concrete wall looked impenetrable. As I easily passed through the checkpoint into the occupied territories of the West Bank, many Palestinians were waiting on the other side of the turnstiles to cross in the opposite direction.

The place they were leaving was a revelation: dusty and uneven roads, signs in Arabic and virtually no Westerners or Israelis, most of whom are legally barred from entering the territories. I arrived in the centre of Ramallah to discover a teeming, chaotic environment. On the walls, posters advertising Mars Bars and portraits of newly elected Palestinian Authority Chairman Mahmoud Abbas were pasted cheek by jowl.

I visited Yasser Arafat's compound, or Muqataa. As I approached the site through the carpark, I saw destroyed buildings inside the compound, the aftermath of a major attack by the Israeli Defense Force (IDF) in 2002. Arafat's request to be buried in Jerusalem had been vetoed by the Israeli authorities, and thus his grave stood inside the Muqataa, housed in a glass-encased room guarded by Palestinian soldiers. I was the only visitor, but I noticed floral wreaths from Norway, France and other European countries. The place was strangely moving, perhaps because of Arafat's contradictory life and his decidedly mixed achievements; he was a man both loved and feared, a dictator and freedom-fighter.

Later, I met Chris Sidoti, a former Australian human rights commissioner, now based in Geneva and working with various NGOs. He had been leading a human rights conference in Ramallah. After dinner, a handful of young Palestinian journalists from the city took us to a smoky, underground pool hall. The men were all in their early twenties, with various levels of English fluency, and were studying either law or media. I was told about frequent delays at Israeli checkpoints. One of the young men had seen a woman giving birth at Qalandia checkpoint the day before. Another told of waiting sometimes three hours a day to simply get to university. 'It's hard to like the Israelis', one said. They talked of feeling trapped. Chris said that being in Ramallah was like living in a Third World country, while the First World beckoned 10 kilometres away in Jerusalem. I left them all at around 11 p.m. and travelled back to the checkpoint. It was virtually empty aside from a handful of Israeli soldiers. Palestinians weren't allowed to leave after early evening, but foreigners could get back into Jerusalem until midnight. An IDF solider waved me towards her, opened my backpack and asked for my passport. 'Why do you want to be in Ramallah?' she said. 'There is nothing to see there.'

Listening in Jerusalem

The following day I attended a conference at Jerusalem's American Colony Hotel, entitled 'Human Rights in Times of Conflict, Human Bombs and Targeted Killings: The Human Rights Perspective'. Professor Eyal Ben-Ari, a specialist in sociology and anthropology and director of the Jerusalem-based Harry S Truman Research Institute for the Advancement of Peace, argued that the IDF's attitudes towards human rights had improved greatly during the 1990s. There was 'growing transparency of IDF actions', he claimed, and demonising Arabs was now 'a rarity'. 'Targeted killings', the act of murdering perceived political opponents, was 'given cultural legitimacy in Israel'. He suggested that the intifada had given Israelis the confidence to support the killing of suspected 'terrorists'. I found his views unconvincing, not least because I knew many Israelis were blissfully unaware of, or complicit with, their government's extreme anti-terror measures. Besides, innocent civilians were often killed during such operations.

The next speaker, a Palestinian, discussed why a handful of Palestinians are drawn to suicide bombing. Lawyer Mohammed Abu-Harthieh attempted to get inside the minds of such people. 'We know we cannot match [Israel's] balance of power, but we can match the balance of terror', he said. When Israel responds with collective punishment rather than targeting individual responsibility, he argued, it is a clear violation of international law. The conference revealed the chasm between the two peoples and the vastly different perspectives on human rights. Israelis were portrayed as righteous while the Palestinians appeared weak and humiliated.

It was a depressing and negative discussion of human rights, but West Jerusalem itself nevertheless seemed to assert the possibilities of a relatively harmonious coexistence between the peoples of Israel. I particularly loved the Old City, a small portion of land populated by Jews, Muslims, Christians and Armenians. The Muslim quarter was dark and its alleys filled with shops selling spices, silver and jewellery. One sign caught my eye: 'Industrial Islamic Orphanage School'. The Jewish quarter revealed men with dark, heavy beards, dressed in the religious Jewish uniform. Some of them were accompanied by their wives; the women walked a few steps behind as they carried the luggage for their husbands—a surreal sight.

The Western Wall was impressive, if disturbing. Religious men offered to place tefillin, leather objects used in prayer, on my arms or head. I declined; they persisted; I refused again, and they became irritable. Nearby a bar mitzvah was in progress. A Jewish boy recited from the Torah, attended by his male relatives, while the women in his life looked on from a distance, standing on chairs placed on a dividing line extending from the middle of the wall.

Nearby is East Jerusalem, almost a completely different world from the rest of the city, predominantly populated by Palestinians and increasingly isolated by Israeli checkpoints and the 'security' fence. Successive Israeli governments have deliberately aimed to isolate and punish Palestinians in an attempt to force them out of the city. Palestinians rightly demand that East Jerusalem be declared the capital of their state, an issue that has a long and fraught history. During my time in the area, I barely saw any Israelis. It was like visiting an Arab country in the heart of the Jewish state.[8]

One evening, I arranged to meet Fadia Daibes and her husband Said in an East Jerusalem hotel.[9] Fadia is a consultant in the Palestinian water sector, and Said a musician. They are a well-travelled couple, fluent in English, evidently well educated and middle class. 'Most tourists don't come to East Jerusalem', Fadia told me, 'because the media and guides say it's dangerous and full of thugs'. In reality, the lives of roughly 250 000 Palestinians in the area are very difficult:

> We're Palestinians but have Israeli ID cards and Jordanian pass-
> ports. Officially, we are not Palestinian. We have no sports cen-
> tres. There is nowhere for us to take our children on long walks.
> Often I have a meeting in the occupied territories and the
> checkpoint closes so you have to cancel. After a while, you just
> make less of an effort to go.

In the mid-1990s, according to Fadia, life for Palestinians in East Jerusalem was 'privileged':

> We could go abroad easily, get permits or exit visas to anywhere.
> After the second intifada in 2000, we were locked in. I used to
> go and shop in a mall in Israel very close to here, because they
> had very nice clothes. Now I don't have the guts or I feel
> ashamed of myself if I go. I feel like a prisoner in Jerusalem. I
> can't easily go to the West Bank [because of the excessive wait-
> ing at checkpoints] or to West Jerusalem, so we have one or two
> entertainment restaurants here that we go to. When I do go to
> Ramallah, with all the blocks and the wall, I still feel it's more
> freedom than here.

Fadia had recently won an award from a Swedish philanthropic organisation dedicated to environmental rejuvenation for her work on water-conservation issues. As she talked about the regional water crisis, I began to see that it was a metaphor for the larger Israel–Palestine conflict. The Jordan River, a major supplier of water for the region, is diminishing fast and is filled with sewage.[10] In Israel and the occupied territories, the Israeli authorities control the distribution of water. The topic was virtually ignored during the Oslo agreement of the 1990s. 'We [the Palestinians] just followed our emotions that we wanted all the water and that doesn't work. They delayed the water issue to the final status negotiations, and when Rabin was assassinated everything was blocked', Fadia explained.

Fadia paints a damning picture [11] of Israel's disregard for the water needs of the Palestinian people. Former Israeli water commissioner Meir Ben Meir quotes the official line: that international law does not apply to Palestinians because Palestine is not recognised as an independent state. Palestinians should buy water from the Israelis, he said. Fadia concluded that long-term sustainable agreements were the only way forward.

Although she believes in cooperation between Israelis and Palestinians, she said that too often this amounts to little more than dinners being held between the two sides rather than concrete plans being laid. She is critical of organisations such as the World Bank and the European Community for shifting their attention from development to emergency relief:

> The World Bank cancelled all the water-development programs and shifted them into emergency, which is fixing a pipe here, fixing a trench there, all the bits and pieces that were damaged by the IDF. Maybe they fix it today and then the IDF will come tomorrow and destroy it again.

She demanded international sanctions against Israel: 'Many donors are in fact subsidising the occupation. I say don't stop the emergency program, but it must be done in parallel with long-term development'.

If Fadia Daibes saw her ideal solution to the conflict implemented, there would be a Palestinian state on the 1967 borders, shared water resources, a divided Jerusalem and shared responsibility on border and security.

From Jenin to troubled Hebron

I wanted to visit the large West Bank town of Jenin, so with a handful of Palestinian passengers I took an overpriced minivan ride across the West Bank. Well-kept Jewish settlements dotted the small hills, alongside poor, dusty Palestinian towns. Farmers carried their produce on goats. The landscape was surprisingly green, and often beautiful.

The roads near Jerusalem and the settlements were smooth, but these soon turned into a pot-holed mess (often caused by Israeli tanks, I was told). We crossed a handful of checkpoints. I noticed that cars with Israeli plates could pass straight through while Palestinian vehicles were checked individually. Access to towns such as Jenin was hassle-free for me, as I was travelling around the West Bank in a period of 'relative calm'. Had I come even a few months earlier, I was constantly reminded, I would probably have faced great difficulties passing Israeli checkpoints.

Jenin's town centre was eerily deserted, the shops closed. It was Friday afternoon, a time of Muslim prayer. In the empty silence, I noticed that thousands of posters covered the walls. Written in Arabic, they showed men carrying guns promoting martyrdom in front of Jerusalem's Dome of the Rock. The faces of assassinated Hamas leaders Sheikh Ahmed Yassin and Abdel Aziz Rantisi seemed to be everywhere.

The place was dusty and unclean, and the buildings decayed. I walked around the deserted market and a few people appeared and stared. I found my way to the refugee camp, site of an infamous Israeli invasion in 2002. A number of children started to follow me and to throw large stones in my direction. I shouted at them to stop but to no avail. I picked up my pace but the kids wouldn't let me out of their sight. At last an old man appeared and screamed at the kids to cease. He spoke very broken English but told me that the children probably thought I was Israeli. 'Not many people come here other than the Israelis', he said. That I was wearing green trousers resembling military fatigues probably didn't help me!

The camp contained many re-built houses and walls. Water ran along the cramped, steep paths. I could see hundreds of houses sitting on small hills in the distance. I was expecting to see visible reminders of the Israeli incursion, but only traces of the destruction remained. When I found the Palestinian Red Crescent office, I learnt that the United Arab Emirates and Saudi Arabia had funded programs to rebuild the refugee camp.

One small building housed a makeshift hospital and a handful of male nurses and doctors. They were friendly and spoke broken English. One man, with growing rage in his eyes, said, 'Sharon is the biggest terrorist. Tell the world this!' I started chatting with Abdul Raouf, a nurse.[12] He was 32 and had once lived in Zurich for a couple of years. 'After 9/11', he said, 'life for Muslims and Arabs in Europe was very hard; they think we're all terrorists'. He told me about life under occupation, about ambulances being fired upon and destroyed by the IDF. A burnt-out ambulance sat outside the Palestinian Crescent building. A few years earlier an IDF sniper had taken aim at the ambulance, and the vehicle had caught fire. Inside the building I met the Palestinian doctor who had been in the ambulance. After 15 months' treatment in a Jordanian hospital, the man still looked sickly. He had several visible skin grafts, and the skin on his face appeared tight.

Raouf told me of many pregnant women dying at checkpoints because the Israelis wouldn't allow their ambulances to pass. He earned 40 shekels for eight hours' work and worked as a cleaner at another hospital to supplement his income. 'Everybody here wants peace, to make a living and space for our children to play', he said. 'This is our land. The Jews should go back to Europe.' When I said that the Jews could not go back to Europe, he acknowledged that it was impossible: 'They say that we should go to Jordan or Syria, but that's not right. We will stay. Most people here think we can live with the Jews, but I don't think so'. He told me about a public hospital in Jenin that had 28 stretchers for beds and was trying to deal with 64 sick children in only seven rooms. Next to the Red Crescent building was the Palestinian police headquarters, still half destroyed by the Israelis. I saw a handful of men in uniform trying to march in time.

As depressing as Jenin was, nothing there prepared me for my visit to Hebron. According to the Bible, Hebron is one of the most spiritual places in historical Palestine, and this is partly why it has become fiercely contested territory. Often virtually inaccessible because of intense violence between the IDF, Palestinian militants and Jewish settlers, no place better exemplifies the apartheid-like policies of the Israeli state. Around 500 settlers live among 170 000 Palestinians, and successive Israeli governments have supported the fundamentalist Jews who openly advocate Palestinian 'ethnic cleansing'.

Unlike other West Bank cities, where I was comfortable discovering places and people myself, in Hebron I followed advice and found a guide. Gunhild Louise Forselv, a tall, lanky Dane whose blonde hair drew attention to her, was a senior press officer with the Temporary International Presence in Hebron (TIPH). The TIPH is a civilian observer mission staffed by personnel from Europe; it was set up after a massacre in 1994, when a settler killed Palestinian worshippers. Its main task is to monitor and report misconduct by either side in the conflict, although they are not permitted to intervene directly and have no military or police functions. The official TIPH mandate is to assist in efforts to 'maintain normal life in the City of Hebron, thus creating a feeling of security among Palestinians'. I soon discovered just how difficult that was.

'We have no agenda, such as ending the occupation', Gunhild told me. I asked her how the IDF responded to their presence ('our relationship is average'), the settlers ('they dislike us, often calling us "Nazis"') and Palestinians ('kids sometimes throw stones at us out of frustration, but mainly we are liked'). The city is divided into an H1 area and an H2 area, an arrangement agreed upon in the 1990s. The intention was to delegate responsibility to both the Palestinian and Israeli authorities, but in reality the arrangement resulted in de facto Israeli control. The result is a Palestinian population virtually kept prisoner in their own homes with their markets and roads closed.

Driving in a four-wheel drive with reinforced windows (for protection against Jewish extremists), we entered H1, where Palestinians are allowed to walk but not drive. The buildings were run-down, and IDF patrols stopped almost every Palestinian man. The streets were virtually deserted, however. 'This is supposed to be the busiest day of the week', Gunhild told me, 'but everybody stays inside'. We spotted a couple of young male settlers with dark beards and untucked white shirts, both carrying automatic weapons. These were representatives of the infamous 'hilltop youth', an extremist Jewish rabble who threaten violence against Ariel Sharon and regularly attack Palestinians.

We entered H2 and got out of the car to look around. I was told to keep my hands visible at all times and not to make eye contact with any Jewish settlers. 'Sometimes they've beaten up members of the TIPH', Gunhild said. In this part of town, only IDF and settlers' cars were allowed. Palestinian land and houses were routinely stolen for 'security purposes'. Areas that were once thriving were now routinely deserted. Many boarded-up shop fronts were sprayed with the Star of David, a crude way for settlers to claim the property as their own. Comparing this behaviour to 1930s Nazi Germany was considered outrageous, Gunhild said. The Christian Peacemaker Teams released a series of photographs taken in Hebron in recent years that showed the attitudes of many settlers to the Palestinians.[13] Some of the graffiti in English included: 'Die Arab Sand Niggers'; 'Exterminate the Muslims'; 'Watch out Fatima, we will rape all Arab Women'; 'Kill All Arabs'; 'White Power: Kill Niggers'; 'Gas the Arabs' and 'Arabs to the Gas Chambers'. It was hard to believe that anybody, let alone Jews, would want to emulate Nazi behaviour.

As we walked through the deserted streets, Gunhild told me that many Palestinians were not allowed to walk down the same roads as Jews, forcing them to leave their homes through neighbours' doors or alleys. Only old men were still selling their wares because they were too old to move away and start a new life. Fences, gates, barbed wire, aggressive IDF soldiers and constant settler provocation made Palestinians prisoners in their own city. The West Bank settlers were more extreme than those in

Gaza, according to Gunhild: 'It's more religious here, rather than political'. The week before I visited, a 15-year-old Palestinian boy had been shot dead by the IDF. He allegedly wielded knives while approaching the soldiers. We both wondered why the boy had to be killed. Gunhild said young soldiers wanted to prove their masculinity and show who was boss. Boredom was a significant factor. The IDF have complete control over the area, being able to issue orders to demolish houses, bar access, close shops, take land and impose curfews.[14]

Virtually all the shops in the souks were closed. Sheets of wire mesh were suspended above the markets. Gunhild explained that this was to prevent settlers, living on the levels above, from throwing rubbish and faeces onto the Palestinians, although the meshing was already groaning under the weight of discarded bottles, clothes and rubbish. As we walked through the market, a Palestinian man approached Gunhild and told her that he and his friends had been sitting and talking in their courtyard when a soldier stationed above them in a guard tower had told them to 'go home'. No reason was given for the directive.

The difficulty of TIPH's mission was underlined early in 2006 following worldwide Muslim outrage over the publication in a Danish newspaper of cartoons that were seen as insulting the prophet Muhammad. Around 300 Palestinians attacked the observer mission in Hebron, threw stones, smashed windows and tried to set the building on fire. Sixty unarmed TIPH members were inside at the time but were unharmed. A week before the protests, eleven Danish members of the mission had left Hebron after receiving threats from local Arab extremists. Gunhild told Associated Press that TIPH had decided, in consultation with the Hebron governor, to keep a low profile and to temporarily cancel patrols.[15] She claimed that Palestinian groups had guaranteed the mission's safety just days before the attack.

Wide-eyed near Gaza

I wanted to enter Gaza but Israeli authorities claimed I didn't have appropriate press credentials. Fellow journalists also told me that Israeli authorities were notoriously suspicious of independent reporters unattached to a major news organisation. A 2003 Israeli directive demanded that all foreign nationals who enter Gaza, including United Nations (UN) workers, sign a form that absolves the army of responsibility if they kill or injure you. It is especially aimed to restrict non-violent direct action against the Israeli military, namely by the International Solidarity Movement (ISM).[16]

I travelled as close to Gaza as possible and rested at Kibbutz Nirim, around 2 kilometres from the border and situated in the Negev desert.

My hosts were Sam and Mara Wisel, now in their seventies, who had migrated from Melbourne to Israel in the late 1950s, keen to live the Zionist dream of building a new nation from scratch.[17] Sam, a solid man with white hair, beard, an Akubra hat and large, worn hands, still used words such as 'proletariat' and 'bourgeoisie'. 'I wanted to come here', he said, 'to be a hard working man with my hands and work the land'. 'I was very gullible', Mara, a petite woman who is fiercely critical of IDF conduct in the territories, told me. Both Sam and Mara retain Australian accents and a strong love for their birth country. They have two children living in Australia, an academic and an artist, and another son who is a senior commander in the IDF and often works covertly in the West Bank. His career choice is a sensitive subject. Mara regrets it, but Sam told me he thinks Ron is 'a good kid who would never do anything wrong'.

The kibbutz felt peaceful. With its green surroundings and 1960s-style concrete architecture, it was like being in a time warp. A few times we ate at the communal dining room, akin to a school cafeteria but with better food. Mara and Sam's apartment was small but decked out with any number of modern appliances.

The local landscape was agriculturally rich, with greenhouses dotting the horizon, noticeably different from the West Bank's rocky, ragged terrain. Several monuments commemorated the lives of Israelis who fell in the conflicts from 1948 to 1967. One plaque referred directly to Kibbutz Nirim: 'In memory of the heroic stand of a handful of Kibbutz Nirim members, who unaided repelled the invading Egyptian army on 15 May 1948, the day of Israel's Declaration of Independence'.

The Negev has been transformed from a desert into rich, fertile farming land, and many *kibbutzniks* reside in the area. Nirim is relatively small, with around 600 members; some kibbutzim have thousands of residents. I was told that some young people no longer wanted the traditional kibbutz lifestyle, and only around 2.1 per cent of the Israeli population lived on kibbutz. Even during their peak in the 1960s and 1970s, no more than 6 per cent of Israelis resided on kibbutz. Once privatisation arrived, the collective spirit started to erode, according to Mara and Sam. I had always presumed that those on kibbutz were politically left-leaning. Not anymore. Many on Nirim were rightists, opponents of the Gaza withdrawal and supporters of the settlers. How had this happened? The post-1967 period was a watershed, Mara and Sam said. A hardening of hearts and a firmer resolve against the Arabs resulted in a determination to keep the occupied territories. By the early 1970s, the fundamentalist settler movement was on the rise, and the country started becoming 'less egalitarian between social and economic classes'. All these factors contributed to the couple's increasing disillusionment with Israel.

As we drove through the Negev countryside, studded with red poppies, I was struck by the absence of Arabs. We approached the entrance of a Gaza settlement block, Gush Katif. Land appropriation was common in the area, with Jewish-only roads and farmers paying residents of Khan Younis a pittance to work in their greenhouses. It was exploitation under conditions of virtual slavery. When I visited, it was only a few months before the planned withdrawal from Gaza, but Mara said she'd heard on the radio that millions of shekels were still being spent on facilities for the settlements, including a library.[18]

On the way back to the kibbutz, we spotted a Bedouin family tending their sheep and were invited into their camp for tea. The family was wary but soon warmed to our presence. A man aged in his twenties, his striking wife and young child all lived under a plastic sheet along with his two brothers. There are about 150 000 Bedouin living in the Negev, about half in urban centres and half in traditional Bedouin rural villages, which the Israeli government refuses to recognise. The result is that rural Bedouin are not connected to national infrastructure and are left without access to water, electricity, sewage, health services, educational facilities and roads. Mara and Sam have long worked to improve their rights.

We sat on Mara and Sam's outside veranda and heard the constant whirring of F-16s overhead. 'Until about three weeks ago, you couldn't sit out here', Mara said. 'There was gunfire, loud helicopters and explosions within earshot all the time.' Sam maintained his faith in the country, its media and its government, despite vehemently disagreeing with much of the current situation. Mara was more pessimistic. 'The spell has been broken here some time ago', she said. She and a group of friends protested every Friday afternoon at the road to Gush Katif—'we haven't missed one in four years'—holding up signs for the settlers inside to read: 'Come back to Israel. We welcome you'.

Sam and Mara impressed me as honest people who had lived their lives according to a combination of Marxist, revolutionary Zionist and pro-Palestinian sympathies: 'We only learnt about what really happened in 1948 much later with the New Historians [such as Ilan Pappe and Benny Morris.]'. Mara acknowledged that their initial ignorance of the events was because 'nobody told us, or we didn't want to hear or we were brainwashed. We very much wanted to believe the dream'. I enjoyed hearing about their belief in an alternative to capitalism and the ways in which they had put this into practice over the years. 'We were both Zionists from the beginning, but we were always very conscious and very sensitive about the Arab issue', Sam said. 'We accepted at face value the equality of Jews and Arabs in Israel.'

The couple's idealism is not completely shattered. 'I still do believe that Jews need a national home', Mara said. 'I remember we even thought of once going to South Africa to fight against apartheid. Israel was that sort of business. We were going to do a little more than just live and die as a nuclear family.'

Sam's family had lived in Palestine for generations before they migrated to Australia. None of his relatives had died in the Holocaust. Sam identified strongly with the Australian working-class culture in which he grew up. He thought he saw its egalitarian impulse in Zionism:

> I felt that Zionism also recognised the right of other peoples. I've often heard the argument, even to this day, that if we have the right to demand national independence, so do others. I can see in the Jewish communities in the world, in America, Australia and England, the Jewish question has been paramount, and they don't recognise that if you're a Zionist, you're a Zionist for everybody.

The 1982 Lebanon war was another turning point for Sam and Mara. Sam was one of the first to protest against the war in Tel Aviv, a mere three weeks after its beginning. 'That would have been unheard of before', Sam said. 'People certainly disagreed with Israeli actions but would never dare say it in public.'

Mara struggles with disillusionment: 'I often say to Sam that I'm losing hope and maybe we should move back to Australia. I think it was first when Sharon became Minister of Defense. The second time was when he became Prime Minister. I said I can't stand this any longer, but I'm still here'.

The following day I met Alon Schuster, Mayor of Sha'ar Hanegev, the region where Sam and Mara live.[19] Sha'ar Hanegev advertises itself as 'fulfilling David Ben-Gurion's vision of settling the Negev and making the desert bloom'. Six thousand citizens are scattered across 45 000 acres, and some are re-establishing relationships between Israeli and Palestinian communities. A large photo of Ariel Sharon was displayed in Schuster's office. I asked him about it. 'I'm a leftie', he said, 'but I support Sharon because I think he is the best accomplisher of my agenda. He is doing what we were dreaming by pulling out of Gaza. He's a son of a bitch but he's our son of a bitch now'.

A bit like Guy Spiegelman, Schuster believes that Zionism has achieved its aims and it is now time to reinvent the ideology. But again it is complicated: he believes in a Palestinian state, but refuses to accept Israeli responsibility for the failure to establish it.

As we talked I discovered that, as for Sam and Mara, Lebanon had been a turning point for Schuster: 'I volunteered for the war in Lebanon because I believed in supporting the decision of a democratic state. But three weeks later I was publicly protesting the wrongness of the campaign'. I asked him if he supported soldiers who refused to serve in the occupied territories because of their objection to the occupation. 'In a democratic society, good people shouldn't be acting like that', he said. 'The army needs good people to stop the bad people.' Sam had expressed similar views the day before in relation to his son. Perhaps this was his way to deal with his son's role in the IDF.

Meeting a refusnik

I was keen to meet an Israeli refusnik. Matan Kaminer refused to serve in his country's army and paid the price, spending nearly two years in prison.[20] In 2004 Kaminer joined five others in one of the more high-profile cases of this relatively new movement in Israel's militaristic society. The three sentencing judges said they were guilty of a 'very severe crime which constitutes a manifest and concrete danger to our existence and our survival'. During their 21-month gaol term, their families launched an effective public relations campaign to highlight their plights. One of Kaminer's colleagues-in-arms, Haggai Matar, told the *Guardian* that Israel was punishing them especially harshly because they had gone public and could 'affect other people'.[21]

I found Kaminer to be a highly articulate 22-year-old and unlike anyone else I've ever met. Sitting in his small, messy student apartment in Jerusalem, he told me that his father had refused to serve in the Lebanon war and had gone to prison for his beliefs. Despite being part of the radical Left in Israel, Kaminer said that he had felt moderately optimistic during the 1990s and the Oslo agreements:

> I remember thinking when I was 10 or 11 that when I was 18 there wouldn't be any need to go to the army. With the outbreak of the second intifada, the Zionist Left evaporated and what remained was to be radical. We were told that you were either for [Ehud] Barak and the proposals he made to the Palestinians—accepted by most of the Zionist Left—or you disagreed and said that any

acceptable offer would have to include the Palestinian capital in East Jerusalem and a settlement to the refugee problem. For me, refusing to serve in the occupied territories was a political act.

Kaminer's ideological opposition to the occupation stems from the belief that 'being ruled by another people ... is as far from democracy as you can get'. A declared anti-Zionist, Kaminer said that the definition of Zionism had changed radically over the years: 'Noam Chomsky said that 50 years ago I was called a Zionist and now I'm called an anti-Zionist, even though my views haven't changed'. The palpable fear and racism within Israeli society towards Arabs and Palestinians are because 'we want to be a western European country and the Palestinians are not from those origins'. His objection to Zionism is based on its inherent bias towards one people over another. During Kaminer's court martial, the authorities threatened that the five men would have to enlist again after their sentences since they had never served their full terms in the IDF.

Yet other conscientious objectors had started to come forward. In December 2003, thirteen reservists from Israel's elite military commando unit sent a letter to Ariel Sharon explaining their refusal to serve any longer in the occupied territories.[22] They joined a growing group of individuals, from former security chiefs to reserve pilots, who, by the early part of the decade, had started openly questioning official government policy.[23]

In the same month, a group of elite soldiers released a letter of refusal to the public. It began, 'We, reserve combat officers and soldiers of the Israeli Defense Forces, who were raised upon the principles of Zionism, self-sacrifice and giving to the people of Israel'. It succinctly summarised the 'corruption of the entire Israeli society', declaring that 'We shall not continue to fight beyond the 1967 borders in order to dominate, expel, starve and humiliate an entire people'.[24]

Kaminer told me that his refusal started by gathering a handful of friends together while still at school and issuing a high school seniors' letter that articulated the reasons for their proposed action. They began as 62 people and within a year had gathered 350 signatures. Despite their principled stance, he said, 'most young Israelis are completely oblivious to any possibility of revolutionary change' and are fearful of refusing military service because of the known consequences. Kaminer reminded me that not everybody goes into the army in Israel: 'Twenty per cent of the population are Arab citizens of Israel and another 10 per cent are the ultra religious Yeshiva students who also get exempted. Something like 30 to 40 per cent don't complete their service at all'. During his time in gaol, he found many of the other prisoners were less than sympathetic with his political stance. He was not physically abused but often threatened or simply ignored.

His ideal solution to the conflict is a one-state solution, with Palestinians and Israelis living together, but he acknowledges that separate states are a more realistic option for the foreseeable future. The right of return is a more complex problem. The idea that every Palestinian refugee has to return exactly to where they came from is unacceptable:

> Most of the refugees today were not actually born there, and they are second, third and fourth generation. There is not really anywhere to return to. Many of the places have been completely destroyed and the ones that remain are mostly occupied by other people, so to right a wrong that was made years ago, and throw people out of their homes now, is a mistake. I don't think the Palestinians want them there either.

Kaminer continues his activism as he believes the current direction of the Jewish state is leading to further tension with the Palestinians. He now works for Rabbis for Human Rights, an Israeli NGO dedicated to resisting Israeli oppression of Palestinians.

A day with Amira Hass

The following day I spent in the West Bank with Amira Hass, one of Israel's leading journalists.[25] 'I'm called "a correspondent on Palestinian affairs"', Hass once said, 'but it's more accurate to say that I'm an expert in Israeli occupation'.[26] Between 1993 and 1997, she reported exclusively from Gaza and wrote a book about her experiences, *Drinking the Sea at Gaza*.[27] Now she is based in Ramallah and reports on life in the occupied territories for *Haaretz*. As a child of secular Holocaust survivors, she inherited a strong sense of justice and sympathy for the struggle of persecuted peoples. She loves Israel despite being an avowed non-Zionist.

When few other journalists questioned the official version of events and their consequences, Hass understood—not least because she was living among those the Israelis were trying to suffocate—that Israeli policy in the West Bank and Gaza was leading to inevitable failure: 'The only Israelis this generation of Palestinians know are soldiers and settlers. For them, Israel is no more than subsidiary of an army that knows no limits and settlements that know no borders'.[28] Her stories generate masses of emails from readers, some of which are vitriolic. She told Robert Fisk in 2001 that some messages compared her to the Nazis; others hoped that she would suffer from breast cancer, and many argued that there would be no peace until all Palestinians were expelled.

I met Hass—a plump woman, dressed in black and wearing a white scarf and trainers—at a central bus stop just outside Jerusalem. An *Haaretz* photographer accompanied us, and our driver and guide was Dror Etkes, settlement watch coordinator for Israeli group Peace Now. We travelled to a German school on the outskirts of Beit Jala. There are 830 boys and girls at Talitha Kumi School, a German Evangelical Lutheran Institution; 70 per cent are Christian and 30 per cent are Muslim. Students from Bethlehem and the West Bank learn together in a coeducational environment. There is a dormitory for boys, though they stopped accepting girls from Gaza in the mid-1990s because of Israel's closure policies. Girls were often unable to visit Gaza or return to school after a visit.

Most students only attended school three days a week because of the difficulty of getting home to Palestinian towns and villages. Free movement was a significant problem for staff as well as students. The school's music teacher, who lived in Bethlehem, had written a Christmas song that was aired on Israeli television. Despite this, when she requested a permit to enter Jerusalem to buy a new piano, the Israeli authorities refused and gave no reason.

The school's principal, Dr Georg Duerr, told us that the proposed path of the fence would restrict access to students living a mere half-kilometre from the school. Israelis authorities informed him that a 'humanitarian tunnel' would be built to facilitate easier access. Duerr said that he held little faith in official guarantees as past experience taught him to believe virtually nothing they said. 'Our school is trying to make a model of harmony', he told us. Duerr worked in South Africa during the years of apartheid and opened a school that allowed both white and black students. The similarities to current-day Israel were highly unfortunate, he said.

Talitha Kumi is a beautiful school with bright, airy rooms. From the roof, we were treated to wonderful views of the lush valleys soon to be criss-crossed by the wall. Etkes said that Israelis were currently 'battling between hating Arabs and hating settlers, but hating Arabs was a stronger feeling'. Many Israelis increasingly felt that settler extremism had crippled the Jewish state economically and socially, but ingrained anti-Arab racism permeated every level of society. Hass responded pessimistically: 'Maybe in 50 years, the economic situation will be so bad that things will change, but not before then. Things will only change with Israeli,

Palestinian and international pressure. And when the Left offers more than slogans'. She has an infectious laugh, but remained resolutely serious throughout the day.

We drove to the Efrat settlement. My companions commented that every time they visited it appeared to have expanded further. Fences sprang up, then were moved; Palestinian land was taken, and new Jewish-only roads were funded. We went through Tamar settlement, situated on a hilltop near Bethlehem. Some men were erecting power poles and looked at us suspiciously. The mobile homes at Tamar were illegal, but Etkes said that the authorities turned a blind eye. There were panoramic vistas from the settlement and I could see how Palestinian towns were being surrounded by Jewish settlements.[29]

We drove on to the settlement of Beitar Illit, a massive development whose many red-roofed houses blotted the landscape. Empty land behind was slated for further development. Shrinking Palestinian towns sat on one side, soon to be surrounded by the wall and more settlers. Hass was exasperated. She said she'd seen such developments even during the 'peace process' years. Bypass roads for Jewish-only traffic were everywhere, but we didn't use them, as cars were sometimes ambushed by Palestinian militants.

We stopped in a Palestinian village and were invited into a house. One of the men there knew Hass's work. As we sat in the lounge room, Hass told me that the Palestinians were 'resigned mainly, not angry' about the wall and imposing settlements. The view from our guest's roof was spectacular, but the ultra-Orthodox Beitar Illit settlements were now virtually on their doorstep. He told Hass that a few weeks before our visit, a few of his friends had tried to meet up with some Israeli activists, including Matan Kaminer, from peace group Ta'ayoush. When the IDF discovered the Israelis were coming, they placed a military cordon around the town and restricted access. Another time they demanded the phone numbers of all the participants meeting in a house. They stood outside, Hass was told, 'as if they were going to shoot us'.

Etkes and Hass said that most Israelis had no idea about what really went on in the occupied territories. There was almost full media complicity with Israeli authorities, they told me. Hass said that *Haaretz* was the only outlet that would publish her work, though her current editor wasn't always supportive and sometimes held pieces or placed them at the back of the paper. The last intifada had caused the Israeli media to question less and to accept more government spin, Hass said.[30] She found fault with the other side, too: 'It's frustrating that often the Palestinians don't protest or complain until the bulldozers arrive [to demolish their houses]'.

Her work consistently gives voice to perspectives rarely articulated in mainstream Israeli society. 'What drives me is anger, the injustice of it all', she said. 'Sometimes I get very frustrated and have to turn away and read fiction. Somebody has to write what happens so nobody can say they didn't know. It's important that Jews write about this. It's who we are and we shouldn't hide it.'

Maintaining the rage

Along with Amira Hass, Gideon Levy is Israel's other truly maverick journalist. Having worked at *Haaretz* for over 20 years, he's spent many of these writing solely on the occupation. 'I want to write about what Israelis are doing on my behalf', he told me.[31] A tough-looking man with cropped hair, Levy reminded me of Hass, with a seemingly endless supply of determination and anger.[32] He doesn't see himself as being like Hass, however:

> We come from different backgrounds. Amira was raised in a communist community and she came already loaded with a lot of political ideals, while my development was much more gradual because I was just an ordinary guy and not very political. I worked for four years with Shimon Peres when he was leader of the Opposition. I became more radical later.

Levy said that the occupation had become more brutal during his years of reporting:

> I can recall the famous scene during the first intifada, broadcast on CBS, that showed Israeli soldiers breaking the bones of Palestinians with stones. Everyone was shocked by that scene and it was broadcast all over the world. It was, we thought, the most terrible thing that we could imagine. Today I wouldn't even mention it because kids are killed like flies.

He argued that Israelis have been conditioned to believe that 'Palestinians are not human beings like us', otherwise 'they would never be able to live with the thought that they were doing such terrible things to other human beings'. He told me how world Jewry both supports and condones Israeli brutality:

> For them, military strength is the only strength. American Jewry, and maybe in Australia too, offer the ultimate self-orientation:

'We are the ultimate victim' and nobody else has the right living here, especially after the Holocaust. Every time I hear this slogan that Israel is the only democracy in the Middle East, I don't know if to laugh or cry, because a state with one of the most brutal and cruel military occupations in the world isn't a democracy.

Levy calls himself an 'anti-Zionist' although he believes Jews living in Israel have every right to live there. He imagines a two-state solution and a return of some of the Palestinian refugees:

Listen, we absorbed one million Russians in ten years, more than half of them were not Jewish. So why, for God's sake, can't we absorb half a million Palestinians who were born here, who own this land, whose memories are here, whose everything is here? They belong to here ten times more than all the Russians and the Europeans and maybe me. After this solution will take place, we may realise that it's better for both states to federate or become one state.

Despite having a high profile in Israel, his media appearances have significantly decreased in recent years. Levy used to have a weekly television show but is now rarely asked to participate on radio or television talk shows: 'They take someone from the extreme Right and from the centre and never from the radical Left. There have been tensions at *Haaretz* but generally they can live with me'. Although he receives hate mail, including death threats, he believes that some reaction is better than indifference.

He holds the Israeli media heavily responsible for hiding the true face of the occupation and showing 'our' victims but never 'their' victims in the same light:

We face a deeper problem of self-censorship, not because somebody tells them to be like this, but because they believe that their place is to sit in the bulldozer who ruins the house and not with the families who are left behind. If they show something they will show the bulldozer and not the families who are left. They will tell you about the so-called reasons why the house was demolished but they will never check. They will say today Israel assassinated a big terrorist, but they will never check whether he was such a big terrorist. Every settler who is scratched by a stone will get two pages in a newspaper and nobody will mention the Palestinian family who lost three children. It's easier for Israelis to dismiss Amira [Hass] because she lives in Ramallah and not here. With me it is harder because I am here and part of it.

'I think deep in their hearts, most Israelis are really racist', he told me sadly. He compares present-day Israel to apartheid in South Africa:

When you drive a road in the West Bank which is a road for only Jews, what is it if not apartheid? When you cross a checkpoint which is only open for Jews, what is it if not apartheid? If you are an Israeli citizen of Palestinian origin who tries to find in this liberal neighbourhood an apartment to rent and you have terrible difficulties doing so because you are Palestinian, what is it if not apartheid?[33]

Despite this attitude, he loves his country: 'I wouldn't live in any other place in the world. I'm part of it; I was born here and I think I will never leave'.

Levy supports sanctions against the Israeli state, believing that only outside help can end the occupation: 'I think if the American President wanted to end the occupation, it could end in two months. But we will never have it because of the Jewish lobby'. He encourages Europe to play a more active role but understands the historical difficulties: 'Europe is neutralised because of the Holocaust. Every time there is just a small voice against Israel, immediately this whole mechanism is saying "anti-Semitism" and "Europe, don't you dare". Israel today is an immoral state, one of the most immoral states in the world'.

Israel's Chomsky

One of the most trenchant critics of the Israeli political and media establishment is linguist Tanya Reinhart. Like Noam Chomsky, she attacks the media for the responsibility they must bear for the failed peace process. A columnist for Israel's mass circulation daily *Yediot Aharonot*, she spends six months of every year teaching at the Netherlands' University of Utrecht and the rest of the year at Tel Aviv University. Her book *Israel/Palestine: How to end the war of 1948* is a devastating critique of the Israeli establishment and its desire, in Reinhart's interpretation, to provoke a Palestinian intifada in October 2000. When Sharon described Israel's war against the Palestinians as 'the second half of 1948', she wrote, 'there can be little doubt that what they mean is that the work of ethnic cleansing was only half completed in 1948, leaving too much land to Palestinians'.[34]

A central aspect of Reinhart's book is its forensic analysis of the failed peace talks at Camp David in 2000, between Ehud Barak and Yasser Arafat. The book was released in Hebrew in 2005, and *Haaretz* reviewer Yitzhak Laor praised Reinhart's ability to expose the fallacy, still accepted by many, that the Israeli leader had offered the Palestinians 'the lot, they rejected the offer and then they launched an attack on us'.[35] Former head of Israel's Military Intelligence Amos Malka told *Haaretz* in 2004 that every effort was made by the political and military elite to turn Palestinian disquiet into war.[36] When Sharon visited the Temple Mount in 2000, the Israeli response to Palestinian protests, orchestrated by Sharon and Ehud Barak, was deliberately brutal. In the first days of the uprising, soldiers in the territories fired 1 300 000 bullets, according to *Haaretz* in June 2004.[37] 'The intent was to score a winning blow against the Palestinians and especially against their consciousness', according to the report. 'This was not a war on terror, but on the Palestinian people.' Reinhart argued that this was a deliberate attempt to crush Palestinian nationalism once and for all, and that the media sold the propaganda line that the intifada seriously threatened Israel's very existence.

One would expect such revelations to cause a massive stir. And yet Reinhart knows that Israeli society has remained mute. The majority of Israelis are fed up with the occupation, she told me, so

> how do you get this majority to stay obedient? The only way is to convince them that the government is doing everything possible to find peace and it's just impossible. The first intifada brought a change in Israeli public opinion. We began to understand that the occupation has a price, that it's not coming for free.[38]

She wrote in May 2005 that one must read the *Guardian* and watch Aljazeera in order to find out what goes on in Israel.[39] 'The spokesman of the Israeli regime writes the news, the media prints and broadcasts it and the analysts recycle it', she said. I asked whether she had considered leaving Israel permanently and she told me that she and her husband 'talked about it all the time. We talk about a red line and that line is being crossed'. The week before my visit, Reinhart's husband had one of his poems pulled from *Haaretz*. 'You can't call Sharon a murderer in public anymore', she complained. Surely Sharon's bloody record should be a legitimate target of satirists, artists and writers, she said.

The grandfather of the peace movement

My last interview was, perhaps appropriately, with Uri Avnery, the 'grand-father' of the Israeli peace movement. We met in his central Tel Aviv apartment overlooking the city and the Security Services building. His lounge room was filled with numerous bookshelves, artefacts from around the world and two framed photos of himself and Yasser Arafat. One was of their first meeting in 1974 and the second was taken at a more recent peace conference, where Arafat approached him and they embraced. Avnery is in his eighties, with piercing eyes and a white beard and hair, but he remains optimistic about the prospect of peace, and is highly engaged.

Avnery's life has reflected the history of his country. He was a soldier in pre-state Israel, is a writer and journalist, and a former politician and founder of numerous left-wing political movements including Gush Shalom.[40] Avi Shavit wrote in *Haaretz* in November 2004 that Avnery's major political contribution was to bring Yasser Arafat 'into our lives'.[41] 'Arafat will be remembered as one of the greatest leaders of the second half of the twentieth century', Avnery predicts.[42] Nevertheless, Avnery's voice is marginalised within Israel itself, though the Internet has allowed many more to read his weekly columns.

During our long conversation, Avnery was part philosopher and part pragmatist. 'Zionism has not changed', he said, 'but circumstances have changed. Zionism is becoming more powerful and therefore the possibility of taking hold of ever-greater parts of Palestine is real. It's a war. War prevents seeing the other side as it is. Ariel Sharon is the epitome of all this. He's the ultimate terror fighter'.

Avnery argues that Sharon is the direct heir to founding father David Ben-Gurion:

> Ben-Gurion was determined to have a Jewish state as big as possible with as few non-Jews in it as possible. He was determined to reach this in stages, achieving at every stage only that what was achievable. Sharon is very much the same. He is immovable. He wants all of Palestine to become a Jewish state with not a single Arab in it. He is not fanatically blind and he does not want to overreach himself, so he wants to use the circumstances of every stage in order to achieve what is possible, leaving it to the future to achieve more.[43]

He dismissed the self-proclaimed leaders of the Israeli peace movement Peace Now and the Labor Party as the 'moderate parts of the Zionist enterprise'. 'They have very little to do with peace', he said. The real peace movement, however, had had immense influence:

> Fifty years ago, there were not 10 people in all of this country who even recognised the existence of a Palestinian people, not to mention a Palestinian state. It was unthinkable. Today, the fact that the Palestinian people exist is accepted by practically everyone. Most people considered it treason when we made contact with the PLO in the 1970s, including the government of Israel. Today the Left generally supports Sharon. You have this curious duality in Israeli life, which amazes people, including Israelis. In the public opinion polls, the majority accept our point of view, more or less. While in the same opinion polls, the majority supports a right-wing leadership, which is doing the exact opposite. This is not new; it has been around for as long as I can remember.

Avnery wants Israelis to see themselves as an 'Israeli civilisation, not a Jewish civilisation'. What does he mean?

> The settlers and their allies, a considerable minority in Israel, want a Jewish state in the real sense of the word. Separation between state and religion is quite unthinkable for them. They want a state ruled by the rabbis, according to Jewish religious law, very much like the Islamic fundamentalists. Against this you have the majority who want a democratic state ruled by Parliament. I've been saying since before the state of Israel that a Jewish democratic state is a contradiction. There is a law that says you cannot stand for elections if you deny this is a Jewish democratic state.

The USA and Australia share a deep affinity with Israel for 'unconscious reasons', he said. 'Namely, trying to eradicate the local population and committing genocide. For Americans, Israel is really not just a second America, but justifies American history. America, I believe, has never come to terms with its own history.'

According to Avnery, the future national identity of Israel is the next major challenge.

Guess who's coming to dinner

Although I had never visited Israel, I have family there, based in Ramat Hasharon, about a 20-minute drive from central Tel Aviv. I had met some of these relatives years before in London, where some then lived, and distinctly remembered their bellicose views on the conflict.

Ronnie and Lilly Green, both in their sixties, welcomed me into their home. Ronnie is a warm, gregarious man with a strong English accent. I told myself it would be best to avoid mentioning the conflict, but he knew I was researching a book. I offered the briefest of explanations of its likely content. 'Your book will have the wrong views', he told me. Over the coming two days, I experienced a barrage of Ronnie's vitriol. Some 'highlights':

Germany is the devil. I've never been there and never will. And my children, luckily, share the same view. We have no German products. I don't think Israel should have accepted Germany money [soon after its birth] or support for at least 50 years. But when it's a matter of survival, it's a difficult decision.

You can't be pro-Palestinian without being anti-Israel. But you can be pro-Israel and pro-Palestinian.

I've never read in the Israeli press any incitement or hatred of Arabs. Never.

We should be harder against the Palestinians, crush them, until they realise that we aren't going anywhere. Only force will make them understand.

The world hates Jews and hates Israel. They always have and always will. They hate now that we're strong.

I don't care if the Palestinians are suffering. We must come first.

The checkpoints, the wall and bypass roads are all necessary to keep Palestinians from killing Jews.

I don't know of any Arab or Palestinian academic, protester or individual, except for a few, that don't hate Israel and Jews.

His passion was violent and astounding. I tried to stop the conversation numerous times, but he refused, determined to convince me how wrong I was: 'The only good book on this subject is Alan Dershowitz's *The Case for Israel*', he told me. 'He understands . . . I used to be left-wing but not when I realised that they hate us. It's not their land. It's ours.

The country hasn't been hijacked by right-wing fanatics and the settlers. I'm willing to compromise, probably on Jerusalem and the territories.' This last sentence contradicted many of his previous statements, but he refused to elaborate.

Other members of the family were invited over for a Sabbath meal. Ronnie and Lilly's daughter, Danielle, was equally confrontational. 'In Israel', she said, 'people are very political and we all have very strong views on everything'.

I was mildly reassured when Ronnie told me that, despite our disagreements, 'Blood is thicker than water. We're family'. A few hours later a suicide bomber ripped through a crowd waiting for entry into a popular Tel Aviv nightclub, killing five people. It was the first such attack inside Israel for many months. Emotions were frayed inside the house. Ronnie paced in front of the television and lectured me on the reasons why negotiations could never work with 'these people'. I didn't know what to say.

I felt saddened by Ronnie's attitude. I wondered if I'd be just as intolerant if I lived in Israel. There was a complete lack of empathy or understanding of the other side, and there was demonisation of Arabs, and hatred of the UN and France. Israel was the eternal victim, continually fighting for its very existence. 'We used to allow Palestinians to work here [in Israel]', he said, 'but now we don't anymore, thankfully'.[44]

In an article he wrote to mark the sixtieth anniversary of Auschwitz, Tom Segev described the condition that seemed to afflict my cousins, and many others I met in Israel. The Holocaust had created an Israeli society unable or unwilling to see other's suffering. In Segev's words:

> The hatred of Arabs has become legitimate. A state in which so many of its citizens survived the Holocaust is supposed to be strict in its observance of democracy and human rights ... Ironically, the oppression in the territories is encouraging anti-Semitism, and in various places in the world it is even endangering the safety of Jews.[45]

Before my travels, I had hoped to discover voices of optimism in Israel and Palestine, and I did, here and there. It was clear that some Israelis were ready for a different future, ready for a different Zionism, even if their own thoughts about it were sometimes self-contradictory, and they were still struggling to see the way ahead. There was concern about the impact of continued conflict, not only on Palestinians in the occupied territories, but on the future of Israel itself. Progressive voices had been marginalised for too long, partly a result of Palestinian suicide attacks and hardening Israeli attitudes. The Oslo years may have been initially embraced by the wider Israeli and Palestinian populations, but an ever-deepening occupation soon turned this hope into hatred for many Palestinians.

The overriding sense was one of frustration. Palestinians knew their voices weren't being heard on the world stage, and Israelis felt persecuted in the court of global opinion. I had little sympathy for the latter. Operating an illegal occupation for nearly 40 years must have a cost. I felt ashamed during much of my time in Israel, and this became even more acute while travelling around the West Bank. I was embarrassed to be a Jew in a country that so openly and brazenly discriminated against non-Jews. Especially given our history, this situation was deeply shaming and morally unacceptable.

I sensed a growing awareness, however, that the current direction was doomed. When a former deputy director of Mossad can publicly lambast the IDF as 'soulless and merciless',[46] one knows the tide must be turning. The likely outcomes are less clear. My relatives' callousness, while shocking, shouldn't have surprised me. After all, successive Israeli governments wouldn't have been able to get away with such murderous policies had it not been elected by a majority of voters in a free country with a relatively open press.

The trip made me question the role of my journalism. Was I simply trying to report the situation on the ground, a reality often ignored in the Western media? Or did I have a broader agenda: was I trying to show the precarious position of an undemocratic Jewish state in the middle of an autocratic Arab world? Ariel Sharon said in 2001: 'Israel may have the right to put others on trial, but certainly no one has the right to put the Jewish people and the State of Israel on trial'.[47] That kind of hypocrisy permeates the attitudes of many Jews and Israelis to their homeland. I realised I needed a better understanding of where this hypocrisy came from. I needed to know more about Zionism, and the related issue of antisemitism.

ZIONISM AND ANTISEMITISM

4

THE PROBLEM OF ZIONISM

*Zionism is a kind of romantic nationalism fundamentally at
odds with liberal values.*

Norman Finkelstein, 2001[1]

*There was a strong element of self-righteousness and short-
sightedness in the early Zionists and they overlooked the
presence of the Arab population and its significance. They had
the self-righteousness of victims preoccupied with their own
victimisation to the degree that they could not even imagine
that they could commit any kind of injustice to another.*

Amos Oz, 2004[2]

WHEN THE FATHER of Zionism, the Austrian journalist and playwright
Theodor Herzl, promulgated his vision for a Jewish homeland in 1896,
he imagined a secular state in the Middle East with few aspects of traditional Jewish culture, a nation that had more in common with the countries of central Europe than with the rest of the region. His seminal
pamphlet *Der Judenstaat* (*The State of the Jews*) was praised by some as the
only true solution to the eternal problem of antisemitism, but was
ridiculed by others as idealistic nonsense.[3] And indeed, if the aim of a

Jewish state was to provide stability and security for Jews, then Herzl, if he were alive today, would be sorely disappointed by the way things have turned out.

Israel today is a nation at a crossroads, with a population of about 5.3 million Israeli Jews and nearly 1.4 million Israeli Arabs. About another four million Palestinians are registered as refugees by the UN. As the distinguished Israeli philosopher Yeshayahu Leibowitz observed after the Six Day War: 'A state governing a hostile population of 1.5 to 2 million foreigners is bound to become a security service state, with all this implies for the spirit of education, freedom of speech and thought and democracy. Israel will be infected with corruption, characteristic of any colonial regime'.[4]

There is plenty of evidence that the state of Israel has become a colonial oppressor, just as Leibowitz feared, including a brutal occupation, Jewish-only roads in the occupied territories and racially discriminatory policies in Israel proper. I witnessed it myself during my visit to the occupied territories in early 2005. This development has not gone unnoticed, or unopposed, by a minority of Israeli Jews. As Professor Mordechai Kremnitzer of Jerusalem's Hebrew University said, commenting in 2004 on the IDF's policy of demolishing the houses of Palestinians whose relatives had allegedly committed terrorist acts: 'The destruction of houses is a callous violation of international law that is impossible to defend under principled examination. I am certain that in another twenty years, there will not be a single person in Israeli society who does not say home demolitions are barbaric and shameful'.[5]

Zionism is normally seen as a nationalist, ethnic or religious movement, but what if it is examined from the perspective of race? Professor Ilan Pappe, lecturer in politics at Haifa University, and one of Israel's leading dissenting intellectuals, argues that Zionism today should be seen as an 'exclusionary ideology' because 'it's the kind of ideology which defines who belongs and who doesn't belong in the state of Israel, and obviously anyone who is not a Jew does not [truly] belong'.[6] What has gone wrong? How did Zionism's dream of a utopia turn into a humanist's nightmare?

The birth of Zionism

The history of the conflict in Israel–Palestine is one in which almost every fact is contested and fiercely debated, and Palestinian and Zionist narratives compete for historical supremacy. The ferocity of these historical debates has only intensified since the 1967 war, which led to the oppressive occupation of the Palestinians in Gaza and the West Bank. To understand the true reasons for the conflict, one must comprehend the birth of the Zionist movement, for the real roots of today's conflict in Israel–Palestine can be clearly traced to those early days of European colonial thinking at the end of the nineteenth century. Herzl's seminal essay on the Jewish state shamefully ignored the indigenous Arabs of Palestine, even though it is clear that Herzl realised that the Palestinians would not simply disappear and make way for massive Jewish immigration.[7] It was perhaps the first but certainly not the last time that the Palestinians were treated simply as if they didn't exist.

The trial of Alfred Dreyfus in 1894, which Herzl covered as a journalist, was the catalyst for his Zionism. Dreyfus was a French military officer unjustly accused of treason by sections of a society driven by antisemitism. Jewish secularists had long argued that assimilation was their best hope for acceptance in European society, but Herzl, himself an assimilated Jew, believed that the Dreyfus affair proved definitively that they were wrong. In his writings, he drew on elements of an established Jewish intellectual tradition that had originated in post-Enlightenment Eastern Europe in the 1850s. According to Pappe, 'its practitioners abandoned centuries of religious dogmatism for reason and science, in search of solutions for the particular problem of Jewish existence in Europe'.[8] Judaism was no longer seen as merely a religion but as a nation.

The first Zionist Congress was held in 1897 in Basel, Switzerland. Conservative rabbis regarded Zionism as being against God's will and thought Jews should remain in exile until the Messiah's coming (some religious Jews still champion this cause). For most attendees, however, Herzl's idea, while seemingly outrageous, had irresistible appeal. Herzl wrote in his diary: 'At Basel I founded the Jewish state. If I said this out loud today I would be answered with universal laughter. Perhaps in five years, certainly in 50, everyone will know it'.[9] In part, Herzl drew strength for the cause from antisemitism, understanding that it could be harnessed to convince European leaders to support Zionism in order to solve the problem of Judeophobia in their countries. Herzl once commented that antisemitism served to 'inhibit the ostentatious flaunting of conspicuous wealth, curb the unscrupulous behaviour of Jewish financiers and contribute in many ways to the education of the Jews'.[10] He was not alone in thinking that Jewish behaviour was directly related to antisemitic attitudes and could therefore be altered.

The indigenous population of Palestine was regarded as a distraction from Zionism's grand plan and so was ignored. This denial has become a mainstay of Zionist thought. Herzl clearly understood the ingrained Jewish desire for a Holy Land: '"Next year in Jerusalem" is our old phrase', he wrote in *Der Judenstaat*. 'It is now a question of showing that the dream can be converted into a living reality.' He imagined a social state created and sustained by a massive influx of skilled labourers, engineers, farmers and workers. The kibbutz, a collective farm system, was judged the most appropriate way to order society, primarily because it was thought to be the best way to avoid the use of indigenous labour. The early Jewish settlers, mainly from Eastern Europe, faced a hostile environment but arrived to claim the land and start a new life.[11] They were imbued with a sense of romantic nationalism and enjoyed support from the growing Russian Jewish community.

Establishing a new state required patronage and serious financial backing, neither of which was initially forthcoming. Herzl tried wooing the leaders of the fragmenting Ottoman Empire, as well as Kaiser Wilhelm, Pope Pius X and the King of Italy, all without success. Soon enough, however, he found that the British were more amenable to his vision. The British suggested the so-called 'Uganda plan' whereby a Jewish homeland would be established on land in Kenya, and Herzl embraced it enthusiastically. But the offer was rejected in 1904 by the Zionist Congress, one year after his death.

Even at this embryonic stage of Zionism, the language of Jewish racial superiority permeated many public and private writings. There was a distinct lack of pluralism within Zionist thinking about the Palestinians. The attitudes of Jewish colonialists are exposed in an 1891 piece by Zionist essayist Ahad Ha'Am: 'Truth from the land of Israel' revealed that settlers 'treat the Arabs with hostility and cruelty, trespass unjustly on their territories, beat them shamelessly for no sufficient reason, and boast at having done so'. He explained this behaviour in terms of psychology: 'They were slaves in their land of exile and suddenly they have unlimited freedom, wild freedom ... This sudden change has produced in their hearts an inclination toward repressive despotism, as always occurs when the "slave becomes the king"'.[12]

Only twelve Zionist settlements existed in Palestine by the early twentieth century, but with increasing British support for the Jewish project, Palestinians were already losing the international public relations war. The land was controlled by the Ottomans, but their influence was starting to wane. The borders stretched from today's south-east Gaza to the Litani River, now in Lebanon. The indigenous population noticed the ever-increasing number of Jews on their land, and they fought back. Before World War I, the Jewish population in Palestine was 85 000 of a total population of around 700 000.[13] Skirmishes occurred frequently between newly arrived Zionist landowners and the traditional holders of that land. This was inevitable considering that uninvited colonists were slowly but surely taking control of large swathes of Palestine. 'In the eyes of some Zionists', writes former Australian ambassador to Israel Peter Rodgers, 'the fact that Palestinian nationalism was a response to the growing presence rather than being something "organic" made it inferior'.[14]

By the end of World War I, the Ottoman Empire was finished as a force. The British—and, to a lesser extent, the French—ruled the region. Zionist organisations had ingratiated themselves with the colonial powers for many years. The Arabs, on the other hand, had been promised independence by the British and the French, and felt entitled to it. But between them, the United Kingdom and France redesignated Arab countries as 'areas of influence', which they ruled as mandates. The Zionist project gained sympathy with a colonial power that regarded it as providing a unique opportunity to transplant European values into a hostile Arab world. In 1922, Winston Churchill, Secretary of State for War from 1919 to 1921, argued that the Jews were in Palestine 'as of right and not on sufferance ... It should be formally recognised to rest upon ancient historic connection'.[15]

'A national home for the Jewish people'

The British plans for Palestine were crystallised in 1917 in the Balfour Declaration. This official diplomatic instrument finally gave the Zionists a decisive strategic victory: 'His Majesty's Government view with favour the establishment in Palestine of a national home for the Jewish people'. The British were keen, at least officially, to placate the inevitable Arab indignation: 'It being clearly understood that nothing shall be done which may prejudice the civil and religious rights of existing non-Jewish communities'. Yet the declaration did not mention these groups by name, such was their tendency to dismiss the indigenous inhabitants.[16]

How could the Balfour Declaration produce anything but distrust between the competing peoples? After all, the Jewish population at the time was around 85 000, while the Arab population was estimated at 700 000.[17] Establishing a national home for the minority could only infuriate the vast majority of residents. In the 1920s, Zionist colonial ambitions for a Jewish state in Palestine grew. More land was appropriated, some bought from Arab owners. The Zionists' justification for their plans had a strong historical precedent, as has been noted by progressive historian Norman Finkelstein: 'From the British in North America to the Dutch in South Africa, from the Nazis in Eastern Europe to the Zionists in Palestine, every conquering regime has invoked the same claim that the territory appointed for conquest was deserted'.[18] Most Palestinian leaders soon became aware of the true aim of the Zionist leadership: transfer. The notion that the entire indigenous population should be moved into neighbouring Arab countries was expressed not only by extremist elements, but also by leading figures such as Ben-Gurion and Herzl himself.[19]

As Y Weitz, head of the Jewish Agency's colonisation department, wrote in 1940: 'Between ourselves it must be clear that there is no room for both peoples together in this country ... there is no other way than to transfer the Arabs from here to neighbouring countries, to transfer all of them: not one village, not one tribe, should be left'.[20] Transfer remains a potent idea for many Israeli Jews. A June 2002 poll by Tel Aviv University's Jaffe Centre for Strategic Studies revealed that 46 per cent of Israelis had considered the idea of expelling the Palestinians and thought it a good idea.[21] Where they would go exactly remained unclear. Distrust and outright racism towards the Arab population remain potent political forces.[22]

By the mid-1930s, amid ongoing Arab riots against the British and Jews, British intervention appeared the likely outcome, although an unwelcome one for the Jewish settlers. For ideological and political reasons, the Zionists were keen to prove to their colonial benefactors that it was they, and only they, who could create a viable state in the region. To concede that Palestine was already inhabited was a concession they were unable to make: the idea that the land was unpopulated remains one of the most potent myths in popular Jewish thought.

With another world war brewing, a 1937 royal commission led by Lord Peel recommended partition as the solution to the already intractable conflict. The British partition proposed a two-state solution, with separate Jewish and Arab homelands and curbs on Jewish immigration. Neither side accepted the idea, mainly because each felt betrayed by a lack of British honesty. Both sides hoped to be British favourites and receive the spoils of imperial closeness. Unfortunately, both sides were misled.

In the words of Pappe:

> the nature of Zionism should have made cohabitation an impossibility. The construction of a Zionist identity in Palestine was not a mere intellectual exercise. It was implemented by such an extensive colonization of the land that even the elitist, quasi-aristocratic

Palestinian national leadership could impress upon the nation the danger now lurking at the door of every Palestinian home.[23]

In 1937, David Ben-Gurion, a leading Zionist who became Israel's founding prime minister, expressed the feeling of many in the Jewish camp when he wrote to his son Amos of the longer-term goals of Zionism, including the goal of establishing a Jewish homeland across the entire land of Biblical Israel: 'The rest will come in the course of time. It must come'.[24] Ben-Gurion believed that the partition of the state of Palestine was just the beginning, not the end, of the Zionist enterprise.

The impending war in Europe gave the British an increasingly pragmatic view of their role in the Middle East. Simply put, they needed Arab countries' support, and while they appeared to be giving the Zionist leadership whatever they wanted, they were too preoccupied with the war effort. The 1939 White Paper, while superficially more balanced than the Peel plan, was a clumsy attempt at appeasing Palestinian sensibilities. Its essential aim was to maintain the status quo until the situation in Europe became clearer. A limit on immigration meant that incalculable numbers of Jews, now destined for the Nazi death camps, were unable to escape. A number of Zionist organisations brought Jews into Palestine illegally, but their success was limited.

During this period Zionist terror groups emerged. Violence against Palestinians and the British steadily grew, and the Stern Gang became just one of the more extremist groups determined to achieve its aims through whatever means were at their disposal; the underlying aims were to dispossess as many indigenous groups from the land as possible and to get rid of the British. A 1943 Stern Gang document, 'The newspaper of the fighters of Israel', claimed the 'enemy' had a 'moral perversion admitted by all'.[25] Furthermore, 'neither Jewish morality nor Jewish tradition can negate the use of terror as a means of battle'. 'Craftiness and murder' were acceptable means of victory when used in the name of God, the Lord of Israel. The group's most infamous act was the 1946 bombing of the British wing of the King David Hotel in Jerusalem, in which 91 people, including 17 Jews, were killed.

The rise of Nazism in Europe prompted a sudden change in Palestinian loyalties, but not for the reasons offered by Zionist propaganda. Alan Dershowitz, in his book *The case for Israel*, claims that 'the Palestinian leadership with the acquiescence of most of the Palestinian Arabs actively supported and assisted the Holocaust and Nazi Germany and bear considerable moral, political and even legal culpability for the murder of many Jews'.[26] This is gross exaggeration. It is true that the prominent Palestinian leader Haj Amin al-Husseini offered his services to Hitler, regarding Nazi Germany as a vital ally against Zionism. To suggest that Husseini was one of the architects of the 'Final Solution', as is claimed in Israel's Holocaust memorial Yad Vashem, attributes undue infamy to the religious leader.

According to Israeli sociologist Baruch Kimmerling, the misleading portrayal of Husseini as a major figure in Hitler's grand plan for the Jews is calculated, and fits with a determinedly negative characterisation of Arab resistance.[27] The argument of the Zionist lobby has remained the same for decades: Arabs have never accepted the existence of a Jewish state in the land of Palestine and are therefore antisemites, determined to complete what the Nazis began. The fact that the indigenous population may have opposed the imposition of a Jewish state for other reasons is never conceded. Kimmerling suggests that it is dangerously misleading to regard the Arab resistance to the Jewish presence and to the gradual conquest of the land as an expression of historical antisemitism: 'Ironically, the Zionist effort to "Nazify" the Arabs—a strategy that began in the 1940s—ends up diminishing the extraordinary genocidal crimes committed by Nazi Germany'.[28]

Such accounts also overlook the complicity of some Zionists who worked in cooperation or even collaboration with the Nazis. The leadership of the Jewish Agency negotiated with the Nazi regime in the 1930s, ensuring that extensive capital flowed into Palestine. Soon after Hitler's rise to power, the German Zionist Federation, the Jewish Agency and the German Finance Ministry encouraged the emigration of around 60 000 German Jews to Palestine. They received partial payment in German export goods, even though they were forced to leave their assets in Germany. Israeli historian Tom Segev writes that on the eve of the Holocaust, the Israeli Jewish leadership was focused predominantly on saving Jews who could help the cause of Palestine.[29]

By 1945 there were millions of displaced persons across Europe and around 330 000 Jewish Holocaust survivors searching for sanctuary. The Nazis had killed six million Jews, and the Zionist leadership, with Ben-Gurion at its head, saw a unique opportunity to exploit Jewish suffering for the purpose of gaining world sympathy for the establishment of a Jewish homeland.[30] Jews suffered untold horrors in Europe, and many were now seriously ill, malnourished and disoriented. Ben-Gurion's world view remained deeply Palestine-centric. In 1938 he said:

> If I knew it was possible to save all children of Germany by their
> transfer to England and only half of them by transferring them
> to the Land of Israel, I would choose the latter, because we are
> faced not only with the accounting of these children but also
> with the historical accounting of the Jewish people.

Israeli historian Idith Zertal argues that, because of Ben-Gurion's highly
successful lobbying, Israel soon acquired the right to speak for living Jews
as well as the six million killed.[31] Ben-Gurion suggested granting symbolic
citizenship to the victims, essentially turning them into martyrs for the
Jewish homeland.

At the end of World War II, the British Empire was rapidly unrav-
elling, and its role in Palestine was reduced to one of relinquishing control. The world order had changed in a matter of years. By the spring of
1948, Jews and Arabs were engaged in a civil war, and each side was inflicting horrors on the other. The Arab Liberation Army, comprising
Palestinians and volunteers from other Arab countries, attacked Jewish
communities in Palestine.

The Palestinian leadership, through its association with the Nazi
leadership, had fallen out of favour internationally, while the Holocaust
mobilised the support of Jews and the world powers in an unprecedented
way. Western guilt in relation to the destruction of the Jewish people in
the Nazi death camps virtually guaranteed the establishment of a safe
refuge from future genocidal actions. The formation of a Jewish state was
now only a matter of time. According to Edward Said, it is by no means
exaggeration to say that by 1948, the Zionists had already won the political battle for Palestine in the world's eyes, at least in terms of ideas, rhetoric and image.[32]

When the newly created UN General Assembly passed Resolution
181 on 29 November 1947 and recommended the partition of Palestine,
Palestinian and Arab leaders generally rejected it, perhaps not fully realising the world's determination to create a Jewish homeland.

Hard-line elements in the Zionist movement also rejected partition.
Soon after the UN declaration, the mass expulsion of Palestinians began
in earnest. Some left after their leaders lost battles against the Zionists,
but far more were thrown out during Jewish retaliation against Palestinian
attacks on settlements. 'Ethnic cleansing' commenced.[33] The desire of
the Zionist leadership—transfer—had begun to be fulfilled. The aim was
clear: to rid the land of as many Palestinians as possible. Jewish military
forces proceeded in the knowledge that world opinion, moral legitimacy

and sympathy were on their side. More than 400 Palestinian villages were destroyed and many hundreds of Palestinian Arabs were killed and raped. A culture of death and martyrdom flourished in the Israeli state.[34] The glorification of Zionist deaths in the cause of Israel's formation left the new nation almost addicted to sacrifice. Its war dead were considered to be better role models than the Diaspora Jewry, who were sometimes portrayed as weak and ineffectual, and as having been blindly led to slaughter in the Holocaust.

The most infamous massacre of Palestinians took place at the village of Deir Yassin on 9 April 1948.[35] Two Jewish paramilitary groups, the Irgun and Lehi, had attempted to break the Arab siege of Jerusalem and had murdered about 110 Palestinian men, women and children. Afterwards, Menachem Begin issued the following statement:

> Accept my congratulations on this splendid act of conquest. Convey my regards to all the commanders and soldiers. We shake your hands. We are all proud of the excellent leadership and the fighting spirit in this great attack ... Tell the soldiers: you have made history in Israel with your attack and your conquest. Continue this until victory. As in Deir Yassin, so everywhere, we will attack and smite the enemy. God, God, Thou has chosen us for conquest.

The Jewish state now proposed by the UN would cover around 54 per cent of Palestine and nearly half of its one million inhabitants would be Arab.[36] With little or no regard for the plight of the indigenous inhabitants, the world considered the Jewish struggle to be more important than the needs of Palestinians; Palestine soon ceased to exist as a functioning entity. Official Zionist history teaches that the vast majority of Palestinian refugees—about 750 000—fled upon the orders of their Arab leaders. The reality was altogether messier, and no evidence exists to prove the Zionist case. In fact, the Palestinian population was largely urged to remain where it was.[37]

Nakbah: the catastrophe

Israel, not unlike Australia, was reared on myths of racial and cultural superiority and long resisted any serious examination of the effects of colonial actions on the indigenous peoples. In the 1980s, revisionist historians in Israel began revealing the true nature of Israel's 'War of Independence'. They concluded that partition was never completely accepted by the mainstream Zionist leadership; the indigenous inhabitants did not all leave after receiving orders from Arab leaders; surrounding Arab states were not completely opposed to the young Jewish state; the war was not simply a battle between a weak and defenceless Jewish David and an aggressive Arab Goliath; and Israel's postwar role was not solely peace-loving.[38]

Yet the myths about this war have only intensified since 1948. Ilan Pappe argues that each side continues to deny the history and pain of the other:

> The catastrophe that befell the Palestinians would be remembered by them in the collective national memory as the *Nakbah*, the catastrophe, kindling the fire that would unite the Palestinians in a national movement. Its self-image would be that of an indigenous population led by a guerrilla movement wishing without success to turn back the clock. The Israelis' collective memory would depict the war as the act of a national liberation fighting both British colonialism and Arab hostility, and winning against all the odds.[39]

The state of Israel was born on 14 May 1948, with Ben-Gurion reading a statement heralding a new Jewish age. Israel had consumed much of Palestine, except the West Bank and East Jerusalem (controlled by Jordan) and Gaza (administered by Egypt). By now, only 20 per cent of Israel's population was non-Jewish. The Declaration of Independence pledged that Israel would be based on the notions of peace, justice and liberty as conceived by the Prophets of Israel, that it would uphold the principles of the UN charter and that it would give equal rights to the country's Arab citizens.[40]

Many facts of 1948 remain hidden. Benny Morris, one of the leading Israeli historical revisionists (or 'New Historians'), has extensively researched the period. In a startling interview published in *Haaretz* in 2004, Morris discussed Israel's early crimes against the Palestinians.[41] He told of the many massacres and rapes carried out by Israeli forces in 1948 and contended that expulsion orders originated with Ben-Gurion himself. 'Ben-Gurion was right', Morris argued. 'There are circumstances in history that justify ethnic cleansing . . . A Jewish state would not have come into being without the uprooting of 700 000 Palestinians . . . The need to establish this state in this place overcame the injustice that was done to the Palestinians by uprooting them.' Once regarded as mildly progressive—he even spent time in gaol for refusing to fight in Israel's Lebanon war—Morris's attitude had apparently shifted, reflecting a deeper psychosis in contemporary Israeli society.

According to Morris, Ben-Gurion didn't go far enough in 1948: 'If he had carried out a full expulsion—rather than a partial one—he would have stabilized the State of Israel for generations'. This argument goes to the heart of a dominant strand of Zionist thinking: time and time again, supporters of Israel justify the killing and persecution of Palestinians as necessary to protect and maintain the Jewish homeland.

Despite the 'ethnic cleansing' that accompanied it, Israel's birth was greeted with near universal support, particularly in the West. The USA, the Soviet Union and Australia welcomed the Jewish state. The Arab states, including Egypt, Jordan and Syria, were less satisfied with Israel's 'War of Independence'. A Jewish homeland was born in the ashes of the Holocaust, at a time when many Jews in Europe had nowhere else to go. Zionism had been a conquest ideology from the very beginning and was now reaping the rewards for its years of romancing the major powers. The times suited Zionism.

In October 1953, 69 Palestinians were massacred in the West Bank town of Qibya by Israeli forces led by a young commander named Ariel Sharon. The aim was to punish and warn the Palestinians that overwhelming force would be used to crush any Palestinian infiltration of Israeli land. These kinds of activities continued indiscriminately. In 2001, Sharon explained his thinking, exposed at Qibya: 'I know the Arabs and the Arabs know me ... I have seen war and I know its horrors but the Jews have only one small country and it must be defended'.[42]

The 1956 Suez War saw Israel, the United Kingdom and France invade Egypt to reverse Egypt's nationalisation of the Suez Canal. Israel, which dearly wanted to expand its territory, exploited Western insecurity during this period to become the region's superpower. France offered the Jewish state nuclear technology, and Israel was soon well on its way to building covert weaponry.[43]

In the 1960s, relations between Jews and Palestinians continued to deteriorate. With the world's eyes averted from the Palestinian refugees, the seeds of resistance were sown. For much of the West, the Palestinians simply didn't exist. This attitude was exemplified in Joan Peters's book *From time immemorial,* which was widely praised when it was published in 1984. Peters, a former CBS journalist who served in the Jimmy Carter administration as an expert on Middle Eastern affairs, claimed that the Palestinians were not indigenes but had come to Palestine in the years before 1948. Most damningly, she suggested that the Palestinians had only moved in because of economic opportunities provided by Jews. *Ipso facto*, the Zionist campaign was legitimate. Her theory was debunked in 2001 by Norman Finkelstein—(not to mention Middle East historian Yehoshua Porat years before him). Finkelstein writes that 'the fraud in Peters's book is so pervasive and systematic that it is hard to pluck out a single thread without getting entangled in the whole unraveling fabric'.[44]

The Palestinians' plight was not helped by the refusal of many neighbouring Arab countries to assist them, though the politicians' rhetoric remained bellicose. It has been far too convenient to let the Palestinians remain the political football of the Middle East, an unresolved 'problem' always to be blamed solely on Israel.

The riveting capture in 1960 of Adolf Eichmann, one of the chief Nazi architects of the Holocaust, concentrated world attention on the Jewish state. Kidnapped by Israeli agents in Argentina, Eichmann was placed on trial in Jerusalem in 1961 and subsequently executed. His guilt was beyond question, but more fundamental issues emerged. Ben-Gurion wanted the event to become a defining moment in the legitimisation of Zionism. According to Hannah Arendt, Israeli Attorney General Gideon Hausner suggested that Israeli nationalism was the only way to ensure Jewish survival.[45] For many Israelis, it was the first moment that they felt themselves to be, literally or symbolically, Holocaust survivors, imbued with a sense that another Holocaust was imminent. Israel's leaders talked up the threat posed by their Arab neighbours. The almost sacred need for Israel's existence was once again dramatically demonstrated, the need to defend and extend its borders dramatically justified.

The Eichmann trial brought about a fundamental shift in world opinion, which swung decisively towards Israel. Israel cast itself as the eternal victim, a nation that was destined to succumb to continual external threat unless it had the support of the world powers and the right to defend itself at all costs. Baruch Kimmerling explains this mentality as 'the unburdening of ... almost any moral restrictions, or even obedience to internal or international laws, whether it came to the making of nuclear weapons, the [future] occupation of West Bank, Gaza and Lebanon'.[46]

The Six Day War

In June 1967, the Six Day War changed the face of the Middle East. Israel's Arab neighbours, especially Egypt, decided that Israel had to be removed from the map and attacked, but the result for them was military devastation. In less than a week, Israel trebled the land under its control, gaining territories such as the Gaza Strip, West Bank, Sinai and East Jerusalem.

Now Israel entered an even more militaristic age, and the Western world's love affair with the Jewish state intensified. The US administration of Lyndon Johnson accepted Israel's conquest, with only an occasional dissenting voice. Jewish elites in the USA also 'discovered' Israel, as the superpower realised the strategic significance of Israel to its regional ambitions. Conservative American commentator Norman Podhoretz wrote that, after June 1967, Israel became 'the religion of American Jews'.[47] The USA was impressed with Israel's show of force and realised that a significant strategic ally was keen for its assistance. The Soviet Union's growing influence over the Arab states required a counterbalance, so US financial, military and political support was forthcoming. American Jews argued that they were now defending the USA against the vicious Arab invaders, and Israel was positioned as the frontline of the struggle.

Egypt, Syria and Jordan had been defeated in a matter of days, and the Israeli leaders—many of whom had long held ambitions of creating a 'Greater Israel' encompassing the West Bank (Judea and Samaria in their language)—took their chance. In a speech to a left-wing Israeli think tank after the war, Ben-Gurion suggested keeping Jerusalem but giving back all other conquered land to the Arabs. He feared that the Jewish state would be distorted and the country's soul corrupted. By this stage, the nation's founding prime minister was an old man whose values differed from those of the Israeli mainstream. As BBC journalist John Simpson explains, 'Ben Gurion represented an Israeli tradition whose day was already passing—the old Israel, socialist and neutral'.[48] His comments were ignored.

Despite US acceptance of the war's outcome, there was concern at the UN, and on 22 November 1967 the Security Council approved Resolution 242, making it clear that Israel should withdraw 'from territories conquered'. Israel has never complied with this ruling and the USA's power of veto has always ensured that the resolution is not enforced. While the resolution was unanimously passed, it also called for the establishment of defensible borders for all relevant parties (Israel, Syria, Egypt and Jordan.) To the present day, Israel has insisted that a cessation of Palestinian 'terrorism' is a prerequisite for negotiations. While the international community demands an end to the occupation, US support has enabled Israel to avoid taking concrete steps.

Overnight, Israel became an occupying force with control over one million Palestinians in West Bank and Gaza. A British foreign correspondent, James Cameron, remarked with awe, 'Zion was not born nineteen years ago with the birth of the state of Israel, but today, in its great and rather frightening exultation, with the Jewish nation suddenly translated from David into Goliath'.[49] Ariel Sharon, then a general in the army, flew over much of the captured land just after victory and, according to Yael Dayan, daughter of Israel's then Minister of Defense, Moshe Dayan, wrote on a piece of paper to her: 'All of this is ours'. 'He was smiling like a proud boy', Dayan said.[50] Sharon's vision of a Greater Israel was widely accepted within Israel and throughout the world.

Menachem Begin underlined what was at stake in 1969: 'If this is Palestine and not the land of Israel, then you are conquerors and not tillers of the land. You are invaders. If this is Palestine, then it belongs to a people who lived here before you came'.[51] He was wise enough to recognise the necessity of negating Palestinian rights to their own homeland.

One of the immediate results of the occupation was an improvement in the fortunes of the PLO. Formed in 1964 and led by Yasser Arafat from 1969 until his death in 2004, its explicit aim was the creation of a Palestinian state. At one time the PLO advocated a Palestinian state that would replace the entire state of Israel, but more recently it has sought only the occupied territories of the West Bank and Gaza. The PLO leadership has dismissed both Zionism and Arab nationalism as detrimental to the long-term aims of Jews and Arabs, aspiring now to the establishment of a viable democratic, secular state in Palestine (though it took many years for the PLO to accept the concept of a two-state solution).

In the late 1960s, Arafat assumed the leadership of the PLO and began a program of resistance to the occupation, mobilising the Palestinian people in a common cause. When Arafat addressed the UN General Assembly in 1974, dressed in his trademark black and white keffiya, he confidently stated: 'I am a rebel and freedom is my cause ... I have come bearing an olive branch and a freedom fighter's gun'. Despite accusations of corruption and ingrained cronyism, Arafat became a potent symbol of Palestinian resistance. 'He made it impossible to look at the Middle East, and at Israel, without also seeing the Palestinians', wrote Israeli commentator Amos Elon.[52]

The settlement movement

The occupation was criticised by opponents within Israel from the beginning, but it took many years before anything resembling a sizeable 'peace' movement developed. Instead, in the months after the Six Day War, the settlement movement emerged in response to a perceived need to unify and secure the territories that had been seized. In April 1968, the messianic movement emerged in Hebron and gained support from the government. Messianic Zionism uses biblical laws and teachings to justify Jewish control of the West Bank and Gaza.[53] Over the years, this movement has grown, becoming a serious threat to the Jewish state and demanding the establishment of a religious state governed by rabbinical law. This group initially believed, along with most Israelis, that the settler outposts would provide Israel with solid defences and would determine future borders if and when peace negotiations took place. Underlying these delusions was the idea that the Palestinians would simply accept being ruled as prisoners in their own land.

In the 1970s, settlement-building began in earnest in the occupied territories, creating conditions that are still apparent in the twenty-first century. A 1980 report by the World Zionist Organisation settlement department explicitly articulated a policy of dispossession and biblically inspired greed:

> Being cut off by Jewish settlements the minority population will find it difficult to form a territorial and political continuity. There mustn't be even a shadow of a doubt about our intention to keep the territories of Judea and Samaria for good ... The best and most effective way of removing every shadow of a doubt about our intention to hold onto Judea and Samaria forever is by speeding up the settlement momentum in these territories.[54]

The settler movement soon gained political, judicial and military support. Palestinian land was stolen, and even when the Supreme Court occasionally decided against the settlers, the decision was ignored by authorities. The messianic urge infected virtually all sides of Israeli politics. The settlements took on the appearance of middle-class suburbs, with all mod cons. The desert was literally made to bloom, but at a horrible cost.

Today more than 400 000 Jews live on occupied territories. To understand the rise of the messianic settler movement is to comprehend the modern Israeli state. Ariel Sharon said in 2001, 'the settlements represent the best of Israel. To abandon them would go against Jewish history and morality'.[55] The growth has been massive, despite successive US administrations appealing, tentatively at best, for cessation.

In 2003, Labor MP and former speaker of the Israeli parliament Avraham Burg launched one of the most pointed attacks on the Zionist project by a mainstream politician: 'It turns out that the 2000-year struggle for Jewish survival comes down to a state of settlements', Burg wrote, 'run by an amoral clique of corrupt lawbreakers who are deaf both to their citizens and to their enemies'.[56] Burg argued that the settlers had bribed and convinced the entire Israeli establishment that their mission had to continue uninterrupted. He observed that 'Israel, having ceased to care about the children of the Palestinians, should not be surprised when they come washed in hatred and blow themselves up in the centres of Israeli escapism'.

Shlomo Gazit, former head of Israel's military intelligence, writes that Israel was initially determined to maintain an 'enlightened occupation' but ignored 'the historic lessons of the collapse of empires in the twentieth century at the end of the colonial era'.[57] The Palestinians studied Zionist history closely and learnt the lessons of the Jewish underground movement in the years before 1948. Gazit argues that the expanding settlements and oppressive Israeli presence in the West Bank and Gaza can only be explained in terms of corruption of power and the deliberate provocation of the Palestinians. Israel viewed the territories 'in a classic colonialist manner' and saw them as the natural market of its goods. 'Israel's policy and behaviour pushed the Palestinians into the most dangerous position', Gazit writes, and 'they had nothing to lose'.[58]

Both major political parties in Israel, Labor and Likud, have essentially supported the massive expansion of the settlements. The 1947 partition plan gave Israel 55 per cent of Palestine, and an extra 23 per cent was taken in the 1948 war. The 1967 war saw the remaining 22 per cent taken across the 'Green Line' (the pre-1967 armistice line.) Mass confiscation of land, acts of collective punishment, arrest without trial and house demolitions became the norm. Virtually every Geneva convention related to areas under occupation was abused. Rabbi Zvi Yehuda Kook, the most influential religious figure in the territories, declared that the West Bank and Gaza belonged to the Jewish people and could never be given back to the Palestinian people.[59] With notable exceptions, the vast majority of the Israeli population accepted this rationale. 'The tokens of Israeli exceptionalism were everywhere', writes historian Bernard Avishai. 'Zionism had been proven right by, of all things, Zionism's might.'[60]

For the Palestinian people, the occupation had a devastating effect. Many became cheap labour within the Israeli economy and were badly treated and underpaid. This exploitation contributed to the formation of religiously based Palestinian movements such as Hamas and Islamic Jihad. These groups provided social services and support, and conducted an ongoing resistance to Israel. In the first 20 years of occupation, Palestinians were actively excluded from discussions on the future of their land. A 1986 *Le Monde* article by Israeli journalist Amnon Kapeliouk explained that Israeli government policy from the mid-1970s actively sought to delegitimise any form of Palestinian nationalism, especially the PLO.[61] By being portrayed as a terrorist organisation, the PLO and its claims were automatically diminished, and most Western powers, especially the USA, accepted this characterisation.

Despite extensive US support for Israel, numerous covert channels existed between the Central Intelligence Agency (CIA) and the PLO. Beginning in the 1970s, the PLO's chief of intelligence, Ali Hassan Salameh, received the approval of Yasser Arafat to work with the US government, providing information on terrorist groups—the PLO, of course, was then regarded as a terrorist outfit itself—in the hope that its own political goals could be furthered as a result of the USA's closeness to Israel and the USA's influence in the Arab world. It was a fraught relationship and proved that the USA was prepared to deal with a group then regarded as hostile.[62]

The Yom Kippur War and the war in Lebanon

Israel's Arab neighbours remained unhappy with Israel's position in the occupied territories. Egypt and Syria launched an offensive war against Israel on 6 October 1973—the day of Yom Kippur, the holiest of the Jewish year. Although Israel claimed victory after less than three weeks, its invincibility was shattered, and four years later, Israel returned Sinai to Egypt, a direct consequence of the war. The Soviet Union played a part in supporting and arming Egypt, though the USA provided valuable resources to Israel during these trying years. Many Arab states soon fell into the arms of the Soviet Union, embracing its aid and military hardware. Their newfound allegiances were clear, making any calls for Palestinian self-determination seem hypocritical at best.

With US and French assistance, Israel had already built a nuclear capability by the mid-1970s, and by the decade's end, President Jimmy Carter had given Israel access to satellite intelligence, providing valuable information on its Arab neighbours. When Israel illegally bombed Iraq's nuclear reactor at Osirak in 1981, President Ronald Reagan was dismissive: 'boys will be boys'.[63] Israeli Prime Minister Menachem Begin knew that he had the world's most powerful country in his pocket. 'If the nuclear reactor had not been destroyed', Begin said, 'another Holocaust would have happened in the history of the Jewish people. There will never be another Holocaust. Never again! Never again!'[64]

Officially Israel has always maintained a policy of deliberate ambiguity on nuclear weapons, though practically it has maintained a consistent position: that no Middle East country other than itself has the right to possess these weapons. This is a view shared by the USA, which is more than happy to ensure that Israel is the only nuclear state in the region. Israeli nuclear whistleblower Mordechai Vanunu, who exposed Israel's nuclear secrets in the mid-1980s and suffered 18 years of harsh imprisonment, has felt the wrath of Israel as a result of his decision to discuss his country's nuclear status.

There was much soul-searching in Israel after the Yom Kippur War—principally because Israel was unprepared for attack—and the Jewish state's supposed invincibility was questioned for the first time since its birth. However, Israel's mainstream still failed to appreciate the national aspirations of the Palestinians, and the war did nothing to change this. Most Israelis never travel to West Bank or Gaza, and mainstream media rarely offer perspectives on the occupation other than those of government officials.

The Israeli establishment's desire to eradicate the Palestinian leadership took its most extreme turn with the 1982 invasion of Lebanon. In an attack conceived by then Minister of Defense Ariel Sharon and designed to destroy Palestinian resistance based across its northern border, Israel laid siege to west Beirut and caused the death of 17 000 Palestinians and Lebanese, many of whom were civilians. Using US-made cluster bombs and cutting off supplies to the beleaguered city, Israel did severe damage to its international image. For the first time, the West glimpsed a rapacious and aggressive state that had been given moral immunity throughout much of the world.

Journalist Robert Fisk, then of the London *Times*, was one of the few who witnessed the massacres at the Sabra and Chatila refugee camps committed by the Christian Phalangist, Israel's dysfunctional allies. He articulated the rationale of the invasion: 'In Israel, "terrorist" means all Palestinian Arabs—and very often, all Arabs—who oppose Israel in word or in deed'. 'Bad terrorists', explained Fisk, those who fought against the occupation and Israeli oppression, were the sort who the Israeli authorities believed 'should be "cleansed" from society'.[65] 'Good terrorists', however, were sympathetic to Israel and graced with other titles, such as 'fighter' or 'soldier'. Israel justified its war on the 'terrorist' infrastructure to its north by characterising the Palestinians as 'mindless barbarians'[66] and a people who simply had to be eradicated because they opposed the Jewish state. It wasn't until 2000 that Israel fully withdrew its forces from Lebanon. Even though a flawed commission of inquiry in 1983 found that Sharon bore personal responsibility for the atrocities, he was never formally charged.

In 1982, there were over 300 000 Palestinian refugees in Lebanon, and many of them were radicalised by the invasion. The Lebanon war led to a hardening of Palestinian nationalism, the opposite of what the Israelis had intended. Lebanon was Israel's Vietnam, a war the Jewish state didn't need and, increasingly, didn't want. Although the Israeli peace movement began to gain traction after the war in Lebanon, its arguments for the return of the occupied territories had little impact on government policy.

The major peace group in Israel is Peace Now. It regularly organises protests of hundreds of thousands in Tel Aviv, as well as campaigning against the settlements. Many leftists criticised the group, however, when it supported Sharon's Gaza withdrawal in 2005. Gush Shalom, led by veteran journalist and politician Uri Avnery, is far smaller and receives little media coverage, but still works with Palestinians in solidarity against the occupation. Any number of other groups exist, along with various NGOs, which predominantly campaign for an end to the occupation and the establishment of a two-state solution.

In reality, Israel knew its continued expansion would never receive real US censure or serious cuts in support. Even though Israel is now a strong state, US financial support continues. Today it receives assistance valued at roughly $3 billion annually, making it the largest single recipient of US aid.[67] From the US perspective, this support allows new US weapons to be tested, helps subsidise the US arms industry and provides a representative for US interests in the region.

Yet Israel is far more than just a reliable strategic partner in the Middle East. Stephen Zunes, assistant professor in the Department of Politics at the University of San Francisco, argues that US officials have talked of 'moral' reasons for supporting the Jewish state. Brent Scowcroft, former national security adviser to George Bush Senior says George W Bush is 'mesmerised' by Sharon. 'When there is a suicide attack', Scowcroft told the *Financial Times* in 2004, 'Sharon calls the President and says, "I'm on the front line of terrorism," and the President says, "Yes, you are . . ."'.[68]

Ever since the formation in 1973 of the right-wing Likud Party, its *raison d'être* has been to romanticise the nationalist cause, highlight the historical attachment to the land and take a strong stand against a perceived irrational Arab opposition. In its ideology, the West Bank is sacred, holding a special place because of its strategic, cultural and religious importance. To Likud, the West Bank is the true prize of a long-term peace deal.

But whether Sharon's Likud Party or Labor is in power, state ideology has remained fairly consistent over the years. The Left and Right are united in their belief in a Greater Israel, despite the rhetoric that suggests a desire to negotiate with the Palestinians.[69]

From intifada to the Oslo Accords

When the first Palestinian uprising occurred in 1987, it had been a long time in the making. The reasons for the intifada ('resurgence' in Arabic) were simple. Most Israelis may not have seen it coming, but when a government uses a people as a constant bargaining chip and as cheap manual labour, instituting apartheid-style policies, the results are predictable. Remarkably, children were the initial instigators of the uprising. A few thousand teenagers, armed with slingshots, stones and Molotov cocktails, led the charge against the occupation forces. Within weeks, the Palestinian cause was world news and sympathy followed. Thousands were killed and injured, and not just from the use of live rounds; many were systematically beaten and abused by Israeli forces.

The effects of the three-year intifada were profound. The Palestinians would not surrender, and Israelis soon realised that they were fighting a public relations battle against enormous odds. The IDF used draconian methods to try to stamp out the uprising: torture, cutting off electricity and water, demolishing houses, arbitrary arrest without trial and destroying olive groves (the sole source of income for many Palestinians).[70] By the beginning of the 1990s, the mutual distrust and hatred had rarely been as high.

A 1987 UN General Assembly resolution, opposed by Israel and the USA, provided insight into the ongoing ability of the Jewish state to conduct itself without rebuke, and with continued US support, in the occupied territories. Israel's actions were beyond criticism. The resolution condemned 'terrorism wherever and by whomever committed', noting that peoples under 'colonial and racist regimes and foreign occupation' have the right 'to struggle' for 'self-determination, freedom and independence'. It did not give the Palestinians *carte blanche* to commit terrorist acts in Israel proper, but behaviour in the occupied territories was to be seen in its proper context. Much of the world agreed. When the PLO finally agreed to recognise the Jewish state in 1988, Israel's belligerence was becoming increasingly internationally unacceptable.

The PLO did not support the US-led invasion of Iraq in 1991 that followed President Saddam Hussein's annexation of Kuwait. The movement did not endorse Saddam's aggression, but it hoped the Iraqi challenge to the USA might bring much needed attention to the issue of Palestine. This was a tactical blunder, and the PLO was diplomatically isolated. Kuwait and Saudi Arabia even cut off aid, causing a financial crisis. The US government publicly stated it wanted to engage in a resolution of the Israel–Palestine conflict but accepted Israeli requests for the PLO to be excluded from major discussions. Once again, peace was to be imposed without the consent or involvement of the leading Palestinian body.

The 1990s saw a flurry of peace deals, US overtures, recriminations and vast settlement expansion. In the wake of the first Gulf War, the Oslo agreement was sold to the world as a peace process. Negotiated at the highest levels of the Israeli and Palestinian leaderships—the PLO was now seen as an acceptable negotiating partner—its stated aim was the transfer of Gaza and parts of the West Bank into Palestinian control and the creation of a path towards Palestinian self-determination. Arafat was the central figure in these negotiations, and many of his Palestinian colleagues were sidelined. Perhaps pragmatically, yet naïvely, the PLO agreed to exclude from discussion the issues of Jerusalem, settlements, security and borders— a decision that was to prove fatal because Israel had no desire to enter final-stage negotiations, preferring to stall and offer symbolic gestures.

The sight of Yasser Arafat, Israeli Prime Minister Yitzhak Rabin—a former national military hero—and US President Bill Clinton signing the Oslo Accords at the White House on 13 September 13 1993 appeared, briefly but falsely, to herald a new beginning. In his memoir, Clinton later related the arduous process of bringing Arafat and Rabin together. Rabin agreed to a handshake but not the traditional Arab gesture of a kiss. Clinton described Rabin's comments about the chances of peace as 'heartfelt and genuine towards the Palestinians', but found Arafat a 'showman' who used 'tough words to reassure the doubters back home'.[71] Clinton's greater sympathy appeared to lie with the Israelis.

Clinton recalls a private lunch with Rabin soon after the White House signing. Rabin told Clinton that he had come to realise that the land occupied since 1967 was 'no longer necessary [for] security, and, in fact, was a source of insecurity'.[72] Furthermore, expressing ideas now more widely accepted within Israel itself, Rabin observed that if Israel were to hold on to the West Bank permanently, the country would have to decide whether to give the Palestinians there the right to vote in Israeli elections. With their higher birth rate, they would outnumber Israelis within a few decades. Rabin said that if they were denied the vote, Israel would no longer be a democracy, but an apartheid state.[73]

Yet despite the fanfare with which the accords were greeted, the real conditions under which Palestinians lived ensured that their quality of life would deteriorate for the remainder of the decade. During the Oslo negotiations, Israel demolished nearly 300 Palestinian homes in East Jerusalem.[74] In 1993–2000, 740 homes were destroyed and 480 kilometres of settler-only roads were built.

Throughout the Oslo process, the settler population doubled. Thirty new settlements were established, including cities such as Kiryat Sefer. Israel stole 200 square kilometers of Palestinian farm land for settlements and Jewish-only infrastructure. The Palestinian Authority received control of only around 18 per cent of West Bank and 60 per cent of Gaza. Shlomo Ben-Ami, one of the Israeli negotiators in the late 1990s, wrote in 1998 that the aim of Oslo was to establish a situation of 'permanent neocolonial dependency' for the occupied territories.[75] The blame for these failures can be shared between the Israeli, Palestinian and US governments. The underlying thinking remained constant. The Israelis, supported by the USA, had no intention of allowing a true flowering of Palestinian statehood or independence. The military occupation, one of the longest of the twentieth century, remains the most effective way of controlling the Palestinian people.

Yet many Palestinians hoped that the Oslo agreements would finally bring change, and this was reflected in their initial support, which did not last long. Most Palestinians, wrote Camp David negotiators Hussein Agha and Robert Malley in 2001, 'were more resigned to a two-state solution than they were willing to embrace it; they were prepared to accept Israel's existence, but not its moral legitimacy. The war for the whole of Palestine was over because it had been lost'.[76] Ominously, Palestinian suicide bombing commenced in 1994, the year after Arafat and Rabin's famous appearance on the lawns of the White House. Born out of frustration with the Oslo process—and no tangible evidence that the occupation was ending—Islamist groups such as Islamic Jihad and Hamas engaged in a campaign of terror that rattled the Israeli populace but not the political elite.[77] Yasser Arafat often condemned these acts, though Israel consistently claimed he both supported and legitimised them. The suicide bomb is a brutal weapon that has led to a hardening of Israeli hearts and heads. Since 1994, more than 700 Israelis have died in more than 120 suicide attacks.

Many Israelis expressed optimism that a negotiated settlement would end decades of animosity, but the right wing and the settler movement saw Rabin's overtures as tantamount to betrayal. In October 1995, Ariel Sharon and (future prime minister) Binyamin Netanyahu attended a rally organised by the extremist Chabad and Zu Artzenu. The mob chanted for the death of 'Oslo criminals' Rabin and his Cabinet Minister Shimon Peres, calling them '*Judenrat*'.[78] In late 2004, Jewish settlers in Gaza, facing eviction, wore yellow stars evoking Jewish persecution in Nazi Europe.

Rabin was assassinated by a right-wing settler, extremist Amir Yigal, on 4 November 1995. Yigal killed Rabin because he said the Prime Minister relied on Arab votes to push the Oslo Accords through the Knesset. In reality, Rabin had no interest in taking on the settler movement—his moves towards peace were essentially rudimentary. He would offer nothing more than a mini-state. The reality during this process was an acceleration of Israeli land confiscation, a growing settler population, increased restriction on Palestinian movement within the territories, and the employment of violent means of repression, including house demolitions.

Rabin's murder was religiously based, sanctioned by fundamentalist rabbis in the USA and Israel who believed that it was God's will to prevent the return of territory within Greater Israel. Rabin had been accused of encouraging Palestinian terror—and not just by fanatics. Many in Likud shared this view. In mid-1995, after a suicide bombing in Tel Aviv, Netanyahu accused Rabin: 'You Yitzhak Rabin, I accuse you of direct responsibility for stirring up Arab terror and for the horror of this massacre of Tel Aviv. You are guilty. This blood is on your head'.[79] In the all-pervading climate of pessimism after Rabin's death, Netanyahu was elected prime minister, and served from 1996 to 1999.

The 2000 peace talks

The July 2000 Camp David summit, with President Clinton, Israeli Prime Minister Ehud Barak and Yasser Arafat, was a damaging failure, one that has ultimately created a new set of myths. The talks came about because Barak convinced the world that the Israeli population was finally ready to 'break every imaginable taboo' and find peace with the Palestinians.[80] Clinton was happy to assist in this process, while Arafat's control over his people was deteriorating, leaving him with few political cards.

It is generally accepted by the international community that Israel made an unprecedented offer—an end to the occupation and share Jerusalem—and that Arafat refused, without even presenting an alternative. The truth lies somewhere in the middle: contrary to popular myth, Arafat wasn't solely to blame. 'There is no partner for peace' became a familiar refrain from the Israeli side, and is still heard today when the government talks of its unilateral plans for a security fence and for partial disengagement from the West Bank. The Camp David negotiations are perhaps the most misunderstood peace talks of recent years.

Ambiguity reigned supreme during the negotiations. Nothing was ever put into writing, only expressed verbally.[81] All the important issues were discussed, including the right of refugees to return to land stolen by Israel in 1948, the establishment of East Jerusalem as the Palestinian capital and the return of the entire West Bank and Gaza to Palestinian hands. Yet Arafat and his associates, while deserving some criticism, were not offered anything of real substance at Camp David.[82] Israel's proposal divided Palestine into four separate cantons surrounded by Israel: the Northern West Bank, the Central West Bank, the Southern West Bank and Gaza.[83] Going from one area to another would have required the Palestinians to cross Israeli sovereign territory, subjecting their movement within their own country to Israeli control. Trade and commerce would also have been affected, leaving the Palestinian economy in Israeli hands. This kind of Palestinian state would have had less independence than the Bantustans created by the South African apartheid government. In the years since, the Jewish state has created a similar system, with ever-growing restrictions of movement, through checkpoints, Israeli-only roads and border closures.

Israeli scholar Tanya Reinhart explains that at Camp David, 'Barak was neither aiming for reconciliation nor genuinely attempting to move closer to an end of the conflict'.[84] The USA placed pressure on the Palestinians and Israelis, but eventually blamed Arafat alone for the collapse of the talks. Clinton has written that he was stunned[85] by Barak's offer to 'put Jerusalem on the table'—the first time that had ever been done by an Israeli leader—and tried to convince Arafat to accept the offer. He was not being offered anything close to being acceptable, however, with the proposal leaving Palestinian ghettos surrounded by Israeli enclaves.[86] Final-deal negotiations on the status of Jerusalem and the return of Palestinian refugees were not even initiated.[87] 'The Palestinian leader who will give up Jerusalem has not yet been born', said Yasser Arafat.[88] In 2003, Barak himself wrote that his proposal did not give anything away.[89] The outbreak of the second intifada—sparked by Ariel Sharon's provocative visit to the Muslim holy site Haram al-Sharif in October 2000—was indicative of the Palestinians' response.

The Israelis elected Ariel Sharon's Likud Party to government in March 2001. After the World Trade Center attacks on 11 September, President George W Bush re-engaged in the Israel–Palestine conflict, advocating the need for a Palestinian state: 'My vision is two states, living side by side in peace and security'.[90] A so-called 'Road Map to Peace' was engineered, though time after time, pressure has been exerted only on the Palestinian side. Moreover, the powers in the Bush administration, some of whom are fundamentalist Christians and Christian Zionists,[91] have ensured that the 'Road Map' is worth no more than the paper on which it is written. Domestic political factors, such as Bush's reliance on the religious Right and on powerful Washington Jewish lobbyists, allowed Sharon to continue his unprecedented campaign of terror in West Bank and Gaza and of settlement expansion. The Iraq invasion in 2003 received support and assistance from Israel and its US lobby, and it is no secret that Iran and Syria are potential future targets of Israel and the USA.

The future

Israel is sitting on a demographic time bomb. With current birth rates, it is likely that within a decade Palestinian Arabs will achieve a majority between the Jordan River and the Mediterranean. The result will be a majority population ruled over by a minority. This is one of the stated reasons for Sharon's 'disengagement' from Gaza, involving the withdrawal of around 8200 settlers and the establishment of a Palestinian state. Critics rightly argue that this is simply a ploy, allowing Israel to solidify and expand West Bank settlements and to complete the 790-kilometre wall that runs straight through Palestinian land and splits villages. Israel says it's to protect its citizens from terror acts. Palestinians claim it's a shameless land grab.

Israeli human rights group B'Tselem says that settlement expansion, not security, is the primary consideration in Israel's decisions regarding the route of the wall.[92] Palestinian residents have even taken their complaints about the wall's route to the Israeli courts. A Tel Aviv Magistrates Court ruled in March 2006 that the planned wall near East Jerusalem would cause disproportionate harm to the Palestinian residents nearby and should be stopped.[93]

Israel's 'security fence' has existed in the minds of numerous Israeli politicians for many years, even during the first intifada. The idea of separating the two peoples gained currency within Israel especially during the years of the second intifada. Some of the barrier is wire mesh while other sections are high concrete walls. In 2003 a total length of 650 kilometres was approved by Sharon's Cabinet, and building commenced. The barrier snakes across the West Bank and frequently surrounds and steals Palestinian land and towns. Israel claims the fence has saved numerous

Israeli lives from Palestinian terror, while the Palestinians rightly claim that Israel is using the fence's path to determine future borders of the Israeli state. Israel's Supreme Court has ruled that sections of the barrier violate Palestinian human rights but has accepted Israel's justification of the fence as a security measure. The international response has been largely negative. In 2004 the International Court of Justice found that the barrier broke international law, primarily because of its negative impact on the Palestinian residents along its route and because of Israel's attempt to construct the wall on occupied territory, rather than along the 1967 'Green Line'.

The possibility of a contiguous Palestinian state becomes all but impossible with a security barrier snaking across occupied land. During my visit to the West Bank in early 2005, I spoke to many Palestinians who told me of their inability to reach their land because of the wall or of the severe difficulty experienced by their children in reaching schools only a few kilometres away. It was hard not to conclude that the Israeli authorities cared little about the wall's effects on the Palestinian population.

I believe that the true goal of Sharon's plan is to maintain control of the most fertile ground while relegating responsibility for the Palestinian population to a local administration. All three major political parties in the 2006 Israeli elections essentially argued for the same outcome: for the Palestinians to disappear, or be made invisible to Israeli eyes. Sharon's unilateral strategy has survived his incapacitation. Some 30 years ago, Moshe Dayan explained the thinking that continues to this day: Israelis should tell the Palestinians in the territories that 'you shall continue to live like dogs, and whoever wishes, may leave, and we shall see where this process will lead'.[94] The occupation should remain permanent in one form or another, he argued.

The situation for the Palestinians remains dire. The death of Arafat in 2004 and election of Mahmoud Abbas as President in January 2005 was seen as heralding a new era. However, the Hamas victory in the 2006 Palestinian elections—primarily intended as a rebuke to the corruption and stalled peace negotiations conducted by Fatah—signalled a rocky road ahead, given that the USA and Israel have refused to negotiate with the democratically elected Palestinian government. Peace will not arrive without fundamental changes. 'Every Western pundit or official who pontificates about Palestinian terrorism needs to ask how forgetting the fact of the occupation is supposed to stop terrorism', Edward Said wrote in 2001.[95] Arbitrary arrest, incarceration without trial, the killing of civilians, inhumane roadblocks and settlement expansion all lead the Palestinians to one conclusion: the Israelis, and their US backers, aren't serious about peace.

The Israeli state continues to enact legislation that proves its desire to divide the nation racially. In the summer of 2003, the Knesset passed a law that prevented the unification of families where one partner is an Israeli (Arab or Jewish) and the other is a person from the Arab world.[96] Israeli citizens could marry non-Jews from anywhere else in the world and live with them in Israel, but if they married Arabs of Palestinian origin resident in the occupied territories, they would not be allowed to live together as families in Israel.

The 1950 Absentee Property Law attempted to legalise Israel's control over Palestinian land in what became Israel. The law gave Israel the 'right' to seize land owned by people defined as 'absentees'. 'Absentee' was defined as a Palestinian who between 29 November 1947 and 18 May 1948 fled any of those areas of Palestine that became Israel. The result was that thousands of Palestinians who had once lived in the West Bank would lose ownership of their property. In July 2004, the Sharon government attempted to implement the Absentee Property Law in East Jerusalem. Israeli politician Yossi Beilin called this development unprecedented: 'Neither from the left nor from the right, no one dared to do this'.[97] The nation's Attorney-General ruled the move illegal.

Despite the dispiriting effects of war on the outlook of both peoples, a poll in January 2005 revealed that 54 per cent of Palestinians supported a two-state solution along the 1967 lines with no large return of refugees.[98] A large number of Israelis also desperately want peace, despite their overwhelming support for Sharon and his unilateralist Kadima Party. But until the underlying issues are addressed and Jews and Arabs learn to understand and respect the other's history and trauma, no number of peace deals will bring a lasting settlement.

A long history of racist superiority lies at the core of Israeli attitudes to the Palestinian people and the failed resolution of the Israel–Palestine conflict. The irony in all this, of course, is that Jews themselves have suffered antisemitism through the ages, and continue to suffer. The racism that Israelis have perpetrated and the racism that Jews themselves endure cloud the Zionist view of Israel's behaviour. Israel's ongoing occupation and decades of oppressive policy in the occupied territories prove that the Palestinians have always been seen as an inconvenient nuisance. The historical effects of antisemitism on the Jews are a major factor in Israel's behaviour today. The next chapter examines the background of this insidious disease and its modern consequences. It also analyses the ideological and intellectual struggle to separate anti-Zionism from antisemitism.

5

THE PROBLEM OF ANTISEMITISM

Criticising Israel is not anti-Semitic and saying so is vile. But singing out Israel for opprobrium and international sanction—out of all proportion to any other party in the Middle East—is anti-Semitic, and not saying so is dishonest.

Thomas Friedman, 2002[1]

IN SEPTEMBER 2005, large protests in Washington DC exposed a fault line in the anti-war movement. More than 100 000 people gathered to call for an end to the Iraq war and the withdrawal of US troops. The crowd consisted of various peace groups, politicians and activists. David Frum, former speech-writer for George W Bush and resident fellow at the neo-conservative think tank the American Enterprise Institute (AEI)—a leading backer of the Iraq war—wrote later that the rally had a strong 'anti-Jewish focus'.[2] He claimed that someone at the protest carried a sign advertising a website, 'nowarforisrael.com'. The site's homepage featured a caption proclaiming: 'Meet just a few of your Jewish Supremacist Warmongers', and above it were photos of a number of prominent Jews, Richard Perle, Ariel Sharon, William Kristol, Paul Wolfowitz, Elliot Abrams and Douglas Feith.

Frum also took exception to two of the speakers, George Galloway and Lynne Stewart. Galloway, a British MP, had once referred to Israel as 'this little Hitler state on the Mediterranean' and is a fierce critic of the Israeli occupation; Stewart, a lawyer, had represented Sheik Omar Abdul Raman, the blind sheik convicted of being involved in the 1995 plot to blow up the UN and other New York landmarks. She was convicted in February 2005 for passing on messages from the sheik to his followers, who were supposedly intent on committing terrorist acts, and when she spoke at the rally was on bail awaiting sentence.[3] It was not only neo-conservatives and hawks who asked why the principal organisers of the rally, ANSWER (Act Now to Stop War and End Racism) had chosen such divisive figures to address the crowd, or why they would provide a major platform for Stewart when her associations merely gave easy comfort to critics.

Amy Lansky is a PhD student in California—'very much on the left when it comes to the war and Israel'—and after watching the rally on CNN she wrote an email to progressive Jewish group Tikkun.[4] She claimed that the anti-war movement 'does not, in its heart, sincerely welcome Jewish participation'. She praised the speech of Cindy Sheehan, whose son died in Iraq, but felt uncomfortable with everyone else who addressed the rally. She argued that the demonstration looked extreme from the outside, and the inclusion of Arab speakers, who discussed Arab liberation, self-determination and Israel, rather than Iraq, played 'very badly to the average American. It looked "fringe" rather than mainstream'. She suggested the anti-war movement should 'focus on the war and America, not on Israel/Palestine and the broader Arab struggle'.

Although the 'broader' Arab struggle is directly related to US meddling in the region, Lansky's unease highlights a growing ideological divide in the anti-war movement between those who simply oppose US involvement in the Iraq war and others, whose agenda is to blame and demonise Israel. Frum dismisses the vast majority of anti-war protestors who simply want an end to the Iraq quagmire, seeing something more sinister at the heart of the protest movement: 'It is revealing something that at the core of these so-called peace marches you will find a leadership that strongly supports acts of war targeted against Americans and Jews. You will see that the radical Left and extremist Islam—while they may disagree ideologically—can find common cause'.

Many other commentators and writers have drawn a similar connection between criticism of Israel and antisemitism, and argue that such attacks are on the increase. These writers include conservative British author and columnist Melanie Phillips, along with Nick Cohen, a columnist for the *London Observer* and the liberal British journal the *New Statesman*. Phillips gave a talk to the London Society of Jews and

Christians in April 2004,[5] in which she argues that much current debate on Israel 'goes far beyond legitimate criticism and turns instead into irrational and malevolent hatred . . . Whereas previously the aim was to eradicate the Jews, now it is to eradicate the Jewish state'. Cohen expressed similar views in the *New Statesman* in October 2005,[6] arguing that the liberal Left 'has been corrupted by defeat' since the end of the Cold War and is increasingly aligning itself with 'whichever causes sound radical, even if the radicalism on offer is the radicalism of the far right'.

There is a growing body of writing concerned with the so-called 'new antisemitism'. Jewish writers differ on the problem but many agree that a 'war against the Jews'[7] is occurring. Phyllis Chesler, a professor of psychology and women's studies at Duke University, writes in *The new anti-Semitism: the current crisis and what we must do about it*[8] that 'anyone who denies that this is so or who blames the Jews for provoking the attacks is an anti-Semite'. In the past decade, claims of resurgent antisemitism have played a significant part in debates about Israel and, more broadly, about peace in the Middle East. This chapter asks how real this resurgence is, and how much it is related to the charged atmosphere that surrounds the question of Israel's recent conduct.

A short history of antisemitism

Evidence of discrimination against European Jews goes back hundreds if not thousands of years, yet its history is not necessarily well known. Many Australians, even those of British descent, are probably unaware that Jews were expelled from England in the mid-fourteenth century and not allowed to return for 350 years. The term 'antisemitism' was not coined until 1879, when German journalist Wilhelm Marr argued in his book *The victory of Judaism over Germanism* that the Jewish people were an alien race. He founded the Anti-Semitic League, and by 1881 an Anti-Semitic Petition had gathered 225 000 signatures and was presented to Chancellor Otto von Bismarck.[9] It declared that Jews were not interested in equality with the German people and were attempting to subvert German society. By 1882, an official Anti-Semitic Party won a handful of seats in the German Reichstag.

Marr's understanding reflected stereotypes of Jews that had existed for centuries in Christian Europe and even in Roman and Greek times. According to this view, Jews are a distinct people, different from all others. The composer Richard Wagner—Hitler's favourite—once said, 'I hold the Jewish race to be the born enemy of pure humanity and everything noble in it'. Wagner's personal dislike for Jews—he hated their voices and mannerisms—can be traced back to his belief that they were a disruptive force in German society and should fully assimilate.[10]

Brian Klug, senior research fellow in philosophy at St Benet's Hall, Oxford, and a founding member of the United Kingdom's Jewish Forum for Justice and Human Rights, explains this blind hatred:

> An anti-Semite sees Jews this way: they are an alien presence, a parasite that preys on humanity and seeks to dominate the world. Across the globe, their hidden hand controls the banks, the markets and the media. Even governments are under their sway. And when revolutions occur or nations go to war, it is the Jews—clever, ruthless and cohesive—who invariably pull the strings and reap the rewards.[11]

In nineteenth-century Europe, the rapidly liberalising political climate of the United Kingdom offered the least problematic environment for Jews. In 1858 Lionel de Rothchild was allowed to sit in the House of Commons after the law restricting the oath to only Christians was amended; in 1868 Benjamin Disraeli, a conservative politician from an Anglicised Jewish family, became prime minister. But elsewhere, the position of Jews remained tenuous, even though they had lived throughout the continent since Roman times. Rising nationalist sentiment meant that groups of people were increasingly identified by their biological descent.[12] Jews were seen as an insular community—some of whom wanted to return to Palestine—and accused of creating a state within a state. For this reason, many Europeans mistrusted the true intentions of the Jewish population. Of course, the vast majority of Jews simply wanted to integrate within their respective countries.

French Jews excelled in virtually every field, but the 'Jewish oath'— required for all Jews in European courts until it was abolished in the nineteenth and twentieth centuries—was designed to humiliate and isolate them by insisting that they prove their loyalty to the French state. Moreover, there was a widespread belief among Christians that Jews would perjure themselves in Christian courts. The Comte de Clermont-Tonnerre told the French National Assembly in the years after the 1789 Revolution (expressing a view still widely held a century later) that 'The Jews should be denied everything as a nation, but granted everything as individuals ... If they do not want this ... we shall be compelled to expel them'. His comment reveals how burgeoning liberal values could coexist with the French establishment's continuing discomfort with Jewish community identity. The French Supreme Court removed the oath in 1846, and despite ongoing persecution and victimisation, French Jews were spared excessive violence.[13] In the last decade of the nineteenth century, the Dreyfus affair (discussed in chapter 4) highlighted institutional antisemitism in the French establishment.

By the end of the century, Jews owned more than 50 per cent of the banking institutions in Austria–Hungary and held many positions of influence in the Hungarian and Austrian aristocracy.[14] Their prominence led to unease. In Germany by this time, most Jews were middle-class and either self-employed or entrepreneurs. The political and voting system was based on personal wealth, allowing them to form a powerful bloc disproportionate to their size.[15] Left-of-centre parties were largely favoured, as socialists believed Jews should receive the same benefits as every other group in society. Discrimination still occurred—in the army, universities, diplomatic service and bureaucracy—but Jews maintained a strong social conscience and cared for other, less fortunate, members of society.[16]

Against the backdrop of gradual Jewish emancipation, the late nineteenth century saw the rise in Europe of a pseudo-Darwinian racial ideology that divided people into two distinct groups: 'Aryans' were the fittest and most likely to survive, while Jews and Blacks were at the bottom of the racial hierarchy. It was thus considered appropriate to oppose Jews on racial grounds. German nationalist academic Heinrich von Treitschke was a proponent of these ideas and fought against what he saw as an impediment to Germany's rise in world stature. In his *History of Germany in the nineteenth century*, he argued that Jews were a destructive element in Germany and were better suited to 'radical' France.[17] Treitschke wrote that Jews 'were chiefly attracted towards the French [nation], not merely from reasonable gratitude, but also from an inner sense of kinship...To the Jews, German veneration for the past seemed ludicrous, but modern France had broken with her history.'[18] France was a 'raw state, created, as it were, by pure reason', and therefore Jews would feel more at home there. Even Karl Marx, a converted Jew, concluded that, through Jewish wealth and the evils of capitalism, Jews had a destructive influence on society. Society could only be saved, in his view, with the destruction of Judaism, which would bring an end to capitalism as well.[19]

Across Europe, resurgent antisemitism was driven by a belief that Jews were to blame for economic problems and for polluting traditional ways of life. These attitudes were strongly promoted by many journalists, politicians and writers, and even fostered by the Roman Catholic Church. It was argued that Jews conspired to control the media and banking institutions. The result was that 2.1 million Jews left Europe between 1881 and 1914, most emigrating to the USA.[20] Others moved to Australia, Argentina, Canada and South Africa.

In 1881, pogroms in Russia signalled growing antipathy to Jews across Eastern Europe, and there were innumerable pogroms in the following decades. In May 1882, Tsar Alexander III of Russia introduced the 'May Laws', which stayed in effect for more than 30 years. They resulted in the banning of Jews from rural areas and towns of less than 10 000 people, and imposed strict quotas on Jews who wanted to undertake secondary or higher education. In the early years of the twentieth century— the exact year remains unclear—the Russian tsar's secret police published the *Protocols of the Elders of Zion,* a booklet that laid out the supposed plan of Jewish leaders to gain world domination. This hoax publication was designed to discredit Jews and to blame them for the 1905 Russian Revolution. A little-known tsarist official, Serge Nilus, edited a number of versions of the document and tried to prove its Jewish origins. The 1911 edition included a reference to a source stealing the book from (fictional) Zionist headquarters in France.[21] Another source claimed it had been read out at the first Zionist Congress in Basel, Switzerland, in 1897. The book was translated and distributed throughout Europe after World War I until it was exposed as a forgery by the London *Times* in 1921.[22] Used extensively by Hitler and the Nazis as evidence of the evils of Judaism, it remains a seminal text of antisemitic thought and attempts to 'prove' that Jews control and manipulate the world. By 1917, when the Russian Revolution brought the Bolsheviks to power on an anti-religious platform, Jews remained isolated and persecuted.

In Germany, a great many Jews—including some of my own family— participated in World War I in an attempt to prove their patriotism. Despite Jewish sacrifice, antisemitism continued unabated. German Walther Rathenau, writing to a friend in 1916, lamented that 'The more Jews are killed [in action] in war, the more obstinately their enemies will prove that they all sat behind the front in order to deal in war speculation. The hatred will grow twice and threefold'.[23] But the nation's economic troubles after the war created a perfect breeding ground for scapegoating Jews, and contributed to the extreme ideology of the National Socialists and to the elevation of Hitler in 1933.

German novelist Jakob Wassermann argued in 1921 that Jew-hatred was the ultimate German hatred.[24] Wassermann believed that Germans 'were emotionally resistant to accepting Jews as their equals and given to scapegoating them for every crisis, setback or defeat. Hatred of the

Jews could encompass every conceivable sexual frustration, social anxiety, jealously, animosity, bloodlust and greedy instinct that Germans were otherwise unable to exorcise'.[25]

Nazi ideology highlighted the perceived secret power of Jews deriving from their self-proclaimed 'chosen people' status. The Nazis, however, saw themselves as the only group of people who could lead Germany into a brighter future. As mainstream Zionist historian Robert Wistrich observes, 'there could not be two chosen peoples. The character of Hitler's messianic pretensions necessitated the removal of that very people who had embodied chosenness for three millennia'.[26]

Hitler's war against the Jews was determined and genocidal. From 1933, the civil rights of Jews were gradually revoked, and the 1935 Nuremberg Laws heralded the beginning of the end. Marriage between Jews and non-Jews was banned, and Jews were no longer classified as German citizens, removing their right to vote. The following year Jews were banned from professional positions, causing their social influence to evaporate. Jewish children were banned from German schools in 1938, and by the following year virtually all German Jewish businesses were bankrupt or had been bought out by the Nazis.

The large Jewish community in Poland was the hub of Eastern European Jewry and, despite discrimination, remained vibrant until Germany's invasion in 1939. Germany's invasion of Poland, France, Denmark, Belgium, Norway and the Netherlands signalled a rapacious Nazi expansion across Europe, and the policy of eradicating the Jews accelerated. Jews were soon herded into ghettos and forced to wear yellow stars. The 'Final Solution'—the systematic destruction of European Jewry—was planned in 1942, and death camps across Poland and Germany became the final resting places for millions of Jews, homosexuals, gypsies and anyone classified as 'subhuman' because they were thought to challenge the superiority of the Aryan race.

Postwar antisemitism

After World War II and the establishment of Israel, many Holocaust survivors travelled to Palestine to start new lives. In the wake of the Holocaust, Western governments viewed antisemitism through a radically different prism. Many felt so guilty about their behaviour before and during the war that they were determined to treat Jews with greater fairness. There were many instances of memorialisation of the Holocaust experience. Germany's generous and contentious financial contributions to Israel in the early 1950s, for instance, can be regarded as an act of penance, as can subsequent legislation that gave property rights back to the original Jewish owners. Yet antisemitism was far from obliterated. The British journalist and author George Orwell noted that although antisemitism was probably less prevalent in the United Kingdom than it had been 30 years before, there was still widespread mistrust of Jews in his country: 'There is more anti-Semitism in England than we care to admit, and the war has accentuated it, but it is not certain that it is on the increase if one thinks in terms of decades rather than years'.[27]

The rise of communism across Eastern Europe allowed governments there to continue to discriminate against Jews and officially deny Hitler's attempted genocide. The communist government in Poland refused to return pre-war property in the years after the war, and ongoing pogroms and persecution prompted over 100 000 Jews to leave for British-controlled Palestine before 1948. Polish involvement in the Nazi reign of terror was largely covered up, and only surfaced fully after the fall of communist power in 1989. The Six Day War in 1967 led Poland to sever relations with Israel and to show greater support for the Soviet-backed Arab states. Shortly afterwards, a government-led campaign equated Jews and Zionists, implying Jewish disloyalty to Poland.

The Soviet Union's attitudes to Jews and Zionism were complex but by the 1970s had resulted in cruel persecution. As leader, Stalin supported the formation of Israel in the hope that British influence would decrease in the Middle East. Through much of the Cold War, however, the Soviet Union provided political and financial backing to many Arab countries. In Eastern Europe, Soviet authorities refused to acknowledge Nazi crimes against the Jews, and since official policy dictated strict socialist principles, political Zionism was labeled 'bourgeois nationalism'.[28] Soviet Jewry suffered greatly during the communist years, and authorities regularly shut down synagogues and published antisemitic material. By the early 1960s, Jews in the USA started campaigning for the rights of Soviet Jewry to live in peace or emigrate, and within a decade, many Jews left and settled in Israel and the USA.

The USA was a major destination for Jewish migrants, with a Jewish population of approximately one million by the turn of the twentieth century and roughly six million today. New York became the major Jewish centre in the country (with a Jewish population of around 1.75 million people in 2006). The Jewish population of the USA has largely assimilated, and the 2001 National Jewish Population Survey found 4.3 million Jews with some religious or cultural connection to the Jewish community, though a rising intermarriage rate contributed to a predominantly secular Jewish community.

Although it rarely degenerated into violence, American antisemitism flourished in the early part of the twentieth century and contributed to the establishment of Jewish quotas in clubs, universities and employment. In 1922, for example, Harvard University President A Lawrence Lowell advocated restricting Jewish participation because he believed only 'establishment' Americans should attend his prestigious institution. The years after World War II saw a softening of this antagonism and led to Jews being more widely accepted, although the USA did not formally abolish various anti-Jewish quotas and discriminatory measures across the education system until the 1960s.

The American Jewish community was the largest and strongest in the world before World War II, yet it was incapable of averting the Holocaust or persuading the US government to allow greater Jewish immigration before the war.[29] A number of mainstream Zionist groups were opposed to allowing greater Jewish immigration. The push for this came mainly from non-Jewish political groups on the Left, some of which had a disproportionate numbers of Jews in both leadership and membership. Despite its horrors, the Holocaust was generally overlooked or downplayed in US public debate until the 1960s. This was partly the result of Jewish organisations' concerns that openly dwelling on the trauma of the Holocaust would promote the image of Jews as victims.[30] Historian Norman Finkelstein argues that mainstream Jewish groups also played down the Holocaust to fall into line with the US government's Cold War priorities.[31]

Israel played a relatively minor role in US strategic thinking until the Six Day War, when, Finkelstein suggests, Jewish leaders 'discovered' the Holocaust in order to bolster US support for the Jewish state: 'Whereas before 1967 Israel conjured the bogy of dual loyalty, it now connoted super-loyalty'.[32] It soon became increasingly difficult to openly challenge Israeli actions and US support for them. Finkelstein explains that a favourite tactic of the 'post-1967 born-again Zionists was tacitly to juxtapose their own outspoken support for a supposedly beleaguered Israel against the cravenness of American Jewry during the Holocaust'.[33] The Zionist religion had been born.

In the Muslim world, antisemitism existed before the troubles over Israel and Palestine. Pogroms on Jews in Iraq and Algeria, for instance, were not uncommon before World War II. Blind antisemitism, blood libels—Jews were accused of sacrificing humans and using their blood in rituals—and government-sponsored bigotry contributed to an atmosphere of hostility towards Jews and Israel.[34] Arab scholars realise that this trend must be challenged.

Traditionally European antisemitism has been foreign to the Islamic world, although Nazi iconography and conspiracy theories have gained greater prominence since the establishment of Israel. In December 2005, the Iranian President, Mahmoud Ahmadinejad, denied that the Jewish Holocaust had occurred, prompting outrage in the West. 'Anyone who believes in social justice and opposes racist oppression', writes Joseph Massad, lecturer in Arab politics at Columbia University, 'must be in solidarity with all holocaust victims, especially European Jews, 90 per cent of whom were exterminated by a criminal and genocidal regime'. But he adds: 'Such a person must equally be against the Zionist abduction of the holocaust to justify Israel's colonial and racist polities'.[35]

Contemporary antisemitism

In June 2005, the front page of London's *Independent* newspaper prominently featured a photograph of the defaced Rothschild mausoleum, where generations of Jews had been buried since the mid-nineteenth century.[36] 'Jew Boy Dead' was daubed on one intricately built tomb. The paper reported that the number of antisemitic attacks in 2004 had been the highest on record in the United Kingdom. A leading British MP argued in late 2005 that 'anti-Semitism is back in fashion'.[37] The United Kingdom's Chief Rabbi, Jonathan Sacks, said in early 2006 that a 'tsunami of anti-Semitism' was spreading across the world and included Holocaust denial and hatred of Jews.[38]

In 2003, the Vienna-based European Union Monitoring Center (EUMC) identified Germany, the United Kingdom, France, Belgium, and the Netherlands as EU member countries with increases in antisemitic attacks in 2002 and 2003. In France, for example, there were six times as many attacks as in 2001. Of 313 xenophobic, racist or antisemitic attacks, 193 were classified as antisemitic.[39] The report stated that there were 'many incidents of Jewish people assaulted and insulted, attacks against synagogues, cemeteries and other Jewish property, and arson against a Jewish school'.[40] Although far-right groups remained likely perpetrators, an increasing number of disaffected Muslim youths were also involved.[41]

Such attacks are often flagrant, and deeply offensive, yet statistics need to be treated with caution. A previous EUMC report—unpublished because of its flawed methodology—had cited, as an example of antisemitism, the actions of Greta Duisenberg, wife of the president of the European Central

Bank, who had unfurled a Palestinian flag from her Amsterdam apartment.[42] And evidence of increased attacks on Jews needs to be read in the context of data on racial violence generally. In 2005, the EUMC found that Jews, Muslims, North Africans, immigrants and refugees or asylum seekers were the groups most vulnerable to race attacks in Europe, but immigrants and refugees were the main targets, by a large majority.[43]

While there is certainly evidence that antisemitic attacks are on the rise in Europe, a broad resurgence of antisemitism is far from proven.[44] In part this reflects the difficulty in measuring changes in antisemitic attitudes as opposed to antisemitic acts.[45] But, more profoundly, at the heart of the current debate lie fundamental questions about the relationship between Judaism and the Zionist project, and about the nature of contemporary antisemitism. In an era when the Holocaust looms large in our understanding of history, and the Zionist concept of a modern Jewish homeland has become reality, many Jews argue that contemporary antisemitism presents a different face from that of the monstrous persecution of the 1930s and 1940s.[46]

The reasoning behind antisemitic attacks is rarely definitively articulated. Several studies point to 'vague motivations', rather than to specific issues or political actions. Islam has undoubtedly spread in past decades, and many Zionist groups claim that Europe's increasing Muslim population is leading the new antisemitism. Yet the European Monitoring Centre on Racism and Xenophobia released a report in 2004 that suggests the largest group of perpetrators are in fact young, white Europeans inspired by a far-right ideology.[47]

Europe's Muslim population is growing: 10 per cent of the French population, for instance, is now Muslim.[48] This change is creating unease. In November 2005, the bleaker suburbs of Paris saw many nights of rioting by Muslims of North African origin. Their frustration was caused by high unemployment, institutional racism and poor assimilation. 'You feel you will never make it because you are Arab', explained French-Arab journalist Nadir Dendoune.[49]

Mainstream opinion is increasingly of the view that Europe's Western liberal values are incompatible with those of the growing Islamic population. When the Washington-based Pew Research Center conducted a survey on global attitudes in 2004, a year after the start of the war in Iraq, it found that Europeans held much more negative attitudes towards Muslims than towards Jews.[50] It also found that Jews were regarded more highly in France, Germany and Russia than they had been in 1991 at around the time of the Gulf War.[51]

By comparison, there is evidence of a change of attitude on the subject of Israel. A poll released by the EU in 2003 found 59 per cent of citizens identified Israel as the world's greatest threat to world peace—more than for Iran, the USA, Iraq or North Korea.[52] It might seem logical to conclude that many Europeans disapprove of Israel's conduct but distinguish it from the conduct of Jews generally. This analysis is supported by a 2004 survey conducted for the Anti-Defamation League (ADL) in the USA, which reported a fall in antisemitic attacks across Europe but a rise in hostile views towards Israel. The ADL suggested governments were becoming more successful in preventing violence in the Middle East from seeping into Europe through the large Muslim population. It also undermined the view that anti-Zionism can be equated with anti-semitism because many individuals were able to express disquiet in relation to Israel without slandering all Jews in the process.[53]

Yet the findings were seized on by many supporters of Israel, including the Prime Minister, Ariel Sharon, as evidence that the ancient hatred had returned with a vengeance. Emanuele Ottolenghi, research fellow at St Antony's College at Oxford University—and an extreme right-winger, friendly with the Zionist Right—wrote that secular Europeans will only fully accept Jews 'if they renounce a core component of their identity: that is, their sense of Jewish peoplehood as expressed through their attachment and commitment to the democratic state of Israel and to the Zionist enterprise'.[54]

Among Jewish intellectuals and leaders, opinion about the so-called resurgence in European antisemitism is clearly divided, as a BBC forum conducted in the wake of the EU's poll suggests. Yaron Ezrahi, a professor of political science at the Hebrew University of Jerusalem, argues that this so-called resurgence is just a convenient excuse to avoid the international consequences of Israel's conduct:

> The right-wing in Israel describes every criticism of the country as a form of anti-Semitism. It is very convenient for the present government—which is the most right-wing in Israel's history and headed by a prime minister who has not taken the smallest initiative in the direction of a diplomatic effort in the peace process—to blame everything on anti-Semitism.[55]

Robert Wistrich, director of the Jerusalem-based Vidal Sassoon International Center for the Study of Anti-Semitism, articulates the Zionist position:

There is a clear feeling from the Israeli point of view that what is at stake now is the very legitimacy of the state of Israel in a moral, historical and political sense. When we get to a point when it is becoming acceptable in many places in Europe and even in mainstream opinion to label Israel as a Nazi state, or, in more diplomatic language, an apartheid state, the Israeli citizen feels that their very right to exist in any form, whether politically or as a nation, is being challenged.[56]

For many Israelis, personal experience of systematic discrimination, or even of repression, has blurred the distinction between anti-Zionism and antisemitism. Take the case of Natan Sharansky, a minister in several Israeli governments who resigned from Cabinet in May 2005 in protest over Ariel Sharon's plans for disengagement in the occupied territories. Born in the Ukraine in the era of Stalin, Anatoly Sharansky, an intellectual and a courageous dissident, spent several years in a Siberian prison camp for his outspoken representation of Soviet Jewry. The state of Israel welcomed him with open arms after he was released in an East–West prisoner exchange in 1986: 'While criticism of an Israeli policy may not be anti-Semitic, the denial of Israel's right to exist is always anti-Semitic', Sharansky wrote in 2004, and it is not difficult to see why he would feel that way.[57]

Sharansky believes that legitimate criticism of Israel moves into antisemitism when it meets the criteria of the '3D' test: double standards, demonisation and delegitimation.[58] Singling out Israel for human rights abuses, while ignoring Syria, Iran, Cuba or China, reeks of antisemitism. Comparisons between Nazi Germany and current-day Israel 'can only be considered anti-Semitic'.[59]

Of course present-day Israel isn't Nazi Germany. Such comparisons are false and intellectually dishonest. After all, Palestinians are not being herded into gas chambers in the West Bank. Comparison of Israeli and Nazi actions is ultimately futile. 'If the Israelis are no better than the Nazis', explains Asaf Romirowsky, an associate fellow of the conservative Middle East Forum, 'then the Nazis' actions were no worse than the Israelis'.[60]

This argument cuts both ways. By invoking other nations' human rights abuses, Zionists such as Sharansky avoid discussion of Israeli responsibility for the continued military occupation of the territories captured in 1967, and for the killing of Palestinians in the territories. 'Israel's occupation of the Palestinians is not the moral equivalent of the Nazi genocide of the Jews', writes Sara Roy, a senior research scholar at the Harvard University Center for Middle Eastern Studies and a child of Holocaust survivors.[61] 'But it does not have to be. No, this is not genocide but it is repression and it is brutal. And it has become frighteningly natural.'

France's antisemitic equation

France, which has both the largest Jewish and the largest Muslim populations in Europe,[62] has found itself at the forefront of European controversies over Israel, with polls showing that many oppose Israeli tactics against the Palestinians. Influential Zionists such as Alan Dershowitz and Natan Sharansky believe that the French have become 'knee-jerk anti-Israel'.[63]

Jewish sensitivities have been inflamed both by general French attitudes to Israel and by a documented increase in antisemitic attacks. This sensitivity was highlighted by a French court's extraordinary finding in 2005 that the editor of Le Monde and the authors of an opinion piece were guilty of 'racial defamation' against Israel and the Jewish people.[64] The court ordered editor Jean-Marie Colombani and the three writers to pay a symbolic one euro in damages to Lawyers Without Borders and the France–Israel Association. The France–Israel Association and Lawyers Without Borders had claimed that a 2002 article titled 'Israel/Palestine: the cancer' contained points that 'targeted a whole nation, or a religious group in its quasi-globality' and should be defined as racial defamation. They argued that the article referred to 'Jews' when it actually meant 'certain Israelis'.

A paragraph in the article read:

The Jews of Israel, descendants of an apartheid named the ghetto, ghettoize the Palestinians. The Jews who were humiliated, scorned and persecuted humiliate, scorn and persecute the Palestinians. The Jews who were the victims of a pitiless order impose their pitiless order on the Palestinians. The Jews, scapegoats for every wrong, make scapegoats of Arafat and the Palestinian Authority.

The attorney who represented the paper warned that the decision had ominous implications for fair comment. 'The article was a critique of a policy, of [Prime Minister Ariel] Sharon's policy, it wasn't a racial criticism', lawyer Catherine Cohen said:

The remarks were taken out of context; the plaintiffs argued that they were against Jews, but a few paragraphs later, the piece says that all occupiers behave the same way. This is a very serious matter for intellectuals, for commentators who express their point of view on a very complex issue.

The French umbrella group for Jewish associations, CRIF (Conseil Représentatif des Institutions Juives de France), praised the decision, which has since been upheld on appeal: 'We have always considered that criticism of Israel falls under the category of the free and democratic exchange of ideas', it said, 'but that debate cannot express itself as a demonisation of Israel nor of the Jews'.

The rest of the Western media virtually ignored the finding. An article finally appeared in the *Wall Street Journal Europe* in early June,[65] and this led to a handful of follow-up articles in *Haaretz*, the *Jerusalem Post*, the *Guardian* and a few others. 'One would have thought that such a verdict would prompt wide-ranging coverage and lead to extensive soul-searching and public debate', journalist Tom Gross wrote. 'Instead, there has been almost complete silence, and virtually no coverage in the French press.'[66]

Antisemitism is a fact of life in France, and the Jewish community has had to accept the reality that the number of attacks will often reflect the level of bloodshed in the Middle East.[67] In July 2004, the Israeli Prime Minister, Ariel Sharon, caused a storm of controversy when he encouraged French Jews to emigrate to Israel and escape 'the wildest anti-Semitism'. Theo Klein, the honorary president of CRIF, responded that the French Jewish community could take care of its own problems. 'It's not up to him to decide for us', he said. 'The Jewish community has been in France for 2000 years, it is completely integrated. I see discomfort, yes; worry, certainly, but not danger.'[68] Patrick Gaubert, of the pro-Zionist International League against Racism and Anti-Semitism (Ligue Internationale Contre le Racisme et l'Antisémitisme, or LICRA) also slammed Sharon. 'These comments do not bring calm, peace and serenity that we all need', he said. 'I think Mr Sharon would have done better tonight to have kept quiet.' The *Independent* discovered that many ordinary Jewish Parisians shared Sharon's concerns and concluded that, although he was being provocative, his words reflected genuine concern over rising antisemitism, often perpetrated by Arab youths.[69]

The brutal kidnapping and murder of 23-year-old Jew Ilan Halimi by a gang of African youth in early 2006 sparked renewed calls for action against antisemitism. The leader of the gang said that they picked Halimi because he was a Jew and presumably rich.[70] The French interior minister, Nicholas Sarkozy, said that the crime was motivated by antisemitism. 'We have a duty to the memory of Ilan Halimi, to his family, his parents, his friends and above all, to the Jews of France, to establish the truth', he said.[71]

The crime caused outrage across France. Tens of thousands of French citizens protested, and the marchers included government and Opposition representatives, Jewish groups, anti-racism campaigners and leaders of various religious groups. Roger Cukierman, head of CRIF, said, 'It's important for French society to realise that little anti-Semitic and racist prejudice can have terrible consequences'.[72]

The *Guardian*'s correspondent in Paris, Jon Henley, says that the Zionist lobby in France is 'moderate and low-key, light years removed from what you would see in the US'.[73] CRIF is close to government, he argues, and is always present in talks on all relevant topics. For example, the group was deeply involved in the process to ban Islamic headscarves and Jewish skullcaps from state schools in the name of secularism. Despite this, Henley says that the French Jewish community is 'well anchored and relatively unconcerned by sporadic acts [of violence]'. He has witnessed a Jewish community that is far better integrated, better educated, more privileged and wealthier than the Muslim community, although Muslim resentment towards Jews is certainly a growing problem. France's failure to integrate the ever-growing Muslim community over the last decades has also contributed to this frustration.[74]

Henley's optimism is not shared by all. The National Consultative Commission on Human Rights released its annual study in March 2005, revealing that racist, antisemitic and xenophobic attacks in France had soared from the previous year and largely targeted Jews and Muslims.[75] In the past five years, thousands of French Jews have moved to Israel, with around 3300 emigrating in 2005, the highest number in 35 years.[76] The rise in antisemitic attacks caused the Chief Rabbi of France, Joseph Sitruk, to encourage Jewish men to stop wearing their skullcaps in public, 'to avoid becoming a target for potential assailants'. France's education minister, Luc Ferry, instituted a program in early 2003 to stamp out antisemitism and racism in schools. He said terms such as 'dirty Jew' and 'Alien Sharon' were now common playground insults.[77]

Many argue that the Middle East conflict has been imported to France. 'The political climate is too pro-Arab', one Jewish mother, whose young child had been abused at school because of his religion, told the *New York Times*.[78] Sammy Ghozlan, a retired police officer who operates a clearing house for information on antisemitism in France, argues that many Jews feel the 'honeymoon period [is] over' and that antisemitism will become more common.[79] Henley suggests that public opinion in the country is indeed overwhelmingly pro-Palestinian and is reflected in the media coverage of the Middle East. He wonders, though, whether the pro-Palestinian sentiment or anti-Israel media coverage came first. The last few years have seen a slight shift in this government and media perspective, however, and according to *Le Monde*, 'it's now up to the Palestinians—the occupied—to prove their goodwill'.[80]

French Jews generally lean to the right politically, says Maurice Safran, editor-in-chief of the weekly *Marianne*, and he argues that the majority see Sharon as the 'true leader'.[81] 'For the left, as well, Sharon has become the new hero', he says. 'The moment he declared he would continue the peace process after the disengagement, he captured them, too. The French Jewish left may not fight for Sharon, but it will quietly support him.' When a government-commissioned report concluded in 2004 that anti-Zionism amounted to a form of antisemitism, it was clear the Zionist lobby had successfully convinced the author that questioning the right of Jews to their own homeland was in itself antisemitic.[82]

French Jews are undoubtedly feeling uneasy about the growing wave of violence perpetrated by Muslim youth, sometimes against Jews themselves. When riots hit Paris in late 2005, a Jewish director of a high-tech company told *Haaretz* that his community was disappointed the state didn't punish the Muslims involved more severely. 'The Muslims won and the French went on the defensive', he said. 'And who will pay the price? Us Jews, as usual.'[83] It is not surprising, then, that Zionists such as Dershowitz and Sharansky identify France as being particularly dangerous for Jews. It is worth remembering, however, that the French state is undergoing a massive identity crisis as it attempts to integrate the ever-growing Muslim population, and Jews remain relatively prosperous and safe.

When arguments spin out of control

One of the most remarkable aspects of the whole Israel–Palestine debate is how intense the rhetorical defence of Israel has become in recent years, particularly in the USA, and how it inevitably equates anti-Zionism with antisemitism.

The American historian Norman Finkelstein argues that antisemitism has not, in fact, increased and that the 'main purpose behind these periodic, meticulously orchestrated media extravaganzas [by Jewish groups] is not to fight anti-Semitism but rather to exploit the historical suffering of Jews in order to immunize Israel against criticism'.[84] He explains that Jews inflate the antisemitic threat when there are 'renewed international pressures on Israel to withdraw from occupied Arab territories in exchange for recognition from neighbouring Arab states'.[85] For making such statements, Finkelstein has been labelled 'anti-Semitic, anti-Israel, anti-American, Holocaust revisionist and terrorist sympathizer' by Columbia University students trying to block his planned visit to their campus.[86]

Reading the US Jewish feminist writer Phyllis Chesler, one could be forgiven for thinking that the 'Palestinianization of the western academy and media' is threatening the very lifeblood of Western civilisation. In her view, anything other than complete compliance with the US and Israeli agenda is akin to supporting terrorists, and individuals such as Norman Finkelstein and Israeli historian Ilan Pappe should be shunned because they encourage antisemitism.[87]

Similarly, conservative US columnist George Will accused the Left in 2004 of being infected with an 'anti-Semitic chic'.[88] He claims critics of Israel no longer openly slam Jews, and prefer to mouth anti-Zionist slogans. Even raising opposition to US foreign policy or the neo-conservative movement was an expression of antisemitism, Will wrote. Alan Dershowitz, an eminent American civil rights lawyer, member of the Harvard Law Faculty, and long-time supporter of Israel, claims that he has 'never heard a mere critic of Israel called anti-Semitic'.[89] This is surely untrue. I have been accused of antisemitism, and worse, on many occasions simply because I have dissented from the official line on the conflict. In *The case for peace* he argues that 'anti-Semitism and hate speech directed against Israel and its supporters will continue, regardless of what steps Israel takes towards peace'.[90]

In both *The case for peace* and his earlier book *The case for Israel*, Dershowitz attempts to prove that the Jewish state 'in all its years has killed fewer civilians than any other comparable country'.[91] He believes that Israel has been unfairly targeted, especially in universities across the USA, and is demonised beyond any other nation on earth. He blames the Palestinian leadership for the failure of a Palestinian state to materialise and praises Israel 'for the way it stood up to terrorism'.[92] *The case for Israel* concludes that Israel is largely blameless in relation to the current situation. This thinking inevitably leads to the labelling of anybody who disagrees as an antisemite.

In a review of *The case for peace*, Amy Wilentz, a former Jerusalem correspondent for the *New Yorker*, commented on its 'obsessive pages of attack and vitriol':

> Dershowitz doesn't believe that Israel bears a responsibility for what has happened in the Middle East. The problem, as he sees it, has two root causes: anti-Semitism (including the anti-

Semitism of American academe, all of Europe, the United Nations and most human rights organisations) and the late Palestinian leader Yasser Arafat. (Arabs also see the problem as having two root causes: European and American imperialism in the Arab world and Jewish intransigence concerning Israel.) Thus the second half of the book looks justifiably at anti-Semitic writing and teaching in the Arab world as an impediment to any real peace with Israel. Dershowitz uses this section to attack what he calls 'organised hatred' which for him also includes the Nobel Peace Prize committee, the poet Amira Baraka, the leftist linguist Noam Chomsky, journalist Alexander Cockburn and ... controversial Holocaust 'expert' Norman Finkelstein.[93]

Finkelstein, a lecturer in political science at DePaul University and author of several controversial books, including *The Holocaust industry*, which argues that Jewish groups are financially exploiting the Holocaust, rejects the claim and charges the Zionist lobby with creating a politically convenient myth: 'This shameless exploitation of anti-Semitism delegitimises criticism of Israel, makes Jews rather than Palestinians the victims and puts the onus on the Arab world to rid itself of anti-Semitism rather than on Israel to rid itself of the occupied territories'.[94]

Finkelstein analyses mountains of human rights organisations' records and discovers, despite counterclaims by Dershowitz, that Israel is a serial human rights abuser and is allowed to continue its transgressions under US political, financial and military cover. 'The most fundamental—and telling—fact about the chapters of *The Case for Israel* devoted to human rights issues', writes Finkelstein, 'is that never once does Dershowitz cite a single mainstream human rights organisation to support any of his claims'.[95] Dershowitz prefers to trash their legitimacy instead.

However, Dershowitz argues justifiably that some in the progressive movements need to move past the extremist language and polemics, and the comparisons to Nazi Germany, and to engage with the issues maturely. The anti-globalisation movement has indeed appropriated elements of antisemitic rhetoric in recent years, and Dershowitz is right to challenge this. He has also targeted the US linguist and social activist Noam Chomsky for his allegedly anti-Israel and antisemitic views. In both *The case for peace* and *The case for Israel*, he accuses Chomsky of 'flirting with Holocaust denial'[96] and, along with Finkelstein and progressive journalist Alexander Cockburn, hijacking US university campuses 'to intimidate many moderate voices for peace and the two-state solution'.[97]

Chomsky says that Israel 'cannot be compared to Nazi Germany' but highlights 'points of similarity, to which those who invoke the analogies want to draw attention', namely its treatment of the Palestinians.[98] Chomsky's principled stance against all state violence, including Israel's, is the main reason he is seen as such a threat. In 1967, he says:

> Israel won a dramatic military victory, demonstrated its military power, in fact, smashed up the entire Arab world, and that won great respect. A lot of Americans, especially privileged Americans, love violence and want to be on the side of the guy with the gun, and here was a powerful, violent state that smashed up its enemies and demonstrated that it was the dominant military power in the Middle East, put those Third World upstarts in their place.[99]

Chomsky believes that Israel will only exist 'as long as US state interests are being served and preserved'.[100] The risk he sees is that if those interests suddenly shift, the Jewish state will be 'finished' and 'anti-Semitism will shoot up'.

As a Jew himself, Chomsky has accepted that his views will regularly be met with vitriol. So how does he deal with it now? 'As long as my parents were alive, it was bothersome', he tells me:

> They more or less agreed with me … I mean they lived in a Jewish ghetto their whole lives and to hear this kind of stuff about their son was very hard. So I cut some corners in the early years. I would say things in a muted way, so it didn't hurt them.
>
> I never wanted to be [part of the intellectual elite]. I pulled myself out of that in 1957. I wouldn't go to the stupid parties if they invited me. But a close friend of mine, [the late] Edward Said, it bothered him, because he wanted to be part of polite, elegant New York society. He dressed well; he played squash with them. And to be slandered and vilified [as an antisemite] was very hard for him.[101]

An increasing number of anti-war marches target Israel and praise Palestine, but Dershowitz is wrong to conclude that this proves antisemitism is rife. Sharansky argues that many critical of Israel speak out because they see the Jewish state as 'the last vestige of colonialism'.[102] It is a charge that Dershowitz is unable to convincingly deflect.

Antisemitism in Australia

Australia is not exempt from this debate. Antisemitism does exist here, of course, and may even be on the increase, but the reasons for this are more complex than Zionist supporters would have us believe. Attacks on Australian Jews between October 2003 and September 2004 were 50 per cent above the average for the past 14 years, according to a report issued in December 2004 by ECAJ.[103] There were 455 reported attacks in the recorded period, including racist graffiti, eggs thrown at Jewish people on their way to religious events and the words 'kill the Jews' being burnt into the lawn of the Tasmanian Parliament. The entrance of a Jewish organisation in Melbourne was daubed in graffiti written with excrement, reading 'Kill All Jews'.[104] The report claimed that the incidence of anti-semitic graffiti was 30 per cent higher than the average of all the years since the ECAJ started gathering information in 1989.

Nevertheless, the report commented, the vast majority of Australians were not anti-Jewish, and the attacks were generally less violent than in years past. Jeremy Jones, a former president of the ECAJ, offered words of reassurance to members of the Jewish community: 'Every day there are millions of interactions between Jews and non-Jewish Australians, so every year there are hundreds if not thousands of millions of these inter-actions'.[105]

Australian writer Dawn Cohen has argued that 'many progressive Australians fear that taking anti-Semitism seriously means abandoning the suffering of Palestinians. They need to locate Jewish victimhood in the linear past so that the Jewish community can occupy the mutually exclusive category of oppressor'.[106] She believes that if you scratch the 'surface of your average Aussie, you will discover the view that a Jew complaining about Australian anti-Semitism is a wimpish drama queen'.

While Jewish community leaders such as Jones seem relatively content with general Australian attitudes to Jews, they denounce as anti-semites those Australians—by implication from the Left and far Right—who accuse Israel of being 'Nazi-like', committing 'Holocausts' or maintaining 'concentration camps'.[107] As previously noted, such labelling is counterproductive and factually inaccurate, but for Jones even debating the Zionist lobby during the 2003 Hanan Ashrawi affair is a sign of antisemitism. According to Jones, commentators who dare to suggest the existence of a 'Jewish lobby' are guilty of 'invoking hostile anti-Jewish caricatures'.[108] His targets have included *Australian* columnist Phillip Adams and the *SMH*'s Alan Ramsey. During the controversy that erupted when the 2003 Sydney Peace Prize was awarded to Palestinian Hanan

Ashrawi, Ramsey wrote that Ashrawi's Palestinian identity was 'enough to ensure a virulent campaign of distortion and ridicule by Jewish critics to brutalise her image'. Adams damned the 'so-called Jewish lobby' for 'its efforts to suppress and censor' its opponents.

The editor-in-chief of AIJAC's *Australia/Israel Review* (*AIR*), Tzvi Fleischer, shares Jones's concerns. He argues that there are certain themes in the Australian media that prove the existence of the 'new anti-Semitism':

> These include the alleged financial and media power of the Jewish lobby; an extreme demonization of Israel and extravagant assertions about the supposed worldwide effects of its policy toward the Palestinians; conspiracy theories about American Jewish neoconservatives; and a tendency to claim that anti-Semitism is a response to Jewish behavior and attitudes.[109]

Shaming Israel's critics

As many critics of Israel's recent conduct can attest, those who attempt to shame Israel will in turn be shamed by Israel's loyal supporters. Jewish critics of Israel are not immune from such shaming—indeed they are often even more vigorously attacked. During an international conference on antisemitism in Jerusalem in February 2004, some participants argued that antisemitism was being fuelled by critical coverage of Israel's policies in the 'left-leaning' newspaper *Haaretz* and by negative comments made by left-wing Israeli politicians.[110] As Akiva Eldar responded in *Haaretz*:

> It is much easier to claim the entire world is against us than admit that the state of Israel, which rose as a refuge and a source of pride for Jews ... has become a genuine source of danger and a source of shameful embarrassment to Jews who choose to live outside its border.[111]

Leading British human rights lawyer Geoffrey Robertson QC makes a similar point. 'Notwithstanding the recrudescence of anti-Semitism in some parts of Europe', he writes, 'the promised land remains the country where Jews are most at risk'.[112] This should surely cause Zionists to pause and wonder whether the Jewish state must take some responsibility for its parlous international standing. Ned Curthoys, teacher in the School of Humanities at the University of Technology, Sydney, offers a similar argument about the need for honest debate: 'If Jews are to counter an intensified if unorganised anti-Semitic recrudescence in the West and the Middle East, then the most hopeful solution for Jews today is to recognise a diversity of Jewish voices rather than trivialise genuine anti-Semitism'.[113] Blaming murderous Arabs and European antisemitism for all of Israel's woes may hearten Zionist supporters, but it is an increasingly untenable position.

Conflating legitimate criticism of Israel with antisemitism—calling critics of Israeli policies antisemitic—is a strategy intended to stifle criticism and dissent. Not every anti-Zionist is antisemitic; to assert that they are makes it more difficult to distinguish between real antisemitism and harsh but often warranted criticism of Israel. Israel and Judaism are separate and should not be automatically connected. Likewise, antisemitism is not anti-Zionism, though the two can be connected and are sometimes conflated.[114] Reading a commentator such as Alan Dershowitz, one could be forgiven for thinking that 2006 is 1933 Germany and that anyone who dares challenge Zionist or Israeli myths is a closet Nazi; his hysteria presumes nothing less. Yet as Amy Wilentz reminds us, 'Dershowitz doesn't believe that Israel bears a responsibility for what is happening in the Middle East'. And that is the nub of the issue. Yes, antisemitism must be fought, but suggesting that antagonism towards the state of Israel is unrelated to Israeli action make as much sense as claiming that rising anti-Americanism has no connection with the quagmire in Iraq. Shaming critics into submission does nothing but inflame tensions while ignoring the vitally important task of examining modern antisemitism.

The resurgence of antisemitism will continue to be debated, and can be regarded as part myth, part political statement and part fact. One of the important battlegrounds in this debate is that of media coverage as the mainstream media are increasingly charged with contributing to a rise in antisemitism. The following chapters consider these media debates both in Australia and overseas, examining the role of government, media and powerful lobbyists in shaping, influencing and censoring the coverage of the Israel–Palestine conflict.

ADVENTURES IN LOBBY LAND

6

THE POLITICS OF ZIONISM IN THE USA

Wherever you look in the Congress there are the tell-tale signs either of the Zionist lobby, the right-wing Christians, or the military-industrial complex, three inordinately influential minority groups who share hostility to the Arab world, unbridled support for extremist Zionism, and an insensate conviction that they are on the side of the angels.

Edward Said, 2003[1]

SUCCESSIVE US administrations have offered little more than lip-service to the principle of an even-handed approach to the Israel–Palestine conflict. This is partly the result of decades of dedicated activism by the Zionist lobby. As Republican Senator Gordon Smith, a member of several Senate committees including the powerful finance committee, said recently:

> Obviously one of the greatest commitments that we have is to Jewish people and the State of Israel to try and manage the difficult process of the peace there and securing that nation, and doing so in a way that, if possible, is just to the Palestinians. It would be foolish for people to think that somehow we are neutral.[2]

This attitude permeates both sides of politics. Republicans and Democrats—and American Jews generally find the latter more electorally appealing—have become mouthpieces for whichever government presides in Tel Aviv. Regardless of who holds power, most major political parties in the USA, Australia and other Western democracies offer nearly unqualified support for Israel's policies in the occupied territories and for 'security measures' implemented by the Jewish state. Western media organisations also generally adopt pro-Israeli, and often one-sided, perspectives on the conflict. The Zionist lobby can take at least some of the credit.

In both the USA and Australia there are powerful connections between politicians and Jewish lobby groups. The American Israel Public Affairs Committee (AIPAC) is probably the most powerful international lobby group in the USA. There is overwhelming sympathy in Congress for the cause of Israel, and AIPAC is often the conduit through which this support is voiced. Australia's most influential international lobby group, AIJAC, is similarly instrumental in maintaining the nexus between domestic politics and Middle East affairs. Both AIPAC and AIJAC cultivate close relationships with government, and target politicians who don't accept the official line on the conflict in Israel–Palestine, whether they are Jewish or not.

The power, influence and scope of the Zionist lobby are often discussed yet frequently misunderstood. Allusions to an underhanded Jewish influence on politics and the news media are counterproductive and create unnecessary antisemitic stereotypes, yet paradoxically, a serious examination of the motives, activities and behaviour of the lobby is rarely attempted, even though the material is often on the public record. This chapter sets out to investigate the role of the Zionist lobby in pressuring US politicians to place Israeli concerns high on their agendas, and in shaping media coverage of Israel and Zionism.

The influence of AIPAC

After visiting the USA, Gershon Baskin, who runs a moderate Israel–Palestine media think tank in Jerusalem, wrote in the *Jerusalem Post* that US foreign policy towards Israel was almost solely dictated by the wishes of AIPAC:

> Meeting people in the halls of Congress to exchange views, the first questions I was asked were: what does AIPAC have to say about that? Have you spoken to AIPAC? There is little doubt that AIPAC has successfully instilled a strong sense on the Hill

that anything that concerns the US/Israel relationship must be checked with them first.

He went on to chastise both government and Jewish leaders for a lack of real leadership:

> It is quite remarkable how lacking in independence the US Congress is with regard to US policy on Israel. It is equally remarkable that most of the official Jewish establishment organisations in the US lack any vision regarding how best to help Israel achieve peace and stability. The status quo of only backing whatever the Israeli government does, while at the same time placing severe limitations on the ability of the US administration to assist the Palestinians, is not really acting in the best interests of Israel.[3]

AIPAC's annual conference in Washington is a monumental affair, drawing thousands of delegates, Israeli politicians, and Democrats and Republicans to parrot the officially sanctioned line. In 2004 delegates shouted 'four more years' as they welcomed George W Bush to the podium. Bush credited AIPAC with 'strengthening the ties that bind' Israel and the USA, and praised 'our shared values, our strong commitment to freedom'.[4]

In 2005, a walk-through model of Iran's uranium-enrichment process was the centrepiece of the conference, and Israel's Prime Minister, Ariel Sharon, addressed the event. The US Secretary of State, Condoleezza Rice, offered the usual platitudes and suggested that 'some in the Arab media have even asked why the only real democracies in the Middle East are found in the "occupied lands" of Iraq and the Palestinian territories'.

Even Hillary Clinton, Democrat Senator for New York, climbed on board, praising the 'liberation' of Iraq, the 'professionalism' of the US military, Sharon's 'extraordinary stand' on 'disengagement' and his 'deep concern' over Iran, then telling delegates:

> What you are doing today is not only on behalf of AIPAC, not only on behalf of Israel, not only on behalf of the strong and enduring relationship between the USA and Israel; it is truly on behalf of the kind of world we want for our children and, for those lucky enough, grandchildren.

AIPAC's political funding

AIPAC has become the leading source of funds for Zionist causes in the USA. Jewish Americans make up less than 2 per cent of the US population yet provide substantial funding to political campaigns, and predominantly to Democratic candidates.[5] Mitchell Plitnick, director of policy and education for Jewish Voice for Peace, argues that a 'great portion comes from wealthy Jews who historically have shown little attachment to Israel, but great attachment to the liberal-leaning ideals of the Democrats'.[6] Yet AIPAC's fundraising is legendary primarily because there is so little opposition or competition to its activities. The organisation has an annual budget of US$19.5 million, a staff of more than 130 people and around 60 000 members.[7]

The exact amount of money given by AIPAC to political campaigns remains unclear, although the US Federal Electoral Commission provides some insights. Between 1997 and 2001, 46 members of AIPAC's board gave well over US$3 million to various candidates, and one, David Steiner, a New Jersey real estate developer, gave more than US$1 million.[8]

AIPAC board members are chosen by the amount of money they give, rather than their ability to support AIPAC members. In an investigation of AIPAC political funding in 2002, published by *Prospect* magazine, Michael Massing writes:

> An examination of AIPAC giving on the FEC Web site turns up many of the same recipient names from across the political spectrum: Joseph Biden, Christopher Bond, Barbara Boxer, Hillary Clinton, Susan Collins, Dianne Feinstein, Charles Grassley, Tom Harkin, Dennis Hastert, James Jeffords, Trent Lott, Nita Lowey, Mitch McConnell, Patty Murray, Charles Schumer, Paul Wellstone, and so on. In all, hundreds of members on both sides of the aisle receive substantial pro-Israel contributions. This giving packs all the more punch because of the lack of a counterweight by pro-Arab and pro-Muslim PACs.[9]

AIPAC focuses its lobbying on members of Congress, rather than on presidential candidates. Massing explains the process by which candidates are cultivated:

> Consider the case of Tom Daschle. When, as a four-term congressman, Daschle first ran for the Senate, in 1986, his opponent was considered no friend of Israel. Daschle's own record

was not particularly distinguished on matters Israeli, but AIPAC and other Jewish groups, intent on nurturing him, helped organize a round of fundraisers in different locales. In the end, say former AIPAC officials, these events netted Daschle roughly one-quarter of the $2 million he spent on the campaign. Daschle has received similar amounts in subsequent races. And as he's ascended the Democratic ladder in the Senate, his votes on the Middle East have reliably reflected AIPAC's perspective. Similarly, when Trent Lott was rising in the House under Newt Gingrich, AIPAC assigned some of its wealthy southern members to cultivate him. The Mississippian became a strong supporter of Israel.[10]

Other factors in US policy on Israel

While there is no doubt that AIPAC influences the USA's policy-making, its aims tend to coincide with the superpower's own perceived strategic interests in the Middle East. Despite the power of the Zionist lobby, other factors also shape US support for Israel. They include: the politics of oil; the arms industry and its influence in Congress; the sentimental attachment of US liberals to Israel's internal democratic institutions; the Christian Right's messianic beliefs; racist attitudes to Arabs and Muslims; and the failure of progressive movements to challenge US policy on Israel successfully.[11]

Socially and philosophically, mainstream US culture identifies with the Zionist ideal of Israel as a Western liberal democracy blooming in the desert, constantly fighting for its existence against irrational Arab forces. Indeed, this ideal has much in common with the USA's own foundational mythology. The sentiment shared by many conservatives and liberals is partly admiration for Israel's democratic norms and its social institutions, such as the kibbutz, and partly relief that an oppressed minority has finally found sanctuary.[12] 'Through a mixture of guilt regarding Western anti-Semitism, personal friendships with Jewish Americans who identity strongly with Israel, and fear of inadvertently encouraging anti-Semitism by criticising Israel', writes American historian Stephen Zunes, 'there is enormous resistance to acknowledge the seriousness of Israeli violations of human rights and international law'.

Just as important have been the politics of oil. George Bush Senior, President from 1989 to 1993, was often criticised by Zionists for his lacklustre support of Israel in the face of competing priorities. As economics editor for *National Review Online*, Larry Kudlow wrote, 'He saw the world through the lens of oil politics. He and then-Secretary of State James Baker were viewed as clearly tilting US–Mideast policy toward Saudi Arabia and away from Israel'.[13] In this role, Bush Senior played hardball with Israel, particularly over problematic issues such as the continued expansion of illegal settlements in the occupied territories. In 1991, Israel's right-wing government asked Washington for a loan guarantee of US$10 billion in commercial paper, seeking a new credit line to finance the resettlement of Jews leaving the Soviet Union. President Bush had just driven Saddam Hussein's army out of Kuwait in the first Gulf War and was soon to attend a Middle East peace conference in Madrid. His administration did not want to undermine the conference by massively subsidising the settlement of a million new immigrants to Israel on Palestinian land in the West Bank, the area where Yitzhak Shamir's government was likely to place many of them.

This is where the lobby comes in. In just one day about a thousand AIPAC-connected lobbyists reportedly visited congressional offices demanding that members urge Bush to release the money immediately. The Zionist lobby was more than willing to threaten the withdrawal of future financial support from Senators across the country. Bush responded that he was 'up against some powerful political forces', a comment some criticised as antisemitic. Israel eventually received the funds, and Bush even apologised for causing any undue offence. A report on the episode written by Jeffrey Blankfort includes an extensive list of both Democrat and Republican politicians who lined up to offer unconditional support for Israel during this period, and of the large amounts of money they have received, both before and after, from Zionist sources.[14]

Some Americans question the power of the Zionist lobby. Mitchell Plitnick from Jewish Voice for Peace argues that 'American policy depends on the popularity of Israel in the US. The "almighty lobby" still needs to devote huge resources to PR to maintain that. Its power, as formidable as it is, is largely based in public perception of its strength and the absence of serious opposition'.[15] Opposition does exist, but the vast majority of politicians and journalists prefer to ignore it. It is possible that one day Arab and Muslim voters and lobby groups will have as much influence in US politics as Jews. American Muslims are now believed to outnumber American Jews, and Islam is one of the fastest growing religions in the USA, but these changes are yet to be reflected in the political process.

There is reluctance in Congress to embrace the Palestinian cause.[16] After the death of PLO leader Yasser Arafat, *Haaretz* reported that it was exceedingly difficult to convince congressmen and women that the Palestinian Authority should be given any financial assistance at all;

Zionist lobbyists were doing their job. 'There is still the notion that the PA is corrupt and not effective', said Edward Abington, former US consul to East Jerusalem.[17]

For evidence of AIPAC's continuing influence, consider the case of Georgia congresswoman Cynthia McKinney. An African American with a longstanding antipathy towards the establishment view of the Israel–Palestine conflict, she truthfully observed in the aftermath of September 11 that many people had profited from the 'war on terror'.[18] Her pro-Palestinian line cost her her seat in 2002 after five consecutive terms (though she regained her Congress position in 2004).[19] When she questioned the Israeli occupation of Palestinian land, Jewish organisations, including AIPAC, offered financial support to her rival, Denise Majette. According to *Haaretz* in July 2004, Jewish activists were attempting to prevent her election to the Congress. ADL spokesperson Deborah Lauter told the paper that 'the American Jews have every right to participate in American politics, like any other special interest group'. True enough, but McKinney's statements had only ever been about the USA's unbalanced support for the Israeli government and its brutal occupation. It was a perspective that Jewish groups would rather not be aired in the public domain. Indeed, it is increasingly important to Zionist groups that they win over the leaders of the Latino and Black communities, and this priority is reflected in the consistent pro-Israeli votes of congressional delegations, despite the fact that these votes provide no benefit to their constituents.[20] The record shows that this lobbying is highly effective.

The Democrats and Israel

Bill Clinton's presidency (1993–2001) was in some ways dominated by the Oslo Accords, the second intifada and the Camp David negotiations. Clinton was popular in the Jewish community and strongly supported the Jewish state, but many Zionist groups objected to his placing pressure on Israel to talk with the Palestinians and to withdraw from occupied territory. It now appears that the Zionist lobby, and its Christian Zionist friends, successfully pressured Clinton to soften his stance towards Israel in the late 1990s.[21] Extraordinary claims have recently been made by conservative Christian leader Jerry Falwell, who has suggested that the scandal over Clinton's affair with Monica Lewinsky was used against him in the cause of Israel.[22]

Gershom Gorenberg, a Jerusalem-based journalist, explains how the relationship between extreme elements of the Zionist lobby and Christian fundamentalists developed during the Clinton years and has only strengthened during the presidency of George W Bush. These Christian fundamentalists are less interested in the survival of the State of Israel than in the 'rapture', or apocalypse. 'Clinton was not a soul-mate of this philosophy, unlike Bush, but was captive to their vast influence', Gorenberg argues.[23]

During the 2004 US presidential election, both major parties shamelessly pandered to Jewish voters and pushed ideas at the extreme end of Israeli politics.[24] The Democratic candidate, John Kerry, was keen to shore up his party's traditional Jewish support base, and released a position paper entitled *Strengthening Israel's security and bolstering the US/Israel special relationship*.[25] He supported the isolation of PLO leader Yasser Arafat and the maintenance of Jewish settlements in the West Bank, and he praised Israel's 'security fence'. Kerry applauded Sharon's plan to withdraw unilaterally from Gaza, as well as the maintenance of some Jewish settlements in the West Bank in any future peace deal, and insisted that Israel and the USA only talk to the Palestinians if they reject 'terror'.[26] Whatever Bush offered on the conflict, Kerry echoed 'me too'.

It did not hurt the cause of Israel when Kerry, a New Englander, discovered a year before the presidential election that both his paternal grandparents were born Jewish, later converting to Catholicism. Kerry's Jewish wife, Theresa Heinz Kerry, was heavily involved in the fight for the rights of persecuted Soviet Jewry in the former Soviet Union, and has long been a strong supporter of Israel.[27]

Kerry has told anecdotes about travelling in Israel that suggest he feels an emotional involvement in the issue.[28] One of the sites he has visited is Masada, the ancient ruins of a fortress near Jerusalem where the Jewish Zealots made their last stand against Roman rule in 73 CE: 'We stood on the edge and we yelled "*Am Yisrael chai!*" ["the nation of Israel lives"]. And boom, across came the echo, the most eerie and unbelievable sound. And we sort of looked at each other and we felt as if we were hearing the souls of those who had died there, speaking to us'.[29]

Howard Dean, the liberal former governor of Vermont and current chairman of the Democratic National Committee, who was bested by Kerry for the Democratic presidential nomination, appears to have gradually hardened his line on the Middle East, and his statements on Israel are almost indistinguishable from the Republicans'. During the 2004 presidential election, Dean criticised the Iraq war and attempted to gain the Democratic nomination by challenging those who gave the Bush administration authority to invade Iraq. By 2005, however, he told an audience of the American Civil Liberties Union, 'Now that we're there [in Iraq], we're there and we can't get out ... I hope the President is incredibly successful with his policy now'.[30] Democrats had become fearful of slamming Bush's Iraq policy, worried they would be accused of being anti-American or pro-terrorist.

In 2002, Dean told the US Jewish newspaper *Forward* that his view on Israel was 'closer to AIPAC' than Israeli groups such as Peace Now. He rarely expressed discomfort with the official government line on Israel during the 2003–04 presidential campaign. In May 2005 he told AIPAC's policy conference that 'Israel's fight against terrorism is also America's fight', promising that 'when it comes to American support for Israel and its security, there are no critical differences between Democrats and the President'.[31]

AIPAC and the National Jewish Democratic Council run annual trips to Israel for US politicians. The aim is to instil an understanding that Israel's security is paramount. When Dean travelled to Israel in September 2005 with AIPAC president Steve Grossman, he said that 'with each trip to Israel, I gain a better understanding of the central role that Jerusalem plays in the hearts and minds of the Jewish people'.[32] He made no mention of East Jerusalem or of Palestinian demands for it to be a future capital of a Palestinian state. A diary of the trip, posted on the National Jewish Democratic Council website, failed to mention meetings with any Palestinians or a visit to the occupied territories.[33]

There is no doubt US involvement in the war in Iraq has influenced Democratic feelings about Israel and the Middle East. Near the midpoint of George W Bush's second term, the Democratic policy on Israel is virtually identical to the Republicans', and seems unlikely to change even if a second Clinton enters the White House. Hillary Clinton, a leading Democratic contender for 2008, has clearly outlined her position on Middle East policy, which includes maintaining permanent military bases in Iraq (to ensure 'quick-strike capabilities' in the region), threatening military strikes against Iran, and allowing 'no more excuses for the Palestinians' such as the claim that they are committed to 'peace'.[34] Her strongest commitment in the Middle East is to Israel: 'The security and freedom of Israel must be decisive and remain at the core of any American approach to the Middle East. This has been a hallmark of American foreign policy for more than 50 years and we must not—dare not—waver from this commitment'.

Clinton is a member of the Senate Armed Services Committee, and represents one of the most Jewish parts of the country, so her record on Israel is unsurprising for a so-called liberal. A supporter of the invasion of

Iraq, believing it to be an essential component of the US 'war on terror', Clinton has visited US troops in Iraq and Afghanistan, and remains committed to the occupation, although she now says she wouldn't have authorised the Iraq mission had she known about the lack of weapons of mass destruction (WMDs), the absence of a long-term plan, and flagging international support.[35] Anti-war campaigner Cindy Sheehan, whose son was killed in Iraq, has accused her of being a 'political animal who believes she has to be a war hawk to keep up with the big boys'.[36] While the media increasingly treat Clinton's policies on most issues as little more than cynical political ploys to attract an increasingly fearful and conservative US public, her attitude to Israel is simply consistent with that of the political majority.[37]

During an address given to New York's Yeshiva College in December 2005—a few weeks after returning from Israel, where she stated that the 'security fence' was 'against terrorists, and not against the Palestinian people'[38]—she made her attitude clear: 'Israel is not only our ally; it is a beacon of what democracy can and should mean. If the people of the Middle East are not sure what democracy means, let them look to Israel'. She continued: 'If Americans did not understand it [Israel's sacrifices] before 9/11, it is abundantly clear now that we must stand beside Israel and make it clear we guarantee Israel's security. In defeating terror, Israel's cause is our cause'.[39]

The lobby and George W Bush

George W Bush takes a conservative Christian stand on Israel–Palestine, supporting the state of Israel. In a speech to the American Jewish Committee in 2001, Bush explained his position on Israel:

> One of our most important friends in the world is the State of Israel ... a small country that has lived under threat throughout its existence. At the first meeting of my National Security Council, I told them a top foreign policy priority is the safety and security of Israel.[40]

Yet Bush received only 19 per cent of the Jewish vote in 2000 and achieved little better in 2004.[41] After the 2000 election, senior Bush administration officials courted Christian fundamentalist groups and reassured them that the President was wholly committed to Israel.[42] Although Christian conservatives voted in greater numbers for Bush in 2004, the majority of Jewish voters continued to favour the Democrats.

Nevertheless, the neo-conservatives around Bush have strong connections to the Israeli cause through lobby groups and think tanks such as the Jewish Institute for National Security Affairs (JINSA) and the extraordinary Project for the New American Century (PNAC).

Formed in 1997 during the Clinton presidency by a group of hawks and conservatives, PNAC's stated aim was to 'rally support for American global leadership' by restoring what it described as a Reaganite policy of military strength and moral clarity to the conduct of US international relations. Its principal founder was William Kristol, who had worked for Vice-President Dan Quayle in the Bush Senior administration and is now editor of the conservative, Murdoch-funded *Weekly Standard*. Those who lent their names to its statement of principles have all subsequently been strongly associated with the Bush Junior administration, including Dick Cheney, Donald Rumsfeld and Paul Wolfowitz. Other prominent figures who jumped on board included conservative commentator Norman Podhoretz; former Unocal adviser Zalmay Khalilzad, now US ambassador to Iraq, former deputy secretary of state Richard Armitage and defense adviser Richard Perle.[43] One of the PNAC's first missions was to tell President Clinton that US policy on Iraq was not working. In a letter to Clinton—written in January 1998, more than five years before the US invasion of Iraq—they argued that Iraq was intent on acquiring WMDs, and that the USA should depose Saddam Hussein:

if Saddam does acquire the capability to deliver weapons of mass destruction, as he is almost certain to do if we continue along the present course, the safety of American troops in the region, of our friends and allies like Israel and the moderate Arab states, and a significant portion of the world's supply of oil will all be put at hazard.

We urge you to . . . turn your Administration's attention to implementing a strategy for removing Saddam's regime from power. This will require a full complement of diplomatic, political and military efforts. Although we are fully aware of the dangers and difficulties in implementing this policy, we believe the dangers of failing to do so are far greater. We believe the US has the authority under existing UN resolutions to take the necessary steps, including military steps, to protect our vital interests in the Gulf. In any case, American policy cannot continue to be crippled by a misguided insistence on unanimity in the UN Security Council.[44]

As its letter to Clinton showed, the group, which included several prominent Jews, was sympathetic to Israel.[45] In 1996, Perle and other hawks had written a policy document for Israel's Likud Party, entitled 'Clean break', which advised the Jewish state to abandon the Oslo Accords, maintain and expand settlements in occupied territory and launch the overthrow of Saddam Hussein.[46] The authors of 'Clean break' included James Colbert of JINSA. PNAC and 'Clean break' sought a major reordering of the Middle East, principally to benefit Israel, but also to bring about the installation of Western-friendly regimes.

Bush's controversial ambassador to the UN, John Bolton, has also had a hand in PNAC lobbying, as a signatory to the 1998 letter to Clinton. Bolton has been a loyal supporter of Israel over the years. As a member of the State Department under Bush Senior, he led a successful campaign in 1991 to revoke the infamous 'Zionism equals racism' resolution passed by the UN's General Assembly in 1975, which officially denied the right of self-determination for the Jewish people.[47]

Under George W Bush, before his UN appointment, he was a hawk-ish Undersecretary of State for Arms Control and International Security Affairs, supporting the US war in Iraq, and associated with lobby groups close to Israel's Likud Party.

When Bush nominated Bolton for the US ambassadorship early in 2005, the Senate resisted his confirmation because some members were concerned that his bellicose outlook would leave the world, in a post Iraq environment, even more suspicious of US intentions. The Zionist lobby came out fighting. Tom Neumann of JINSA claimed it was offensive to the Jewish community for his nomination to the UN job to be delayed. 'We should remind our elected representatives', he said. 'The Jewish community will always be grateful.'[48] Similar views were expressed by David Harris, Executive Director of the American Jewish Committee.[49]

AIPAC strongly supported Bolton, not least because he advocated action against Iraq and Iran, and an open-ended commitment to Israel. A senior, anonymous Jewish official told the Jewish newspaper *Forward* in 2005 that 'it would sure help to have Bolton in the UN and credible [Zionist] lobbyists in Washington'[50] to 'impact' US policy towards the Islamic state. 'What we need today on Iran', said JINSA's Neumann, 'is someone like Bolton who will show the world that we're tough'.[51]

Bush ultimately used his presidential powers to install the UN ambassador, although Bolton must face Senate confirmation again in 2007. The episode reveals that AIPAC's agenda is closely aligned with the Bush administration's and that a small number of mainly Jewish, neo-conservative ideologues have disproportionate influence over US policy in the Middle East, and actively undermine any attempts at restricting Israeli actions.[52]

The influence of the Zionist perspective in US policy during the George W Bush administration has been remarkable. In 2004, during a visit by Sharon to the White House, President Bush announced that he accepted Israel's insistence that it would not withdraw from its large settlements in the West Bank. In the process, he effectively reversed more than 20 years of official US opposition to the settlements, and the strategy previous US leaders had adopted of holding out the future of the West Bank settlements as a bargaining chip in peace talks. He also accepted Sharon's unilateral strategy of withdrawal from Gaza and the building of a security fence, calling it 'historic and courageous'.[53] While US officials have since argued about what settlements may stay or go, President Bush has endorsed the dangerous go-it-alone strategy that Israel has embarked on.

Now Iran, which has been on AIPAC's agenda for several years, is the next item on the neo-conservatives' to-do list.[54] The Bush administration has used fierce rhetoric against the Islamic regime and threatened military action. Vice-President Dick Cheney told the AIPAC 2006 conference that the country must not be allowed to develop nuclear weapons and that 'the United States is keeping all options on the table in addressing the irresponsible conduct of the regime'.[55] Secretary of State Condoleezza Rice told a US Senate panel in March 2006 that 'Iran is the single biggest threat from a state that we face', echoing similar statements about Iraq in 2002 and 2003.[56] Almost absent from public debate is the possibility that threatening, bombing or invading Iran has nothing to do with WMDs and all about protecting Israel and fears that Iran, the world's fourth-largest oil producer, will shift its petrodollars into Euros, thereby breaking the US dollar monopoly. Before the 2003 invasion, Saddam was threatening to make the same move.[57]

Israel has long been determined to stop Iran from developing nuclear weapons, and Cheney has given Israel political cover to carry out an attack against the Islamic state. 'Israel is our ally', he said in February 2005, 'and in that we've made a very strong commitment to support Israel, [and] we will support Israel if her security is threatened'. In March 2006, John Bolton addressed the annual AIPAC conference in Washington about the 'threat' of Iran's nuclear intentions.[58] The US ambassador to the UN sent a clear signal to the international body, saying that a failure by the UN Security Council to address Iran would 'do lasting damage to the credibility of the council'.[59] He promised that the USA would protect Israel against Iranian aggression:

While Mr Ahmadinejad, president of the Islamic Republic of Iran, has clearly failed his lessons in history, indulge me a moment, if you will, to offer him up at least one lesson on current events: our commitment to Israel's security and the alliance between the United States and Israel are unshakeable. The work AIPAC has done to forge and strengthen those ties should serve as a powerful reminder to any leader now or in the future that, simply put, there will be no destruction of the state of Israel. The greatest example of democracy in the Middle East is of course Israel.[60]

The wider AIPAC agenda was expressed by Daniel Gillerman, Israeli ambassador to the UN, who told delegates that, 'while it may be true—and probably is—that not all Muslims are terrorists, it also happens to be true that nearly all terrorists are Muslim'. He concluded: 'Thank God for AIPAC. This is for us the greatest guarantee and insurance policy for the survival of Israel. Please don't ever change'.[61]

AIPAC's Iran scandal

AIPAC's reputation took a battering in 2004 with the announcement that two senior US government employees were being investigated by the FBI for allegedly passing on classified documents concerning Iran to Israel.[62] A Pentagon analyst, Larry Franklin, was indicted, and pleaded guilty to discussing sensitive material with Steven Rosen, director of AIPAC's foreign policy division.[63] Franklin received a 12-year gaol sentence for sharing information with an Israeli diplomat.[64] Rosen had spent 23 years with AIPAC, and during that period cemented strong relationships with the most influential players in Washington.[65] Years before joining AIPAC, Rosen was a professor of politics at Brandeis University. The *New York Sun* wrote in June 2005 that during this time 'his politics became increasingly conservative and pro-Israel'.[66] Former AIPAC Middle East analyst Keith Weissman was also caught up in the scandal, and was prosecuted along with Rosen.

Franklin had leaked sensitive material about Iran to Israel via AIPAC. What were representatives of AIPAC doing in Franklin's office, an office that dealt, among other things, with forming the plans for war in Iraq?[67] The second most senior diplomat at the US embassy in Baghdad was also brought into the investigation, for allegedly passing classified information to Rosen.[68]

The FBI investigation hampered Israel's efforts to guarantee swift action against Iran, according to *Forward*. 'Pro-Israel activists in

Washington are privately worrying that the shake-up at AIPAC ... will make it even harder for Jerusalem to convince the White House that quick action must be taken against Iran', it reported.[69] The initial agenda of AIPAC was for the USA to invade quickly, occupy and pacify Iraq, and then prepare an assault on Iran. Because of the disastrous Iraqi occupation, alternative plans were hatched.[70] The neo-conservatives and Zionist supporters now had to resort to Plan B: an attack on Iran by Israel. In March 2005, the London *Times* reported that Sharon had already given an '"initial authorisation" for an attack [on Iran] at a private meeting last month on his ranch in the Negev desert'.[71] Such planning was inconceivable without US support and approval.

The ramifications of the scandal were profound, but American Jewish leaders remained uncharacteristically silent (at least publicly) during the initial phases of the FBI investigation. *Haaretz* correctly commented that the controversy had caused many Jews to address the issue of 'dual loyalty', whereby their love for the USA and their love for Israel often pulled them in opposite directions.[72] Dr James Zogby, president of the Arab–American Institute, argued in May 2005 that many American Jews were 'growing increasingly troubled by the heavy-handedness of this approach to electoral politics and the "strange bedfellows" created by an "Israel first and only electoral agenda"'.[73]

When Douglas Feith, Under Secretary of Defense, resigned in January 2005, his departure provided another insight into the FBI investigation. The accused Pentagon analyst, Larry Franklin, was a Defense employee; Feith's role in the AIPAC scandal—if any—remained unclear, although he was questioned by the FBI, and it is this interview that appears to have uncovered the existence of a spy—Franklin—working under Feith and former deputy secretary of Defense Paul Wolfowitz. Feith was one of the leading facilitators of the Iraq war and produced suspect intelligence that allegedly proved a link between Saddam and al-Qaeda. He was a dedicated Likudnik—during the Clinton years, when he was associated with JINSA and PNAC, he had helped to pen the 'Clean break' policy document for Likud. Juan Cole, a professor of modern Middle East and south Asian history at the University of Michigan, followed the case closely, and wrote on his website:

> Having a Likudnik as the number three man in the Pentagon
> is a nightmare for American national security, since Feith could
> never be trusted to put US interests over those of Ariel Sharon.
> In the build-up to the Iraq War, Feith had a phalanx of Israeli

generals visiting him in the Pentagon and ignored post-9/11 requirements that they sign in.[74]

Nevertheless, in 2005, when the USA invoked military sanctions against Israel over arms deals with China, Feith was reportedly behind the move. Israel had sold China unmanned aerial vehicles and replacement parts for Harpy attack drones.[75]

Any suggestion that senior members of the Bush administration might have been working hand-in-glove with the country's leading Zionist lobby during the period of the Iraq war, and that their sabre-rattling in relation to Iran might also have been influenced by this relationship, warrants the most thorough investigation. The story—little reported in the Australian and US media—reveals the tawdry relationship between AIPAC and the upper echelons of the US administration.

The media goes blank

The mainstream media in the USA seemed to be unsure about how to respond to such serious charges. All the major newspapers reported the case, yet failed to engage with the major issue raised, namely Israel's relationship with the US establishment. The *New York Sun* ran a feature in June 2005 that exposed the backgrounds of the major AIPAC players and how they were connected to the Bush administration.[76] It was a rare and commendable piece of investigative journalism.

The commercially owned news media in the US follow the intimate relationship between the USA and Israel in their reporting—including US support for Israeli political and military manoeuvres—but generally fail to investigate the 'special relationship' between the two nations, the amount of US aid given annually, or the influence of the Zionist lobby on policy. News articles regularly describe the hardships of Palestinians in the occupied territories and occasionally even demonstrate an understanding of their grievances, though the real reasons for their predicament are often ignored. Former executive editor of the *New York Times*, Max Frankel—he was at the paper for 50 years and was executive editor from 1986 to 1994—wrote in his memoirs that he 'was much more deeply devoted to Israel than I dared to assert ... Fortified by my knowledge of Israel and my friendships there, I myself wrote most of our Middle East commentaries. As more Arab than Jewish readers recognised, I wrote them from a pro-Israel perspective'.[77] This situation remains largely unaltered today.

When Israel was preparing to 'disengage' from Gaza in August 2005, Ariel Sharon's government asked for over US$2 billion in additional aid.

A CNN poll asked whether US taxpayers should be footing the bill, and a remarkable 94 per cent answered no.[78] The cable news channel had featured a report on the amount of money spent annually on Israel—it revealed that the US government had provided over US$140 billion in assistance to Israel since the early 1970s—and had asked, 'How much is enough?'. It was a rare discussion point and surprising to see on CNN.[79]

The victory of Hamas in the Palestinian elections in January 2006 provided a window on the connections between the Bush administration, the Zionist lobby and the leading mainstream media. The week before the poll, the *Washington Post* reported that the US government was pumping millions of dollars of foreign aid into the Fatah-run Palestinian Authority in an attempt to bolster its election chances.[80] The writers argued that the program 'highlights the central challenge facing the Bush administration as it promotes democracy in the Middle East'. Like the blatant efforts of the USA and Britain to change Iraq's first democratically elected leadership, it laid bare the hypocrisy underlying US rhetoric about bringing democracy to the Middle East.

The *New York Times* echoed the Israeli agenda. 'America is engaged in a global armed struggle against terrorism', the paper wrote in early March 2006 after the Bush administration said it would not financially support Hamas.[81] 'It is firmly allied with Israel and is committed to Israel's survival.' The day after the Hamas win, the *Times* accepted the official Israeli perspective that there was 'no negotiating partner' and implicitly supported further unilateral separation from the Palestinians.[82] After the Kadima Party won Israel's general elections in late March 2006, the *Times* was 'heartened by anything that leads to an Israeli withdrawal from land that Palestinians must control if the area is ever going to evolve into two peaceful, co-existing states', it wrote. Crucially, however, 'Hamas has yet to earn itself a seat at the negotiating table'.[83] There was virtually no acknowledgement of any US responsibility for the parlous relationship between the two parties, or the role of the Zionist lobby in pressuring successive administrations to impose 'peace deals' rather than negotiate them.[84] Recent polls suggest that the USA's reputation in the Middle East has never been weaker, primarily because of the Iraq war and the nation's fanatical support for Israel, yet the mainstream media are content to portray Israel's interests as synonymous with those of the USA.[85]

A straitened climate of debate

The continuing confusion between anti-Zionism and antisemitism, and Zionists' attempts to attack critics by conflating the two are stultifying US media coverage. The antisemite slur distorts public debate, sometimes in bizarre ways. One of the strangest examples followed Mark Felt's admission that he was the secret source known as 'Deep Throat' in the Watergate scandal. Felt, former second-in-charge of the FBI, provided information to the *Washington Post*'s investigation of the scandal, which brought down President Richard Nixon in 1974. Ben Stein, a writer, actor, economist and lawyer, wrote in the *American Spectator* in May 2005 that Nixon was a 'hero' because 'he was fighting for peace'. Felt, however, was a traitor. 'It's been reported that Mark Felt is at least part Jewish', he wrote:

> The reason this is worse is that the same time Mark Felt was betraying Richard Nixon, Nixon was saving Eretz Israel. It is a terrifying chapter in betrayal and ingratitude. If he even knows what shame is, I wonder if he felt a moment's shame as he tortured the man who brought security and salvation to the land of so many of his and my fellow Jews.[86]

Since attempts to suppress Norman Finkelstein's latest book about antisemitism were revealed in early 2005, national and international commentators have drawn attention to the straitened climate of media discussion of Israel in the US press. '[T]he parameters for debate are relatively narrow compared with the rest of the western world', the London *Guardian* commented.[87] It quoted Colin Robinson of the New Press, Finkelstein's first publisher: 'The atmosphere for publishing critical stuff on Israel here is very intimidating'.

As discussed in chapter 5, Finkelstein's book, *Beyond chutzpah: on the misuse of anti-Semitism and the abuse of history*, was an attack on Alan Dershowitz's book *The case for Israel*. Finkelstein, an assistant professor of political science at DePaul University, Chicago, claimed that Professor Dershowitz had plagiarised parts of Joan Peters's discredited *From time immemorial*, the 1984 work that tried to prove that the land now known as Israel was essentially empty before Jews arrived and that Palestinians had no real right to call it their own. Finkelstein also attacked other aspects of *The case for Israel*, notably its central contention that 'no nation in the history of the world that has faced comparable threats to its survival—both external and internal—has ever made greater efforts as, and has ever come closer to, achieving the high norms of the rule of law'.

What might have remained an academic debate reached the pages of the national press. The *New York Times* reported that Dershowitz had counter-charged Finkelstein with making up quotes and making up facts.[88] The Harvard professor was clearly worried about his reputation being sullied by a relatively unknown academic, as well as the establishment view of Zionist history being seriously challenged. The *Boston Globe* quoted Dershowitz, who threatened Finkelstein's publisher, the University of California Press, with a law suit: 'I told the UC press, "If you say I didn't write the book or plagiarized it, I will own your company"'.[89]

The news media loved the stoush but generally refrained from fully investigating the arguments put forward by Finkelstein. It was largely left to alternative publications, such as the *Nation,* and overseas papers, such as the *Guardian,* to explain why Dershowitz was so defensive and why the University of California Press—slammed by Dershowitz as 'very hard-left' and 'very anti-Zionist'[90]—had the right to publish *Beyond chutzpah.* An Associated Press article,[91] republished in many major US broadsheets, discussed the plagiarism charges laid by Finkelstein but almost completely avoided any mention of Israel and its actions, themes central to the spat. Jon Weiner, professor of history at the University of California Irvine, offered a rare dissenting view in the *Los Angeles Times.*[92] He wrote that Dershowitz had reason to be concerned because Finkelstein demolished the law professor's portrayal of Israel as a noble state.

What emerges from press coverage over several months is that Dershowitz made concerted efforts to prevent publication of Finkelstein's book. When Dershowitz discovered that the New Press in New York planned to release the book, he reportedly obtained the home addresses of the New Press board and urged them not to publish it. The publisher at New Press, Colin Robinson, commented: 'I got four letters from Dershowitz in three months'. After the University of California Press acquired the book, Dershowitz was so determined to stop publication of the book, according to Weiner, that he briefed a well-known law firm to write strongly worded letters to the University of California, to seventeen directors of the press and nineteen members of the press's faculty editorial committee.[93] He also wrote to the Californian Governor, Arnold Schwarzenegger, in early 2005 to protest.[94] Schwarzenegger's legal affairs secretary wrote back to Dershowitz: 'You have asked for the Governor's assistance in preventing the publication of this book [but] he is not inclined to otherwise exert influence in this case because of the clear, academic freedom issue it presents'. 'Thus the star of "The Terminator"', writes Weiner, 'sought to teach a lesson about academic freedom to a Harvard law professor'.

Dershowitz is a well-known defender of the First Amendment—an important section of the US Constitution that protects freedom of speech, press, religion, assembly and petition—but told the Associated Press that he saw nothing incongruous about trying to convince University of California Press not to publish Finkelstein's book.[95] He wanted the book to be printed, he argued, ideally by a less respectable publisher, so he could 'devastate (Finkelstein) in the court of public opinion'. 'The First Amendment only protects honest mistakes', he said. 'It doesn't protect deliberate falsehoods.' Yet tellingly, after the book's release—and Finkelstein's central allegation that Dershowitz had passed somebody else's ideas as his own—he brought no defamation action against Finkelstein. A number of reviewers have commented that careful examination of the documents Finkelstein presents in *Beyond chutzpah* makes it difficult not to conclude that he is right to question Dershowitz.[96]

The 'Israel lobby' affair

The controversy that legitimate critiques of Israel and the Zionist lobby generate in the USA was on display again after the release in March 2006 of an academic paper by two US professors, John Mearsheimer and Stephen Walt, on the 'Israel lobby', published under Harvard's Kennedy School of Government logo.[97] They claim that the USA has been 'willing to set aside its own security and that of many of its allies in order to advance the interests of another state'. The authors argue that the Israel lobby has managed to convince Americans that 'US interests and those of ... Israel are essentially identical', when in fact they are not.[98] They make it clear that they support the 'moral case' for Israel's existence but rightly argue that it is not in jeopardy. Mearsheimer and Walt dismiss the sort of conspiracy depicted in the *Protocols of the Elders of Zion* but point out that the pro-Arab lobby groups are comparatively weak, allowing journalists, politicians and lobbyists to push Israel's interests at the expense of US interests.[99] One of the 'most powerful weapons' of the lobby, they write, is to accuse critics of antisemitism. Their report—measured and rationally argued—concludes that the Zionist lobby wields an unhealthy influence over the media and body politic in the USA.

Although the report's credibility wasn't helped by public endorsements by white supremacist David Duke and the Islamist Muslim Brotherhood[100]— the authors distanced themselves from both—the ensuing attacks on the report reveal that there is deep sensitivity in the USA when it comes to even raising Israel's influence on foreign policy. Alan Dershowitz called the paper 'trash' and claimed it 'could have been written by ... Noam Chomsky, and some of the less intelligent members of Hamas'.[101] The Harvard law professor went on to say the authors were 'bigots' and had written a report that closely resembled the *Protocols of the Elders of Zion*.

One of the report's authors told *Forward* that the paper was originally commissioned in 2002 by one of the USA's leading magazines, the *Atlantic Monthly*, 'but the publishers told us that it was virtually impossible to get the piece published in the United States'.[102] The abuse kept on coming. The ADL described it as 'a classical conspiratorial anti-Semitic analysis invoking the canards of Jewish power and Jewish control'.[103] Harvard soon decided to remove its logo from the study and insisted on a more strongly worded disclaimer that stated the work reflected the views of the authors only.[104] Veteran American Jewish commentator Earl Raab argues that many American Jews believe that if the USA ditches Israel, it would also be abandoning American Jewry. The line between antisemitism and legitimate criticism of Israeli policy is therefore often deliberately blurred.[105]

The American Civil Liberties Union argues that the First Amendment to the US Constitution exists 'precisely to protect the most offensive and controversial speech from government suppression. The best way to counter obnoxious speech is with more speech. Persuasion, not coercion, is the solution'.[106] Yet although the First Amendment covers the whole spectrum of views, from the moderate to the extreme, it is difficult to find open and honest debate about the Middle East in the US media; the Zionist lobby is simply too effective. One has to read the British or European press for a more thorough examination of the conflict, and to find voices debating the meaning of Zionism openly and freely. The following chapter focuses on the United Kingdom and some of the remarkable dissenting voices that have been heard there in discussions of Israel.

'One of the saddest consequences of Israel's colonialism has been the moral coarsening of the Jewish-American community', writes Michael Lind, a Whitehead Senior Fellow at the New America Foundation think tank.[107] He notes that the success of the Zionist lobby has meant that Arabs and Palestinians are discussed 'in terms as racist as those once used by southerners in public when discussing blacks'. 'Since 1967', he continues,

> the need to justify the rule of Israel over a conquered helot population has produced a shift from humane idealism to unapologetic tribalism in parts of the Diaspora, as well as in Israel. It is perhaps no coincidence that the most important non-Jewish supporters of Israel in the US today are found in the Deep South among descendants of the segregationist Dixiecrats.

7

THE UNITED KINGDOM'S CLIMATE OF DISSENT

For too long the accusation of anti-Semitism has been used against anyone who is critical of the policies of the Israeli government, as I have been. Even Tony Blair was recently described as a 'common anti-Semite' in an Israeli newspaper. Being Jewish is no defence from this charge.

London Mayor Ken Livingstone, 2006[1]

THERE IS NO question that the general public mood in the United Kingdom is more sympathetic to the Palestinian cause than in the USA. Performing at a benefit in October 2004 for the children of Palestine, the lead singer of popular rock band Primal Scream, Bobby Gillespie, commented: 'Everyone knows who is under the boot and who's got the mouthful of broken glass. The Palestinians are a prisoner nation, refugees and exiles treated like ghosts. Now we want them to feel our solidarity'.[2] The concert reflected the growing public awareness of the Palestinian struggle. Gillespie compared the situation to the 1980s, when his father, a union leader, made trips to Nicaragua to support the Sandinistas against US aggression. 'It was the obvious thing to do then', he wrote, 'and it's the same today with Palestine'.

This mood perhaps partly explains the 2005 electoral win of George Galloway, a former member of the Labour Party and leader of the Respect Party. A socialist party formed by Galloway, Respect campaigned strongly against the Iraq war but also opposed privatisation, and supported the trade union movement and the Palestinian cause. Galloway unseated Oona King, a Black Jewish Labour member who had supported the Iraq war. Galloway is a long-time critic of Israel, Zionism and its treatment of the Palestinians. He was accused of accepting financial kickbacks from Saddam—a charge he vehemently denied, though some of his former associations were highly questionable, not least his friendship with Iraq's former deputy prime minister Tariq Aziz. In early 2005 he volunteered to appear before a US Senate committee and was questioned by right-wing Republican Senator Norm Coleman about his relationship with Saddam Hussein. Galloway denied the allegation that he had accepted kickbacks and aggressively counterattacked, questioning the extent of the political donations AIPAC had made to Coleman.

Galloway has called for a boycott of Israeli goods, and his win is almost certainly related to the high percentage of Muslims in his electorate. Although King has criticised Israeli policy, she heard that her heritage was targeted. 'I have been told by several people that members of Respect have told them not to vote for me because I am Jewish', she told the *Evening Standard*. Galloway was accused of stirring up racial hatred.

While it is not always easy in the United Kingdom to have rational debate about the Israel–Palestine conflict, there is nevertheless much more space in the public domain for such discussion, compared with both the USA and Australia. A broader range of opinion flourishes as a result, among both Jews and non-Jews.[3] The distinguished Jewish Labour MP Gerald Kaufman wrote in the *Guardian* in 2004 that the only way to stop Palestinian oppression was to impose sanctions and a weapons ban on Israel because 'such a policy brought down apartheid South Africa'.[4] He expanded on these points in the *Guardian* in 2005.[5] After leading the first British parliamentary delegation to the Palestinian Authority, he wrote: 'What we saw is never seen by ordinary, decent Israelis . . . who, since they dare not venture into the occupied territories, have no idea of the persecution of Palestinians being carried out in their name'. A founding member of the Jewish Forum for Justice and Human Rights, Brian Klug, appeared in the same paper, arguing that it is both acceptable and necessary for Jews to question the main tenets of Zionism.[6] It is not anti-semitic, he writes, to challenge Israel's occupation of West Bank and Gaza, the spread of Jewish settlements in the territories, the discriminatory treatment of Palestinian inhabitants and 'the institutionalised bigotry against Israeli Arabs in various spheres of life'.

Only half of one per cent of the United Kingdom's 60 million inhabitants claim Jewish heritage. Numerically, the United Kingdom's roughly 300 000 Jews are a much smaller interest group than either the 1.5 million Muslims living in the United Kingdom or the 5 million or more Jews living in the USA.[7] The composition of the Zionist lobby in the United Kingdom is more complex than that of its US equivalent, and its influence is more complex as well. The Board of Deputies of British Jews is a democratically elected national representative body and claims to represent a cross-section of British Jews. It does not have the same political or financial power as AIPAC, but is close to Tony Blair's Labour government (as well as to the Tories) and is the largest Jewish body in the country.

Addressing the 2005 Board of Deputies president's dinner, attended by the United Kingdom's Chief Rabbi and a host of MPs, Blair praised the work of the board in maintaining rights and freedoms, and argued that 'the country would be immeasurably poorer without the Jewish voice'. Blair confirmed his commitment to the official Zionist line. 'I am, and always will be, a strong supporter and friend of the Jewish community and of the State of Israel', he said. The Palestinians were mentioned in passing. 'Today, a true friend of Palestine is one who supports its moderate leadership, not those who seek to undermine it'. Only the Palestinians commit terror, Blair implied, not the Israelis: 'Those who trade in terror are enemies of peace'.

There is more nuance in Blair's view of Israel than in Bush's, partly because of his nation's role as a former imperial power and its historical involvement in Palestine. Since World War II, and the rise of the USA as a superpower, the United Kingdom's imperialist urges have decreased but the change in its international role is merely one of emphasis. As the historian Mark Curtis writes, 'Britain's role remains an essentially imperial one: to act as junior partner to US global power; to help organise the global economy to benefit Western corporations; and to maximise Britain's (that is, British elites') independent political standing in the world and thus remain a "great power"'.[8] Since 1948 Israel–Palestine has provided almost endless opportunities for successive British governments to talk the language of peace while supporting Israel's territorial expansion.[9]

Yet the United Kingdom's own recent troubled history in Ireland profoundly colours the attitudes and understanding of Britons. It's not that long since the Irish Republican Army (IRA) was conducting a terror campaign in the heart of London, or since the human rights of those openly supporting the cause of Irish nationalism were sometimes severely constrained. In an essay for the Jerusalem Center for Public Affairs, Dean Godson, an associate editor of the *Spectator*, claimed that many British officials saw strong similarities between Israelis and the Irish Protestant Unionists. Both were perceived 'as "Afrikaners" or "settler" groups who have driven out indigenous peoples' and must be pulled down a peg or two. Godson predicted that the lesson the British had learnt in Northern Ireland—that, eventually, political concessions are inevitable—would ultimately benefit the Palestinians. The British 'believe that the IRA—like the Palestinians—has a great number of good excuses to go back "to war". That process, of depriving the insurgents of "excuses", inevitably comes at the expense of Unionists and the Israelis'.[10]

The British government has long championed a 'balanced' approach to the Israel–Palestine conflict and claimed to understand both sides equally. But the reality has been very different.[11] In the aftermath of the United Kingdom's involvement in the 2003 Iraq war, it was understood that one of the conditions under which Blair had agreed to Bush's request for support was progress on Israel–Palestine. George W Bush's endorsement of a two-state solution and implementation of a 'road map' to achieve this goal were to be a 'reward' for Blair's assistance in supporting the US-led invasion of Iraq. Blair received nothing of the sort. After Sharon's visit to Washington in March 2004, when the Bush administration gave its blessing to Israel's new strategy of unilateralism, a group of more than 50 former diplomats wrote to Blair, denouncing the decision to accept a number of illegal West Bank settlements. 'Our dismay at this backward step', they wrote, 'is heightened by the fact that you yourself seem to have endorsed it, abandoning the principles which for nearly four decades have guided international efforts to restore peace in the Holy Land'.[12]

A few months later, 347 British Jews wrote to the Board of Deputies of British Jews arguing that the time had come to 'distinguish the interests of the community in Britain from the policies adopted by Israeli governments ... These issues must be brought into the open. Silence discredits us all'.[13] Andrew Samuels, a professor of analytical psychology at the University of Essex and a signatory to the letter, applauded this stance: 'The debate in international Jewry about the need to separate Jewish identity from Jewish nationalism, and hence to feel free to criticise Israel's policies, has turned out to be crucially important in getting world governments to think in an equitable way about the Middle East'.[14]

Brian Humphreys, a member of the Board of Deputies, offered a lame response to the petition: 'Although the "official" Board line is not to criticise the Government of Israel there are a significant number (although still a minority) of Deputies who do voice contrary opinions at the Board, when discussions on Israel take place'. A signatory to the petition, the Turkish-born writer Moris Farhi, commented: 'If the light unto the nations chooses the path of tyranny, what hope for mankind?'[15]

Ken Livingstone, dissenter

In this climate of robust debate, the expression of genuinely radical views is possible, and when they occur, genuine tensions can develop. London Mayor Ken Livingstone is an outspoken critic of Israeli policy, and the Jewish establishment's response to his criticism provides a perfect example of its sensitivity. Livingstone was born in 1945 and told the *Guardian* in February 2005 that he 'grew up in a world in which all the horror of what the Nazis did unfolded over years. The incident of the Holocaust just infuses all my politics—and I do look for parallels'.[16] He has a track record of tossing grenades into the debate. In 1984 he said the Board of Deputies of British Jews was 'dominated by reactionaries and neo-fascists'. In 1987—the year he became MP for Brent East—he compared Camden Council's housing policies to Hitler's oppression of homosexuals. He observed in 2000—the year he became Lord Mayor of London—that 'capitalism has killed more people than Hitler'.

Long known as 'Red Ken' because of his left-wing outlook, Livingstone joined the Labour Party in the early 1980s. His relationship with Labour often proved rocky as the party moved further to the right. He has spent his life advocating gay and lesbian rights, and used the powers of London Transport to ban homophobic advertisements on the Underground, buses and taxis. He fought South African apartheid, and after becoming leader of the Greater London Council in 1981 encouraged Black people to build stronger communities.

Early in 2005, Livingstone was involved in a verbal stoush with a Jewish journalist. The Mayor had been attending a party at London's City Hall to mark the twentieth anniversary of the first occasion on which an MP had publicly declared his homosexuality.[17] Oliver Finegold identified himself as an employee of the *Evening Standard*, and repeatedly questioned Livingstone about how the evening had gone. Livingstone ultimately responded by asking whether Finegold was a 'German war criminal'. Finegold answered that he was Jewish and he found the question offensive. 'You are just like a concentration camp guard', Livingstone continued. 'You are just doing it for the money, aren't you?'[18] The *Standard* is the sister newspaper of the *Daily Mail*, which supported the Nazis during the 1930s. Livingstone refused to apologise for his outburst, although he publicly acknowledged that the Holocaust was the worst crime of the twentieth century.[19]

Livingstone, who has since argued that he was effectively off duty, apparently felt harassed by the reporter. Nevertheless he provided little reason for the outburst, though he later accused Associated Newspapers, which owns the *Evening Standard*, of running a 25-year vendetta against him. He told the London Assembly that if 'I could, in anything I say, relieve the pain anyone feels I would not hesitate to do it, but it would require me to be a liar. I could apologise but why should I say words I do not believe?'.[20] The Standards Board of England announced in August that a disciplinary hearing would be held to investigate charges that Livingstone 'failed to treat others with respect and brought his authority into disrepute'. By November, he told the SomethingJewish website that the Board of Deputies, the Tories and the *Evening Standard* were behind a campaign to oust him.[21] He even stepped up his attack on the Zionist lobby: 'The Board of Deputies—and the *Jewish Chronicle* is their mouthpiece—have this idea that anyone who's critical of Israel gets denounced as being anti-Semitic, so as a result the average spineless politician never says anything about the Middle East again'. Finally, he spoke of the possibility that he might have Jewish roots. 'Then I could be a self-hater, couldn't I?' he joked.

The Jewish community's outrage at Livingstone's concentration camp comment was spontaneous. Michael Whine, head of the Community Security Trust (CST), an official body that deals with security for the United Kingdom's 300 000-strong Jewish community, said the mayor had behaved 'like an anti-Semitic thug'. A group of Holocaust survivors demanded an apology: 'Only two weeks ago the nation gathered together to mark the Holocaust ... You have made light of our suffering and abused the memory of those that perished'.[22]

The offence Livingstone caused was compounded by the fact that he had supported controversial Sheikh Yusuf al-Qaradawi, a leading Islamic cleric. While condemning the September 11 attacks in the USA, Al-Qaradawi has condoned suicide bombing as a legitimate means of resistance for Palestinians. The Qatari-based religious leader has been banned from the USA, but not from the United Kingdom.[23]

The deputy mayor of London, Nicky Gavron, a Jewish daughter of a Holocaust survivor, defended Livingstone. She told the *Guardian* that her leader was a colourful character who used juxtaposition to shock but that he was not an antisemite. He used 'the [Iraq] war and Hitler as a moral reference point. But I wouldn't work for him for a minute if he was anti-Jewish'. He had also called George W Bush 'the most dangerous man on the planet' and commented that he looked forward to seeing the Saudi royal family 'swinging from lamp-posts'.[24]

Livingstone did not back off. In March 2005 the *Guardian* published an article in which the mayor labelled Ariel Sharon a 'war criminal who should be in prison', and accused Israel of 'ethnically cleansing' Palestinians on their land, building illegal settlements and 'organising terror'.[25] He also expressed his belief that the 'contribution of Jewish people to human civilisation and culture is unexcelled and extraordinary' and referred to his cooperation with Jewish groups in fighting the far-right National Front. Livingstone's article was a robust defence of his record and a plea for readers, and especially Jews, not to conveniently confuse legitimate criticism of Israel with antisemitism. He argued that growing suspicion of Israelis and Jews was directly related to the actions of Sharon, and to deny this was dishonest. 'Relations with the Board [of Deputies]', he wrote,

> took a dramatic turn for the worse when I opposed Israel's illegal invasion of Lebanon, culminating in the massacres at the Palestinian camps of Sabra and Shatila. The board also opposed my involvement in the successful campaign in 1982 to convince the Labour party to recognise the PLO as the legitimate voice of the Palestinian people.

Livingstone challenged the Board of Deputies' perspective: 'The fundamental issue on which we differ . . . is not anti-semitism—which my administration has fought tooth and nail—but the policies of successive Israeli governments'. Livingstone insisted that Zionist lobbyists and the Israeli government were deliberately exaggerating the extent of antisemitism in Europe to obscure the truth about its treatment of the Palestinians. 'The reality', he insisted, 'is that the great bulk of racist attacks in Europe today are on black people, Asians and Muslims'. All racist attacks should be stamped out, he said, but 'for 20 years Israeli governments have attempted to portray anyone who forcefully criticises the policies of Israel as anti-semitic'. It was an unprecedented attack.

The response was swift. Zvi Heifetz, Israeli ambassador to the United Kingdom, condemned Livingstone for airing his 'anti-Israel' comments at a time when there was 'a tangible sense of renewed hope for peace in the Middle East'.[26] Sharon had taken 'courageous actions to advance peace'; the Lebanon 'operation' was justified, and there was a danger that the mayor's comments would serve, 'however unintentionally', to strengthen the antisemitic 'venom' that existed in the United Kingdom. Heifetz argued that there was no connection whatsoever between a rise in Judeophobia and Israeli actions. In this respect, his remarks weren't dissimilar to Tony Blair's comments after the London bombings, when the Prime Minister suggested that the Iraq war was wholly unrelated to the attacks.

In late February 2006, an unelected three-man Adjudication Panel for England found Livingstone guilty of breaching the Greater London authority's code through his comments and of damaging the reputation of his office. They recommended a one-month suspension.[27] Karen Pollack, chief executive of the Holocaust Educational Trust, supported the ban—as did the original complainants, the Board of Deputies of British Jews—though many unions, MPs and political allies argued that an unelected body should not be able to suspend an individual who had been elected by millions of Londoners.[28] A few days later, however, a High Court judge froze the suspension and allowed Livingstone to continue the fight against the 'McCarthyite' decision to ban him.[29]

Livingstone went on the offensive, defended his record of fighting 'every manifestation of racism, anti-semitism and every other kind of discrimination' and joked that, 'as far as I am aware, there is no law against "unnecessary insensitivity" or even "offensiveness" to journalists questioning you as you try to go home'.[30] He saved his strongest vitriol for Jewish groups—and he specifically referred to the Board of Deputies—for labelling as antisemitic anybody 'who is critical of the Israeli government ... Even Tony Blair was recently described as a "common anti-semite" in an Israeli newspaper. Being Jewish is no defence for this charge'.[31]

Livingstone received wide support in the *Guardian* letters page, but one letter stood out. Michael Halpern claimed that the Board of Deputies of British Jews 'professes to be the official voice of British Jewry ... of which I am one'.[32] He said the body was not representative of Jewry, 'but only a number of individual synagogues and their respective members', and that the complainant in the case against Livingstone, Jon Benjamin, was 'an unelected, paid official of that organisation'. There are 'many thousands of Jews in the UK who (vehemently) disagree with policies of the Board, and their methods and uncritical support of the Israeli government'. It was like a breath of fresh air, as the kind of Jewish voice that is usually silenced declared that dissent was alive and well.

The London bombings

In the wake of the July 2005 bombings, Livingstone was again in the spotlight. He told the BBC that he opposed all violence and had no sympathy for the bombers. He argued, however, that British and US intervention in the oil-rich Middle East contributed to hatred of the West: 'We've propped up unsavoury governments, we've overthrown ones we didn't consider sympathetic'. He also pointed to the 'running sore' of the Israel–Palestine conflict. 'A lot of young people see the double standards, they see what happens in Guantanamo Bay, and they just think that there isn't a just foreign policy', he said. He accused Israel of actions 'which border on crimes against humanity'.[33] He then told Sky News that 'the Palestinians don't have jet planes, don't have tanks, they only have their bodies to use as weapons'. For good measure, he said that he didn't distinguish between members of Likud and Hamas, branding them 'two sides of the same coin ... They need each other in order to attract support'. Sharon responded days later. 'Hamas is a murderous terrorist organisation', he said, 'which has murdered and wounded thousands of Israelis. The comparison drawn by the mayor of London was grave and inappropriate. It indicates ignorance and basic misunderstanding of reality'.[34]

Livingstone was accused of justifying suicide bombing, although he had condemned it. His point was to try to explain why some people were driven to extreme acts, and he made the entirely reasonable observation that Israel's brutal occupation had consequences. The Palestinians were 'under foreign occupation and denied the right to vote', he went on, 'denied the right to run your affairs, often denied the right to work for three generations, I suspect that if it had happened here in England, we would have produced a lot of suicide bombers ourselves'. He said that the West's double standards had 'infected' the way people viewed Britons who join the IDF and those who engage in jihad:

> If a young Jewish boy in this country goes and join the Israeli army, and ends up killing many Palestinians in operations and can come back, that is wholly legitimate. But for a young Muslim boy in this country, who might think: I want to defend my Palestinian brothers and sisters and get involved, he is branded a terrorist.[35]

The Jewish community was outraged. Jon Benjamin, director general of the Board of Deputies, described Livingstone as 'a lackey of the Muslim agenda in this country'. The fact that Livingstone had rightly compared terror in the United Kingdom and Israel—and tried to find reasons for such heinous acts—was 'outrageous'. Israel's ambassador to the United Kingdom, Zvi Heifetz, said the mayor was wrong to 'differentiate between the victims based on their nationalities'. Then Israeli Foreign Minister Silvan Shalom suggested that Livingstone had a 'mental condition' and 'to distinguish between the blood of innocent Israeli civilians and the blood of others is unacceptable'.[36] Shalom had made a perhaps inadvertent admission. Jewish blood was more important than that of others, whether they be Palestinians or Arabs. A few days later, Shalom's wife, Judy Nir-Mozes, said on a television chat show in Israel that 'it's not all bad for the English to find out what [suicide bombing is] like'.

Ronnie Fraser, chairman of the Academic Friends of Israel, said the fact that the mayor could get away with such comments said 'something about mainstream British society, where attitudes towards Israel have become anti-Semitic': 'Ken Livingstone has always had this extremist hatred of Jews and Israelis. Why should we be surprised? He has always been consistent in this'.[37] Fraser was merely the latest to conveniently conflate Israel and Jews, and to suggest they were one and the same thing.

In August, Livingstone responded to his critics in another *Guardian* column.[38] He once again denounced suicide bombing, called for British withdrawal from Iraq and urged Muslims to cooperate with authorities to find the extremists in their ranks. Furthermore he argued, in relation to Qaradawi, that 'if supporters of the Palestinians should be banned on the grounds that Palestinians kill children, then consistency would require banning Israeli leaders, who have been responsible for killing several times more Palestinian civilians'. In a sharply directed attack at his Jewish critics, he wrote that banning Qaradawi would be akin to insisting that British Muslims be treated with respect while banning 'their religion's most eminent representatives': 'Imagine how the Jewish community, many of whom do not agree with the policies of the Israeli government, would react if Israeli leaders were banned because of military actions that have killed thousands of Palestinian children'.

Livingstone's support for Qaradawi is based on his belief that he is 'one of the world's most eminent Muslim religious leaders', and though the mayor disagrees with his views on homosexuality, 'whatever his individual views, he is seen as a moderate and is fiercely opposed to al-Qaeda'. He believes that treating the British Muslim community with respect requires more than lip-service and that 'every major British Muslim organisation—even those disagreeing with him, such as Imaan, the organisation of lesbian and gay Muslims—believes Qaradawi should be admitted'.

Livingstone is a provocative figure, though he remains popular in London. Even liberal Labour MP Gerald Kaufman said that his remarks to the *Evening Standard* reporter were 'crass and insensitive' and showed a 'culpable lack of judgement'.[39] Alan Dershowitz argues that Livingstone is 'racist' and 'anti-Semitic' because he has called Ariel Sharon a 'war criminal', though the mayor's record on social issues remains impressive.[40] Livingstone's comments were ill advised for a public figure, and probably designed to shock, and he should have apologised, though it is important to note his ability to separate real antisemitism and valid criticism of Israeli government policy. This distinction is something Zionist groups would rather not be acknowledged. Being proudly pro-Palestinian, pro-Israeli, pro–human rights and pro-peace makes Livingstone an easy target for his critics.[41]

Outraged of Clapham

It is still difficult to debate the Israel–Palestine conflict honestly. After the screening of journalist John Pilger's documentary *Palestine is still the issue* on the United Kingdom's ITV in 2002, elements of the Zionist lobby, from both the United Kingdom and the USA (where the film had not been screened) bombarded him with abuse and hate mail.[42] The murder of his family was 'not a bad idea'. He was likened to Holocaust denier David Irving and labelled a 'demonic psychopath'. A person called Arie Karseboom told Pilger that he must be a Nazi Party member or have an Arab wife, as there was no other way to explain his focus on Palestinian injustice.

When 50 000 people gathered in London in the same year to show their solidarity with Israel, one speaker, Richard Harris, the Bishop of Oxford, was jeered by the crowd for suggesting that Palestinian suicide bombers lacked hope.[43] Such explanations for attacks against Israel were unwelcome in a crowd that was content simply to label any form of Palestinian resistance as terrorism. Former Israeli prime minister Binyamin Netanyahu addressed the rally, as did Peter Mandelson, a close friend of Tony Blair's and a former, now disgraced, Labour politician. Mandelson, whose father is Jewish, told the crowd that 'the Holocaust is the reason for Israel's existence and for its right to live in security'.

A *Guardian* feature has catalogued the verbal threats received by Jewish activists who oppose the Israeli government.[44] 'Self-hating Jews' sometimes were the target of vicious accusations and even violence. Aljazeera even uncovered an antisemitic hate-mail campaign against Jewish peace activists in London in early 2004.[45] 'The highly conservative Jewish Board of

Deputies now estimate opposition to the Sharon government within the UK Jewish community at about 30%', they wrote. 'Some right-wing Zionists are turning on their co-religionists with vitriol.' *Aljazeera* found British Jews who had received messages such as 'Hitler killed the wrong Jews' and 'Too bad Hitler didn't get your family'.

In the wake of the London suicide bombings in July 2005, there was much finger-pointing at Western Muslim communities and at extremism within their ranks. The *Independent*'s Yasmin Alibhai-Brown, a non-White Muslim, wrote a few weeks after the attacks that the sensitive position of British Muslims was being exploited by the United Kingdom's Zionist lobby.[46] 'Interviewers regularly push Muslim spokespeople into an admittance that Palestinian suicide bombers are an exact equivalent of the London blasts', she wrote. 'The suffering is the same but the two situations cannot be compared. Israel wants to cleanse itself of any culpability.'

Attitudes towards Muslims have changed since the bombings. 'Islamophobia' has become the new antisemitism. An opinion poll in early 2006 found that four out of 10 British Muslims want sharia law introduced into some parts of the country, and 20 per cent feel sympathy with the London bombers.[47] Such statistics only cause intolerance towards the Muslim community to increase. Conservative columnist Melanie Phillips argues that the British are blind to a new war against the Jews 'merely because they have the temerity to seek to defend themselves from being wiped out', and contends that the Israel–Palestine conflict 'is not the cause but the result of Muslim anti-Semitism'.[48] Expressing hatred of Jews has rightly become a social taboo, but damning Islam and Muslims has become acceptable and is even encouraged. Witness the London *Times* columnist Julie Burchill writing in *Hareetz* in February 2006:

> Anyway, from now on I think I'll get just a few less accusations of racism when I point out that Muslims can be a bit, well, narrow-minded. Mind you, it's a long hard struggle trying to make bleeding-heart liberals see sense. Especially when you live in a country where a sizable part of the print and broadcasting media are such guilt-ridden cretins when it comes to Islam that if they saw Osama bin Laden and Saddam Hussein sexually sharing their own grandmother, they'd swear the poor old lady asked for it.[49]

The idea that a mainstream columnist might offer similar observations about Jews is inconceivable, and yet Zionist groups prefer to focus on Livingstone rather than addressing the real sources of intolerance in twenty-first-century Britain. As far as I am aware, no mainstream Jewish group has condemned Burchill's comments, or others like them, and I suspect that it's principally because she is such a strong supporter of Israel.

Despite these worrying trends, the United Kingdom remains far more tolerant of dissenting views on the Israel–Palestine conflict than the USA or Australia. This is partly because of the diversity of its media owners and its healthy multicultural constituencies. It is difficult to imagine a controversial figure such as Ken Livingstone surviving and thriving politically in the USA or Australia. The political environment in Australia is radically different—more conformist and slavishly pro-Israel—and the next chapter examines the complex relationship between Australia's Zionist lobby, government and mainstream media elite.

8

ZIONISM IN AUSTRALIA

*If you [Australian Jewry] have worries it should not be about
goyim, but about your internal enemies—Australian Jews*

Isi Leibler, speech at Melbourne's Crown Casino, 2003[1]

*There is no Jewish lobby. If there were, what would it lobby for?
'Jewishness'? Chopped liver? The wearing of hats in the age of
air-conditioning?*

Mark Dapin 2004[2]

AUSTRALIA'S GEOGRAPHIC DISTANCE from Israel has had an intriguing
effect on the country's Jewry. Australia has the highest rate of emigration to Israel per capita in the Western world, and a great number of Jews
regularly make financial contributions to Israel. A 1991 survey of Jewish
students on university campuses found that 77 per cent envisaged themselves contributing regularly to Israel once they became salary-earners.[3]
Such close identification with the Jewish state is based on a strong desire
to maintain an ongoing connection with the homeland, which is seen as
a significant source of inspiration.

Danny Ben-Moshe, director of Social Diversity Research at Victoria
University, argues that identification with Israel continues to be a central

feature of Jewish Australian identity.[4] Australian Jews engage with the Jewish community and with politics for a variety of reasons:

> For some Jews it is based on the Jewish ethic of *tikkun olam*,[5] of making the world a better place. For others, it is based on the Jewish historical experience of anti-Semitism that makes fighting racism obligatory, and still others are motivated by practical concerns for organised Jewish life in Australia.

The community has developed greatly since the formation of Israel, and although the Australian Zionist lobby does not hold as much sway as its US counterpart, its influence over the political and media elite is considerable. As in the USA, a narrow set of boundaries is imposed, and little dissent is tolerated. While many Jews and community groups are socially progressive on issues such as refugees and Aborigines, attitudes towards Israel are usually uncompromising and conservative. A 1991 study in Melbourne found that most Jews mixed extensively with other Jews and expressed a commitment to Jewish continuity.[6] Such powerful social cohesion at least partially explains the often blind devotion to Israel and its actions. Within the Jewish community, differences over aspects of Israeli policy sometimes flare briefly into intense debate before appeals to Jewish unity snuff it out. Overall, especially since the 1967 war, the Australian community's loyalty almost always lies with the Jewish state, no matter what it does, to whom or how.

Jews and Australian society

Jews have lived in Australia since White settlement began in 1788—as many as 14 of the first convicts were of Jewish descent. They generally assimilated within society, achieving positions of influence in politics, business, the professions and the arts. General Sir John Monash, one of the most celebrated Australians, was born of German-Jewish parentage and became a national military hero, considered by many to be the most outstanding Allied general on the Western Front in World War I. 'We Australian Jews in this remote outpost of the British Empire are Britishers to the backbone and spinal marrow', shouted the *Jewish Herald* at the end of World War I.[7] The experience of the Holocaust and the birth of Israel transformed the priorities of Australian Jewry and led to the arrival of around 35 000 Jews, primarily from Europe, between 1945 and 1960. By the late 1990s, there were more than 100 000 Jews resident in Australia, and the Jewish community was prosperous and influential.

As in the USA, the strong support within the wider Australian community for the existence of Israel derives largely from the fact of the Holocaust and the idea of Israel as a Western liberal democracy. Although the lobby threatens and challenges influential Australians, both Jewish and non-Jewish, to toe the Israel-first line, it is clear that Australians' support and sympathy for the Israeli struggle against 'terrorism' can be counted on, even without Zionist pressure.

From 1947, as Minister for External Affairs in the Curtain and Chifley Labor governments, Herbert Vere ('Doc') Evatt led Australia's push at the UN to recognise the Jewish state in the ashes of the Holocaust, and the ALP's early support of Israel is something many Jews have never forgotten. During the 1950s, the government of Robert Menzies, while supporting Israel, largely served British and US strategic interests.[8] By the time of the 1967 war, however, Jews felt comfortable that the major political parties strongly supported Israel's military strength and position. This bipartisan approach has largely continued to this day.

A history of sectarianism and reactionary social attitudes, and the involvement of the Left in Labor politics have nevertheless complicated the ALP's attitudes from time to time. The conduct of Israel came into sharper public focus in the late 1960s and early 1970s, after it seized the Gaza Strip and the West Bank in the Six Day War. Australian Jewish support for Israel intensified, because the community perceived that the Jewish state's very existence was at stake. Philip Mendes, a senior lecturer in the Department of Social Work at Monash University, writes that 'the left discovered the Palestinians, and the romance with the PLO began. Israel was stereotyped as a powerful oppressor state and a tool of western imperialism involved in suppressing the national rights of the Palestinians'.[9] Although both the ALP and Liberal Party supported Israel's takeover of the West Bank and Gaza, on Australian university campuses there was growing support for Palestinian nationalism.[10]

By the time of the 1973 Yom Kippur war and Arab oil embargo, Prime Minister Gough Whitlam—in a speech at the New South Wales Zionist Council's celebrations for Israel's 25th anniversary—suggested that although Australia's position on Israel was one 'of neutrality... we are not neutral on the question of the sovereignty of Israel [and] the right of Israel to defend her borders'. In other words, Australia's position clearly endorsed Israel's right to exist within internationally recognised borders, yet still upset Jewish leaders. What of the right of Palestinians to defend their borders? There was a strong whispering campaign trickling down from the Jewish community's leadership recommending against a vote for the ALP. Years later, Whitlam claimed that elements of the Jewish community had tried to blackmail him to change his Middle East policy.[11]

In recent decades, Australia's Muslim population has grown swiftly, and Muslims now outnumber Jews by nearly 3.5 to one.[12] However, the Muslim population is disparate and its members often poor. The community will need to develop greatly before it poses a serious challenge to the influence of the Jewish community.[13]

A recent reputable opinion poll revealed that less than half the Australian population are passionately pro-Palestinian or pro-Israeli.[14] The poll asked people whether they were more sympathetic to the Israelis or to the Palestinians, and 24 per cent nominated the Israelis and 23 per cent the Palestinians; 33 per cent said neither or both, and 20 per cent were unsure. I found the level of support for the Palestinians startling considering the anti-Arab atmosphere of the political environment since September 11. Nevertheless, one Zionist lobbyist argued the poll was 'the result of relentless bias against Israel in large sections of the Australian media'.[15]

The Zionist lobby in Australia

Several state and national organisations represent the Jewish community in Australia. The two major federal governing bodies—ECAJ and Zionist Federation of Australia (ZFA)—claim to present a unified front on issues such as Israel and antisemitism. Although both represent mainstream Zionism, they have minimal influence on Australian policy towards Israel. The ECAJ has, however, played a central role in campaigning for Soviet Jewry, immigrant assistance and Jewish schooling, as well as unsuccessfully chasing Nazi war criminals. The ZFA is mainly focused on fundraising for Israel. Both organisations publicly endorse a two-state solution but essentially accept whatever position is advanced by the Israeli government of the day. According to Suzanne Rutland, an associate professor and chair of the Department of Hebrew, Biblical and Jewish Studies at the University of Sydney, the historical record shows that the ECAJ and ZFA have close associations with both the major political parties, and both organisations claim to have no political bias.[16] Both groups offer strong support for the Howard government, not least because of its strong support for Israel.

A number of other Zionist advocacy groups exist. The NSW JBD and the Jewish Community Council of Victoria both exercise influence over the Jewish community in their respective states. They are the largest component bodies of the ECAJ. Both groups lobby government and the mainstream media—especially Fairfax, the ABC and SBS—though their overall effect is debatable. On the progressive side, the Australian Jewish Democratic Society (AJDS) encourages a more inclusive and questioning debate on the Israel–Palestine conflict and was formed in 1984 out of frustration that only 'official leadership' viewpoints were being heard.[17] The AJDS remains marginal in mainstream Jewish debate, and although its views often appear in the *AJN* letters pages, its position is generally considered to be out of step with consensus Zionism and too supportive of Palestinian self-determination.

By far the most powerful organisation within the Jewish community is AIJAC. Bernard Freedman, Canberra correspondent for the *AJN*, argues that the ECAJ, ZFA and other 'leading' Jewish organisations are 'barely recognised and mostly ignored' in Canberra, while AIJAC is most visible 'when Jewish issues attract the interest of the non-Jewish media'.[18] Simply put, AIJAC is the only well-funded Jewish group in the country, and the best organised.

Based in Melbourne[19] and funded by private donations,[20] AIJAC describes itself on its website as 'the premier public affairs organisation for the Australian Jewish community'. It takes a high-profile, assertive stand on many issues, yet is not accountable to the community through elections. This sometimes causes tensions within the Jewish community, as was the case during the Hanan Ashrawi affair, when its aggressive lobbying was criticised by other Jewish groups.[21] AIJAC's office-bearers are appointed by its board, led by taxation lawyer Mark Leibler. The *AIJAC Review* National Editorial Board includes Mark Dreyfus QC—friend of Labor MP Michael Danby and the Labor-endorsed candidate for the Victorian seat of Issacs—and Supreme Court Justice Howard Nathan. AIJAC's current executive director, Dr Colin Rubenstein, is a former lecturer in politics and Middle Eastern Affairs at Monash University. He stood unsuccessfully for Liberal Party preselection in 1990.

Launched in 1974 as Australia/Israel Publications, in 1977 the AIJAC's think tank introduced a fortnightly publication, *Australia/Israel Review* (*AIR*, later known simply as AIJAC's *Review*), edited by journalist and community leader Sam Lipski. It was initially distributed free to trade unionists, parliamentarians, journalists, academics and church leaders, and by the late 1980s had a subscriber base of around 3600. Michael Danby, who is now a federal Labor MP and still close to the lobby, succeeded Lipski as the magazine's editor, focusing on Australia's far-right movement. By the early years of the new century, *AIR*'s focus had shifted to Australian politics and the hardening of public attitudes towards the Middle East conflict.

AIJAC is well connected to both the Liberal and Labor parties. A number of Jewish businessmen also play an influential role as advocates for Israel and Zionism, even though they are not directly involved in groups such as AIJAC. The Liberals have been most successful in attracting Jewish financial support. According to returns lodged with the Australian Electoral Commission (AEC) in early 2004, Mark Leibler's firm, Arnold Bloch Leibler, gave the Victorian branch of the Liberal Party A$7500, while Jewish business figures including Frank Lowy, Harry Triguboff and Richard Pratt donated hundreds of thousands of dollars to Liberal Party coffers.[22] The ALP also received significant funds from leading Jewish businesspeople, including Lowy.

Frank Lowy, Australia's second richest man, is a close friend of John Howard. Former Liberal Party fundraiser and Fairfax chairman Ron Walker told the *Australian Financial Review* in 2004 that Howard was 'exceptionally close' to Lowy. 'He would, maybe, talk to him every week, if not, every fortnight', Walker said. 'Often he [Lowy] will ring him from overseas and tell him what world trends are. The Prime Minister trusts him and listens to his advice on international issues particularly issues relating to the state of Israel.'[23]

Businessman Rabbi Joseph Gutnick, a strong supporter of right-wing Israeli governments and the settler movement in Israel travels regularly between Australia and Israel. He has reportedly donated at least A$30 million to Jewish causes and has supported Likud's Binyamin Netanyahu.[24] Gutnick expressed his support for the ALP during the 2004 federal election campaign, saying he was disappointed with the Howard government's 'mishandling' of Pauline Hanson and immigration. 'I went away [from meeting Mark Latham] confident that he is a supporter of Israel', he said.[25] Few other Likudnik figures are so strongly aligned with the ALP.

And long before Lowy or Gutnick came on the scene, there was Isi Leibler. The elder brother of Mark, Isi Leibler is a multi-millionaire who made his fortune in the 1970s by creating Jetset Tours.[26] Leibler now resides in Israel, and says that John Howard's support of the Jewish people and the war in Iraq has made him popular there: 'I think this little guy is going to come out of all this as a real man of history. I think he's been absolutely outstanding'.[27]

AIJAC and the Howard years

AIJAC claims to be politically non-aligned. The *AJN* featured a letter in December 2003 in which Mark Leibler wrote that 'we are non-partisan. This is not simply a claim; it's a fact'.[28] During the ALP's long stint in office from 1983 to 1996, the party's closeness to the Zionist lobby was well known, as was Bob Hawke's strong personal support of Israel. But the Howard years have been marked by a special affinity between the Liberal government and the Zionist lobby group in the wake of the World Trade Center attacks of September 11, which gave rise to a belief that Israel's struggle against terrorism was now also the West's. 'In this post 9/11, post-Bali climate', wrote the *AJN* on Howard's tenth anniversary in March 2006, 'Jews feel safer under Howard'.[29]

When George W Bush visited Australia in late 2003, Mark Leibler was one of a select group of guests invited to John Howard's barbeque for the US President. Earlier that year, Howard was guest speaker at a function to celebrate Arnold Bloch Leibler's fiftieth anniversary. Also present were Minister of Foreign Affairs Alexander Downer, Attorney General Daryl Williams, Minister of Communications Helen Coonan, Opposition Leader Simon Crean and Victorian Liberal Opposition Leader Robert Doyle. Israel's ambassador, Gaby Levy, was also in the crowd. Introducing the Prime Minister, Leibler praised Howard as a wartime leader:

> John Howard is Prime Minister because he has all the qualities that great leaders require ... I believe the Prime Minister's decision to join the 'coalition of the willing', and to commit this country to war [in Iraq] against a totalitarian threat to peace, demonstrated strength, courage and vision ... I personally believe his [decision] was the right one, for Australia and for the ultimate cause of a more peaceful world. The Prime Minister's decision, will, I believe, be vindicated by history.[30]

AIJAC were strong supporters of the Iraq invasion and publicly campaigned for Australian involvement.[31] A few months after the start of the Iraq war, Jewish leader Sam Lipski even said Howard's decision to help topple Saddam 'earned a pride of place in Zionist military history' because, in his view, Israel had been made safer thanks to Australian grunt.[32]

Howard's description of the Israel–Palestine conflict could have come from the mouth of Leibler himself. 'A couple of weeks ago', Howard told the crowd at the Arnold Bloch Leibler anniversary celebration,

> I met the former Prime Minister of Israel, Ehud Barak, when he visited Australia. I could only reflect with sadness on the fact that some three years ago things seemed bright, and the star

of a peace settlement seemed to blaze quite brightly in the sky at that particular time. I remember my personal experience of going to Ramallah [to see Arafat] at the behest of the Israeli Government, and accompanied by several people who are in this room tonight. It looked as though the courage of that man, Barak, had brought us close to some kind of settlement. Sadly his courage was not reciprocated and the rest is well known— the suicide bombings, the mistrust and so forth. But we must try again.

Like a dutiful actor following a script, Howard uttered the lines that the pro-Zionist lobby wanted to hear (and that he undoubtedly believed):

Can I take this opportunity, in the wake of the recent events that have occurred in Iraq, to say as a great and staunch friend of Israel, that I believe the world has an historic opportunity to try and convert some of the events that have occurred in the Middle East to the achievement of some kind of lasting peace.[33]

After Howard was returned to office at the 2004 election, Colin Rubenstein wrote in the *Jerusalem Post* that the victory ensured that 'one of Israel's best friends will remain a force on the international scene for another three years'. Rubenstein's column outlined why the Howard years had been so kind to the Zionist agenda. He applauded the Iraq war—and Howard's decision to keep troops there, which contrasted with ALP leader Mark Latham's pledge to bring them home—Australia's support at the UN for Israel, and its 'determined stance against terrorist groups such as Hizbollah and Hamas, both banned in Australia in the last year'. He damned the 'kangaroo' court—the International Court of Justice—that found Israel's 'security fence' in breach of international law and praised Australia's vote in the UN against forcing Israel to comply with the court's findings. Rubenstein praised the 'liberation' of Afghanistan and Howard's dismissal of Arafat as 'no partner for peace', concluding that 'Howard's [electoral] victory can be seen as an important win for the global war on terrorism'.[34]

The Jewish community has been keen to show Howard its appreciation. Howard collected the 2004 American Liberties Medallion from the American Jewish Committee (an organisation with which AIJAC is formally associated) for his record of 'championing democracy and human rights, and his unequalled friendship towards the United States and Israel'. Previous winners have included Martin Luther King, former Czech leader Vaclav Havel, US presidents Lyndon Johnson and Ronald Reagan, and former US secretary of state Henry Kissinger. At the award ceremony, Colin Rubenstein said the Prime Minister had 'supported the true cause of Middle East peace, without succumbing to the sirens' song of wishy-washy moral equivalence. He never shirked his responsibility to condemn terrorism, and has never evaded his obligation to promote the cause of Arab–Israeli co-existence'. American Jewish Committee chairman Bob Goodkind labelled Howard 'the Don Bradman of Australian politics'. In June 2005, Howard also received the Sydney Jewish Communal Appeal's inaugural award for friendship and commitment to the New South Wales Jewish community. In late 2005 international Jewish group B'nai B'rith announced that Howard had won the Presidential Gold Medal in recognition of 'his Government's consistent support of Israel at the United Nations and throughout the world, combating anti-Semitism'.

Looking back over Howard's public statements, it is possible to trace a gradual change in John Howard's attitude, as the issues of terror and the deteriorating security of the West have brought him closer to the AIJAC view. During British Prime Minister Tony Blair's visit to Australia in March 2006, Howard strongly endorsed a 'man of courage', who in 'the aftermath of the 11th of September 2001 better articulated the reality that that was an attack not just on the people of the United States, but also upon the values and the people of a common family of nations of which we are a part around the world'.[35] Howard includes himself in this post–September 11 understanding, and believes, like AIJAC and Israel, that Western nations have a responsibility to fight Islamic 'terrorism'. Offering Israel almost unlimited support seems to be part of this agenda.

On the Howard government's tenth anniversary in March 2006, the Prime Minister reminded those gathered at Canberra's Parliament House to celebrate the occasion that 'when I sat down to talk to George Bush for the very first time on the 10th September 2001 [in Washington] I had no idea, he had no idea that the world was to change forever the following day'.[36] Howard has deliberately chosen to align his legacy with that of the Bush administration and its military misadventures in Iraq and Afghanistan, and has acknowledged that Australia's involvement in Iraq was partly driven by duty to the US alliance.[37] 'There seems to be a sort of affinity between Australia and Israel', writes Colin Rubenstein, 'almost an overlapping destiny'.[38] Howard's 'emotional commitment' to the Jewish state, Rubenstein argues, has followed in a tradition of active Australian involvement in the Middle East since World War I.

During an interview in 1998 with the *AIR*, Howard explained that he had made many Jewish friends while at university and this had deeply affected his attitude towards Israel and the Jewish community.[39] 'I always had a very strongly supportive attitude towards Israel', he said, 'and I felt that on occasions, the attitude taken by the former [Labor] government did not totally reflect the reality that for most of Israel's existence, neighbours have wanted to destroy her'. However, he called for Palestinian self-determination—'I understand the Palestinian aspirations and I think they've got a right to self-determination like everybody else'—and expressed concerns at 'some aspects' of Israeli settlement policies. He was also asked about Aboriginal reconciliation, immigration and Pauline Hanson, issues that had caused 'anxiety' in the Jewish community as a result of his government's decisions.

During a speech in January 2002 to the American Jewish Committee in New York, Howard explained his post–September 11 thinking: the Palestinian people 'do have legitimate aspirations', but the attacks on September 11 made Australia realise the world had changed and 'I want to say how strong Australia supports actions being taken by the United States government ... in the name of the world to fight terrorism'.[40]

At the UN, Australia has increasingly taken Israel's side. AIJAC and the wider Jewish community praised Howard when he condemned the outcome of the UN World Conference against Racism in Durban in September 2001. Arab countries tried to isolate Israel over the occupation, and to single it out for particular attention in attempts to delegitimise the Jewish state. The USA and Israel eventually walked out of proceedings and complained of anti-Israel bias. AIJAC said that the event 'turned into a display of the very evils they were supposed to combat' and that 'Australia took a vitally important role in moderating the proceedings' by dismissing international calls to accuse Israel of racism.[41]

In December 2005, Foreign Minister Alexander Downer explained to an audience of the United Israel Appeal that when the Coalition parties first came to power in 1996, the protocol for the Australian government was to vote at the UN in 'good company', with the USA and the Europeans. Jews have long complained about the UN's anti-Israel and antisemitic bias. 'Now, where we see an unbalanced resolution condemning Israel we vote against it—irrespective of who stands besides us', Downer said. Australia is an 'independent and morally-upright nation' and the Howard government 'an unqualified supporter of Israel'.[42]

The Israel-first doctrine was on display in July 2004 when Australia became just one of six countries that voted against a UN resolution ordering Israel to destroy the 'security' wall through the West Bank. The vote received little media coverage, though the precedent was significant. One hundred and fifty members of the UN assembly supported the resolution, while only six voted against it—the USA, Israel, Marshall Islands, Micronesia, Palau and Australia. The decision was made in the shadow of a World Court ruling that called on Israel to tear down parts of its barrier. Australian Federation of Islamic Councils (AFIC) president Ameer Ali said the vote sent a message to the Muslim community that the government cared little about the Palestinians.[43]

Downer defended the decision. 'It isn't reasonable to Israelis that they can't erect a security barrier to protect the people of Israel from suicide-homicide bombers', he said. He told the October 2004 annual assembly of the State Zionist Council of Victoria that diplomats in New York had advised him that Australia should align itself with the EU and Canada and abstain. 'In a nanosecond, I said we will not change our vote', he said. 'We will vote against this, we will vote even if we're the only country in the world that votes with Israel on this resolution, we'll still do it because this resolution is wrong.'

The ALP's foreign affairs spokesman, Kevin Rudd, thought that Australia 'should have abstained'. *SMH* columnist Alan Ramsey, however, thought that abstaining was 'even more pusillanimous than voting "no"'.[44] 'It is strange how the other 150 nations have got it wrong again', one letter writer mused in the *SMH*.

When I was in Israel, I asked people who knew Australia how John Howard was perceived. The vast majority who had heard of him simply knew that Australia had participated in the Iraq war but not about our support of Israel. *AJN* journalist Chemi Shalev told me, 'If you take away the American component then probably John Howard is Israel's best friend in the world'. Like Isi Leibler, he was sure this was the general perception in Israel: 'If you tried to find three countries that are most similar in their view of the world—good versus evil and priorities—you would find Israel, Australia and the United States'. Shalev said that in a 'post–September 11, post-intifada world, Jews are much more black and white than they used to be [about security issues], and much less tolerant of grey areas'.[45]

The ugly language of Zionism

Isi Leibler's views represent the acceptable face of the Zionist lobby. As a former president of the ECAJ, Leibler moved to Jerusalem in 1999 and was senior vice-president of the World Jewish Congress until 2005.[46] His commentary on the Israel–Palestine conflict, and the Diaspora's role in supporting Israel, has calcified down the years. Today it is an example of the worst bigotry found in the Zionist lobby. Leibler wrote in the *Jerusalem Post* in October 2002 that Palestinian society

> is no less suffused with evil than were the people of Germany under Hitler ... The Jews have faced no such evil since the Nazis. That should not be construed as a racist statement or a primitive demonisation of an entire people. It is calling a spade a spade. US President George W. Bush refers to evil states. Our Palestinian neighbours who seek the destruction of the Jewish people represent the essence of evil and barbarism. And now is the time for us to say so to the world at large, loud and clear. We are not suggesting that the Palestinian people are intrinsically or genetically more evil than the Germans were under Hitler. We are saying that, like the Nazis, the Palestinian leaders have succeeded in indoctrinating their people and transforming them into a society which is inspired by evil.[47]

It's a far cry from 1960, when a more idealistic Leibler argued that the Australian Jewish community's priority was fighting antisemitism but that public relations activities should be 'on the positive rather than defensive line'. Furthermore, 'the Jewish community must be at the forefront and willing to co-operate with all elements from left and right who are dedicated to the concept of an open society without which pluralism and full Jewish life is impossible'.[48] But by the 1970s Leibler's optimism had dwindled as he complained that the memory of the Holocaust had receded to the point where 'the protective shadow of Auschwitz, which for nearly 20 years acted against manifestations of open anti-Semitism from "respectable" quarters is no longer applicable. Jews are now openly defamed without engendering a sense of guilt or conjuring an association with Nazi genocide ... It is as if Nazism never happened'.

Leibler visited Melbourne in December 2003, at the time of the Hanan Ashrawi controversy, and decried dissenting Australian Jews as a danger within:

> If you [Australian Jewry] have worries it should not be about goyim [non-Jews], but about your internal enemies—Australian Jews who publicly criticise those who exposed that bad woman, Hanan Ashrawi ... The days that Jews feel they cannot express

their views and lobby against enemies of Israel, that is the day when the Jewish community begins to unravel.[49]

An incident in 2003 further highlighted the pressure exerted by powerful members of the Zionist lobby. Leibler was reported to be concerned with John Howard's comments on Israel's threats to destroy Hamas. The Prime Minister had said that 'the hyper-escalation by the Israelis is very unhelpful and I don't think it's in the interest of Israel'. Leibler wasn't having any of it and suggested Howard needed a little counselling on the matter. 'I believe his statement was based on insufficient information', he said. Leibler said he was to see the Prime Minister and express his views: 'I have been extraordinarily proud of John Howard's approach to the Middle East. I remember three years ago when Howard met Arafat in Gaza, how Arafat made all sorts of promises. Howard assured me then he would stand by Israel, and he has'.[50]

This kind of absolutist position has overwhelmed all others within the Liberal and Labor parties. The response to a federal or state government that does not toe the staunchly Zionist line on Israel is a stern telling off, political pressure and the threat that the 'Jewish vote' will look elsewhere. While academics Geoffrey Brahm Levey and Philip Mendes argue that the influence of the 'Jewish vote' on the body politic is greatly exaggerated by the mainstream media,[51] it suits the Zionist lobby's agenda to hype its influence and to pressure the major parties into submission.

AIJAC's post–September 11 agenda

AIJAC's agenda has shifted since September 11. The organisation saw in the Bush administration an opportunity to further its Israel-first agenda in Australia, and found a willingness among Australian politicians to follow its lead. Murdoch's *Australian* newspaper, in particular, has published any number of AIJAC 'analysts' and visiting international scholars, mostly with a message of military might over diplomacy and of the dangers of 'appeasing terrorists'.

AIJAC strongly supported Sharon's 'courageous decision' to disengage from Gaza in 2005 because it proved 'Israel's ongoing commitment to peace, despite four and a half years of terrorism'.[52] Claiming that the move 'has the potential to substantially bolster the peace process, providing that the Palestinians demonstrate a reciprocal willingness to take constructive action', AIJAC's attitude towards the conflict was clear: each and every move made by Israel displayed a sincere commitment to peace, while the Palestinians were incapable of 'marginalising their extremists'.[53] Sharon's incapacitation in early 2006 led Rubenstein to argue that Israel's newfound unilateral approach would 'give Palestinians a state whether they want it or not'.[54] How such an arrangement could bring peace—and those who slammed this plan were 'rejectionists', according to Rubenstein[55]—was not explained. 'Spurning opportunities for peace is a long established Palestinian pastime', wrote AIJAC's Ted Lapkin in the wake of the Hamas victory in January 2006.[56] AIJAC simply doesn't like, or trust, Arabs or Palestinians.

Lapkin is a relatively recent recruit to the AIJAC team, but since his appointment as director of policy analysis, it's been hard to miss his opinion pieces in the Murdoch and Fairfax press, usually defending the virtue of the US, British and Australian governments in the 'war on terror'. He was born in the USA but grew up in Israel, and served as an Israeli officer in the IDF, fighting in the Lebanon war. He has also served as a communications director for a Republican member of the US congress. Before the 2004 US election, Lapkin told the Melbourne *Age* that Bush had 'the same kind of moral clarity' as Ronald Reagan.[57] PNAC's Statement of Principles concedes that 'such a Reaganite policy of military strength and moral clarity'—namely the aggressive projection of US power—'may not be fashionable today'. Reading Lapkin's articles is like being trapped in a small room with a belligerent propagandist: he is an unashamed militarist who defends and supports the use of force by the Allies in World War II, Israel in Lebanon, and the 'Coalition' against al-Qaeda. He finds it politically convenient to conflate all these struggles and to praise the valour of the solider in fighting for 'freedom'.

Lapkin wants Israel to gain a complete military and psychological victory over the Palestinians. He told a 2004 Canberra forum on the conflict that the majority of Palestinian casualties since the outbreak of the second intifada were not civilians but combatants or 'terrorists'.[58] This is factually incorrect.[59] He has written numerous articles defending the US-led military commissions to try 'enemy combatants' such as Australian Guantanamo Bay detainee David Hicks. 'US forces would be within their legal rights to treat captured terrorists as they dealt with Nazi saboteurs during World War II', he wrote in the *SMH* in August 2005: 'With trial by military commission and execution'. According to Lapkin, Hicks was lucky 'to be facing American military justice in 2005, rather than 1945'.[60] In February 2005, he argued in the *SMH* that the reason the USA had freed and not prosecuted Australian Guantanamo Bay detainee Mamdoud Habib was not because of his innocence: 'it is far more likely that the information implicating Habib comes from classified sources that the US is loath to compromise'.[61] The evidence for this? 'I have no access to any classified intelligence material relating to Habib', he later sheepishly admitted. One letter to the editor displayed appropriate incredulity: 'Are these the same sources that told us Saddam Hussein could launch weapons within 45 minutes or that he was buying uranium in Africa, or providing information on the whereabouts of Osama Bin Laden?'[62]

Lapkin's brief as director of policy analysis is broad and serves a greater, often implied, agenda: in his view, Israel's long battle against 'terrorism' is identical to that of Western governments, and similar tactics are therefore justified. He has suggested the use of torture in the case of the 'classic "ticking bomb" scenario' and mocked allegations of prisoner mistreatment at Guantanamo Bay. He wrongly alleged that the men detained at Guantanamo 'were captured on the battlefield while fighting for organisations that systemically violated the most basic tenets of the law of war'. In fact, some were abducted in neutral and allied countries, and many have been tortured.

His articles on the Israel–Palestine conflict are often extreme. When two Israeli agents were discovered in New Zealand trying to obtain false passports—they were later charged and sentenced to gaol—relations between Israel and New Zealand deteriorated. Israel apologised in June 2005, and diplomatic relations between the countries were restored. Lapkin portrayed the incident as relatively insignificant and charged New Zealand Prime Minister Helen Clark with being soft on terrorism because a number of bogus New Zealand passports were being sold on the Bangkok black market. Since Hamas praised Clark's stance against Israel, Lapkin said that Clark had 'made common cause with bedfellows who are not only strange, but downright repugnant'.[63]

Lapkin kept on. Appearing on ABC Radio National's *Perspective* in April 2005, he argued that anti-Zionism was in fact antisemitism, 'the newest face of the oldest hatred'.[64] Paul Haywood-Smith QC, chair of the Australian Friends of Palestine Association, responded in early May and questioned Lapkin's justification of Israel's racist immigration policies. He challenged the claim that Israel was a democratic state—'for its Jewish inhabitants' only—and accused Lapkin and supporters of Israel of 'using defamation themselves to counter legitimate criticism of their racist and expansionist state', declaring that 'I, at least, am not prepared to be intimidated'.[65]

Tensions over Sharon's plan

Although AIJAC is the most influential Zionist lobby group, occasional tensions surface between the leading Jewish groups. AIJAC chastised the NSW JBD in August 2005 for its 'cavalier' attitude towards a 'pro-terrorist

Islamic radical movement with a history of promoting anti-Jewish violence'. NSW JBD president David Knoll had told ABC Radio that he didn't think it appropriate for the government to ban Hizb-ut-Tahrir, an Islamist political group dedicated to establishing a pan-Islamic state. AIJAC argued that Knoll wasn't being tough enough in response to threats to the Jewish community. AIJAC's Mark Leibler ramped up the rhetoric:

> We are in the midst of a war. These are tough times in which tough measures are required to defend liberty against those whose ideal world looks a lot like Afghanistan under the Taliban. After the London bombings, we must take jihadist incitement seriously. Democracy is not a suicide pact.

Hizb-ut-Tahrir, while possibly antisemitic and strongly opposed to Western Middle East policy, appears to be a non-violent organisation.

AIJAC maintains close relationships with most of Australia's Zionist organisations and assists other Jewish groups to gain access to the media. While AIJAC is the best funded and connected, Rubenstein has said he doesn't want to compete with other Jewish organisations.[66]

Nevertheless, Ariel Sharon's plan to withdraw from Gaza genuinely divided Jewish groups, with some seeing it as a retreat from long-established Zionist goals. The debate in Australia paralleled that in the USA, where after months of internal disagreement, the US Jewish leadership declared its support for the 'disengagement' a few weeks before the August 2005 pullout.

A month before 'disengagement', State Zionist Council of Victoria president Dr Danny Lamm announced at a public forum that he was against the plan, and State Zionist Council of NSW president Brian Levitan concurred, calling it 'illegal' and even sending out hundreds of emails urging people to sign a petition. This presented a problem for the Zionist leadership. ZFA president Dr Ron Weiser explained that it was 'entirely inappropriate for any leader to espouse personal views other than to express support for the "democratic process" in Israel'. In other words, toe the line and blindly support Israel, no matter what. An anti-disengagement rally was held a few weeks later and elicited a pointed condemnation from Weiser: 'The rally will only confuse support for Israel at a time when Israel needs all the support it can get'. AIJAC's Mark Leibler supported the right of protestors to make their point but argued that communal leaders should not express views that 'are at odds with the views of the constituency'. Leibler seemed to favour community unity over honest debate.

The issue touched a raw nerve. Rabbi Samuel Tov-Lev wrote to the *AJN*, saying that since Sharon's move was 'anti-Jewish, anti-Zionist and anti everything precious to us', it was the duty of new Zionist and communal leaders to 'protect the Zionist ideas and ideals'.[67] The paper's editorial discussed 'the perennial dilemma of the right of the Diaspora Jews and their leaders to criticise Israeli government policy'. Criticism from the Right was 'far less likely to be utilised or exploited by critics and enemies', but criticism from the Left was 'far more prone to supply ammunition for Israel's detractors'. The *AJN* drew attention to the double standard: 'Many of the same people who are now criticizing Sharon and his pull-out—and defending their right to do so—are the same people who will harshly scold and castigate those who come to their criticism from the opposite end of the political spectrum'. The paper concluded that the criticism of Sharon was likely to set a dangerous precedent.[68]

The vast majority of the Jewish community, including AIJAC and other leading Zionist lobbies, supported the disengagement. A handful of dissenters complained that Sharon's move would destroy the Jewish state, but these voices were few. It was vital to support the Israeli government of the day, and even if some Jews felt uneasy with evacuating Jews from occupied territory, Dr Weiser's position—that of supporting the 'democratic process in Israel'—was clear and widely accepted. The controversy proved that the Zionist hierarchy wasn't representative of the entire Jewish community—both the Left and extreme Zionists are usually ignored—but the loudest voices and mainstream opinion were fairly accurately represented. When Sharon decided to leave Likud and create his 'centrist' Kadima Party in late 2005, the Zionist lobby, hopeful that the move would bring necessary political reforms, almost uniformly accepted Sharon's rationale and virtually endorsed his candidacy.[69]

The ALP under the spotlight

The Labor side of politics is filled with individuals who profess to support the cause of Israel. Former prime minister Bob Hawke was the best friend the Australian Zionist lobby had ever had, until the arrival of John Howard. Hawke still denies the existence of the Zionist lobby, but appears to have mellowed with age, becoming—not unlike public opinion—more sympathetic towards the Palestinians.[70]

The reasons for Hawke's unashamed love of the Jewish state can be traced back to his trade union roots. Biographer Blanche d'Alpuget argues that it was 'impossible to think of another Australian in public life whose upbringing had made him so open to the appeal and difficulties of the state of Israel'. Because his 'whole career had been shaped by a sense of indignation', d'Alpuget wrote, Hawke identified with Israel's determined settler spirit and its labour movement (Histadrut). 'The institutions and problems of the state of Israel were to seize upon the core of Hawke's being', she writes. 'His aspiration for achievement, his capacity for anger, his identification with the "little man", his instinct to rescue.'[71] Hawke himself didn't hold back after his first visit to Israel in 1971: 'The first impression is one that has remained: here was this fantastic blend of informality; an irreverence, a cocking a snook at authority—combined with a very profound awareness of the ever present threat'.[72] Hawke became deeply involved in efforts to rescue Soviet Jews from persecution behind the Iron Curtain, helping them escape to Israel. By the end of the 1970s, Hawke had become close friends with Isi Leibler, a passionate supporter of Soviet Jews and a financial backer of the ACTU. The two men formed a bond, and travelled together to the Soviet Union to meet the refuseniks.

Yet Hawke has become 'more and more frustrated with a lot of the attitude of Israeli governments' from the late 1990s, especially their insistence on settlement expansion. 'They were not helping the cause of Israel or the Palestinians', he tells me. He believes that many in the Jewish community share his concern about Israeli settlement development and say so robustly in public (although he didn't provide any examples of a leading Jewish Australian figure openly chastising the Israeli government).[73] He took a swipe at individuals 'who are concerned with Israel [and] seem to put it into everything; nothing can happen unless Israel is part of it'. Referring to Jewish people and Israelis, he said, 'they tend to relate it to every issue ... which I can understand from their point of view, but it's not the way the world works'.[74] His back-handed criticism of unnamed members of the Zionist lobby would have been unthinkable during his years in power.

Hawke's criticisms show the need for independent political thought in the ALP. Nevertheless the experience of the ALP suggests that in recent years Zionist lobbying has been highly effective and dissent pretty much unacceptable. When a number of backbenchers spoke out in favour of a Palestinian state and against the harshness of the occupation in 2002, pro-Zionist lobbyists put great pressure on then federal Labor leader Simon Crean to renew his party's commitment to Israel and to denounce the irrationality of the 'renegade' members of his party. During the year-long controversy, the ALP was accused of being pro-Palestinian—political death in the current environment—and the Zionist lobby challenged

Crean's leadership in an attempt to quash any opposition to the accepted Zionist narrative.

ALP backbencher Julia Irwin, MP for Fowler in Sydney's western suburbs, proposed a private member's bill in late 2002 that condemned Israel's occupation of Gaza and the West Bank, and supported Israel's right to exist within 'secure borders' and the establishment of 'the state of Palestine based on the pre-1967 borders'. Labor MP for Melbourne Ports, Michael Danby,[75] tried to stop the motion from even being discussed. Irwin called Danby a 'bully', a man determined to refuse parliamentarians even the opportunity to discuss the Israel–Palestine conflict.[76] The debate went ahead: Irwin discussed the need for UN intervention in the crisis; Danby slammed Irwin, and the content of the speeches received almost no media coverage.

By August 2003, after nearly six months of incessant pressure on Crean to rein in his backbench, the Labor leader barred Irwin, Danby and Labor MP Leo McLeay from speaking during a parliamentary debate on the Middle East. Only shadow foreign affairs minister Kevin Rudd, former leader Kim Beazley and Crean himself were allowed to speak. Crean had received a complaint about the debate from the then president of the ECAJ, Jeremy Jones, and clearly decided, in an attempt to appease the Zionist lobby, to silence any dissenters. The *SMH* reported that the issue was causing a lot of political heat for the Labor leader and that Crean's decision was motivated by a fear of losing Jewish votes and donations.[77] Crean realised that it simply wasn't worth wasting political capital to defend the rights of some backbenchers. He knew that the Zionist lobby wouldn't stop undermining his leadership until he bowed to their pressure.

Irwin claimed the 'Jewish lobby' had 'hijacked' the party. Former New South Wales ALP MP Leo McLeay hit out at those trying to silence Irwin. 'It amazes me how intolerant . . . the pro-Israel lobby can be', he said. 'If you are not an enthusiastic supporter of the Sharon version of the Berlin wall, you are considered to be anti-Jewish. When will the Jeremy Joneses of this world understand that criticism of the Israeli government and its actions is not ant-Semitism?' Irwin protested that the 'Jewish lobby' was responsible for a 'code of silence' forbidding any parliamentary debate about the conflict.[78] She quoted an email from an unnamed 'senior media commentator' that warned her about taking 'on the most implacable, arrogant, cruel and powerful lobby in the country'. The email predicted that she would be 'singled out for vilification and, if possible, political destruction'. She refused to name her source because the commentator had 'felt the full force of the Jewish lobby's fury a long time ago and had gone through hell'. Crean chastised Irwin in private, arguing that 'the reference to the Jewish lobby is offensive because that's the typecasting of everyone'. Irwin had been blunt but honest, and Crean was desperately trying to douse the flames.

Liberal MP Christopher Pyne, chairman of the Australia–Israel Parliamentary Friendship Group,[79] told ABC Radio's *World today* that the motion was 'pandering to the pro-Palestinian position' and argued that Crean should have stopped its debate.[80] Then Jeremy Jones said Irwin had 'conjured up the bogeyman of a powerful Jewish lobby [that] might appeal to anti-Semites, but certainly not to any reasonable observer'. He went on to dismiss Irwin's private member's bill by ridiculing her, saying that her 'ignorance' on the conflict was on display and 'then she complains about people who might point out her ignorance'.[81]

Crean tells me it frustrates him that if one person in the Labor Party takes a particular position, condemning Sharon and the occupation, some argue that it is the official ALP position. He spoke to a 'lot of the Jewish leadership' because 'I'm close to them and have known them for decades'. He discussed the matter with Mark Leibler, Colin Rubenstein and Stephen Rothman, former president of the NSW JBD, and asked them to identify the source of the allegation that the ALP was anti-Israel and antisemitic. Crean now says that 'Rubenstein never questioned my commitment in terms of recognition of the state of Israel', yet this begs the question why a figure such as Rubenstein would need to approve the political leader's statements.[82]

Crean hoped the criticisms would end after his speech in late August 2003 to the State Zionist Council of Victoria, where he reassured the Jewish community of his party's 'unequivocal and unshakeable' support for Israel. Michael Lipshutz, then president of the Jewish Community Council of Victoria, said that he was happy with Crean's comment but remained concerned about the ALP backbench. 'If they want to condemn Israel, well, that's probably their right to do that in a fair and reasoned way', he said, but refused to explain what criticisms would be acceptable. 'Israel is a country at war', he claimed, as if such a statement absolved a country of any international legal responsibility.[83] Lipshutz later told the *Australian* that 'there is no Jewish lobby in the same way that there is no Italian or Greek lobby'.

The *SMH*'s Alan Ramsey suggested in late August that Crean's speech was at least partly prompted by a number of Jewish donors to the ALP who had expressed concern about the party's Middle East policy.

'So there you have it—money', Ramsey wrote. 'Almost always, in politics, money is at the root of the greatest grovelling.' Ramsey asked what had happened to the ALP's 'even-handed policy', forgetting that the party had never had one. 'The pro-Israel lobby in this country is a powerful, influential and intimidating group', Ramsey wrote. 'Backbenchers such as Julia Irwin and Leo McLeay get left way behind, along with the interests of the Palestinians.'[84]

Irwin contributed an opinion piece to the *Australian* in July 2003 that challenged Zionist advocates to stop threatening to withdraw financial support for the ALP. 'Not because Labor needs the money', she wrote, 'but because it suggests that all party members must toe the line even if their comments broadly agree with Labor policy'. She argued that her original private member's bill was remarkably uncontroversial and had merely called for a safe and secure Israel and an independent Palestinian state. She asked for the input of the Australian Jewish community in formulating ALP Middle East policy. After all,

as in all communities, there is more than one voice and there are many differing points of view among Australian Jews as there are among Israelis. The Israeli Labor party tolerates more diverse views than some in the Australian Jewish community suggest that the ALP should tolerate ... Labor cannot be bought.[85]

Irwin caused further controversy in 2005 by accusing Israel in parliament of building a 'walled ghetto' in disengaged Gaza and a 'concentration camp' for the Palestinians. She suggested Israel's treatment of the Palestinians in East Jerusalem was akin to 'ethnic cleansing'. Labor leader Kim Beazley called the comments 'hurtful and offensive'. Both the Jewish community and the Howard government reacted angrily to her comments, and the Zionist lobby continued to put pressure on the Labor hierarchy to silence such views. Irwin was forced to apologise, and Beazley said she now understood the difference between 'an argument of political difference in parliament and offending people with hurtful words'.[86] Grahame Leonard, president of ECAJ, rejected her apology and said that, 'until she makes a full and unqualified apology to the Jewish community of Australia, we will regard her with the utmost contempt'.[87]

Irwin is not the only federal Labor backbencher who has been censured over her views on Israel. Tanya Plibersek, federal Member for Sydney, sparked outrage during a debate on the Iraq war when she said

that she could 'think of a rogue state which consistently ignores UN resolutions whose ruler is a war criminal—it is called Israel and the war criminal is Ariel Sharon'.[88] Renewed pressure was placed on Crean to 'control'
his backbench, but he responded that the ALP's policy towards Israel
remained solid. 'There has been no change to Labor's longstanding and
deeply held commitment to the state of Israel', he said. This wouldn't
suffice for the Zionist lobby, both within and outside the ALP. Such dissenting voices, according to AIJAC's Rubenstein, were causing distress
within the Jewish community, and 'this drift should be firmly arrested'.

In October 2003, while launching *The challenges of post-Zionism*[89] in
Sydney, Plibersek responded to her critics. 'I think the underlying intent
of this criticism is not that non-Jews have no right to comment', she said.
She went on to explain how for many people there was 'no such thing
as an innocent Palestinian'. Plibersek's speech was a plea for a more
humane form of Zionism. She even felt obliged to begin by condemning
suicide bombing and by asserting that she did not want to see Israel driven
into the sea. None of her previous comments had ever hinted at anything
this extreme, but such was the atmosphere of intimidation generated by
her initial statements.

Virtually absent from the entire controversy was any examination of
the ALP's official policy on Israel. Once you get past the smokescreen of
a supposedly pro-Palestinian agenda, the ALP is as one-sided as the
Liberal Party, and the Zionist lobby knows it—they just want to silence
the handful of dissenters. Indeed, Labor policy on Israel has remained
remarkably static for decades, with only minor tinkering at the edges.
Former Labor Minister for Foreign Affairs Gareth Evans articulated the
rationale for Labor's policy on Israel in the early 1990s. 'There are some
areas of foreign policy where not just hard-headed calculations of interest are involved', he said: 'a little sentiment intrudes as well—and that is
certainly true about Australia's and the Labor government's attitudes
towards Israel'.[90] In other words, the ALP had never claimed to be balanced and was unlikely to change anytime soon. During the height of
the contrived controversy over ALP policy in 2003, the *Australian*
reported that the Jewish community had launched 'pre-emptive strikes
at the first sign of either political party wavering in its support for Israel'
because, according to Mark Leibler, the community expected Australian
politicians to have an 'objective, principled and balanced approach to
Israel and its role in the Middle East'. He then claimed that there was
no desire within the Jewish community for politicians to adopt 'a pro-
Israeli stance'.[91]

Barry Cohen, who served as minister for the arts and environment in the Hawke era, wrote to Crean as far back as September 2002, complaining that, 'at the moment, I can't imagine any Jew with any feelings towards the state of Israel supporting the Australian Labor party' and accusing Crean of leading a party with two 'distinct and separate' policies on Israel.[92] A few weeks after the 2004 federal election, Cohen wrote an explosive article for the *AJN* (republished in the Melbourne *Age* a few days later) in which he described the ALP as a party of ever-shrinking support for Israel, filled with pro-Palestinian supporters. It was OK to be critical of Israel, Cohen said, provided 'the case ... put is not based on the lies spouted by the Palestinian propaganda machine'. The 'left/liberal commentators', especially since September 11, were blaming Israel for all the world's problems, he said. 'How long is it since any Labor leader gave the sort of passionate and accurate defence of Israel we used to hear from Hawke or Kim Beazley?', he asked. There was no moral equivalence between 'a country that seeks to defend its citizens from thousands of terrorist attacks, and the terrorists themselves'. Cohen wanted 'an end to well-known Labor identities marching behind banners equating Israel with Nazism'.[93]

Days after Cohen's tirade—labelled a 'gross exaggeration' by Crean—Plibersek issued a press statement to clarify her position. After saying she supported a two-state solution and a Jewish state, and condemned suicide bombing and the policies of the Sharon government, she declared that 'at no point, have I ever felt that my criticisms of the Sharon government were anti-Semitic, anti-Jewish or threatened the survival of the state of Israel'.[94]

Cohen's comments continued to reverberate for weeks. Labor foreign affairs spokesman Kevin Rudd responded with the usual platitudes. It was as if he needed to prove that his party's commitment to Israel was greater than that of the Howard government. He proudly stated on ABC Radio National's *Religion report* that, for the first time, the ALP platform now explicitly condemned Palestinian suicide bombing. 'I am passionately pro-Israel', Rudd said before praising the 'only Jewish Member of Parliament, Michael Danby'. He had no hesitation in applauding Israeli foreign policy. He noted that former leader of the National Party, Tim Fischer, known for his pro-Arab views and mild criticism of Israel, was not seen as antisemitic simply because he was 'quite supportive of the interests of the Arab States'.[95] Throughout the entire interview, he didn't once mention the concept of a Palestinian state, or the rights of Palestinians in Israel or the occupied territories.

When the *Age* published a comprehensive response by Rudd in December, he at least discussed the need for a two-state solution and mildly criticised the route of Israel's 'security' fence, but it was obvious to which constituents Rudd was speaking.[96] Indeed, after Kim Beazley reassumed the ALP leadership in early 2005, he told the *AJN* that the ALP supported the Howard government's policy of 'being supportive of the Israelis in difficult times', especially during the 'anti-Israel' votes at the UN. He argued that Sharon's 'disengagement' would be the basis of a Palestinian state. 'John Howard is a friend of Israel', he conceded. 'I wouldn't dispute that at all. So is Kim Beazley.'[97]

Michael Danby has positioned himself as the unofficial Zionist spokesman in the Australian parliament and challenges, even forces, members of his own party to show devotion to the cause. As an Opposition backbencher, Danby may not be one of the most powerful politicians in Australia, but his influence within the ALP is rising. Since September 11, and the association of the subject of Israel with a broader 'war on terror', he has repeatedly compared any violence against Western interests with Palestinian action against Israel. He also complements AIJAC's lobbying. Being the only federal Jewish MP means he is listened to as a leading representative of the Zionist lobby. AIJAC's Rubenstein has praised Danby for raising certain issues in parliament and for promoting a particular viewpoint.[98]

Danby's actions and motivations provide insight into the Australian Jewish community and the Zionist agenda he pushes. One of the leading figures in the anti-Palestinian campaign on university campuses in the mid-1970s, Danby became president of the University of Melbourne's Student Representative Council (SRC). In 1977, he was bashed by two men carrying a Maoist banner, apparently because he was a social democrat who campaigned against leftist ideology. Many of Danby's supporters were political conservatives, and some of them began agitating for voluntary student unionism amid claims that the Left-dominated Australian Union of Students (AUS) had donated funds to the PLO. Today, some of these same conservatives, including Treasurer Peter Costello, can be found in the top echelons of the Howard government, where they have actively promoted voluntary student unionism.

Before he was elected to the seat of Melbourne Ports in 1998 (the electorate with the greatest number of Jews in the country), Danby worked in 1983–84 as assistant private secretary to Barry Cohen. Later he became editor of the *AIR* and worked as a professional lobbyist.[99] When Noam Chomsky made his one and only visit to Australia in early

1995, Danby led the campaign against his tour and even his appearance on ABC Radio. In his view, Chomsky should not have been allowed on the national broadcaster at all. It was a view shared by Colin Rubenstein, who wrote in the *AJN*[100] that a person like Chomsky should be introduced as 'a vociferous critic of Israel' rather than merely 'one of the world's best-known commentators on the Middle East'.

In a profile for *Good Weekend*, Danby told writer Mark Dapin that he was a supporter of the Palestinian cause but that the mainstream Jewish community thought differently about the Palestinians: 'A lot of people are just totally sick to death of the Palestinians because a) they never miss an opportunity to miss an opportunity; and b) because of their apparent public support for suicide bombing'. Labor MP Julia Irwin said she'd told Danby that he wasn't 'running for the Israeli Knesset' and that he should focus less on mouthing pro-Sharon platitudes.[101]

Danby reflects the political positions of his Jewish constituency, and it is therefore hardly surprising that he expresses blind support for whatever position is favoured by the Israeli government.[102] It would probably be political suicide to say or write anything else. He also attacks members of the media who challenge the Zionist line.[103] In 2004 he launched an extraordinary attack on the *SMH*'s Alan Ramsey, under the cloak of parliamentary privilege. Ramsey, who has long criticised Danby's blind devotion to Israel, was full of 'chutzpah', and was 'committing the greatest journalistic fraud in Australian media history' by extensively using quotes in his columns and by using words such as 'cheat', 'plagiarism' and 'humbug' throughout his work. 'What we see in Mr Ramsey's columns is not strictly speaking plagiarism—it is grand larceny', he charged. Surprised listeners in the public gallery might have been excused for wondering what direction this attack was coming from, as Danby didn't once mention Israel.

Zionists and the Greens

Whatever disquiet some elements of the Zionist lobby might feel about the Pliberseks and Irwins of the ALP, it's the Greens that elicit their greatest antipathy. The Greens' policy on the conflict is in fact the most balanced because it acknowledges the rights, history and security needs of both Israelis and Palestinians. Their ideal is to end the Israeli occupation, establish an independent Palestinian state, 'specifically recognise those Israeli soldiers who have refused to serve in the occupied territories', dismantle the 'separation wall' and 'support the legitimate rights and aspirations of the Israeli people to live in peace and security in their own independent, sovereign state'.[104]

The implosion of the Australian Democrats has left the Greens as the third force in local, state and federal politics. An increasing number of Jews are involved in the party and have been actively involved in the formulation of its Israel–Palestine policy. The broader Jewish community, however, generally treats the party with suspicion and contempt. During the 2004 federal election, Jewish Greens candidate Dr John Kaye unsuccessfully stood for a New South Wales Senate seat. He told the *AJN* in September 2004 that only the Greens were 'telling the truth' about the conflict and were taking 'a strong and principled stand', something neither the Liberals nor the ALP could reasonably claim. 'I was brought up as a Jew with the story of the Holocaust and the Exodus to Israel', he said. 'That led me to an absolute commitment to where people were dispossessed, where people don't have a homeland, where people are victimised, where individuals are not allowed self-determination.'[105]

Zionists line up to sideline the Greens. In 2004, AIJAC *Review* editor Tzvi Fleischer claimed that Greens Senator Kerry Nettle's problem was not merely with Israel's 1967 occupation but with the country's very existence. Dr Philip Mendes, a self-described 'Jewish left-winger ... who endorses the policies of the Greens on many issues', argued in a September 2004 Anti-Defamation Commission (ADC) report that the Greens were fundamentally pro-Palestinian.

The most notorious example of Greens-smearing is one that suggests collusion between the Zionist lobby and the Liberal Party. On 28 October 2003, Queensland Liberal Senator George Brandis rose in parliament to speak about politics and fascism. After critiquing the Greens' policies, Brandis argued that there were dangerous parallels between the positions of Greens leader Bob Brown, Kerry Nettle and the German Nazi Party in the years 1933–45. He suggested that the Greens' origins went right back to the German '*Volkish*' movement in the mid-nineteenth century: a naturist movement fuelled by a hatred of Jews, which bred a vegetarian dictator named Adolf Hitler. It was a theory borrowed shamelessly from *Herald Sun* columnist Andrew Bolt. Brandis reminded parliamentarians that just as Hitler came to power by rigging elections, 'the sinister and fanatical views represented by Greens politicians can grow and gain strength under the cover of democracy'. A few weeks after the speech, historian Peter Staudenmaier, co-author of one of the books George Brandis used to claim the Greens were Nazis in disguise, claimed that Brandis had twisted his work to suit a particular political agenda. His book, he said, 'says quite explicitly that there is no inherent connection between classical fascism and contemporary Green politics'.[106]

The Zionist lobby is not a homogenous group, nor does the Jewish community share one particular point of view on Israel. It is clear, however, that opposition to an official perspective is little tolerated, and the political and media elite has well and truly learnt the boundaries of debate. It is important to challenge these protocols. The reality is plain to see in our newspapers, parliaments and public debate: the Zionist lobby exercises demonstrable influence over Australia's political elite, and September 11 has made Zionist advocacy much easier by enabling Zionists to conflate Israel's fight against Palestinian terror attacks—and against the Palestinian people—with the West's 'war on terror'. During the Howard years there has been a remarkable dovetailing of government and Jewish community priorities, and indeed, both major political parties support the notion that Israel and the West are engaged in a battle against terror.

In this pro-Israel environment, the Zionist lobby patrols the boundaries of public debate, aiming to silence anyone who occasionally strays from the accepted line. The following chapters examine the ways in which the media have become the central battleground in the Zionist struggle against 'bias', antisemitism and anti-Zionism. Just as politicians who dare question the status quo in Israel are targeted by Zionist critics, editors and journalists are similarly under attack for daring to question Israel's 'war on the Palestinians'.

THE NEWS MEDIA AND THE LOBBY

9

PUBLIC BROADCASTERS UNDER FIRE

*If Arab ambassadors and lobbyists behaved like their Israeli
opposite numbers, would we listen to them? Would we respect
them? Would we run for cover and print only one side of the
story? Would we, hell.*

Robert Fisk, 2000[1]

IN 1991, DURING the Gulf War that followed Iraq's invasion of Kuwait, the
Hawke government attacked the ABC over its coverage of Australia's military involvement. Bob Hawke himself led the attack, dismissing the national
broadcaster as 'loaded, biased and disgraceful'. At the heart of the controversy was a short segment about the war presented nightly by journalist
Geraldine Doogue and featuring a commentator, Dr Robert Springborg,
who had publicly questioned Australia's role in the war.[2] The government
wanted a fixed caption to appear under Springborg's name, declaring where
he stood on the war. After a meeting with Hawke, the ABC's managing director, David Hill, suggested that Doogue and her colleague Andrew Olle
should be taken off air. The head of ABC Television news and current affairs,
Peter Manning, successfully resisted both moves, but not without a damaging public controversy. Seven years later, AIJAC revealed that at the time
it had prepared a dossier on Dr Springborg, which it forwarded to Hawke
and which had been used as part of the government's attack on ABC 'bias'.[3]

In times of war, journalism is a natural breeding ground for controversy: the stakes could not be higher, or the truth more contested. Ever since the September 11 attacks in 2001, Australia's public broadcasters, the ABC and SBS, have been put under intense pressure from AIJAC and others to conform to a news and current affairs agenda that is pro-Israel, pro-American and anti-Arab, just as they were during the first Gulf War. Zionists, Liberal government ministers and conservative cultural warriors argue that they are trying to ensure 'balance'. My investigations reveal years of harassment of reporters and senior management. Sometimes these complaints have coalesced around the reporting of shocking single events, such as the IDF's attack on a refugee camp in the West Bank town of Jenin in 2002, during a search for Palestinian militants. Israel denied it had carried out a massacre there, but reporters later witnessed the burial of dozens of bodies. A UN investigation subsequently determined that 52 Palestinians had been killed during the attacks.[4]

Other complaints against ABC and SBS coverage of Israel have alleged broad-brush bias, making them time-consuming and difficult to adjudicate. Or else the complaints are narrow, even nitpicking, focusing on the use of single words in coverage. At least two complaints of systemic media bias brought by AIJAC against the public broadcasters have resulted in in-depth inquiries.

The consequences are that editors and journalists employed by the public broadcasters increasingly self-censor their stories, or fail to ask the tough questions of politicians or establishment figures. Given the climate, it's remarkable how many hard-hitting and provocative programs are still aired. This chapter is an attempt to join the dots, showing that since 2002, both the ABC and SBS have been under sustained and deliberate attack over their reporting of Israel–Palestine.

2002: the Sharon case

In April 2002, ABC's *Four corners* screened a BBC *Panorama* documentary, 'The accused', on the role of Ariel Sharon in the massacre in 1982 of more than 2000 Palestinians in the refugee camps of Sabra and Shatila in Beirut. Sharon was then Israel's Defense Minister and oversaw the invasion of Lebanon. During the campaign, Sharon's forces allowed Lebanese militia forces into the Palestinian refugee camps to commit massacres.

In the ensuing controversy between the ABC and the Zionist lobby, AIJAC's executive director, Colin Rubenstein, said the program should have been banned: 'The timing is outrageous. The decision to show this program now, even though it has nothing to do with current developments in the Middle East, is about as clear a case of bias as the ABC has ever exhibited'.[5] Critics asked why the BBC was 'focusing on old news'.[6]

Four corner's executive producer Bruce Belsham explained that his program was justified in screening the documentary—the Israeli invasion of Jenin was occurring at the time—making it 'an entirely appropriate time to review some history from the Middle East'.[7] Sharon was the common link between military decision-making in Jenin and 1982 Lebanon: 'His preference for a military solution poses the question: how well-equipped is he to make any future peace?' AIJAC complained in the media about the program but also demanded, and received, an internal ABC investigation.

Another of AIJAC's complaints about the program concerned a statement made on air by Judge Richard Goldstone, a former war crimes prosecutor for the UN. Goldstone was asked if 'responsibility goes all the way to the top, to the person that gave the orders, that potentially makes Ariel Sharon a war criminal?' He replied that if the person in command knew or should have known the likely result of his actions, 'then that person is responsible. In fact, in my book more responsible than the people who carry out the orders'. Rubenstein wrote in the *Age* that Goldstone was just one of those interviewed in the documentary who later claimed that 'they were misled by the BBC'.[8] In a letter to the ABC, obtained by *Media watch*, Rubenstein insisted that Goldstone 'never agreed to speak about the Sharon case'.[9] But Goldstone, in his own letter to *Media watch*, confirmed that the BBC had not misrepresented him and that he was satisfied with the way his words were used in the program. Rubenstein had been caught red-handed. In the AIJAC *Review* he suggested that he had never said publicly that Goldstone had a problem with his representation in the BBC.[10] Rubenstein shifted the goalposts: Goldstone 'does have a problem with the way his comments are widely portrayed by those who have seen the documentary'. This was an entirely different matter.[11]

David Marr, host of *Media watch* at the time, describes AIJAC's conduct in relation to Justice Goldstone and its playing of the Australian media after the fact:

> It's a three-way operation. Now that I know about it, you see that it's occasionally cropping up elsewhere; it's such a clever operation. You first of all put outrageous reports around about what a documentary said, then you go to the talent used in the documentary and put the reports to the talent, who has not yet seen the documentary, and get a comment from the talent. Now

in this case Justice Goldstone was foolish and gave a comment; he should not have given a comment. And you know what he said was on the basis of what he's heard: 'that sounds dreadful; that's not what I believe'. But when he saw the documentary he said, 'that's right, that's exactly what I believe, that's fine, that's true'. But they used his first comments and continued to use them after he publicly rebuked them for misleading him. And this I thought was really, really ruthless.

Marr was surprised by the lack of public discussion afterwards about the conduct of Rubenstein, 'somebody who has a very high cachet in the Jewish community and is a paid lobbyist with access to a prime minister'. Marr argues the revelation should have been

> a wonderful topic for a newspaper to follow up on with an investigation on AIJAC and the way in which they operate … but the feeling is that the mainstream do not see the inner workings of the Jewish community as a story for the mainstream … I think the extraordinary achievement of the Jewish lobby in Australia is to make respectable the notion that Israel has a right to control the West Bank.[12]

Two weeks after 'The accused' was screened, *Media watch* revealed that Rubenstein had written to Victorian Liberal Party powerbroker Michael Kroger, then director of the ABC.[13] Attached to his letter was a dossier alleging anti-Israel bias at the national broadcaster. Kroger faxed the dossier to the head of the ABC Jonathan Shier and head of news and current affairs Max Uechtritz, asking what 'you are doing about the clear anti-Israel bias exposed in Dr Rubenstein's letter'. ABC management then ordered an investigation into the ABC's reporting of the Middle East on virtually all radio and television current affairs programs.

Rubenstein and Kroger were mainly concerned about the tone and choice of words in ABC reporting. Rubenstein's letter to Kroger included the accusation that the ABC Middle East reporter Tim Palmer called a murder victim 'the settler instead of, for example, the shepherd or the Israeli'. Another complaint concerned a *Foreign correspondent* report about trafficking in human organs. Rubenstein acknowledged that human kidneys were purchased in Turkey and sold for transplant in Israel, but believed the ABC should ignore it. 'There are many instances around the world of illegal transplant schemes', he wrote, 'but it is indicative of

Foreign correspondent's anti-Israel preoccupation that they focused on this one'. The closing section of Rubenstein's letter to Kroger got to the crux of the issue: 'The sympathetic coverage to the Intifada by media organisations such as the ABC encourages the Palestinians to persist with this tactic and is therefore partly responsible for the continued bloodshed'.

The ABC's acting director of corporate affairs, John Woodward, dismissed the complaints and claimed the investigation had found no 'pattern of anti-Israel bias'. Kroger refused to respond to the report, and Rubenstein rejected the decision. The ABC offered little more than 'dismissive whitewash', he wrote, and was again blamed for assisting the 'Palestinian leadership' in prolonging the violence and forcing Israel to accept 'Palestinian demands'.[14]

Why did Kroger hassle ABC news management to pursue these spurious claims? Marr believes it was a bullying operation. Kroger often claimed the ABC was against the Howard government, and Rubenstein's dossier merely added fuel to this theory of an anti–Liberal government, anti-American and anti-Israel bias.[15] When a figure such as Kroger demanded the complaints be dealt with, 'that ties everybody up in knots and it makes everybody think twice before [presenting another point of view]'. Marr argues that Rubenstein and Kroger didn't want to acknowledge the existence of different perspectives on the conflict 'that are perfectly respectable and truthful'.[16]

In June 2002, AIJAC's *Review* published an article by associate editor Daniel Mandel entitled 'The ABC of Bias'.[17] In it, *Media watch, Four corners, AM, PM, Lateline*, Tim Palmer and Phillip Adams are all accused of putting a 'politically correct' slant on the conflict. 'This usually means scant or no attention paid to anything that upsets David and Goliath preconceptions ... or perceptions of Muslims', Mandel wrote, 'even if the data is true and noteworthy'. Mandel chastises *Lateline*'s Tony Jones and *AM*'s former host Linda Mottram for labelling Israel's policy of killing enemies as 'assassinations'. It is not appropriate to question this policy, Mandel argues, as 'targeting military personnel in hostilities, including commanders, is entirely consistent with the Hague Regulations'. The article fails to acknowledge that some leading legal experts vehemently disagree with the definition. Amnesty released a report in 2001 that condemns the killings as 'taking place outside any judicial framework'.[18] The group found that most of those killed could have been arrested and charged, and many Palestinians civilians, including children, were killed alongside some of those targeted. UN Secretary General Kofi Annan condemned Israel in 2001 and said the practice violates international law.[19]

Mandel criticises Phillip Adams for 'giving leave and license to regular interviewee Robert Fisk to spout harangues against Israel and popularise fictions about US genocide in Iraq'. Fisk has never alluded to 'US genocide', but does question the actions of US and British forces in Iraq, Afghanistan and Guantanamo Bay. The ABC has a 'culture of bias', Mandel argues, ' a radical agenda, ultimately hostile to both Labor and Liberal ... that is entrenched and seemingly beyond the means of complaints procedures, press councils or board members to address'.

Meanwhile, SBS was having its own problems with the lobby. A documentary by John Pilger, entitled *Palestine is still the issue*, was screened by SBS in October 2002. The film profiled Israel's ever-strengthening military and economic stranglehold on the Palestinians and a group of brave Israelis and Palestinians campaigning for an end to the occupation. Pilger later told me about the furious lobbying of Australian Zionist groups, who attempted to stop the broadcast, and compared it to lobbying over Hanan Ashrawi's peace prize: 'The full New South Wales Jewish Board of Deputies demanded to see the [SBS] director of programs, then demanded to ban the film, while a New York Zionist propaganda group called HonestReporting wrote a generic email of lies and abuse which the Australian lobby used to bombard SBS'. Pilger found it encouraging that the program had gone to air regardless: 'None of this intimidation worked'.[20] He believes that the lobby is losing its power. But it's clear from my own investigations that criticism of SBS has influenced programming decisions.

2003: SBS in the gun

In October 2003 AIJAC released a report alleging systematic bias at SBS news and current affairs in relation to the Israel–Palestine conflict. 'A review of SBS current affairs reveals a decade-long pattern of favouring overwhelmingly anti-Israeli documentaries or material severely critical of Israel, no matter how biased or unreliable', the report claims.[21] AIJAC charged SBS's *World news* with an anti-Israel bias when selecting stories, interviews or perspectives; the news program was also accused of making numerous factual errors, using biased language and graphics, and editorialising. The report claims that SBS rarely acknowledges these errors—'despite official written complaints'—and suggests legislative reform 'to provide for a revised Charter and Codes of Practice that make explicit SBS's obligations with respect to the presentation of news, current affairs and documentaries'.

The report contains several factual errors (including the claim that 'during [Sharon's] term of office, no new settlements have been established', even though numerous new colonies have sprouted up in recent years). It also objects to SBS calling the West Bank, Gaza and East Jerusalem 'occupied Palestinian land'. Why? According to the report, 'It is indisputably the case that this land has never previously been under the sovereignty of either the Palestinian people or a state called Palestine, nor is there any legally binding UN decision or international treaty that says it should be'. Israel and many of its supporters have never accepted UN resolution 242, issued in November 1967, which stresses 'the inadmissibility of the acquisition of territory by war'. The resolution demands that Israel withdraw from the territories it occupied in 1967, including East Jerusalem.

Dateline host Mark Davis is accused in the AIJAC report of being 'aggressive' towards US ambassador to Australia Tom Schieffer during an interview on 19 March 2003, because he had introduced the interview with the observation that Australia 'stands poised to attack a country on the other side of the world [Iraq] that offers this nation no direct threat and many would argue, no perceivable threat in the future'. Aside from alleging bias in programs directly concerned with Israel, the AIJAC report targets others that questioned George W Bush's agenda, especially in the Middle East.[22] Commentary that challenged Australia's role in the invasion and occupation is labelled 'anti-American' bias. Sol Salbe, a member of the Melbourne-based, progressive Australian Jewish Democratic Society (AJDS), questions AIJAC's report, arguing that AIJAC's definition of bias is 'essentially, any program that does not fit into its world view'. He also points to SBS's programming of material investigating the Holocaust: 'The credit it gets for this from AIJAC is—absolutely none':

> Many of the programs shown by SBS actually come from Israel. Some such as *Tekuma* were actually made by the Israeli Broadcasting Authority—the equivalent of our ABC. This one is a good case in point as an example of what AIJAC does not say: 'The screening of the series in Israel caused considerable public controversy, including criticism from then Communications Minister Limor Livnat, for its largely negative focus.' All true, but the argument is disingenuous. What AIJAC omitted to say was that Israel watched a 22-hour Hebrew language series, while SBS showed Australians a highly sanitised six-hour program. Most of the items complained about by Ms Livnat et al. were excised. I for one would like them to have kept the scene

in which a senior Israeli commander explained how his troops burnt Palestinian villages 'as if it were Guy Fawkes Day'.[23]

SBS management treated the AIJAC report seriously, ordering an investigation by the news and current affairs department and the policy section. But in May 2004, the managing director Nigel Milan sent a letter to staff explaining that the investigation had been suspended after a complaint that it had been compromised:

> Any claim that our complaints handling is less than fair and objective cannot be left unanswered. Accordingly, I have decided to seek an external and independent review of the process applying to the handling of the AIJAC complaints. I will advise you once the person responsible for this inquiry has been appointed. I expect this person to receive the fullest co-operation while investigating our handling of these complaints. In order to avoid any prejudice to the inquiry process, neither I nor anyone else involved in the handling of the AIJAC complaints will be permitted to make further comment on this matter either internally or externally. The outcome of the inquiry will be made public.[24]

A senior SBS source later revealed to me what had occurred, providing a fascinating insight into the internal confusion about how to handle AIJAC's claims. Head of policy Julie Eisenberg investigated the complaints and allegedly found even more problems for AIJAC's list. She proposed that SBS add them to a list of apologies that she drafted for Milan to sign as SBS's official response to AIJAC. But head of news and current affairs Phil Martin had drafted a different response, which contained no apologies. Eisenberg called a meeting with Milan and others to discuss SBS's response, but she left Martin off the invitation list and produced her draft response. Martin found out about the meeting and had an argument with Milan, who was considering signing the Eisenberg letter. Milan then issued his intriguing 'compromised' memo to staff, and announced that the 'investigation' would now be outsourced. Following this, Martin threatened to resign unless his response to AIJAC was authorised, and Milan caved in. On 13 July 2004 Milan sent Colin Rubenstein a sympathetic but firm letter, making it clear that while SBS management had met with Rubenstein on a number of occasions—'I regard this opening up of lines of communication as a positive step towards a mutual understanding of the positions of both organisations'—the station would not be accepting the lobby group's complaints. AIJAC was not happy with SBS's response and made a claim to the Australian Broadcasting Authority (ABA), alleging that SBS had breached its Codes of Practice by providing an inadequate response to its original letter of complaint. Attached to the letter that Milan sent Rubenstein was a report by the head of SBS television Shaun Brown, in which he analysed AIJAC's concerns, including an additional complaint from AIJAC about John Pilger's documentary *Breaking the silence*.

One example of Brown's responses to the complaints will suffice. AIJAC's original complaint accused SBS of suggesting that Israel's release of Palestinian prisoners 'is one of the major planks of the Road Map'. 'In fact', AIJAC wrote, 'the prisoner release is not mentioned in the Road Map'. Brown proved otherwise. He quoted from the Tenet plan (proposed by CIA director George Tenet in 2001 in an attempt to commit both sides to a mutual, comprehensive ceasefire): 'Israel will release all Palestinians in security sweeps who have no association with terrorist activities'. Brown pointed out that although the issue of prisoner releases may not be specifically mentioned in the Road Map itself, 'it is clearly part of the Tenet work plan, which, in turn, is tied to the Road Map'.

I submitted a freedom of information (FOI) request to SBS requesting all documentation related to Middle East programs between 2001 and 2003. I eventually received a bundle of documents that confirmed my suspicions: the vast majority of 29 letters of complaint submitted to SBS news and current affairs management about Middle East coverage were from AIJAC's Colin Rubenstein or other AIJAC staff, and all fit a similar pattern. SBS news reports 'lacked fairness and balance' and often contained 'political overtones'. One letter criticised an SBS reporter for using the word 'hard-line' to describe Ariel Sharon, while another was upset that the channel had even mentioned the fact that a Belgian Court had considered indicting Sharon in 2001 for wars crimes in Lebanon in 1982.

AIJAC found a handful of factual errors, but the vast majority of complaints related to journalism that challenged Israel's aggression in the occupied territories, supposedly positioned Israel as the aggressor in the conflict, or ignored Israel's consistent 'striving for peace'. SBS management usually responded firmly and provided responses that supported its journalists. The handful of other complaints to SBS came from pro-Palestinian groups or individuals and complained that Palestinian deaths were not given the same airtime as Israeli deaths. Ali Kazak, head of the General Palestinian Delegation in Australia, asked in 2001 why SBS

Dateline had suggested the Palestinian Authority was a 'dictatorship controlled by one party and one man'. Both sides could clearly be dogmatic and blind to the faults in their ingrained positions.

My SBS source also informed me that SBS management had placed on hold certain documentaries and current affairs segments on the Middle East question that were thought to be too sensitive. When I questioned SBS management about this, they said they were 'not aware of any programs being placed on hold'. But investigating further, I discovered that SBS management had several times rejected documentaries, films and current affairs programs that critiqued the actions of the Israeli government and military.[25] This was primarily the result of intense pressure from Zionist lobbyists at AIJAC and a handful of Liberal and ALP senators. The rejected documentaries included:

- *Ford Transit*, by Palestinian film-maker Hany Abu-Assad, was shown at one of the world's finest Jewish film festivals, the San Francisco International Jewish Film Festival. It received the Spirit of Freedom Award at the Jerusalem International Film Festival and a major prize from Human Rights Watch. This docu-drama tells the story of a Palestinian who drives Israelis and Palestinians from checkpoint to checkpoint across the West Bank and Gaza.
- *Checkpoint*, by Israeli film-maker Yoav Shamir, shows the human toll of the occupation and documents three years of life at checkpoints in the West Bank and Gaza.
- *The wall*, by Moroccan-born, Israeli film-maker Simone Bitton, screened at the 2004 Melbourne Film Festival and won the Spirit of Freedom Award for best documentary at the Jerusalem International Film Festival. It tells the story of Israel's 'separation' fence and its effect on both Israelis and Palestinians.

During a Senate Estimates Committee session in May 2004, ALP Senator Sue Mackay asked Nigel Milan why the three films had been rejected. He took the question on notice and responded soon after. *The wall* was rejected, the committee was informed, 'on the grounds that SBS has recently acquired and broadcast a documentary entitled *Straddling the fence*, which dealt with the same topic as *The wall* in much the same way'. *Straddling the fence* is a report by *New York Times* foreign affairs commentator Thomas L Friedman. While acknowledging the suffering of both Palestinians and Israelis, and implying that the fence would only inflame more hatred, the film failed to explore the claim made in *The wall* that the fence was in fact designed to determine the future border of Israel, rather than being a temporary measure, as claimed by Sharon, his government and supporters.[26] SBS's choice of this film was a safe option. Milan told the committee that the other films were not screened because of 'quality or duplication' concerns. 'In those circumstances', he said, 'it is more appropriate to describe a documentary as "not selected" rather than "rejected"'.

In 2002, comments made by ABC head of news and current affairs Max Uechtritz at a talk in Singapore brought the government's wrath down on the ABC's head. Uechtritz, a former foreign correspondent, discussing the media's coverage of the US-led invasion of Afghanistan in 2001, quipped, 'We now know for certain that only three things in life are certain—death, taxes and the fact the military are lying bastards'. He also observed: 'The lessons of the war? So much technology, so many outlets, so much ignorance'. The federal Minister for Communications, Richard Alston, was incensed, arguing that Uechtritz's 'bias' against the US military had infected the ABC coverage. He charged ABC Radio's *AM* with systematic anti-US bias in its coverage of the Iraq war, issuing a dossier of 68 complaints to the ABC managing director, Russell Balding. ABC Television's *Media watch* soon revealed that the federal director of the Liberal Party, Brian Loughnane, was one source of the complaints.[27] Alston was not acting in response to the public's outrage at ABC bias, as he claimed.

During an interview on ABC Television's *Lateline* in May 2003, Alston explained how suggestions that the Pentagon wasn't waging a 'compassionate war' 'undermined . . . the whole ethos of the military machine'.[28] Alston argued that the ABC hadn't treated military briefings with respect, preferring to take a sceptical approach to official government accounts. Interviewer Tony Jones asked Alston, 'Isn't this the normal scrutiny which independent journalists are expected to apply in something as dramatic as war?' Alston's response was revealing, implying that 'independent analysis' is not the role of a reporter but unquestioningly channelling government spin is.

By early 2005, Alston's 68 complaints had been reviewed and examined both internally and externally, including by the Independent Complaints Review Panel, established after the Hawke government slammed ABC's coverage of the 1991 Gulf War. The ABA was Alston's last port of call for review. It concluded that the vast majority of complaints were without merit, though some displayed evidence of 'bias'. For example, the ABC's description of a White House briefing as part of 'the propaganda war' was found to be derogatory. How this kind of press conference could be viewed as anything other than propaganda is debatable. An insight into the general public's view of the matter was provided by an online poll on Kerry Packer's ninemsn website in 2003. The question of the day read, 'Should the Government be doing more to support the ABC?'. Around 75 per cent of the 26 000 respondents were in favour of the ABC. These were the results of a poll conducted by a commercial news site.

AIJAC crowed about an apology it received from the ABC in late October 2003.[29] ABC Radio's *AM* had claimed in the same month that Israel's withdrawal from the southern town of Gaza had left, according to the UN, '1500 homes flattened'. In fact, the UN had claimed that 1500 people were left homeless and 100 houses were destroyed. The program acknowledged its error both on its website and on air. AIJAC's Colin Rubenstein claimed that this about-face was 'a more responsive approach by the ABC in treating complaints about their many instances of anti-Israel bias'. The suggestion, however, that *AM*'s error was anything other than a simple mistake seems tenuous.

The following month, AIJAC's *Review* claimed that the ABC had 'showed consistent and strong bias against the Iraq war, amounting almost to a campaign, in the way news was selected and presented and the interpretation placed on it'.[30] Naturally, the organisation saw a parallel: 'The same can be said of ABC reporting of the Middle East conflict'. These charges of anti-Americanism were just another example of the increasingly common tactic of complaining of both anti-Israel and anti-American media coverage.

2004: Palestine is still the issue

AIJAC isn't the only organisation to complain about SBS's coverage of Israel–Palestine. The Melbourne-based Anti-Defamation Commission (ADC) used to be a broadly based human rights organisation monitoring the activity of far-right groups in Australia. It has recently moved towards promoting a hard-line position on Israel and is critical of voices it alleges to be against Israel or US government policy. Its chairman, Dr Paul Gardner, is a former lecturer at Melbourne's Monash University. Board members include Malcolm Fraser, Bob Hawke, Neville Wran, Zelman Cowen and Lowitja O'Donoghue. After the October 2002 screening of Pilger's *Palestine is still the issue* documentary on SBS, Gardner wrote a letter to SBS complaining of 'an outrageous example of TV journalism at its worst'. After listing a litany of complaints, Gardner generously wrote that Pilger 'is entitled to his opinion. But his freedom of speech does not guarantee his right to exposure on public television'. The ADC was recommending censorship of an internationally recognised documentary, nominated for a 2003 BAFTA in the current affairs category.

When the film was screened in the United Kingdom on ITV in 2002, Michael Green, chairman of ITV's parent company, Carleton Communications, alleged the film was 'one-sided, factually incorrect and historically inaccurate'. Many Jewish groups bitterly objected to the film's screening. The United Kingdom's Independent Television Commission (ITC) rejected the complaint against Pilger's film, arguing that Israelis, as well as Palestinians, were interviewed, ensuring that the film was balanced.[31]

ADC's rationale was thoroughly familiar: Pilger challenged the ADC worldview, so it was legitimate to question its inclusion on SBS. ADC complained again in 2003 after SBS screened the *Jenin, Jenin* documentary. 'It is a classic case of group libel', Gardner wrote, and 'the person who selected it for screening ought to examine his or her conscience'. The film told the story of the IDF invasion of the Palestinian town of Jenin in 2002 and claimed that excessive tactics were used and numerous citizens were murdered by the Israeli army. Robert Fisk told me in February 2005 that he hadn't called Jenin a massacre at the time, but that given the information he now had, 'I should have'. *Jenin, Jenin* undoubtedly painted a disturbing picture of the Israeli invasion—though it did contain some errors, including a reference to a western wing of a hospital being shelled when the hospital did not have a western wing—and was the first film to be banned in Israel in 15 years. (The ban was later overturned by Israel's High Court.) Being controversial, however, was surely no reason for a film to be censored in Australia.

Gardner was unhappy with SBS's response to his charges, and he issued a press release. While acknowledging the 'difficulties that Palestinians experience, and [having] no objection to programs that present Palestinian viewpoints', he fumed that SBS was 'broadcasting lies' and needed a more effective complaints procedure.

A sign that SBS is adopting a more Israel-friendly agenda was the screening of the propaganda documentary *Jenin, massacring truth* in May 2005. The documentary purports to uncover the Western media's dishonesty when reporting the Israeli invasion of Jenin in April 2002. Israeli soldier Johnathan Van Caspel, present during the incursion, was taken to the United Kingdom and introduced to numerous journalists and editors who had indirectly accused him and his colleagues of committing massacres in Jenin. Many of Van Caspel's friends were killed in the fighting, and the film features scenes of the deceased men's wives and children, accompanied by syrupy music. Alan Dershowitz is featured, accusing the European media of antisemitism, equating anti-Zionism with antisemitism, charging Amnesty and Human Rights Watch with singling out Israel for unjustified criticism, and praising Israel for its record on human rights. Canadian reporter Martin Himel identifies the USA and Serbia as examples of nations that have killed civilians indiscriminately in their histories, while Israel is depicted as always protecting civilians where possible. Van Caspel is incensed that the IDF is seen as anything other than a moral army. The documentary talks up the UN and Human Rights Watch reports that allegedly prove Israel had committed no massacres in Jenin.

What was the real agenda of this documentary? Canadian company CanWest owns Elsash Productions, the organisation that produced the work, and film-maker Martin Himel has worked for parent company Global Television Network. CanWest is a large media company launched by Canadian mogul Izzy Asper in the1970s. Editorial policy at CanWest has always been to support Israel slavishly. David Beers, former chief features writer on the CanWest-owned Vancouver *Sun*, summed up the paper's policy a few years ago: 'Never a bad word about Israel, never a good word about the Palestinians'.[32] Izzy's son, Larry, says that he would screen more balanced programs if 'we could find a commentator on the Middle East that would actually use facts and not innuendo or misguided or misleading statements about the conflict'. What about the facts in the film? Human Rights Watch did indeed report in 2002 that no massacre has taken place in Jenin. However, the documentary conveniently ignored the serious allegations against Israeli soldiers, including the killing and running over by an Israeli tank of a 57-year-old Palestinian man in a wheelchair holding a white flag. The IDF killed a paralysed man in his home when they did not allow his family enough time to remove him, the report stated. Viewers of the film were informed that, despite the tight media control during the Jenin operation and British journalists' claims that they were not given sufficient access, the IDF were in fact taking reporters around the site. In the documentary, we hear *Fox news* journalist Mike Tobin painting a favourable picture of the invasion from the Israeli perspective. This documentary suggests that Israeli statements at the time of the invasion should have been sufficient to convince journalists that no atrocities had occurred in Jenin. The *SMH*'s Jackie Chowns recommended the film unquestioningly, while the Melbourne *Age*'s Brian Courtis was less complimentary. The program, he wrote, was both 'revealing and frustrating. The messengers, you feel, are being encouraged to be far more wary'.[33]

Whose version of balance?

The notion of editorial balance has traditionally guided the work of journalists and media editors. Put simply, it means telling both sides of the story. In the past the concept was often interpreted quite literally, and some newspapers were careful to provide '50/50' space for and against an issue. But does this suffice when reporting on the Israel–Palestine conflict?

Robert Fisk argues that it doesn't. He says that, 'in the realm of warfare ... you are morally bound as a journalist to show eloquent compassion to the victims, to be unafraid to name the murderers and you're allowed to be angry'.[34] He cites examples from his personal experience of reporting:

> When I was close to a pizzeria bombing in Israeli West Jerusalem in 2001, in which 20 were killed, more than half children, I didn't give half the time to Hamas. In 1982, in Sabra and Shatila, I wrote about the victims, the dead who I physically climbed over and the survivors. I did not give 50 per cent to the Lebanese Christian Phalangist militia who massacred them nor to the Israeli army who watched the murders and did nothing.

Fisk's practice reflects a gradual shift in journalism practice over the past 30 years towards the idea that balance is about fairness, and that what matters is that both sides of an issue are ventilated over time. Young reporters were once trained to be neutral, dispassionate, 'objective'. Now, they still learn traditional journalistic techniques, such as the importance of verifying (or disproving) news leads and seeking different angles on each news story. But the emphasis in their training is on actually being fair, rather than on meeting some artificial measure of balance, such as how many centimetres of copy their newspaper has published from each side. The problem with the fairness approach is that it often plays into the hands of media critics looking for examples of media bias in particular stories. Too often, however, accepting 'official' sources as accurate, while dismissing dissenting perspectives as unreliable, results in a disproportionate emphasis on an establishment perspective and in support for state power.

This obsession with 'balance' results in skewed journalism. For example, US media analyst Andrew Tyndall found that, out of the 414 stories about Iraq broadcast on US networks ABC, CBS and NBC from September 2002 to February 2003, all but 34 originated from the State Department, White House and Pentagon.[35] The 'official' truth avoided many uncomfortable facts.

And indeed the fairness approach to reporting seems to trouble AIJAC, as demonstrated in its 2003 complaint that SBS broadcast 'an overwhelming preponderance of material highlighting, or sympathetic to, anti-Israel viewpoints'. AIJAC *Review* editor Tzvi Fleischer defines good journalism as being 'ruthlessly committed to "truth" defined simply, and not hedged by demands to serve supposed "higher truths" which are actually largely subjective opinion'.[36] In AIJAC's opinion, any news story that portrays Israel in a critical light is biased, irresponsible and a sign of anti-semitism. It seems that AIJAC finds it impossible to accept any media coverage that challenges an Israeli government decision or Israeli army manoeuvre or that features a Palestinian or dissenting Jewish point of view. Being pro-Israeli is balanced and non-partisan, while even articulating the Palestinian perspective is biased. AIJAC subscribes to the philosophy articulated by famed Israeli politician Abba Eban: 'The task of Zionists is to show that all political anti-Zionism is either anti-Semitism or Jewish self-hatred'.[37]

Fleischer argues that the main problem with SBS and the ABC is their inability to apply 'oversight mechanisms' fairly and to respond to public concerns, either through Senate Estimates hearings or the Australian Communications and Media Authority.[38] He cites the Alston complaints about *AM* as an example of the ABC's failure to change its ways, clearly unwilling to recognise that the original complaints were ideologically based and an attempt to silence dissent.

It is the job of conscientious journalists to get past the spin of 'official' accounts. Journalist and author Joan Didion took famed US journalist Bob Woodward to task for relying too heavily on such sources, but her critique equally applies to the sanitised journalism desired by AIJAC. 'Fairness', she writes, 'has often come to mean a scrupulous passivity, an agreement to cover the story not as it is occurring but as it is presented, which is to say, as it is manufactured'.[39]

It is not surprising that the concept of 'balance' is so politically charged in the context of the Israel–Palestine conflict. Rupert Murdoch—after receiving the Simon Wiesenthal Centre's Humanitarian Laureate Award in 2006—suggested that criticism of Israel wasn't antisemitic, but then argued that anti-Zionism was unacceptable, as was any other challenge to Israel's actions or legitimacy.[40] Murdoch argued that the Arab world deserved to put under far greater scrutiny than Israel, and he damned the UN for unfairly targeting the Jewish state. 'Modern hate' against Israel was likely to be found, he said, 'in Dutch mosques, Parisian housing projects and American and European university campuses'. He left no room for criticism of the Jewish state. It is impossible to report accurately with such a skewed idea of 'balance'.

The impact on journalists

Receiving and dealing with complaints of bias and/or inaccuracy are part of the professional territory of a journalist. But there is no doubt that concerted campaigns by AIJAC and other lobbyists are wearing down journalists and other media professionals working at the public broadcasters. Such campaigns have a cost, contributing to staff departures and low morale, and impoverishing the culture of media organisations. Furthermore, the fear of being attacked by lobbyists is directly leading to certain subjects or perspectives being ignored or side-lined.

I contacted many senior figures at SBS and the ABC who were interested in speaking about the impact of lobbying on their coverage of Israel–Palestine but were reluctant to be identified. Some were fearful of losing their jobs or being reprimanded. The vast majority wanted somebody to understand the intense pressure put on editors, producers and journalists to not 'rock the boat' or question the pro-Bush and pro-Israeli line coming out of Canberra. The Minister for Foreign Affairs, Alexander Downer, and his press secretary, Chris Kenny, are notorious for issuing veiled threats to SBS and ABC management if they screen a program that is critical of Australian or US foreign policy. A contact at SBS's *Dateline* confirmed that such threats are received regularly by that program; the intention, he said, is to instil fear in the producers so that they don't tackle 'contentious' issues in the future. A senior SBS journalist explained that the Department of Foreign Affairs and Trade is increasingly reluctant to grant access to journalists who want to accompany Australian soldiers in Iraq and Afghanistan, primarily because they fear negative portrayals of 'Coalition' activity.

To its credit, *Dateline* still screens 'risky' stories. A good example is Olivia Rousset's 2004 story about an exhibition of photographs taken by young Israeli conscripts and shown in a small art gallery in Haifa.[41] The pictures were shot in the West Bank town of Hebron, where around 500 right-wing Jewish settlers live among 170 000 Palestinians. Rousset revealed that many soldiers were highly traumatised by their experiences and told of numerous human rights abuses during their time on duty. After the exhibition opened, the Israeli authorities interrogated the soldiers and confiscated video testimony. Exhibition organiser Yonatan Boimfeld said the government was simply trying to 'scare us': 'Imagine what can happen if every soldier who gets out of the army will do another exhibition about Gaza or about Nablus or about Bethlehem. I mean it will be nuts, so they have to stop this wave at the beginning'. It was the kind of story that is unlikely to be seen on any other Australian television current affairs program.

Another example is the world-first screening, in February 2006, of additional shocking photos taken at Iraq's Abu Ghraib prison. The program was criticised by the US government for potentially inflaming tensions in the Middle East—as if the Iraq occupation wasn't reason enough—and John Howard said SBS could only justify the program if it believed the acts 'represented evidence of behaviour not previously investigated'. If not, he said, he didn't see reason to broadcast them because the Americans are 'doing something about it [the abuse]'.[42]

Before leaving in late 2004, Nigel McCarthy was an SBS producer for several years in development within news and current affairs. He recalls the many complaints received from Zionist groups and the process by which they were assessed. 'Complainants are aware that responding to complaints is a time-consuming process, and this is part of their strategy', as is exposing any divisions within the organisation, he says. McCarthy argues that many of the complainants are aware of

> and deliberately disregard the realities of journalism ... Events
> are often reported as they are still unfolding and before a full
> explanation is available or before comment is available from all
> the relevant parties. Attempts to create editorial guidelines that
> restrict journalists because of considerations such as those play
> into the hands of complainants and need to be resisted.[43]

Chantal Chalier, former principal program assessor at SBS, says that SBS management is increasingly shying away from programs that may be critical of Israel because they are 'paranoid about pissing off AIJAC'. The Palestinian narrative is largely avoided because the 'official view' of events is less likely to cause headaches. Chalier says that SBS now wants people who are largely commercially minded and 'more into advertising'.[44] A former SBS programmer who requested anonymity says that 'potentially controversial programs are shunned, sometimes kept from the attention of the preview committee and quietly rejected. This is most clearly the case with documentaries that could be described as "pro-Palestinian"'. Furthermore, the source tells me that board member Christopher Pearson wants documentaries to have 'internal balance', a meaningless term in current affairs journalism.

Former SBS director of programming Rod Webb says that the likes of AIJAC are simply wearing down the current SBS management. 'They're pretty formidable bastards', he says. 'They're terriers—they just keep at it. You know you're dealing with a big outfit that's persistent.'[45] In 2005 Webb's successor Matt Campbell told the *SMH* that 'the last thing most viewers want is another documentary about the situation in the Middle East'.[46] Webb believes this comment says more about 'SBS's current attitude' towards the conflict than it does about viewer preferences, pointing out that 'documentaries on the Middle East invariably rate better than most documentaries on other international "trouble spots"'. He claims that SBS management is split on how to deal with the Middle East; the easiest solution is to avoid aggravating these 'terriers' and to self-censor certain programs. He says that AIJAC is frequently dismissed as extremist in some senior SBS circles, but because of its political clout, its complaints must be responded to, even if editorial standards are compromised in the process.

Former SBS *Dateline* journalist Matthew Carney—now a reporter with ABC's *Four corners*—reported and lived in the Middle East for many years and has noticed an ever-increasing sensitivity to his work, especially on Israel–Palestine. He says that the pressure from Jewish groups on news organisations is linked to a growing recognition in Western society that 'Palestinians suffer'. In the past, Carney argues, there was a perception that the Palestinians 'were these mad people, and they wanted to fight and they wanted to kill; there was no real articulation of . . . their struggle'. He cites his June 2004 story on Hamas in Gaza as an example.[47] The piece examined social and welfare issues, as well as the militias of a 'so-called terrorist organisation'. Only a show such as *Dateline* would profile Hamas, Carney says, because elsewhere in the media 'it's a terrorist organisation, that's been decided and that's it'. He knows the criticism the show received—'you're giving them a mouthpiece'—but argues that as a journalist 'you do have to cover the other side of the story'. This was, of course, two years before Hamas assumed power in the Palestinian territories.

The increased sensitivity in relation to the conflict became apparent in the editing process. 'I had to put everything as "they claim" and "they say". I couldn't report anything, or be seen to report anything as fact', Carney recalls. 'It was becoming quite ridiculous . . . The "alleged" bulldozer, which you can see on the pictures were coming in and destroying houses, was a good example. Now at that point you've got to say this is just absurd, which I did.' The Zionist lobbyists are successful because they are 'relentless': 'They hope they'll wear you down and sensitise the

TV executives to the point where they just couldn't be bothered because they know what's going to happen next'. Carney also says he's never heard from one Arab lobby group in Australia, suggesting that the Zionist perspective is the only one most media figures ever hear.

Boards

The composition of public broadcaster boards has always been contentious, with governments of all stripes attempting to stack them with political appointments, but the Howard years have seen an acceleration of this trend in an attempt to enforce journalistic 'balance'. The make-up of both the ABC and SBS boards has been an increasing source of concern for people who care about the public broadcasters' programming. Political appointments by the Howard government have been a recurring focus of controversy.

The SBS board is chaired by fashion designer Carla Zampatti, a supporter of Liberal Malcolm Turnbull's successful bid for the federal seat of Wentworth and wife of former Liberal MP John Spender. Its members include former Packer and Murdoch television executive Gerald Stone, who agrees with Alston's accusation that the ABC was biased against the Coalition and the war in Iraq, and Murdoch newspaper columnist Christopher Pearson, a former speechwriter for John Howard. On his appointment in 2003, ALP communications spokesman Lindsay Tanner said, 'Not content with stacking the ABC board, John Howard is now stacking the SBS board with political stooges. John Howard is trying to turn the two national broadcasters into propaganda units for the Liberal Government'.[48]

A number of SBS employees regard the board as commercially driven and dangerously conservative, with little or no experience in the complexities of multicultural broadcasting. Professor Amareswar Galla, a board member from 1997 to 2000, commented in the *Age* in 2004 on the lack of ethnic diversity on the board. He said that, 'When I was on the board, it was very diverse and I think it makes a difference. The board is the conscience, and if that conscience doesn't reflect the kind of Australia that we are, then there are problems, no matter how well-meaning people are'.[49] Former SBS program assessor Chantal Chalier suggests that the current board and management 'don't understand multicultural broadcasting; they know about market share, profits and running the place like a corporation'. Almost no one in programming has any links to ethnic communities, she says, and when management talks of 'cultural diversity', 'they're actually talking about people from Britain, New Zealand and Ireland'.[50]

Like SBS, the ABC board has been politicised under both Labor and Liberal governments. The current board is no exception. Seven directors are appointed by the government of the day, and according to the *ABC Act* (1983) 'must be experienced in broadcasting, communications or management, or have expertise in financial or technical matters, or have cultural or other interests relevant to the provision of broadcasting services'. An examination of recent appointments suggests a strong ideological bent. For example, Dr Ron Brunton was a senior fellow at the Institute of Public Affairs (IPA), a Howard-favoured, free-market, right-wing think tank.[51]

Janet Albrechtsen is a weekly columnist for Murdoch's *Australian* and a corporate lawyer who was accused by *Media watch* in 2002 of plagiarising and twisting the words of French and Danish experts to support her claims that a number of rapes of Western women by Lebanese men in Sydney were the result of Islamic values.[52] When Albrechtsen was appointed to the board in early 2005, David Marr questioned her qualifications: 'I have never detected in her work the slightest interest in public broadcasting, except to attack it for doing its job'.[53] Minister for Communications Helen Coonan rejected allegations of bias: 'There's certainly no agenda on the part of the government and I would think there's no agenda on her part or she would have hardly accepted the appointment'.

Appointing Jonathan Shier as general manager of the ABC in 2000 was another attempt by the Howard government to bring some 'balance' to programming. He was extremely unpopular and resigned in 2001. The government's next choice was Kerry Packer's close associate Trevor Kennedy, but the chairman of the ABC board, Donald McDonald, rejected Kennedy's application. Russell Balding was an internal candidate and a relatively non-political figure, and his appointment was seen as a slap in the face to the Howard government and its media cheerleaders.

Political appointments to the ABC board are a significant failing of the current system, according to veteran ABC journalist Kerry O'Brien. The greatest threat, he told the *Monthly* magazine in May 2005, is 'a compromised process at the heart. If you believe in the need for a strong, genuinely independent public broadcaster of integrity then a fundamental part of that process has to be the integrity of the appointment of the board. It has to be free of political interference'.[54] In the week O'Brien's comments were published, the ABC appointed the Prime Minister's former senior broadcasting policy adviser, Gary Dawson, as the ABC's new manager of business strategy and government policy. He was charged with conducting a funding review (in 2004–05, the ABC received total Commonwealth funding of A$774 million) and examining changes to the cross-media laws. Dawson had spent five years in the Prime Minister's office as a press secretary and an adviser.

Since the mid-1970s, ABC staff members have had the right to elect a member of the board, and have always elected strong-willed staff, including the serving staff director, Ramona Koval, award-winning journalist Quentin Dempster and co-founder of Triple J youth radio Marius Webb. The Howard government announced in March 2006 that it would abolish the staff-elected position. Coonan suggested there had been concerns about conflict of interest and the effective running of the ABC board. Koval responded strongly: 'The position is important because it's a balance to the practice of party political stacking'.[55]

Friends of the ABC advocate a process whereby positions on the board would be publicly advertised and board members chosen from a short list developed by an independent committee. The Liberal Party shows no interest in this policy, but the Greens, Democrats and some elements within the ALP have indicated support.

Both major parties appear to support maintaining the status quo on this issue, however. During a 2004 ABC *Lateline* interview, former ALP pollster Rod Cameron said that it would be 'nice in theory' to have bipartisan support and community involvement. Former board member Michael Kroger went even further: 'I'm quite comfortable with the government of the day appointing the board members. I think the last thing the ABC needs is a patsy board who don't have strong opinions'.[56]

The *Australian* newspaper published a poll in 2001 that found that 80 per cent of Coalition voters thought the ABC was doing a good job with news and entertainment, and 50 per cent of Coalition supporters thought the ABC should receive more money. For the years 2002–04, Newspoll found that around nine in ten Australians believed that ABC news and current affairs programs were doing a good job in being fair and even handed. The Australian National University conducted a survey in 2003 that found that 66 per cent of Australians had confidence in the ABC, compared with 31 per cent for the public service, 40 per cent for the government and 33 per cent for religious institutions. This evidence proved that the vast majority of Australians do not believe the ABC to be biased.[57] Rather, ideologues with vested interests are the ones pushing an agenda.

The politicisation of the board is having an effect on the institution's integrity. The Media, Entertainment and Arts Alliance released a report in 2005 into the decline of press freedom in Australia from 2001 to 2005, in the wake of September 11.[58] Along with many examples of governmental meddling in freedom of information, the Howard government's attack on the ABC rated as one of the major concerns: 'A pattern set by the Labor party, the Liberal/National parties have stacked and politicised the ABC Board through patronage appointments'. Furthermore, as former *AM* presenter Linda Mottram wrote in the report, 'anything considered by the powerful to be too tough' can be labelled bias, including analysis of propaganda and spin, the mainstays of war briefings.

The declining independence of the media in Australia was highlighted in a global press freedom table compiled by US-based Freedom House in 2005.[59] Australia ranked thirtieth. Finland, Sweden and Iceland led the table, with New Zealand, Canada, Portugal and the USA ahead of Australia. During the Deakin Lectures in May 2005, ABC chairman Donald McDonald told the audience he was 'wounded' by the low ranking.[60] Visiting US media academic Jay Rosen explained that the survey covered many factors, including access to information, political pressure that influenced reporting, and the legal environment for the media. Online magazine *Crikey* reported that Rosen later told McDonald another reason for Australia's low ranking: political appointments to the ABC board.

Attacks on public broadcasters have undoubtedly increased in the wake of the 'war on terror', aiming to silence those who question official perspectives and to elevate views that reflect acquiescence and patriotic fervour. The ABC and SBS have not escaped these debates, nor should they. At a time when government spin has never been more furious, we need fearless journalists and executives who believe in the tried and true principle of journalistic inquisitiveness. Given the accusations and slander directed at the public broadcasters by lobbyists, Howard government ministers, Labor MPs and conservative media commentators, it is all the more remarkable that controversial programs are still made and aired. Israel–Palestine is one of the touchiest subjects in contemporary news and current affairs, and a senior producer at *Dateline* sums up the dilemma well: 'SBS would show more pro-Palestinian material if it forgot the balance criterion and applied the truth test'.

10

THE OTHER SIDE OF THE STORY

Death gives peace a chance.
Headline on a page-one report of Yasser Arafat's death, 2004[1]

SOMETIMES JEWISH COMPLAINTS about media coverage of Israel are well justified. Take press coverage of Israel's attack on Jenin in 2002. Although Human Rights Watch concluded that Israel's action in Jenin constituted 'serious violations of international humanitarian law, some amounting *prima facie* to war crimes',[2] the official death toll was much lower than first estimates suggested—52 people, some of them Palestinian fighters. In the Melbourne *Age*'s coverage, Paul McGeough unwisely drew a comparison between Jenin and Dresden at the end of World War II,[3] surely destruction on a different scale, while News Ltd's Bruce Wilson compared Jenin to the massacres in Lebanon in 1982, in which over 1500 Palestinians were killed.[4]

Yet whether it's through an absence of Palestinian perspectives, careless use of language or statistics, or the demonising of Palestinian players and interests, the news media err more often in reporting the Palestinian story than they do in covering the Israeli one. As Palestinian pressure groups are not nearly as well organised or influential as the Zionist lobby in countries such as Australia and the USA, inaccurate or unbalanced reporting that damages the Palestinian cause is much less likely to be the focus of comment.

Seeing the Palestinians

Recently a significant study by the Glasgow University Media Group found that many British television viewers had little or no understanding of the Israel–Palestine conflict.[5] When asked, 'Who occupies the occupied territories?', two-thirds of the British sample didn't know, and 15 per cent answered that it was the Palestinians. Almost 30 per cent thought the term 'settlers' referred to Palestinians, and 51 per cent did not know what it meant. The researchers discovered that Israeli spokesmen were interviewed twice as often in British television news reports. According to the authors, Greg Philo and Mike Berry, the mainstream media were not telling the public even the partial truth of the conflict: 'The fact of the military occupation and its consequences is crucial to an understanding of the rationale of Palestinian action'.

They also discovered that casualties from the two sides were reported in different terms, with a disproportionate emphasis on Israeli fatalities: 'In March 2002, when the BBC noted that the Palestinians had suffered the highest number of casualties in any single week since the beginning of the intifada, there was actually more coverage on [all British television channel] news of Israeli deaths'.[6] Words such as 'mass murder', 'atrocity' and 'brutal murder' were used when describing Israeli deaths, as opposed to the characterisation of Palestinian deaths, which were either ignored or dismissed as less important than Israelis.

A number of US-based media lobby groups, such as Fairness and Accuracy in Reporting (FAIR), campaign for greater transparency in mainstream coverage of major issues, including the Israel–Palestine conflict. FAIR was established in 1986 to counter bias and censorship in mainstream reporting. Founder Jeff Cohen appears regularly in the US media, and is a former panellist on Fox News.[7] The group has become one of the leading US groups advocating for media reform, media diversity and avoidance of partisan politics in the independent media debate. It has covered many issues over the years, from Iraq to the anti-war movement, and from Latin America to union-busting.

In 2003, a FAIR report found that the US media almost always reported Israeli deaths but rarely gave dead Palestinians the same courtesy. Journalists' references to periods of 'relative calm' generally meant that there had been few Jewish casualties. In the aftermath of one suicide bombing, the *Los Angeles Times* wrote that the bombings 'broke a six-week stretch in which the people of this war-weary land had enjoyed relative quiet'. FAIR revealed the fallacy of this statement: during this six-week period of 'relative quiet', some 17 Palestinians had actually been killed and at least 59 injured by

Israel's soldiers and settlers, according to the Palestinian Red Crescent Society. This analysis was largely ignored by the mainstream media.[8]

The USA's National Public Radio (NPR), accused by Zionist activists of being anti-Israel, was found by FAIR in 2001 to report disproportionately on the deaths of Israeli minors over Palestinian youths. A May 2005 *New York Times* report revealed that conservatives in the USA were determined to root out the station's 'liberal bias' and to conduct a study 'on whether NPR's Middle East coverage was more favourable to Arabs than to Israelis'.[9] It appears that evidence proving otherwise is irrelevant to those on an ideological crusade.

FAIR's findings are echoed in a study by the pro-Palestinian group If Americans Knew, which claimed a shocking disparity in media reporting of child fatalities in the conflict.[10] It concluded that since September 2000, the *New York Times* had reported Israeli deaths at a rate many times greater than that of Palestinian deaths. 'We found in 2004', they wrote, 'at a time when eight Israeli children and 176 Palestinian children were killed—a ratio of 1 to 22—*Times* headlines and lead paragraphs reported on Israeli children's deaths at a rate of almost seven times greater than Palestinian children's deaths'. The study also criticised the general omission of the cause of death. Palestinian children had mostly been killed by 'gunfire to the head'.[11] This report was compiled using figures obtained from Israeli human rights groups such as B'Tselem and represents a damning indictment of mainstream media negligence in the coverage of Palestinian deaths. The bias revealed in the *Times*' coverage reflects a tendency, even in so-called 'liberal' media, to downplay Israeli violence and the reality of the occupation, and to focus on the supposed irrationality and violence of the Palestinians.

The Australian news media

Anti-Palestinian bias in US and British reporting is reflected indirectly in the Australian news media, which rely heavily on overseas coverage. Many of our newspapers and television channels republish or broadcast reports, opinion pieces, news footage or documentaries from the US and British media, especially the *New York Times*, *Washington Post*, *Los Angeles Times*, ABC America, CNN, London *Times* and *Guardian*. Australian media organisations simply do not have the resources (or in some cases the desire) to compete with these foreign companies.

As in the USA and United Kingdom, the mainstream media outlook in Australia is pro-Israel, but with shades of difference. Rupert Murdoch's papers have shown longstanding loyalty to Israel, and a former editorial-page editor of his *New York Post* newspaper, Scott McConnell, recalls Murdoch telling him, 'Well, it might not have been a good idea to create it [Israel], but now that it's there, it has to be supported'.[12] It is unusual to find the *Australian* or any of his other News Limited papers varying greatly from the official Israeli and US perspective, although from time to time, some journalists, such as Bruce Wilson, have been highly critical of Israeli conduct.[13] The leading Fairfax publications, the *SMH* and the *Age* in Melbourne, have traditionally taken a centrist, though largely pro-Israel, position. Yet despite their occasional scepticism, both these papers, like the *Australian*, tend to accept the view that only heavy US intervention will resolve the conflict.

The Australian broadsheets have correspondents stationed in Israel, while the News Limited tabloids rely on wire services such as Reuters. Both Fairfax and News Limited also supplement their services with British and US coverage. Fairfax subscribes to the *New York Times*, *Washington Post* and *Guardian* wire services, which give it the broadest range of views. The London *Guardian* is perhaps the most critical English-language, mainstream Western outlet covering Israel (with the possible exception of the United Kingdom's *Independent*), while the *New York Times'* audience in its home city includes one of the largest communities within the Jewish Diaspora. Both the *New York Times* and the *Washington Post* have suffered Jewish boycotts over the years because of perceived anti-Israel bias. Supporters of Israel label the papers overly liberal, while other critics accuse them of blindly accepting official Israeli and US perspectives.

Australian journalism has a tradition of producing distinguished foreign correspondents, noted for their independence and courage, and Australian coverage from the Middle East has been no exception. In print journalism, Tony Walker, Paul McGeough and Michael Ware are internationally respected names. At the ABC, Tim Palmer and Christopher Kremmer have covered the region with distinction in recent years.[14]

The 1970s saw a revolution in Australia's attitude to the world, and the ABC led the way in documenting these vast changes. The ABC first opened its Middle East bureau in 1984, and followed with offices in Amman in 1991 and in Jerusalem in 1993. In times of international conflict, the ABC gears up its coverage significantly. At the start of the 2003 Iraq war, it had nine correspondents stationed in the region.[15]

Unlike the ABC, however, commercial television networks in Australia have retreated from in-depth coverage of the Israel–Palestine conflict, as current affairs programs have gone down the path of soft news since the mid-1990s. *60 minutes* and *Sunday* still cover the story, but it is rarely featured on *Today tonight* and *A current affair*, which mostly leave day-to-day political developments in the Middle East to the news bulletins.

The late Richard Carleton's occasional coverage of the issue on *60 minutes* prompted hostile responses from some Zionists, but the reporter noted that the Nine Network trusted him to do his job professionally. In 2004, one of his stories, 'The great divide', explored the building of the fence across the occupied territories.[16] Carleton described the fence as 'Berlin-style', and told me later that he had 'no problem using the term "illegal occupied territory", and I base that on Kofi Annan's position'.[17] His report depicted the humiliating treatment of Palestinians at Israeli checkpoints, and profiled two Jewish groups dedicated to fighting the ongoing militarisation of the Jewish state. Carleton highlighted the difficulty of being a liberal Jew in a society that resisted humanising Palestinians.

At times, Australian journalists such as Carleton, Walker, McGeough, Fairfax's Middle East correspondent Ed O'Loughlin and others have reported with remarkable independence on the unfolding story of Israel–Palestine. Yet their coverage needs to be read in the context of the mainstream Australian media, which are both pro-Israel and pro-USA. Like the Coalition parties and the ALP, the media have supported Israel's existence for more than 40 years, and for much the same reasons (see chapter 8). While the ABC in particular, with its strong contingent of overseas correspondents, provides a distinctively Australian coverage of Israel–Palestine, particularly in its radio news and current affairs, the vast majority of the coverage of Israel–Palestine carried by Australian media is produced for US or British outlets and provides perspectives likely to amplify the importance of the British or US governments in resolving the conflict.

Conditions on the ground

Some of the reasons for journalism that is biased against the Palestinians are structural and practical. Ed O'Loughlin says that discovering the real truth about the conflict is difficult because the Palestinians are poor at providing basic factual information, and the Israelis, while they have efficient information networks, 'are very quick to put out their line, but their information is sometimes unreliable'. Furthermore, security concerns in the occupied territories make access an ongoing problem, and O'Loughlin explains that Israeli soldiers have killed or crippled a number of journalists, with no punishment, during recent years and Palestinian gunmen occasionally ambush people travelling on settler-only roads.[18]

Like most Western reporters covering the conflict, O'Loughlin lives in the Israeli sector. In a report responding to criticism of the *New York Times*' coverage, public editor Daniel Okrent suggested stationing reporters in Palestinian centres. 'The *Times*, like virtually every American news organisation, maintains its bureau in West Jerusalem', he wrote:

> Its reporters and their families shop in the same markets, walk the same streets and sit in the same cafes that have long been at risk of terrorist attack. Some advocates of the Palestinian cause call this 'structural geographic bias.' ... If the reporters lived in Gaza or Ramallah, this argument goes, they would feel exposed to the daily struggles and dangers of life behind Palestinian lines and would presumably become more empathetic towards the Palestinians ... The *Times* ought to give it a try.[19]

The only Western journalist permanently based in the West Bank is *Haaretz*'s Amira Hass, who lives in Ramallah. The fact is that it's much more dangerous to live and work as a reporter in the Palestinian sector, and English isn't the primary language spoken. A 2004 report issued by non-government organisation Reporters without Borders revealed that Palestinian militants often harassed journalists working in the West Bank and Gaza, and 'dozens' of reporters continued to be threatened by both sides while trying to cover the conflict. The level of press freedom inside Israel was ranked 36th in the world, compared with that of the Palestinian territories, where 'acts of violence against the press by the Israeli army' resulting in a ranking of 115.[20]

Having spent many years reporting on the conflict, the ABC's Matthew Carney recognises the challenges of analysing both the Israeli and Palestinian perspectives. It's partly the Palestinians' own fault, he argues. They 'just can't get themselves together in presenting an effective voice to the media', partly because of a 'victimhood mentality'. The articulate, Westernised Palestinian elite were always marginalised and silenced by Yasser Arafat and his cronies. On the other hand, the Israelis have become masters of media manipulation, he says. 'Israelis assume that everyone's a threat and it doesn't matter if you come up to them with great credentials and you write for a pro-American newspaper'.

Carney tells an instructive story from the days of Operation Defensive Shield, when 'Israel re-invaded the West Bank in 2003':

You were assigned your personal IDF person who would take your mobile number ... and then would proceed to ring you, in a very friendly way ... every day, once in the morning, once in the evening, saying 'Hi, how you going? It's Lieutenant Spiegelman. What can I do for you? What story are you doing today? What do you need? Just tell me and I'll get it for you.' And you could say, 'I want a solider that was in Jenin, and I want a collaborator; can you get one?', and they'd say, 'Give me ten minutes, and I'll get it'. That's how they do it; they control it.

So if you're a lazy journalist, of whom there are a lot in the world, all you have to do is just kick back in Jerusalem. The IDF is going to ring two or three times a day, feed you information, and you don't have to go anywhere. If you're tied to daily deadlines, and particularly more for the television networks, in terms of news, this is how they control the media on that level. It was just phenomenal the organisation they put up in about three or four days. If you want to be independent ... there is a cost involved in that as well, in terms of not getting the access on the other side because you're perceived [as] not being in their good books.

One of the most effective means of media control that the Israelis use is issuing press releases after an incident and then restricting access to journalists trying to get to the location of the event, Carney says:

They [the IDF] just lie. On their press releases, if we're talking about incidents where the IDF was alleged to have killed two Palestinian boys, the first response is, 'we were responding to terrorist gunfire from an area. We have the right to self-defence. We can do this under international law'. So then if a journalist bothers to go there and actually interviews people, someone like Amira Hass from *Haaretz*, a journalist who's basically doing their job, and come back, challenge them and actually have convincing evidence, they're forced to admit it. They'll say, 'Sorry about civilian casualties but we're fighting a war on terror'. But most of the time it doesn't get to that second point, and so they have this culture where they can just spin. Most of the journalists based in Jerusalem are going to spin this Israeli line because they simply aren't bothering to go out and see these places.[21]

The language of reporting

Since September 11, much of the Western press has wittingly or unwittingly adopted the language of the Bush administration when discussing 'the march of democracy and freedom' in the Middle East. Australian media have not been immune from this.

The September 11 attacks on Washington and New York opened a new front in the information war between supporters of Israel in the West and media organisations in Australia, the USA, the United Kingdom and Europe. Neo-conservatives in the Bush administration, along with their ideological soul mates around the world, have been able to convince policy-makers and many in the general public that Israel and the USA are fighting the same battle. Long criticised for a perceived bias against the Jewish state, journalists soon found themselves the targets of vitriol if they didn't accept the new orthodoxy, namely that the USA, and indeed the West, is engaged, like Israel, in a battle against Islamic fundamentalism. Israel argued that it too had been waging a 'war on terror' for many years against Palestinian 'terrorism' and Islamic fundamentalism, and that it fully understood the USA's new situation.

In Australia, Peter Manning, a former head of ABC Television news and current affairs, conducted a study of Sydney's major newspapers, the *Daily Telegraph* and the *SMH*, for the twelve months before and after September 11, 2001, and discovered a trebling of the use of the word 'terrorist' in relation to Palestinians.[22] Manning, now an adjunct professor of journalism at the University of Technology Sydney, offered numerous examples of implicit racism against Arabs, and of the media's refusal to follow international norms when discussing the occupied territories. In particular he criticised the work of Ross Dunn, then the *SMH*'s Middle East correspondent. Dunn regularly referred to Palestinian violence as 'terrorism' but never discussed Israeli actions in these terms. He also preferred to use the more benign term 'territories', 'effectively denying the fact of occupation and the consequent illegality of the settlements'. This denial 'infects his view of the reasonability of the actions being taken'.[23]

The mainstream media's definition of 'terrorism' is a constant sore point for supporters of both sides. Daniel Okrent, recently described the *New York Times*' constant struggle when referring to the conflict, and how the paper was attacked both for using, and not using, the 'T word'. Okrent argues that the term 'terrorism' can only be applied to political acts of violence that are aimed at civilians: 'Beheading construction workers in Iraq and bombing a market in Jerusalem are terrorism pure and simple'.[24]

Yet to suggest that any and all forms of Palestinian resistance to an illegal occupation are 'terrorism' or the work of 'militants' ignores the legitimate legal rights of an oppressed people to struggle for their independence. As Manning suggests, '"Terrorism" is accepted as a defining term for Palestinian resistance, whereas an [Israeli] "military campaign" has legitimacy'.

AIJAC argues that the mainstream media selectively use the word 'terrorist' and refuse to label Hamas and Islamic Jihad as 'terrorists'. It seems that AIJAC *Review* editor Tzvi Fleischer believes a journalist should label any individual or group that violently challenges the West as 'terrorist', and the circumstances of the action—even those of legal resistance to occupation—must be ignored. For example, Fleischer was incensed after the death of Yasser Arafat in November 2004 that the mainstream media didn't focus solely on the PLO leader's involvement with 'terrorism', rather than his other life achievements. 'It is a blind spot that is rooted in an ideology that denies there is any such thing as terrorism', he wrote.[25] In this view, Israelis, and Westerners in general, never commit terrorism; only Arabs and Palestinians do.

Such battles over language are having a detrimental effect on accurate reporting of the conflict. In 2001 the BBC ordered its reporters to use the expression 'targeted killings' (of Palestinians) rather than the more neutral term 'assassinations', a direct result of Zionist group pressure and a description used by the Israelis themselves.

Former BBC Middle East correspondent Tim Llewellyn is a frequent critic of the broadcaster's coverage.[26] He argues that the BBC is nervous about its own future as an institution, especially after recent Blair government accusations of bias, and is therefore more likely to 'confuse occupier with occupied'. Llewellyn suggests that the Israelis received negative press around the world during the invasion of Lebanon and first Palestinian intifada, and when the second intifada started in 2000, the public weren't quite sure who started what. 'The Israelis were very quick to capitalise on the Palestinians' lack of communications', he says. 'It was very easy for the Israelis to make it look as if the Palestinians had started the violence.' Llewellyn says the BBC is adopting what it sees as an even-handed attitude, while ignoring the reality that 'the Palestinians are occupied and are fighting for independence'. He believes that if the story was happening in the Balkans or Africa, the BBC would be reporting it very differently. Israeli pressure, coupled with charges of antisemitism if the story is reported fairly, along with the 'emotive quality to the Jewish fate in European society', results in a muted national broadcaster, according to Llewellyn.

Robert Fisk revealed in 2001 that CNN, after constant lobbying by pro-settler groups, stopped referring to Gilo as a 'Jewish settlement', instead calling it a 'Jewish neighbourhood'.[27] The fact that Gilo is a Jewish suburb illegally occupying land outside Jerusalem mattered little. A CNN journalist told Fisk at the time that 'there's a feeling by some people here that what we're doing is searching for euphemisms for what is really happening'.

According to FAIR,

[US] network news shows have characterised Israeli violence as 'retaliation' almost nine times more often than Palestinian violence. This disparity is meaningful. The term 'retaliation' suggests a defensive stance undertaken in response to someone else's aggression. It also lays responsibility for the cycle of violence at the doorstep of the party being 'retaliated' against, since they presumably initiated the conflict.[28]

This inherent bias against the Palestinians, and the journalistic belief that the Israelis are fighting a war inflicted upon them, rather than of their choosing, is critical to how the public views the conflict.

The result of these encroaching dishonesties is the ongoing inability of a Western readership to understand the realities of settlement expansion in the West Bank or the killing of civilians when 'targeted killings' occur. 'A Palestinian shoots at a settlement, we denounce it as mindless but we know why—because they are on his land. But if he shoots at a "neighbourhood" he is a mindless "terrorist" because there is no reason to shoot at a "neighbourhood"', says Fisk.[29]

Meanwhile, back at the ranch

While journalists in Israel are deciding how to report the latest act of violence, back in the office editors and senior news executives are often under siege in relation to the presentation of news about the Israel–Palestine conflict. This pressure comes from several sources. Sometimes it's official pressure from Israel itself.

In early 2005, the BBC bowed to an Israeli demand for a written apology from its deputy bureau head in Jerusalem, Simon Wilson, over his failure to submit for censorship an interview with nuclear whistleblower Mordechai Vanunu. A number of BBC journalists expressed concern at the climb-down. After all, when are the media in a democracy required to submit articles to a foreign government for censorship before publishing them? Wilson had already been banned from Israel after his report appeared.[30] According to the *Guardian*, 'the agreement was to have remained confidential, but the BBC unintentionally posted details on its website before removing them a few hours later'.

Sometimes, as we saw in the previous chapter in the story of AIJAC's attack on the ABC and SBS, the pressure comes from well-established Zionist groups that have a long history and a credible public profile. Radio broadcaster and newspaper columnist Terry Lane has suffered at the hands of the Zionist lobby. He tells me he was strongly pro-Israel in the years after the Holocaust and was even invited to speak at events in the 1970s organised by WIZO, the Women's International Zionist Organisation. By the 1980s, however, he became the target of vitriol from prominent Jews, including Michael Danby and leading Melbourne Rabbi John Levi. His crime was simply to start questioning the actions of the Jewish state. 'Any criticism of Israel is interpreted as anti-Semitism', he says.[31]

In the 1980s, while working for ABC Radio in Melbourne, Lane announced that he would no longer publicly discuss Israel and the Middle East. He had received 'so many vicious and menacing letters' and been subject to 'harassment, vilification, threats and abuse'. The Zionist lobby, he wrote, were 'malicious, implacable, mendacious and danger-ous'.[32] He expressed dismay that as soon as the expression 'anti-Semite' is uttered, 'or, heaven forbid, the sacred formula "six million" ... then I know from bitter experience that there is not one manager or editor in the country who will defend an underling. We are thrown to the jack-als'. He concluded: 'In the end, the truly tolerant have no defence against intolerance. I surrender. To the Zionists I say: you win. To the Palestinians: forgive my cowardice'.

AIJAC not only lobbies media directly, but for 15 years, it has also sent Australian journalists on information tours to Israel. Its Rambam pro-gram—named after twelfth-century Jewish sage Maimonides/Rambam—is designed, in the words of its Sydney-based founder Brian Sherman, to 'lift the veil' on Israel for opinion-makers whose knowledge of the Israel–Palestine issue 'is formed by day to day reports in the media where Israel is largely seen as an occupying force'. Since 2003, around 120 fellows have participated in the program, including unionists, ALP and Liberal MPs, political advisers, journalists and editors. The journalists include: Herald & Weekly Times editor-in-chief Peter Blunden and journalist John Ferguson; the *Australian Financial Review*'s Ben Potter and Robert Bolton; chief editorial writer for the *Age*, John Watson; the *Courier-Mail*'s Dennis Atkins; SBS's Sally Watson, the *SMH*'s Louise Dodson; and Channel Ten's

John Hill. The impact that his participation had on the *Australian*'s Cameron Stewart was evident on his return:

> There is nothing like seeing and getting a better understanding of the geography of Israel and its borders. It took all of three minutes to fly [by helicopter] to the security border and I think it gives a very good example of the security issues that Israel faces. It was a really fascinating time to be there because there were so many changes. While we were there, there were lots of political defections. There was a suicide bombing in Netanya and some rocket attacks.[33]

The week-long program includes meetings with prominent Israeli politicians, a tour of the separation fence, brief meetings with Palestinian leaders in Ramallah and a host of other conservative individuals inevitably speaking from the same song sheet, including former Israeli prime ministers Ehud Barak and Binyamin Netanyahu.[34]

Besides groups such as AIJAC and its US equivalent AIPAC, other Jewish activists are increasingly engaged in media monitoring, contacting journalists and editors and complaining of bias. Several senior journalists in Australia have told me how they have been bombarded with acerbic messages from HonestReporting, a group of self-appointed 'media patrollers', which started in the USA but now has a following in Australia. HonestReporting enlists the public in what it calls Israel's 'media war'. Its website says:

> In news outlets around the globe, journalists regularly misrepresent Israel as the aggressor and Palestinians as the victims. In response, HonestReporting was established to scrutinize the media for anti-Israel bias, then mobilize subscribers to respond directly to relevant news agencies.[35]

Tony Parkinson, a former *Age* journalist, noted for his conservative commentary, experienced the wrath of HonestReporting letter-writers in 2004, who claimed he had compared Israel's murder of Hamas spiritual leader Sheik Ahmed Yassin to the 1985 Palestinian killing of American tourist Leon Klinghoffer on the hijacked *Achille Lauro* cruise ship. Parkinson had done nothing of the sort, and he bit back. The group practised 'rank distortion', he said in an email to the group's Michael Weinstein. 'I have been deluged with some of the most poisonous and vituperative personal attacks experienced in my 25 years in the profession, based entirely on blind acceptance of your scurrilous assertions ... Why don't you go the full distance, and start calling yourself the ministry of truth?'

HonestReporting has also accused *60 minutes* journalist Richard Carleton of 'anti-Israel' bias. In 2001, Carleton dared to try to get inside the mind of a Palestinian suicide bomber and to challenge Israel's policy of pre-emptive military strikes against Palestinian 'terrorists'. The Zionist lobbyists fumed that, 'predictably, *60 Minutes* allows a Palestinian to get in the final word'.[36]

HonestReporting and CAMERA have become virulent and influential Zionist groups affecting media coverage. And while it's hard to gauge the impact they have on news coverage, journalists tell me that it feels like the groups are trying to wear them down so that they will accept a Zionist agenda. CAMERA claims to 'take no position with regard to American or Israeli political issues or with regard to ultimate solutions to the Arab–Israeli conflict' but is in practice completely opposed to any mainstream criticism of Israel. Its tactics include monitoring print and television reports, as well as examples of 'propagandistic assaults on Israel' on university campuses. The group detects bias in virtually every media organisation in the USA. It claims to have 55 000 members and thousands of active letter-writers. During a 2002 CNN program on media coverage of the conflict, CAMERA's executive director, Andrea Levin, argued that while 'we wouldn't say that the entire mass media is anti-Israel', she couldn't find one instance where criticism of Israel was justified.

Australia has its own homegrown version of these organisations—the Media Study Group, which in 2003 released a report analysing 66 articles from the *Age*, including their headlines and photos.[37] Of the headlines studied, the following results were recorded: '0.0% violations were neutral. 1.5% was anti-Arab. 31.8% were anti-Israel. 66.7% contained no violations'. The findings slammed the paper for 'not adhering to required journalistic standards' and criticised its reporting as 'consistently and overwhelmingly one-sided'. Though the study suggests that it 'does not seek to discern whether one party to the conflict is more "right", or to argue the case for one side or the other', any criticism of Israel is deemed to be biased. The study claims to be impartial but uses criteria developed by HonestReporting.

Matters of fact were challenged: using words such as 'occupation', 'settlement' and 'occupied Palestinian territories' were regarded as signs of bias, and more 'neutral' words were suggested. When an *Age* journalist referred to 'the harshness of Sharon's rhetoric' in relation to Israel's actions against Palestinian militant groups, the report objected to such a description of Sharon's language: 'The reporter does not give the context that in the war against terrorism, Mr Bush, Mr Blair and other Western leaders have said no less'. Including such references to other leaders' comments during a news story would be inappropriate and irrelevant, but their omission from the *Age* article was, for the Media Study Group, indicative of the paper's anti-Israel bias. One headline read, 'Israeli land grab tests peace plan'. The report responded: 'This headline seems to lay blame for threatening peace on one side, ignoring significant breaches from the other side'. Implicit in such analysis is the notion that the Israeli actions were justifiable (despite international law and UN resolutions forbidding the behaviour) because of some unspecified Palestinian activity.

The *Age*'s editor, Michael Gawenda, dismissed the findings—initially sent anonymously to him—as a waste of time and as 'incredibly naïve'.[38] The people responsible for the project are not listed on its website. When its authors presented the report at the *Age* office in the Canberra press gallery, they refused to give their names and threatened the *SMH* that it might be next.[39] There were no names on the report, they said, 'because if names are on something people discount it because of who wrote it'. They also asked *Age* journalist Mark Forbes whether the Fairfax Middle East correspondent, Ed O'Loughlin, worked in the Canberra bureau. The authors clearly didn't realise that O'Loughlin was based in Jerusalem.[40]

The impact of these groups varies. For many journalists and editors, dealing with campaigns against 'bias' is time-consuming and certainly gets in the way of doing their jobs. For public broadcasters, such as the ABC and SBS, management is more likely to react positively to complaints and to institute change. Zionist lobbyists are very successful in maintaining constant pressure, as well as engaging allies in the political sphere. The political climate since September 11 has already forced journalists to defend stories that portray the 'other side'. Zionist lobbying and the so-called 'war on terror' have only increased the pressure to conform.

In Australia particularly, but also in the USA, the Palestinian media lobby is weak by comparison. There are no Palestinian equivalents to the Rambam program. Head of the General Palestinian Delegation in Australia, Ali Kazak, regularly complains to journalists and editors about anti-Palestinian bias but says he doesn't have the funds to mount effective lobbying campaigns like AIJAC. His articles and letters occasionally appear in leading papers, but he's routinely ignored by editors. In one letter—obtained through my FOI application regarding communication between SBS management and Middle East lobbyists in 2001–03—Kazak demanded that the channel's news service refer to Israel's 'security barrier' as 'Israel's colonialist apartheid wall'. This suggestion was as inappropriate and biased as anything AIJAC would suggest. However, Kazak has little or no political influence and can therefore simply be dismissed by media executives. The Australian Arabic Council and a handful of other similar groups also lobby the mainstream media to display less anti-Arab and anti-Muslim bias, especially since September 11, though a lack of funds and organisation hampers effectiveness.

In the USA, the Washington-based Arab-American Institute, headed by Dr James Zogby, has close ties to the Democrats and to Palestinian groups. Zogby's opinions occasionally appear in the mainstream media. The Electronic Intifada is also gaining prominence. Launched in 2001, the group aims to 'provide a needed supplement to mainstream commercial media representations of the Israeli–Palestinian conflict'. It is regularly contacted by the BBC, CBC, CNN and various radio stations around the world, and offers an Arab or Palestinian perspective on the conflict.

Antisemitism and the Western press as 'other'

Unbalanced or egregiously inaccurate reporting of Israel is not necessarily antisemitic reporting. Yet the two often seem to be conflated in complaints about coverage of Israel. The main contention is that by highlighting Israel's supposed transgressions, the media isolate Israel in the mind of world public opinion. This leads Jews to conclude that antisemitism is behind the criticisms. The argument leaves little room for serious discussion of Israel's responsibility for provoking Palestinian resistance or the need to examine its oppressive role in the occupation.

Although the vast majority of Israeli mainstream media is strongly pro-government, internal dissent is often tolerated because it comes from within. Criticism of the Israeli government occurs within Israel often at the most unexpected times. During the prime ministership of Binyamin Netanyahu in the mid-1990s, and with violence rising in the territories, even some of his most ardent media supporters criticised the leader for being too brutal. Mass circulation *Ma'ariv* said in 1996 that 'it is difficult to free ourselves from the sensation that we brought this down upon themselves: too many promises unfulfilled, too much forceful talk and too little talk of the hopes of the manifestation of the peace process'.[41] The same sentiment is unlikely to have appeared in the pages of the *AJN*, though the paper's editorial position is certainly not as extreme as that of AIJAC, and may have even slightly mellowed in recent years.

In Australia, far from Israel, it is possible to dismiss critics or dissenters as being far removed from Israeli realities. *Age* journalist David Bernstein argues that Jewish readers are more concerned with what is said and how it's said than with worrying about Australia's overarching policy towards the Jewish state. In other words, there is heightened Jewish sensitivity to media reporting of Israel. Bernstein believes that the large Melbourne Jewish community (the biggest in Australia) is still 'living under the shadow of the Holocaust, and this affects the way they see themselves and the state of Israel. They are very neurotic and should be treated with sympathy'. He says that 'when you actually engage in debate, they're so paranoid and insecure about Israel and the state of Jews, any [media] criticism is seen as an attack on their own essence and [as] displaying antisemitism'. Bernstein feels that, rather than condemning them, 'they should be helped. It's a community that in some ways is sick'. Although the Australian Jewish community is secure in its position within Australia, Bernstein says that they are 'neurotic about the Arabs wanting to destroy Israel if they had the capability and concerned about Israel's long-term viability'.

Bernstein suggests that part of this neurosis reflects their own guilt about Israel:

> People choose not to live there—they live here—and they feel guilty about not living there, and they get caught up in another guilt cycle. They love Israel but not enough to live there. Writer A B Yehoshua always used to say that a Diaspora Jew is neurotic by definition.[42]

Bernstein touches on a central issue in the widespread Jewish response to perceived anti-Israel bias in the media. The Holocaust remains the primary justification and the shield behind which supporters of Israel stand. We are constantly told of Israel's precarious position in the Middle East, surrounded by hostile Arab states. The fact that Israel is the largest recipient of US foreign aid, and is widely regarded as the world's fifth strongest military power, with its arsenal of nuclear weapons, is routinely ignored. The Holocaust 'effect' legitimises Israel's behaviour by silencing critics who don't wish to be regarded as anti-Jewish, anti-Zionist or antisemitic. In Australia, where the profile of the news media is still predominantly Anglo, there is a particular logic to this view, since the media are not part of the Jewish experience. And as we saw above, even in the rare instances where journalists or editors are Jewish (such as Michael Gawenda, a former editor of the *Age*), they are not immune from attack.

Western news values bring added complexity to the debate. Australian journalism is empirical in its methodology; it relies on verification of facts, and places a high value on the credibility of news. It therefore relies partly on journalists' past experience and their instincts about what is valuable or true, as well as a sense of what editors and readers can relate to. Not surprisingly, therefore, Western media organisations principally republish English-language sources and seem reluctant to translate from the vast array of 'world' media. Sources such as the *New York Times*, *Washington Post*, London *Times* and *Guardian* are regularly sourced and reproduced, not only because over time they have developed a reputation for credibility, but also because they seem to be 'like us'. This value system also often extends to the opinion pages. The public editor of the *Chicago Tribune*, Don Wycliff, recently commented that his paper 'features no columnist who can be depended upon to routinely explain and defend Palestinian actions and attitudes as, say, Charles Krauthammer defends Israel's. So on probably the most enduring and insistent foreign policy issue of our time, we routinely do not hear from the other side'.[43] It was a startling but refreshing admission from one of the USA's major dailies.

The effect of this one-sided coverage, however, is detrimental to a broader understanding of the conflict. The lack of Arab or Palestinian sources—and greater suspicion towards them—leads to a skewed perspective, and means debate continues to follow the same old paths. Why are two of Israel's finest reporters on the occupation, Gideon Levy and Amira Hass, never published or interviewed in Australia? Neither journalist has a profile here—despite being successful and controversial within Israel—and Western news editors are probably reluctant to republish work that seems 'exotic' or 'foreign'. And why do they not have a profile here? Because they have not been published here before!

Hass wrote in *Haaretz* in March 2005 on the opening of a new exhibit at Jerusalem's Holocaust Museum, Yad Vashem.[44] She bravely reminded the assembled world leaders that their mere presence in Israel offered support for Ariel Sharon's policies, whether they liked them or not. Let the 'entire diplomatic throng' remember the Shoah on its own territory, Hass said, not in Israel. 'Which of the participants in the ceremony will go to see the roads for Jews only and for Palestinians only', she wrote. 'Will any of them protest the laws discriminating against Israeli citizens, only because they are non-Jews—Arabs—and threaten to impose sanctions unless these laws are revoked?' Hass argued that Israel and its supporters are using the Holocaust to ward off criticism and are continuing to avoid serious discussion about a society 'with built-in discrimination on the basis of nationality'.

Noam Chomsky cautions against overly praising the Palestinian leadership, however. '[Yasser] Arafat and the rest of them would show up here [in the USA] shouting Marxist slogans, pretending to be revolutionaries', he tells me:

> They were just corrupt Third World nationalists who liked to run around, collect their own wares and rob everybody. When 90 per cent of the population is poor, you simply couldn't do that. They had to pretend to be living a global revolution. They're probably the worst national institution of any Third World in history. I've never seen anything like them.[45]

Putting a human face to the Palestinian people and explicitly saying that Israeli policy is immoral should be acceptable in a democratic news media. Why is it controversial to advocate Palestinian human rights and an independent homeland? After all, the Jews already have Israel. Edward Said reminded the world shortly before his death in 2003 that it was far easier for the West to demonise the Palestinian or Arab 'other'—through 'the vicious media and government campaign against Arab society, culture, history and mentality'—than actually attempt to humanise what they don't fully understand.[46]

The death of Yasser Arafat

As a study of misunderstood 'otherness', it is hard to go past Australian press coverage of Yasser Arafat's final illness, and his death on 11 November 2004. The coverage was voluminous, starting in late October and running for at least a month. But while the Australian media uniformly agreed that the passing of such a significant figure warranted extensive coverage, Palestinian voices were few. Instead Western commentators pontificated on the newfound chance for peace, almost all agreeing that the removal of Arafat would help Israelis and Palestinians move closer to a settlement.

John Howard set the tone with his widely reported comment in a radio interview before Arafat's death was announced:

> I think history will judge him very harshly for not having seized
> the opportunity in the year 2000 to embrace the offer that was

courageously made by the then Israeli Prime Minister Ehud
Barak, which involved the Israelis agreeing to about 90 per cent
of what the Palestinians had wanted.[47]

As the Palestinian Foreign Affairs Minister, Nabil Shaath, commented,
in a story carried by the *SMH*, 'There seems to be a problem of empathy, or lack of it. I mean, he [Howard] is probably the only leader in the
world who actually demonised President Arafat after his death, something
that not even the Israelis have done, or the Americans'.[48] Ali Kazak also
remonstrated. Arafat was a 'kind leader', he said, accusing the Australian
government of repeated bias towards Israel.[49]

Arafat led a contradictory life. Born in Jerusalem in 1929—or Cairo,
the facts are disputed—he believed that the only way for Palestinians to
gain independence was through the support of Arab governments. He
founded Fatah in the late 1950s, and the group was initially dedicated
to the destruction of Israel and the establishment of a Palestinian state.
Over the following decades, he lived in Jordan, Lebanon and Tunisia,
before finally being allowed into the West Bank town of Ramallah. By the
mid-1970s, despite supporting acts of terror against Western targets, he
had directly contributed to growing international recognition of the
Palestinian cause. Although his political stance became more moderate
over the years, he was never trusted by the USA or Israel, even after
renouncing violence against Israeli civilians.

There were two themes in the coverage of his death: the first concerned Arafat as an obstacle to peace, the second his very legitimacy as
a leader. The *West Australian*'s editorial on the day after Arafat's death
raised both issues in characteristically blunt terms. The Palestinian would
'not be much mourned in the Western world', the paper wrote, as he was
'widely regarded as an obstruction to peace'. Its hyperbole continued:
'The former guerrilla is most closely associated in Western minds with
the blight of terrorism in the Middle East'.[50]

The *Australian* was predictably negative in its assessment of Arafat's
life. Foreign editor Greg Sheridan described the PLO leader as 'the icon
of Palestinian victimhood'.[51] Leanne Piggott, a lecturer in Middle East
politics at the University of Sydney, also painted a negative picture of
Arafat. He 'never really made the transition from independence fight-
terrorist to nation-builder', she wrote on the opinion page.[52] Nicolas
Rothwell wrote that George W Bush was 'an overt proponent of an
independent Palestine' and that Israel was 'a fellow-victim in the war on
terror'. While hoping that the USA would re-engage deeply in the

conflict, Rothwell seemed indifferent to the occupation and the plight of the Palestinian people. Israel's 'place in the Middle Eastern map remains parlous', the reporter said. The paper's editorial was in no doubt that Arafat 'was a big part of the Middle East problem' and believed his passing 'might mean the two sides can start seriously searching for a solution'.[53]

The *SMH*'s coverage, beginning with the page-one headline 'Palestinians mourn passing of an era', was more measured. Middle East correspondent Ed O'Loughlin, reporting from Ramallah, called the PLO leader 'a former guerrilla fighter' and quoted the common Palestinian mantra 'You are in our hearts, our souls . . . You are our father'.[54] The paper dedicated three pages to the death (its sister publication, the *Age*, featured less than two), reported reactions from around the world and sourced the vast majority of news stories from the US and British press. No analysis was printed from the Arab, Israeli or Palestinian media. President George W Bush was quoted as saying that it was a 'significant moment' for the Palestinians in their search for an independent state. Once again, it seemed it was the Palestinians who needed to prove their worthiness and their seriousness about peace, not the Israelis.

The media objected to Arafat's support for Saddam Hussein in the first Gulf War, and to his history as a guerrilla fighter. The PLO chief was a guerrilla leader in the traditional sense of the word—a believer in fighting a stronger opponent with low-intensity confrontation. He had little choice but to engage in political negotiations in the hope of convincing the Israelis that their occupation was unsustainable in the long term. But at the crux of the media's criticism was Arafat's refusal to accept the 2000 peace deal— the '97 per cent', as the *Australian*'s Greg Sheridan said, of West Bank and Gaza offered to the Palestinians at Camp David.[55] At the heart of this analysis was a refusal to recognise the flaws in the offer from the Palestinian perspective, and to blame Arafat and the Palestinians instead. This view was expressed in racist terms by Ted Lapkin from AIJAC, writing in the *Australian Financial Review* three days after Arafat's death: 'Palestinians are world class rememberers, to the point where they either do not recall things as they happened, or they recollect things that never happened at all'. Lapkin's distaste for the Palestinian people, and indeed the whole Arab world, was palpable. It is inconceivable that his statement could have been published in Australia if it had been made about Jews or Israelis, but this form of anti-Arab sentiment has become acceptable: 'For Palestinians, [the] fundamental unwillingness to admit reality and accept compromise has yielded disaster, defeat and dispossession'. It is the Palestinians' fault that they are without an independent state, Lapkin argued, and continued Israeli expansion into occupied territory is best explained by blaming the Palestinians.[56]

The *SMH*'s editorial, while saying history would judge Arafat harshly for not embracing 'the arduous compromises for peace', at least understood that Arafat and Sharon 'used each other as an excuse to walk away from the negotiating table'.[57] The paper encouraged the USA to 'renew pressure on Israel', although neglected to acknowledge the historically one-sided approach of successive US administrations. The *Age* followed the same line, claiming that in Arafat's 'declining years he had become an impediment rather than an aide to peace'.[58] It argued that Palestinians, if 'they truly want to honour the memory of Mr Arafat . . . must move beyond terrorism as a means to achieve an end', and only then will peace be achieved.

The *Herald Sun* published one of the few pieces by a Palestinian Australian, addressing the question of the failed 2000 talks. Taimor Hazou explained the allure of Arafat and his stature as leader of the Palestinian people. 'No Palestinian leader could have accepted Camp David', he wrote. 'No Palestinian will ever accept a non-contiguous state without East Jerusalem as capital and an adequate response to the right of return.' He expressed the feelings of many in the Arab world when he wrote, 'For Israel and America to talk about finding a "serious peacemaker" is not only a slight on Arafat but on the Palestinian people and their right to choose their own path'.[59] A few days later, *Herald Sun* hard man Andrew Bolt weighed in to redress the balance: 'There is a sickness in Palestinian culture—and an anarchy in its government—that makes talk of peace with its people seem as grounded as the sweet dreams of a sleepwalker in a crowded minefield'.[60]

Did Arafat give peace a chance?

Understanding what really happened at the 2000 peace talks is critical to assessing the coverage of Arafat's death. At Camp David, the Palestinian leader was to meet US President Bill Clinton and be offered, in the words of chief US peace negotiator Dennis Ross, a chance to 'end this conflict' by accepting the offer on the table.[61] Ross claims that Arafat was given sole responsibility for solving the impasse between the Israelis and Palestinians. Arafat was allegedly offered a Palestinian state comprising all of Gaza and nearly all of the West Bank; a capital in Arab East Jerusalem; security arrangements negotiated with international forces; and a right of return for Palestinian refugees to their own state, but not into Israel. Israeli Prime Minister Ehud Barak had accepted these terms, and Clinton had supported them, Ross claims, so it was left to Arafat to abandon fundamental 'historic myths'.

Official history records Arafat's rejection of the offer, the subsequent outbreak of the second intifada, and an ongoing blame game until the PLO leader's death in 2004. The reality is far murkier, however. Two prominent participants—Robert Malley, a member of the US peace team at Camp David, and Hussein Agha, a participant in Palestinian affairs—have rightly stated that

> we often hear about Ehud Barak's unprecedented offer and Yasser Arafat's uncompromising no. Israel is said to have made a historic, generous proposal, which the Palestinians, once again seizing the opportunity to miss an opportunity, turned down. In short, the failure to reach a final agreement is attributed, without notable dissent, to Yasser Arafat.[62]

The Israelis have used the failure of the talks to justify years of aggression and intransigence.

It seems that the underlying Israeli belief—largely shared in the Western media—is that the Palestinians are a barbaric people who have refused successive Israeli offers of peace. Barak claimed in 2000 that he had not 'yet managed to understand from Arafat that he is willing to acknowledge the existence of the state of Israel'.[63] The 1993 Oslo Accords, though, proved that the Palestinians were in fact serious about peace. They had, by agreeing to a two-state solution, given up almost 80 per cent of historical Palestine,[64] and despite years of ongoing settlement expansion, checkpoints and military incursions, many leading Palestinians still called for cooperation with Israel. The mainstream Israeli position was that the occupation would soon cease and a Palestinian state would be formed. The government, however, had no intention of dismantling settlements, and instead accelerated construction.

Although the world has generally accepting the Israeli perspective on the Camp David breakdown, Malley, who took copious notes during the proceedings—and says that virtually no official documentation exists to prove Barak's 'generosity'—concludes that the Palestinians had been rightly cautious in their dealings. He revealed that Israel's offer was in fact conditional on the Palestinians accepting a non-contiguous state with de facto Israeli control. 'No other Arab party that has negotiated with Israel—not Anwar el-Sadat's Egypt, not King Hussein's Jordan, let alone Hafez al-Assad's Syria—ever came close to even considering such compromises', Malley argues.[65]

With full US support, Barak wanted to annex massive settlement blocs in the West Bank without offering full legal rights to the annexed Palestinian residents. He had no concrete list of settlements to be evacuated,[66] and intended to maintain settlements throughout the West Bank and Gaza, making a contiguous Palestinian state impossible. He was not offering East Jerusalem as the capital of any future Palestinian state, but rather the adjacent town of Abu-Dis. Israeli commentator Tanya Reinhart reveals the 'verbal trickery' largely ignored by the world.[67] The area known as 'Al'Quds'—the Arab name of Jerusalem—would be used to describe Abu-Dis. The reason for this was laid out in a 1995 document known as the Beilin-Abu Mazen understandings, and subsequently used by Barak.[68] The document stated, 'Israel will recognise that the [portion of the] area defined as 'Al-Quds' prior to the six days war which exceeds the area annexed to Israel in 1967 will be the capital of the Palestinian state'. Reinhart explains that 'the municipal borders of Jerusalem, under Jordanian rule, were broader on the southeast side than the municipal borders defined by Israel when it annexed East Jerusalem' and included the town of Abu-Dis.[69] Furthermore, Barak proposed that Palestinian residents of East Jerusalem would be the sole responsibility of the Palestinian government, despite their land remaining under Israeli sovereignty.

The Palestinian right of return was always going to be a crucial component of any lasting peace deal. Israel had no intention of allowing an influx of Palestinians into Israel as it wanted to maintain a Jewish majority, so it demanded that the international community solve the problem. Underlying the Israeli and US offer, there was no concession that Israel had been responsible for creating Palestinian suffering in the first place, a central demand of Arafat.

Ultimately, Arafat refused the offers on the table because they were too vague and didn't appreciate the requirements of the Palestinian people. The USA hoped to bring the parties together, but was never an honest broker and always preferred Israeli terms. Barak hoped the Palestinians would accept Israel's rules, then dared to suggest that Arafat was incapable of accepting the existence of the Jewish state. All should share blame, but the power imbalance of the negotiations—the Palestinians had already agreed to give up much of their historical homeland—almost guaranteed a disappointing outcome.

It is true that there was some exceptional reporting and commentary during the Arafat saga, not least from the ABC. Radio National's *AM* featured an interview on 12 November with Hassan Khreishah, elected as speaker of the Palestinian parliament. Journalist Mark Willacy asked Kreishah how he imagined a future Palestinian state. 'Eastern Jerusalem will be the capital of our state', he said, expressing a Palestinian wish rarely discussed at that time. By 15 November, Willacy had gained an interview with Abu Mahmoud, the top commander of the militant Al-Aqsa Martyrs Brigades in the West Bank town of Nablus. Abu Mahmoud warned of a future struggle against more moderate personalities within the Palestinian leadership, including Mahmoud Abbas. This was an important story. No other Australian journalist covering Arafat's death had travelled further into the West Bank than Ramallah.

Yet, overall, the coverage left me with questions:

- Why was Arafat's rejection of the 2000 peace deal rarely presented as anything other than a refusal to accept peace?
- Why was there such an incomplete and inaccurate media understanding of what was offered by Israel in 2000?
- Why were there so few local Palestinian voices heard in the Australian coverage?
- Why do the Australian media run so many overseas reports, but rarely carry perspectives from the Arab or left-wing Israeli press?
- Why do the Australian media seem to accept the argument that the USA will be a central and constructive participant in any future peace talks? After all, from 1990 to 2000, the US provided military aid to Israel worth more than US$18 billion. Since 1993, the Palestinians have received US$1.7 billion in US economic assistance via USAID projects. It's hardly the record of a neutral broker!

The coverage of the Camp David negotiations was another example of how we are generally ill served by our media's reporting of the Israel–Palestine conflict. The predominance of Israeli and US perspectives means that the Palestinian narrative and motivation remain murky. This, of course, suits certain agendas but does not contribute to a balanced view of the competing histories. As this chapter observes, there are several reasons, including a tendency for the media to accept and validate whatever perspective is favoured in the corridors of Washington, London or Canberra. Fine journalists have spent time in both Palestine and Israel, and have listened to both peoples to gain a fuller understanding of the conflict, but far too many prefer to portray Israel as the most aggrieved party.

'In much of the Western world', wrote Robert Fisk in 2002, 'a vicious campaign of slander is being waged against any journalist or activist who dares criticise Israeli policies or those that shape them'.[70] In March 2006, he concluded that the situation had only worsened in recent years. 'You've got to fight', he wrote. 'It's the only conclusion I can draw as I see the renewed erosion of our freedom to discuss the Middle East'.[71] It is simply an attempt to shut us up. It must not succeed.

CONCLUSION: WHERE TO NEXT?

*That is the real question of Israel's existence: whether it can
exist as a state like all others, or must always be above the
constraints and duties of all other states in the world today.
The record is not reassuring.*

Edward Said, 2002[1]

*My friends in Israel say there is a need for two or three states in
Israel: one for the religious, one for the secular and one for the
in-between.*

Alex Dafner, Melbourne Jew[2]

WHEN JEWISH HOLLYWOOD film-maker Steven Spielberg released *Munich*
in late 2005, it was greeted with unprecedented venom within certain segments of the Diaspora. The film details the aftermath of the 1972 Munich
Olympics massacre, in which Israeli athletes were abducted and murdered, and the Mossad's attempts to kill the responsible Palestinian terrorists. As the mission continues, however, the agents start to question
the morality of their actions.

Alan Dershowitz was upset that the Oscar-winner hadn't defended
Israel's 'counter-terrorism' methods.[3] The *Washington Post*'s Charles
Krauthammer was annoyed that Spielberg had even dared to humanise
the Palestinian struggle.[4] Spielberg seemed stunned by the reaction and
said that 'many fundamentalists' within the Jewish community were angry
with him 'for allowing the Palestinians simply to have a dialogue'.[5]
Pulitzer-prize-winning screenwriter Tony Kushner, defending the film in

a backhanded way, observed that there was a desperate need 'in the shock and awe era' to 'understand the enemy'.[6]

It was a sadly typical case of Jewish paranoia. Spielberg is a deeply committed Zionist, but that wasn't enough to satisfy critics who claimed he was indulging in dangerous moral equivalence.[7] In many ways, the reaction to *Munich* represents a useful distillation of the issues raised in this book, and particularly the profound difficulties that inevitably arise when Zionism and its modern manifestation are questioned. Anybody seriously contemplating undertaking a critical examination of Israel, the Palestinians and the Western role in the Middle East can expect to be called antisemitic and anti-Western.

The agenda

Anti-Zionism and antisemitism are not the same thing, however much Zionists might insist that they are. An anti-Zionist can be an antisemite, but the two are not necessarily related. Dr Antony Lerman, director of the Institute for Jewish Policy Research in London, argues that even denying Israel's right to exist isn't by definition antisemitic. 'Not everything negative that happens to a Jew is anti-Semitism', he says.[8] He claims that Diaspora communities are deliberately inflating the antisemitic threat in an attempt to generate sympathy for Israel and its fight against Palestinian 'terrorism'. The 'new antisemitism' is a fabricated fiction, according to Lerman, and a 'just solution to the Palestinian problem' would considerably assist in defusing tensions. When the Jewish community labels any criticism of the Jewish state as treasonous and antisemitic, the labels lose their meaning and real antisemitism may be missed.[9]

It is ironic that Western governments and the vast majority of the Western media elite solidly support Israel and its 'security' measures against the Palestinians, yet Zionist lobbyists still argue that only complete obedience is acceptable. 'One would think', writes Israeli journalist Daphna Baram, 'that Israel was not a nuclear regional superpower possessing the fourth most powerful army in the world, but a shaky sanctuary where Jews are annihilated by the thousands every day'.[10] The only way to defend an illegal and brutal occupation is to be constantly on the offensive, and slamming and threatening opponents often forces them into submission.

Zionism is an exclusionary and racist national ideology that has always overlooked the rights of the Palestinians. After nearly 40 years of occupation, and untold billions spent on the settlement projects, the country is facing unprecedented social problems. A quarter of Israelis now live below the poverty line,[11] and more than half of the Arab house-holds in Israel live in poverty and are discriminated against in their access to education, employment and infrastructure.[12] During my travels to Israel and Palestine, I encountered many Arabs, Palestinians and pro-gressive Jews who realise that the current situation is unsustainable. Israeli journalist Gershom Gorenberg suggests that the settlements are destined to destroy the Jewish state. 'It is clear that Israel's future as a Jewish state depends on ending its rule of the West Bank', he writes. 'Settlements have shackled rather than served it.'[13]

Zionism has achieved its primary aim—the establishment of a Jewish state—but it cannot continue to operate with nineteenth-century think-ing. Traditional Zionism is dying, and many Diaspora and progressive Jews are wondering what will replace it. Ron Pundak, director-general of the Peres Center for Peace in Tel Aviv, calls himself a 'neo-Zionist'. He tells me that 'one of the reasons we don't sign peace agreements with our neighbours is the fact that we are still working according to the assump-tions of the Zionism of 100 years ago'. He fears that Zionism will need to undergo a 'revolution' before it can transform itself into a viable twenty-first-century ideology. 'Old Zionism', he says, is placing the entire enterprise in jeopardy.[14]

Post-Zionism, writes Israeli journalist Tom Segev, 'means that Zionism has done its job ... and must move on to the next stage. Some see this as a goal and others see it as a threat'.[15] What this actually means for the state of Israel and world Jewry is still hotly debated. 'It's proba-bly even harder to define who is a Zionist than it is to define who is a Jew', historian Shmuel Ettinger once said.[16] My interviews with Jews around the world have proved that even raising these existential issues exposes vast discrepancies of thought and conflicting ideals. Surely the future security of Israel depends on a sense of national identity that has moved beyond the primacy of Jewishness.

Israel's treatment of the Palestinians has been nothing short of shameful.[17] Israeli-only roads are now commonplace across the West Bank, and in the months after the Gaza 'withdrawal' in 2005, Israel com-pletely cut off the eastern sector of the West Bank from the remainder of the West Bank. Some two million Palestinians were prohibited from entering the area, ruining livelihoods. Military sources told *Haaretz* the moves were 'security measures'.[18]

Israeli border closures have contributed to an economic siege of the 'liberated' Gaza Strip, and by March 2006 all bakeries in the strip were closed because of a lack of flour.[19] This policy of economic strangulation was best articulated by Israeli prime ministerial adviser Dov Weisglass, who said it was 'like an appointment with a dietician. The Palestinians will get a lot thinner, but won't die'.[20] Such statements are rarely reported in the Western media, though Zionist groups would undoubtedly defend them. Even within Israel, the media often fail to inform readers of the reality of Israel's stranglehold.[21]

One of Israel's rising political stars, Tzipi Livni, highlights the Jewish state's collapsing international image when she observes that today's UN would not pass the 29 November 1947 amendment that called for the establishment of Israel.[22] Israel's legitimacy is now in doubt. The response, however, should not simply be to label critics as antisemites but to begin focusing on justice for both Israelis and Palestinians, and not just on military might.[23] The Jewish state can only ignore majority world opinion for so long.

Despite these uncomfortable realities, the Israeli perspective is far better understood in the West, largely because of the Zionist lobby's activities, but also because Israel's struggle against 'terrorism' is now framed— even more so since September 11—as 'our' struggle against Islamic fundamentalism. The Palestinians are not particularly effective at translating their message for a Western audience, and most Western journalists based in Israel spend relatively little time in East Jerusalem and the occupied territories.

Zionist lobby groups in the USA, United Kingdom, Europe and Australia are highly vocal and efficient at persuading journalists, editors and politicians that Israel must be supported and defended. Ferocious media-monitoring groups such as HonestReporting contribute to this atmosphere of intimidation. They also refuse to tolerate dissenting opinions on the conflict, and actively campaign against Jewish and non-Jewish critics.[24]

The Zionist lobby isn't solely responsible for this situation, but the post–September 11 environment has emboldened the lobby. Public broadcasters are chastised for not being tougher on 'terrorists', and the 2003 Hanan Ashrawi affair proved that even the views of a moderate Palestinian were unacceptable for public consumption. For AIJAC, a good Palestinian is a silent Palestinian. Demographic realities in the West, however, suggest a changing of the guard is imminent. As Muslims grow in number and political potency, the dynamics of the Middle East conflict could change radically. Only then, perhaps, will we understand that the US role has always been a rejectionist one—dedicated largely to maintenance of the Jewish state—and not really that of an 'honest-broker' at all. And only then will there be recognition that the Palestinian leadership has not in fact rejected 'generous' peace deals with Israel over the years; there has never been a fair and balanced offer on the table.

Baghdad to Tehran?

A few months after the beginning of the Iraq war in March 2003, AIJAC's Colin Rubenstein argued that Israelis 'should be grateful to US President Bush and his British ally, Tony Blair, for removing one of the biggest international threats to both Israel and the West and providing a glimmer of hope that Israel's neighbourhood might take a significant turn for the better'.[25] The architects of the Iraq war, many of whom were Jewish or had strong connections to the Israeli establishment, were partly driven by a belief that it would benefit Israel to remove a Saddam Hussein from the Middle Eastern political equation. Now we know the folly of their messianic delusions.[26]

The head of Israel's domestic security agency, Shin Bet, told a group of teenage Jewish settlers in the West Bank in early 2006 that a strong dictator would be preferable to the current 'chaos' in Iraq.[27] Israel was coming to regret its strong support for the war, he argued: 'When you dismantle a system in which there is a despot who controls his people by force, you have chaos. I'm not sure we won't miss Saddam'. It was a remarkable admission. The implication, of course, was that Western-friendly Middle Eastern autocracies were preferable to true democracies, because in the latter, the people were likely to elect Islamist governments hostile to Israel.

Despite the experience of the Iraqi quagmire, Jewish voices are some of the strongest among those advocating military action against Iran's supposed nuclear capability.[28] Iran's President Mahmoud Ahmadinejad has described the Holocaust a myth used to justify the creation of Israel, and has called for the Jewish state to be 'wiped off the map'.[29] The Iranian regime even organised an international conference to debate the 'Holocaust myth', attended by notorious Adelaide revisionist Dr Frederick Toben. Even though Ahmadinejad's predecessor, Mohammad Khatami, describes the Holocaust as a 'historical reality',[30] mainstream Jewish opinion, led by a bellicose USA, seems determined to take action, even with plummeting US public support for the Iraq war. 'The time for unavoidable and fateful decisions may soon be upon us', warned the *AJN* in February 2006.[31] The exact nature of Iran's nuclear arsenal remains unclear, and the International Atomic Energy Agency has yet to produce evidence of a covert nuclear program.

These doomsday predictions are eerily reminiscent of similar pronouncements before the 2003 Iraq war. Larry Derfner, senior journalist and columnist at the *Jerusalem Post*, argues that Iran is going to get nuclear weapons but Israel has the answer: 'more and better nuclear weapons of its own'.[32] It was reported in March 2006 that Israel's special forces were operating inside Iran, searching for the country's uranium-enrichment facilities.[33] The 2006 AIPAC conference focused primarily on the Iranian 'threat', and US ambassador to the UN, John Bolton, said the USA would use 'all the tools' at its disposal to stop Tehran's nuclear capability. Cheered on by the 5000-strong crowd, he warned that the UN Security Council 'must take due note that failure to act in a timely manner and with seriousness of purpose will do lasting damage to the credibility of the Council'.[34] Vice-President Dick Cheney issued similar threats, as did John Howard in Australia. It was as if the Iraq war, and its catastrophic consequences, had never happened.

Anti-Iranian rhetoric only intensified after the Hamas win in the Palestinian elections in late January 2006 and Tehran's offer of financial assistance to the cash-strapped Palestinian Authority. Hamas snatched government from the ruling Fatah Party, formerly headed by Yasser Arafat, by winning 76 seats in the 132-member parliament to Fatah's 43 seats. Israel's ambassador to the USA, Danny Gillerman, said the 'world is witnessing a new alliance between Iran, Syria and Hamas, which constitutes an axis of terror' that could start the 'the first world war of the 21st century'.[35] Perhaps he had borrowed George W Bush's speech-writer.[36] A threatening and militarily aggressive Israel ignores the geographic and political realities of the Middle East. Any kind of strike against Iran would unleash unfathomable consequences. How long can Israel play the regional bully and expect to receive unqualified support from the USA?

Israel maintains a massive nuclear arsenal unchecked by international inspections—assisted in this by the British and French in the 1960s.[37] In comments that should be treated with scepticism, the then British Foreign Minister Jack Straw drew attention to Israel's arsenal, proposing that once the world has 'removed' the threat from Iran, 'then we can get on to work ... in respect of Israel'.[38] A nuclear-free Middle East is surely the only way forward. As was the case with the Iraq war, any conflict with Iran would be heavily promoted by interests friendly to Israel.

The debates we need to have

While the mainstream generally shuns debate on such matters, universities have become the new ideological battleground in relation to the Israel–Palestine conflict. At universities across the USA, centres of Israel studies are becoming the new means of inoculating Jewish students against perceived anti-Israel propaganda. AIPAC regularly runs workshops to 'reposition the American campus to be a tangible asset to the pro-Israel movement' and encourages a 'strong' US–Israeli relationship. Isi Leibler wrote in the *Jerusalem Post* in October 2004 that many young Jews had simply disengaged from the debate because they were intimidated by the aggressiveness of pro-Palestinian 'activists'. Furthermore, he chastised Jews for 'exploiting their Jewishness as a vehicle to maximise their impact' in supporting the Palestinian cause.[39]

When the University of Toronto Arab Students' Collective organised a series of lectures titled 'Israeli Apartheid Week' in early 2005, Jewish groups complained it was racist.[40] The vice-president of B'nai B'rith Canada said the university had shown 'cowardice' by not banning the event. Leading Israeli historian Ilan Pappe was one of the main speakers.

Especially since September 11, there has been an organised campaign by public figures within the US academy itself to label prominent researchers and departments as 'anti-American' and 'antisemitic' because their research is too critical of the USA and Israel.[41] Individuals of Arab and Palestinian background have been specifically targeted.

Take the example of Joseph Massad, from Columbia University's Middle East Languages and Cultures Department. A well-published author and contributing writer for Egypt's *Al-Ahram* and *Palestinian-American*, he was accused by off-campus right-wing Zionist organisations linked to Israel's Likud Party of antisemitism and of likening Israel to Nazi Germany. Virtually none of the complaints came from his students, except for one, who claimed Massad had told a student, 'if you're going to deny the atrocities being committed against Palestinians, then you can get out of my classroom'. Juan Cole, a professor of modern Middle Eastern and South Asian history at the University of Michigan, claims that in the US 'McCarthyism is unacceptable except when criticism of Israel is involved'.[42] Columbia University conducted an inquiry and found Massad not guilty of antisemitism or of punishing pro-Israel students with low grades. That should have been the end of the matter, but a *New York Times* editorial suggested that the Columbia review hadn't been thorough enough and should have examined Massad's views. 'Most student complaints were not really about intimidation, but about allegations of stridently pro-Palestinian, anti-Israel bias', it said.[43]

In February 2005, the New York City Department of Education, after intense pressure from Zionist organisations, the *New York Sun* and pro-Israel politicians, prohibited Rashid Khalidi, director of Columbia's Middle East

Institute, from appearing in an occasional training program for high school students, citing his criticism of Israel. Khalidi was accused of promoting 'pro-Palestinian' views and of intimidating Zionist students. The academic had simply outlined Israel's racially discriminatory laws that cover the occupied territories. Alisa Solomon, professor at the City University of New York, wrote in *Forward* in March 2005[44] that it was sad to see mainstream Jewish organisations buying into the debate. 'For the hawks leading the charge against Khalidi and his colleagues', she wrote, 'the point is not to engage in or promote civil debate on a complicated issue, where there might, in fact, be room for competing narratives. It is to silence the other side'.

Australia is not immune from these controversies. Increasing numbers of Jewish students on campuses across the country are complaining that student unions are willing to denounce racism but are blind to anti-semitism. The national vice-president of the Australasian Union of Jewish Students (AUJS), Simon Nothman, told the *SMH* in late August 2004 that there had been an increase in antisemitic graffiti and posters.[45] 'Jews are the new Nazis' and 'American Jews are the real menace' were two examples. He claimed that the student unions ignored the problems and that Jews often avoided taking part in campus protests and social justice rallies because the events ended up slamming Jews and Israel: 'Whether it's for refugee rights or workers' rights, it's very common for it to be hijacked ... and the crowd later turns against us'.

AUJS conducted a survey among Jewish students in mid-2004 and discovered that 80 per cent of those surveyed felt that they wanted to challenge information presented by lecturers and other students but lacked the confidence and knowledge.[46] The 2004 AUJS winter conference found that standing up for Israel was one of the major concerns of the students. They had felt intimidated by posters, invited speakers and 'anti-Israel' propaganda. The definition of such material wasn't clear. Comparing the Jews to Nazis is an unacceptable slight, but posters proclaiming 'Free Palestine' should clearly not be classified in the same way.

Prominent Zionists, such as Alan Dershowitz and Israeli politician (and former Soviet refusenik) Natan Sharansky, have written extensively about why Israel is failing to engage students on campus. Both men charge the Left with infecting the anti-war movement with a virulent anti-semitism. Dershowitz recounts an experience where he was approached at a speaking engagement in Boston by protestors holding signs that read, 'Dershowitz and Hitler, just the same, the only difference is the name'.[47] He was rightly offended, but alleges that the individuals reflected the Left's increasing hatred of Israel. Sharansky agrees, claiming that 'Jewish activity on campus is directed almost entirely inward, when Jewish organisations feel like walled fortresses in enemy territory'.[48] Intimidation is clearly unacceptable, but both Dershowitz and Sharansky write like Israel is facing another Holocaust. And they both conveniently ignore Israel's appalling human rights record. When Sharansky says that 'Israel is a democracy in a state of war', he believes this absolves his homeland of any responsibility.[49] Critics are right to challenge this position.

Although the anti-war movement and Left have certainly attracted a handful of rabid extremists and antisemites, it is far too simplistic to suggest that Israel is simply being targeted because Jews live there. Leading US conservative commentator David Horowitz wrote after the Hamas win in Palestine in January 2006 that the Palestinian people 'have joined en masse the Axis of Evil' and that their cause is 'absolutely bankrupt'.[50] Since it was the 'sickest culture on the face of the earth', he argued, any 'secular leftists' in Europe and the USA who support the Palestinians 'reveal their terminal sickness'. Dershowitz, Sharansky and Horowitz are all from radically different backgrounds, but their inability to humanise the 'other' side is as dangerous as suggesting that Israelis are no different from Nazis.

A contentious subject that is routinely avoided in Australia is that of a one-state solution to the conflict, the idea that Jews and Palestinians should live together in an undivided, bi-national state. Michael Tarazi, legal adviser to the PLO, explained the idea in the *New York Times* in October 2004. 'Israel's overall strategy toward the Palestinians is ultimately self-defeating', he writes:

> It wants Palestinian land but not the Palestinians who live on that land. Many Palestinians are now convinced that Israeli support for a Palestinian state is motivated not by a hope for reconciliation, but by a desire to segregate non-Jews while taking as much of their land and resources as possible.[51]

On the eve of the Gaza 'disengagement' in August 2005, *Haaretz* released a report that was ignored in the world press.[52] For the first time since the establishment of Israel, the proportion of Jews living in the territories under the country's control was below 50 per cent, resting at slightly more than 49 per cent. The demographic reality was already overtaking the political debate.

Palestinians are increasing disillusioned with the idea of peace with Israel, or at least the two-state solution option offered by their leaders.

According to a March 2005 poll by the Palestinian Centre for Policy and Research, which conducts opinion polls in the West Bank, Gaza and East Jerusalem, as many as 65 per cent of Palestinians said they no longer believe that 'a permanent peace with Israel was possible'.[53] The ever-expanding settlement program in the West Bank is seen as making the establishment of a two-state solution almost impossible.

Tony Judt, director of the Remarque Institute at New York University, published a provocative piece in 2003 that articulated the one-state solution.[54] At its birth, Israel 'imported a characteristically late nineteenth-century separatist project into a world that has moved on, a world of individual rights, open frontiers and international law'. The idea of a Jewish state, he argues, 'a state in which Jews and Jewish religion have exclusive privileges from which non-Jewish citizens are forever excluded, is rooted in another time and place. Israel, in short, is an anachronism'. After dismissing suicide bombers as no strategic threat—'and the Israeli military knows it'—he outlines his solution, which requires a 'brave and relentlessly engaged American leadership'. 'The true alternative facing the Middle East in the coming years', he writes, 'will be between an eth-nically cleansed Greater Israel and a single, integrated bi-national state of Jews and Arabs, Israeli and Palestinians'. 'Israel today is bad for the Jews', Judt argues, because its policies are directly contributing to increased intolerance of its actions.

After Ariel Sharon's departure from the political scene in January 2006[55] and the Hamas victory in the Palestinian elections,[56] such a solution seems a remote possibility. Sharon's Kadima Party surged in the polls, and won office, under acting Prime Minister Ehud Olmert. Likud floun-dered, indicating that the unilateral 'legacy' of Sharon is popular with the Israeli public. Olmert outlined his desire to establish 'permanent' borders by 2010 and a complete separation from the Palestinians.[57] He wanted withdrawals from the West Bank but to maintain and expand major settlement blocs around Jerusalem, making an independent Palestinian state impossible. The Israeli political establishment embarked on the demonisation of Hamas,[58] concluding that the party was both inca-pable and unwilling to negotiate. The USA led the charge and even put pressure on moderate Palestinians not to serve in a Hamas government, and ostracising them if they did.[59] After pushing for democracy in the Middle East, the Bush administration suddenly realised that it didn't like the choice of the Palestinian people.[60]

Hamas has a history of launching terror attacks against Israeli civilians and a charter that specifically seeks the destruction of Israel, but numerous Hamas spokespeople have suggested that a negotiated settlement with Israel is a possibility, based on 1967 borders. Israel has rejected this, preferring to act unilaterally. After all, Israel likes to be able to chant the 'no partner' mantra. Leading Zionist groups in the USA and Australia have supported the international isolation of Hamas,[61] even as the head of the its political bureau, Khalid Mish'al, has said that his party does not fight Jews 'because [they] belong to a certain faith or culture ... Our problem is with those who ... imposed themselves on us by force'.[62]

The toxic political environment in recent years has inevitably resulted in efforts to isolate the Jewish state internationally. In May 2005, the British Association of University Teachers (AUT) voted to boycott two Israeli universities, Haifa and Bar-Ilan (who ran a college in the occupied town of Ariel). The decision was eventually reversed, but the media and political responses reflect the broader response to the growing movement against Israeli aggression. The initial AUT vote called on British academics to sever links with Israeli institutions but exempted Israelis who spoke out against their government's oppression of Palestinians. Israeli historian Ilan Pappe openly advocated the boycott,[63] as did Israeli academic Tanya Reinhart. She wrote in Israeli daily *Yediot Aharonot* that although critics claimed Israel was being unfairly singled out, 'it is only because at the moment there is a greater likelihood of success in stopping a small state that Israel became the focus. Still, if an effort is made to save first the Palestinians and at least stop the wall, can we condemn that effort as unethical?'[64]

Worldwide response was immediate. Isi Leibler wrote in the *Jerusalem Post* that 'Israel is a nation under siege, facing existential threats. Is it unreasonable to deny anti-Israeli faculties the use of our universities as staging grounds for campaigns to delegitimise the Jewish state?' He denounced the Israeli academics who called for the boycott and described Pappe as 'the doyen of the haters of Zion in Israeli academia'.[65] 'I think the de-Zionization of Israel is a condition for peace', Pappe said in a September 2002 interview,[66] a view increasingly shared by many around the world.

John Docker, an adjunct senior research fellow at the Australian National University's Humanities Research Centre, is a leading critic of Zionism and initiated the Australian boycott campaign in 2002, along with the University of Sydney's Ghassan Hage. The Jewish community reacted furiously to the boycott proposal. Docker tells me that 'the situation for the Palestinian people has got to the point where their very survival is in question. I support non-violent actions even when they are largely symbolic, as we knew the Australian call might be. We were hoping to achieve a significant symbolic protest against Israel'.[67]

The AUT boycott largely escaped the mainstream Australian media. The *AJN* expressed gratitude that 'this latest wave of depravity has missed Australia' and that 'the winds of extremism' had failed to 'breeze through the colleges and campuses of Australia'. The reason for the boycott was 'plain, old-fashioned anti-Semitism'.[68] (Resident columnist Ruth Wajnryb concurred, complaining that the AUT was measuring Israel 'by a benchmark in morality that is applied against no other state'.[69]) The paper was outraged that the AUT had 'dared compare Israel's treatment of the Palestinians with the blatantly-racist regime of apartheid South Africa' because it had implemented 'so-called colonialist policies'. It may have been comforting to dismiss the AUT as a bunch of radical racists, but worldwide dissatisfaction with the occupation was growing and involved more than just a handful of British academics.[70]

Alongside the academic boycott of Israeli academic institutions, the divestment campaign against companies that support the Israeli occupation has been gathering steam for years. The Presbyterian Church, United Church of Christ, United Methodist Church, Episcopal Church and World Council of Churches (WCC) have all implemented various strategies to express their growing dissatisfaction with Israel's ongoing settlement expansion.

The Presbyterian Church, boasting nearly three million members, led the divestment campaign in mid-2004 with an overwhelming vote at its US general assembly to equate the Jewish state with apartheid South Africa and to cease investing in companies that work directly with occupation forces. By early 2005, the WCC, representing around half a billion Christians worldwide, joined the Presbyterian Church and announced that churches with investment funds 'had an opportunity to use those funds responsibly in support of peaceful solutions to conflict. Economic pressure, appropriately and openly applied, is one such means of action'.[71] After the Church of England announced its plan in early 2006 to divest from Israel, Archbishop of Canterbury Rowan Williams was chastised by the United Kingdom's most senior Jewish leader, Chief Rabbi Jonathan Sacks. The growing movement could no longer be dismissed as Christian antisemitism, but had to be recognised as a legitimate, and desperate, attempt to pressure Israel to conform to international norms.

Israeli military officers are now facing increasing limitations on their movements. In 2005 former head of the IDF's Southern Command

Doron Almog, who had been in charge of the Gaza Strip, had to cancel a trip to the United Kingdom and return without disembarking his plane in London because a criminal complaint had been filed by Palestinians regarding his alleged involvement in war crimes. In December of the same year, two claims were filed in the US Federal Court against Avi Dichter, the former head of Israel's General Security Services, and Moshe Ya'alon, former head of Israel's Intelligence Branch and former chief of staff of the IDF. Both men were accused of committing war crimes. By early 2006, a commander of the IDF was forced to cancel his planned study trip to the United Kingdom after he was warned he could face arrest on his arrival.[72] British law allows private citizens to file complaints against the military personnel of a foreign country.

The Israeli establishment was outraged. Alan Dershowitz offered to defend any Israeli officer who faced charges, expressing disbelief that immunity wasn't an automatic right.[73] One IDF official told *Haaretz* that the countries in question simply didn't appreciate 'the change that [has] occurred in the world following September 11. Israel, like other countries, is waging a battle against terror that operates from among a dense civilian population. Such fighting entails countless legal and ethical dilemmas, but in no way are we talking about war crimes'.[74] In other words, Israel's actions are beyond criticism, accountability and redress. It is as if victims of Israeli actions have no right to challenge the legality, let alone morality, of the Jewish state. Another IDF official complained that Hamas 'terrorists' now have more freedom to travel the world than Israeli officers.[75] One Israeli commentator even said Israel should welcome the potential court cases as an opportunity to 'turn the tables on the Palestinians and expose Palestinian war crimes, in English, for the world to see'.[76] Israeli exceptionalism has never been so unappealing.

Voices of reason

Through these debates, a number of people are speaking out and challenging the mainstream narrative. The Australian political and media elite, however, rarely keeps up. After the January 2006 Hamas victory in Palestine, John Howard stated that there 'will be absolutely no change at all in our total commitment to the preservation of the state of Israel'.[77] Labor leader Kim Beazley was even more bellicose in outlining the ALP's position: 'Israel can't deal with them [Hamas], won't deal with them; the United States won't deal with them, we won't. We recognise the state of Israel and the Israelis' right to live in secure and recognised boundaries'.[78] The Palestinian people, and their rights, were utterly ignored.

In the following months, none of the major Australian newspapers published an opinion piece by a Palestinian to explain the Hamas win. Numerous Middle East 'experts' pontificated on its significance, but once again Palestinians were invisible. The *SMH* editorialised that the death of Yasser Arafat, the Gaza withdrawal and the election of Mahmoud Abbas had 'seemed to offer hope' but that the Hamas victory threw the situation into chaos.[79] Surely the paper wasn't suggesting that the Palestinians themselves were hopeful? The editorial was referring, of course, to the USA and Israel. At least the paper's Middle East correspondent, Ed O'Loughlin, noted the hypocrisy in Israeli demands and pointed out that Ariel Sharon—a man with 'a long history of alleged war crimes'—also rejected the Oslo two-state solution and a halt to settlement expansion.[80]

Perhaps most depressingly, there was little interest in understanding the reasons for the Hamas win. The AIJAC perspective on the conflict—an almost pathological inability to see beyond Israeli interests—was all too apparent. If the media had examined responses in the Arab world, they would have discovered the profound hatred of US policies in the region. An opinion poll conducted by Zogby International in Saudi Arabia, Jordan, Lebanon, the United Arab Emirates and Egypt found that three out of four respondents believed the main motives of US policies in the Middle East were 'oil, protecting Israel, dominating the region and weakening the Muslim world'.[81] The Australian media are still ideologically incapable of viewing the Middle East and Islam outside the narrative imposed by Washington, London and Canberra. Notable exceptions exist, but overall we are poorly served.

A few commentators are bucking the trend, however. Robert Manne, professor of politics at La Trobe University, and one of Australia's best-known intellectuals, seems slightly unsure of his position, though his political stance has shifted from a right-wing and fiercely anti-communist outlook to a more centrist attitude during the Howard years.[82] He grew up in the shadow of the Holocaust—the Nazis killed his grandparents, and his parents escaped to Australia—and identified strongly with the Western powers during the Cold War. He thought the Left was too willing to excuse the mass murderers of the Soviet Union and Cambodia. His break with the Right was prompted by his growing awareness of Aboriginal dispossession and by the Right's denial of the trauma caused by Australia's earliest white settlers. He soon became a strong opponent of the Howard government's asylum-seeker policy and the war in Iraq. He noted in 2004 that many of the leading neo-conservatives behind the war are Jewish intellectuals, including former US deputy secretary of defense Paul Wolfowitz, former Defense Policy Board chairman Richard Perle and editor of the *Weekly Standard* magazine William Kristol. 'Their political trajectory—from reflection on the Holocaust to the liberal wing of the anti-communist movement to neoconservatism—was eerily similar to mine', he writes, but these were the people 'to whose policy influence I was most implacably opposed'.[83]

Manne rarely tackles the Israel–Palestine conflict in his public writing, although a newspaper column he published in December 2004 sparked a furore. In it, he claims to feel a 'tug of loyalty to my [Jewish] people' and then challenges the morality of Israel's brutal occupation. He is not a Zionist, he says, but has supported Israel throughout his life. He argues for a two-state solution, questions the need of Jews for a homeland of their own—'since the end of World War II, the place of Jews in all Western societies has been unproblematic'—and charges Israel with greed and arrogance for not returning all of the occupied territories.[84]

Manne tells me he was told after this column that it took courage to write about the conflict. 'The fact that people say that suggests that even to enter the debate, you pay a price', he says. 'The fact that there is so little interesting debate here means that they [the Zionist lobby] are achieving their aims [by intimidating dissenters].'

He acknowledges that he is not involved in the Jewish community— 'I'm a completely secular Jew'—but he nonetheless challenges the need for a Jewish state. 'It's a betrayal of my belief in liberal democracy to believe that Jews are still under threat and therefore need a homeland of their own', he says. He tells me about an event run by the Jewish community organisation B'nai B'rith a few years ago, attended by lawyer Julian Burnside and former Prime Minister Malcolm Fraser, where he was surprised by the hostility expressed towards Muslim refugees. Zionist leader Sam Lipski explained to him afterwards that for many Jews, this hostility is motivated by 'a gut instinct and a fear of Muslims'.

Writer Arnold Zable, another Jewish intellectual who is a vocal activist for the cause of refugees, tells me that he prefers not to participate in the debate because it is too emotive and vicious.[85] Alex Dafner, who runs the Yiddish show on SBS Radio and is a 'non-Zionist supporter of Israel', is more outspoken. He doesn't believe in Zionism as an ideology but acknowledges that a state is central to the Jewish people. Dafner is highly critical of Israel in its current form: 'It's not socialist; there is real bigotry, religious intolerance and a lack of respect for fellow Jews. My friends in Israel say there is a need for two or three states in Israel: one for the religious, one for the secular and one for the in-between'.

He claims the Melbourne Jewish community is 'the most conservative I've come across, in terms of their unwillingness to debate'. He despairs at the Zionist leadership in Australia and its betrayal of the long tradition of Jewish dissent. 'It's said that only Israelis have the right to criticise Israel's policies, not those in the Diaspora, though we never say that about other societies', he says. Furthermore, 'they've managed to create the notion that the Jewish community is behind Israel' and imply that dissenting voices are 'tiny and not representative'. Although Dafner blames the Melbourne Jewish community's high proportion of Holocaust survivors and their children for the lack of debate, he chastises Zionist groups for hijacking the agenda: 'People often talk about antisemitism and I think it's largely the result of that notion of total support for Israel, right or wrong. It's hard to defend policies which in the long term will be disastrous, such as the current support for the [security] wall'.

Dafner was highly critical of Israel's 1982 invasion of Lebanon, one of the few dissenters at the time. He received hate mail. 'The majority of Israelis who served in Lebanon see it as an unmitigated disaster', he says:

> It was almost regarded as a mini-Vietnam. But the Melbourne Jewish community was vehemently defending it and never really forgave [me]. I still occasionally receive the comment that I am 'anti-Israel' because I dared to speak out against Israeli policy. The greatest sin by far is to criticise Israeli policy rather than having raised debate.

He is dismissive of the hyperbole that often permeates discussion of the Arab world: 'Each time the Jews have gone through vilifying a state or a whole people, then overnight they become moderates and people we can do business with. I often point out: not Israel but the Diaspora is the best protection for the Jews'.[86]

Jews Against the Occupation (JAO) Sydney was formed in May 2003 to represent Jews who support Palestinian human rights and a peaceful resolution of the conflict. It is a small group of less than 100 people, with little media or political influence, but member Barbara Bloch articulates the need for such groups at a time when mainstream Jewish groups see their role as aggressively supporting Israeli government policy without question. 'We support a non-violent negotiated settlement', she tells me. 'I would like to see a bi-national state. I really don't like ethnic/religious absolutism of whatever brand it is and for whatever reasons. I'd like to see Jews and Palestinians sharing this tiny piece of land.' JAO advocates the withdrawal of Israel to 1967 borders and the 'immediate establishment of an international peacekeeping force to end the cycle of violence'. The removal of all illegal settlements and the dismantling of Israel's 'security wall' is part of the group's charter, along with promoting the voices of Palestinian and Israeli women in the debate. The media routinely ignore the group, so while their influence may be minimal, they try to promote wider recognition of events through the dissemination of information and the building of links with other like-minded Jewish and Palestinian groups in Australia and overseas. 'Part of the story that doesn't ever get much of a look in is the occupation itself', Bloch says. 'The Palestinians are under occupation, and the daily life of Palestinians is something we [JAO] feel gets side-lined … There's been a sense in the past that we keep it all inside and don't air our dirty linen in public.' The 2003 Hanan Ashrawi affair changed the dynamic of public discussion, she argues: 'There is another narrative, and certain people are very reluctant to hear that narrative because they may see things they don't like'.[87]

Zionism is being challenged around the world like never before. However, dissenting Jewish groups are travelling a long and frustrating road as they attempt to gain a voice. Ami Eden, national editor of the US Jewish newspaper *Forward*, challenged the establishment Jewish organisations in the *New York Times* in 2005. 'It is time Jews recognise that the old strategies no longer work', he wrote:

> Jewish organisation and advocates fail to grasp that they are no longer viewed as the voice of the disenfranchised. Rather, they are seen as the global Goliath, close to the seats of power and capable of influencing policies and damaging reputations. As such, their efforts to raise the alarm increasingly appear as bullying.[88]

It is still far too politically and morally convenient for Zionist groups to portray Israel as 'disenfranchised' rather than as a global power.

And what of Arab voices? Many Arabs I interviewed spoke of great difficulty in being heard and portrayed fairly in the media. Roland Jabbour is chairman of the Australian Arabic Council, which was launched in the wake of the 1991 Gulf War, to confront racism and the fundamental misunderstandings that the war exposed between wider Australian society and the Arabic communities. Jabbour tells me that the council presents the Palestinian point of view on the conflict, but 'unlike other organisations, we don't make our points by denigrating the other side. We draw a clear distinction between the Israelis, the state of Israel and Jews'. He criticises the Howard government's 'unbalanced' position on Israel, and attributes the anti-American and anti-Western sentiment in the Middle East to the USA's 'blind support' for the Jewish state and Israel's flagrant violation of human rights. He knows that the Zionist lobby in Australia exercises disproportionate influence because 'it is totally suicidal for politicians to be seen to be pro-Arab'.

Jabbour despairs at the negative image of Arabs in the wider community. 'Arabs are continually associated with terrorism and violence, being primitive and anti-Western', he says. This view is so ingrained here, he argues, that it's very unpopular to support the Palestinians: 'It's much easier and safer to be pro-Israeli than to be pro-Arab. One has to continuously explain and defend why one is taking that particular position'.[89]

Jabbour says it's an uphill battle for Australians to unlearn years of Zionist propaganda:

> People seem to make no distinction between an occupied people and those who occupy them. Israel talks about the right of self-defence. How can an occupier claim self-defence but deny the same right to those who are occupied and have the right of self-defence with whatever means are available to them?[90]

Afif Safieh is the Palestinian General Delegate to the United Kingdom. During a speech to the Royal Institute for International Affairs in London in August 2005, he talked of the financial difficulties of running a liberation movement: 'We the Palestinians, we have become the Jews of the Israelis and today, because of our geographic dispersal, we are a "global tribe"'. He said he never compared the Palestinian Nabka to the Holocaust because 'each tragedy stands on its own'. Jews and Gypsies regard Nazism as the greatest barbarity, he said, while Native Americans see the arrival of European settlers, and their attempt at annihilation, as the worst disaster: 'If I were a Palestinian—and I happen to be one—it would be the Nakba. I do not know of a way to measure suffering or how to quantity pain but what I do know is that we are not the children of a lesser god'.[91]

The personal journey

While I have always taken a keen interest in the Israel–Palestine conflict—though I distinctly remember my father criticising me as a young teenager for not knowing about the intifada—in recent years I have experienced a far deeper personal engagement with the issues. My first article on the subject for the *SMH* in July 2003 sprung simply from a desire to articulate an alternative Judaism, one not blindly enamoured with the Zionist cause. The angry response to that piece proved that I had hit a nerve. Since then, I have been heartened by the level of support I've received from within Australia and around the world, encouraging me to engage honestly rather than tarring me with the toxic label of 'antisemite'. I still hope for a day when Zionists will cease using Israel's 'security', or the Holocaust, or the 'war on terror' to justify and excuse actions that are routinely condemned when committed by any other country. Pakistan-born British commentator Tariq Ali told me during his Australian visit in May 2005 that historian Eric Hobsbawm was convinced that if Zionists stayed in power in Israel, the country would cease to exist by the end of the twenty-first century.[92] Israel's current path almost guarantees this outcome.

During my travels in Israel and Palestine, the depth of the problem became apparent. It wasn't only that I felt constantly ashamed by what I saw and heard; I also became aware of the split within Israel itself. The Jewish state is still a relatively new nation, and exhibits signs of a personality disorder. Most Israelis, like the Palestinians, simply want to live in peace and security, though successive leaders, in Israel and the Diaspora, seem determined to undermine this possibility. Many, I believe, have a vested interest in prolonging the conflict. Israel opposes a resolution to the conflict because it opposes the presence of another people on land it has claimed as exclusively for Jews.

The real challenge is to persuade our political leaders and news media to listen to voices that challenge their prejudices and preconceptions. The establishment of an independent, Palestinian state is inevitable, but it will not happen easily, nor without the involvement of many caring people.

EPILOGUE:
THE LEGACY OF THE 2006 ELECTIONS

BACK IN 2003, Israel's Deputy Prime Minister, Ehud Olmert, told the Israeli daily *Yediot Aharonot* that he was opposed to Israel's continued occupation of the Palestinian territories. He warned that if the Jewish state did not pull out, the Palestinian population would soon outnumber Jews.[1] His thinking allegedly influenced Ariel Sharon, who acknowledged that only withdrawal would ensure a sustainable Israel. Olmert, a hard-line Likudnik, was transformed by demographic and political realities. Olmert's change of heart had nothing to do with alleviating the suffering of the Palestinians or assisting their path to nationhood. Rather, he was determined to ensure a Jewish majority in as much of Israel as the international community—namely the USA—would accept. Such pragmatism is central to current Israeli thinking and the Israeli's relations with the Hamas-led Palestinian Authority.

Israel's political landscape was rocked by an earthquake in early 2006. After a stroke, Sharon fell into an irreversible coma on 4 January, and Olmert assumed leadership, leading Sharon's Kadima Party to the 28 March poll. The elections saw the lowest turn-out in the country's history. Analysts concluded that the general public was disaffected with the major parties and preferred to disengage from the political process.[2] The Kadima Party won, but gained far fewer seats than expected (29).[3] Labor, led by former unionist Amir Peretz, won 19 seats, and Binyamin Netanyahu's Likud only 12. Three parties commonly referred to as 'Arab', but which include a Jewish–Arab electoral bloc originating in the Communist Party, won 10 seats. The major revelation, however, was Avigdor Lieberman's far-right Yisrael Beiteinu Party, which won 11 seats.[4] A coalition government was formed between Kadima and Labor.

The results were a clear indication that a desire to make the Palestinians disappear from view has become the norm in mainstream Israeli politics. Gideon Levy wrote in *Haaretz* two days before the poll:

> Contrary to appearances, the elections this week are important, because they will expose the true face of Israeli society and its hidden ambitions. More than 100 elected candidates will be sent to the Knesset on the basis of one ticket—the racism ticket. If we used to think that every two Israelis have three opinions, now it will be evident that nearly every Israeli has one opinion— racism. Elections 2006 will make this much clearer than ever

before. An absolute majority of the MKs (members of parliament) in the 17th Knesset will hold a position based on a lie: that Israel does not have a partner for peace. An absolute majority of MKs in the next Knesset do not believe in peace, nor do they even want it—just like their voters—and worse than that, don't regard Palestinians as equal human beings. Racism has never had so many open supporters. It's the real hit of this election campaign.[5]

Olmert outlined his 'convergence' plan in the months before the election, framing the poll as a referendum on his proposal.[6] He signalled readiness to withdraw from a handful of small settlements in the West Bank but indicated he would maintain and expand one of the largest settlement blocs, including Ma'ale Adumim. The plan will divide the West Bank into two separate areas, with Israel retaining the Jordan Valley, making a contiguous Palestinian state impossible.[7] While Labor favoured negotiation with the Palestinians, Gideon Levy argues that all the major parties, Likud, Kadima and Labor, sought a 'unilateral arrangement' that 'ignored the Palestinians'.[8]

'Much will be said in the coming days about the sea change in Israeli politics, especially the decline of the Likud', the *Guardian* commented after the election.[9] 'But no one should delude themselves that Mr Olmert's maximum offer is anywhere near the Palestinians' minimum.' Olmert stated that he wanted to complete his plan by 2010, though after the election suggested he might start as early as 2008 before the end of US President George W Bush's term in office.[10]

Weeks after the poll, Olmert had revealed his ultimate goal. 'The idea is that we will be separated from the overwhelming majority of Palestinians', he told *Time* magazine.[11] According to polls conducted before the Israeli election, a majority of Israelis and Palestinians are opposed to unilateral moves to resolve the conflict, but Olmert seems determined to push on regardless.[12] He said he hoped to negotiate with the Palestinians before embarking on his 'convergence' plan—while isolating and punishing the Hamas-led Palestinian Authority—though Kadima clearly intends to act unilaterally, and as soon as possible.

There had been another dramatic election earlier in the year, in the Palestinian territories. To the surprise and alarm of many Western observers, Hamas won control of the Palestinian Authority. While the West embraced Kadima's victory and Olmert's unilateral plans, Western nations demanded that Hamas renounce violence and recognise Israel's right to exist, a demand that Hamas refused to meet on the West's terms. Western aid to the Palestinians virtually dried up, leaving thousands of Palestinian workers without pay. US ambassador to Israel Richard Jones claimed that the USA didn't 'want to punish' the Palestinians,[13] despite his government's cuts to financial aid to the Palestinian Authority and refusal to deal with Hamas.[14] Israel also suspended millions of dollars in monthly taxes it collects on behalf of the Palestinian government. The Palestinians' Prime Minister Ismail Haniyeh said that the 'Palestinian people will not give up their government no matter how many sacrifices we have to make. We are prepared to eat salt and olives'.[15]

Immediately after the Kadima victory, the Bush administration invited Olmert to the White House,[16] and the Israeli leader returned the compliment by suggesting that 'Bush will emerge in history as the person who has had more courage to change the Middle East than any person before him ... There is a very strong emotional bond between us, every time we speak we feel it deeply'.[17] US Secretary of State Condoleezza Rice announced that Washington would not rule out supporting further unilateral moves by Israel,[18] and Richard Jones concurred, though he still spoke of 'supporting negotiations because we believe it is the only way to solve the conflict'.[19] In reality, the USA wholly accepted Israel's rejectionist stance.

In Australia, Prime Minister John Howard argued that Kadima 'brings real hope' for the future,[20] while Minister of Foreign Affairs Alexander Downer informed the Victorian United Israel Appeal that Olmert was 'sometimes referred to as the Australian representative in the Knesset' because he had travelled here on a number of occasions. 'The Australian–Israel relationship has never been stronger', Downer said.[21]

Faced with the mandate that Olmert and like-minded Israeli politicians had received in the election, many parts of the mainstream press accepted the inevitability of Olmert's plan. The London *Times* praised Kadima and urged the party to be 'bold where [they] can and if the reply [from Hamas] is a wave of terror attacks, the international community must not be ambiguous in its sympathies'.[22] In Australia, the *SMH* welcomed Israel's 'retreat from Judea' but warned of a high price for dismissing Palestinian demands.[23] Even the *Australian* acknowledged that Kadima's platform 'will not bring the Middle East any closer to a permanent peace' and argued that Olmert's plan 'is less to appease than [to] ignore the Palestinians' and the Hamas government particularly.[24] Not surprisingly, *AJN* congratulated Olmert and the Israelis for realising 'they can no longer hope for a Palestinian partner'.[25] And AIJAC's Colin

Rubenstein argued that 'Israel is moving to give Palestinians much of what they say they want'[26]—except, of course, independence and contiguous territory.

The problem for those who want Israel to pull back from Olmert's plan is that Hamas remains an unknown quantity, saying it wants peace but, on the evidence so far, sanctioning terrorist attacks inside Israel, even if it is not responsible for them. After a suicide bombing in Tel Aviv in mid-April 2006, a Hamas member in Jerusalem told *Ynetnews* that 'Israel and the occupation are responsible'.[27] He reminded readers that 'before the attacks, less than two days before, Israel killed 18 Palestinians'. Such statements, while they might be true, only guarantee international isolation.[28]

Israel and her allies in the West are using the rise of Hamas as an excuse to ignore the claims of the Palestinian people. Israel demands that Hamas recognises the state of Israel and renounces violence, but as Robert Fisk observes, 'if the Israelis want Hamas to acknowledge the state of Israel, then Hamas should be expected to acknowledge the state of Israel that exists within its legal borders—not the illegal borders now being dreamt up by Olmert'.[29]

Haaretz commented that in the months since Hamas's stunning electoral victory in Palestine, the militant organisation was 'acting more responsibly than the Israeli government. Its representatives speak of a new era, of a transition from terror to politics, of continued opposition to occupation via other means, and of aspirations to a long-term *hudna* (cease-fire)'.[30] Israel's official policy has been to isolate Hamas and force its collapse, in the vain hope that the Palestinians will vote next time for more Israel-friendly candidates.[31] Hamas is struggling with a bankrupt economy, violence in Gaza,[32] high unemployment, Western isolation and little aid.[33] Israel and the USA are engaged in disturbingly narrow thinking, however. The failure of Hamas will not bring Middle East peace any closer, and will only inflame extremists on both sides.

Palestinian Prime Minister Ismail Haniyeh argued in the *Guardian* that his people and their leaders were sick and tired of the West's racist approach to the conflict, in which the Palestinians are regarded as inferior.[34] He wondered why the West had not demanded more territorial concessions of Israel and warned the world that Olmert's unilateralism was 'a recipe for conflict'. Palestinian President Mahmoud Abbas agreed. If Israel acts unilaterally, then the conflict will continue.[35] The current path seems to ensure nothing less.

Hamas has said it will abandon its use of suicide bombers,[36] has made an offer of 'quiet in return for quiet',[37] and has shown a willingness to study any Israeli peace offer.[38] Yet its true intentions remain unclear.[39] Palestinian Foreign Minister Mahmoud al-Zahar told a Chinese news agency in early April 2006 that he dreamt 'of hanging a huge map of the world on the wall in my Gaza house, in which Israel did not appear'.[40] A day later, Zahar wrote a letter to the UN Secretary General Kofi Annan, claiming the Palestinians hoped to 'live in peace and security . . . side by side with our neighbours in this sacred part of the world'.[41] Though he later claimed he asked an aide to remove any reference to Hamas accepting a two-state solution, it was a clear indication that being in government was moderating the movement's stand.[42]

Ultimately, however, Palestinians' aspirations and rights are irrelevant to the Israeli establishment. Amira Hass believes that:

> The supporters of convergence and its architects are deceiving themselves by thinking that all these forms of rage won't burst out or that it will always be possible to suppress them. Indeed, it is difficult to predict when and how the rage will erupt, but sooner or later, they will be back disrupting the dreams of comfort and convenience at the expense of another nation.[43]

Average Israelis, she argues, care little about Israeli expansionism, violation of international law, and the human rights and welfare of the Palestinians.[44] They simply want them to live elsewhere. The delusion that underpins Olmert's plan reveals a deep-seated Zionist perspective, despite the rhetoric suggesting that Israel has abandoned decades of settlement expansion. Olmert talks as if the Palestinians should be grateful for the scraps of land and rights his government is offering, rather than understanding their justified rejection.

Palestinian politician Hanan Ashrawi believes that current Israeli thinking is inevitably leading to disaster. 'Now is the time for the US, for the international community, the Quartet, to stand up and say, this is not finished', she says. 'Israel does not have the right to act unilaterally, it does not have the right to wreak havoc and destroy the prospects for a peaceful solution.'[45] Israel has been calling the shots since 1967, always without Palestinian consultation, and clearly believes that the USA will support its attempts to establish 'final borders'. Sadly, once again, the international community has placed a higher value on Israel's vision of its historic destiny than on the humanity of the Palestinians. Although John Howard talks about believing in the 'emergence of an independent Palestinian state', surely he knows that Western support for Olmert will not bring this about.[46]

The Kadima vision is of a concrete wall, with Jews on one side and as many Arabs as possible on the other. Sooner or later, Israel and the Palestinians will have to meet face-to-face, listen to each other's grievances and negotiate with honesty. Only then—and on the condition that both Israel and the Palestinian state achieve safety and security—will this conflict be resolved. Neither side has a monopoly on suffering, but only one party has the power to end the occupation and to recognise that Israel and Palestine are historically destined to share the same homeland.

NOTES

1 The Ashrawi scandal (pages 3–22)

1   Edward Said, 'Dignity and Solidarity', *Al-Ahram*, 26 June – 2 July 2003.
2   Hanan Ashrawi & Jon Elmer, 'Hurtling toward the abyss: Jon Elmer interviews Hanan Ashrawi', OccupiedPalestine.org, 23 November 2003, <www.ccmep.org/2003_articles/Palestine/112303_hurtling_toward_the_abyss>.
3   Tony Stephens, 'Palestinian crusader wins peace prize', *SMH*, 9 August 2003.
4   At the time, Jones was employed by both AIJAC and the ECAJ, causing disquiet within certain sections of the Jewish community, as the agenda of both groups is different.
5   Miftah's goal of ending the Israeli occupation is based on humanitarian, rather than historical or ideological, grounds.
6   Sam Lipski, 'The puzzle behind the Sydney Peace Prize', *AJN*, 3 October 2003. His apology ran the following week.
7   Hanan Ashrawi, 'For The Record No. 34', speech delivered to the Palestine Center, Washington DC, 14 March 2000.
8   ibid.
9   ibid. During this speech, Ashrawi argued that a bi-national state may become the 'de facto solution' if Israel continued its occupation, but warned it would probably still be run by individuals who refused to see Palestinians as legitimate citizens of the state.
10 As quoted in Robert Fisk, 'Interview with Hanan Ashrawi', *Independent*, 8 November 2000.
11 Zionist Organisation of America, 'Hanan Ashrawi, apologist for terror, should be disinvited from Colorado Symposium on 9/11 anniversary', *Campus Watch*, 30 August 2002, viewed April 2006, <www.campus-watch.org/article/id/69>.
12 'Hanan Ashrawi in conversation with Elizabeth Farnsworth', *NewsHour*, PBS Television, 1 November 2001.
13 Robert Fisk, 'The dreamer who relied on emotion and failed to protect his own people', *Independent*, 12 November 2004.
14 'Ashrawi wishes Arafat good health', *Lateline*, ABC Television, 9 November 2003.
15 Gerard Henderson's *Age/SMH* column on 28 October 2003, 'Junk the prize and keep the peace', was typical of the scepticism directed at Ashrawi. The Melbourne *Age*'s coverage was minimal, because of editor Michael Gawenda's view that it was 'a very Sydney story'. *Age* journalist David Bernstein wrote an opinion piece arguing that

Ashrawi, while being passionately committed to the Palestinian cause, was 'a voice of reason and moderation' and that the community's response was entirely inappropriate and likely to inflame accusations of underhanded Jewish influence. His article was rejected by Gawenda, and Bernstein later claimed that Gawenda thought it blamed the Jewish community for antisemitism. Gawenda refused to elaborate on his decision, although Bernstein told me he respected his editor's perspective.

16 Glenn Milne, 'Labor stumbles into another divide', *Australian*, 13 October 2003.

17 Interview with author, Sydney, 26 November 2003.

18 Rees told me he'd taken notes during the conversation with Greiner and passed these onto Ramsey.

19 She had resigned from the foundation when her husband left his position as chairman of the University of Sydney's Graduate School of Management. Nick Greiner was also chairman of British American Tobacco (BAT), which had caused rifts within the university. Sean Nicolls, 'Kathryn follows Nick out the door in protest', *SMH*, 12 August 2003.

20 Jo Mazzocchi, 'Carr opens Lowy Institute', *AM*, ABC Radio, 26 November 2003.

21 'Lowy's greatest goal', *AJN*, 26 August 2005.

22 Mazzocchi, op. cit.

23 Mary Williams, letter to *SMH*, 28 October 2003.

24 Malcolm Turnbull, speech at the Jewish National Fund dinner, Melbourne, 29 May 2004.

25 Tony Abbott, speech to the Victorian Zionist Council, Melbourne, 28 October 2003.

26 ibid.

27 Elizabeth Wynhausen, 'Take the free out of speech', *Australian*, 4 November 2003.

28 *Dr Hanan Ashrawi: a brief introduction*, AIJAC, October 2003, in which the AIJAC rejects Ashrawi's 1996 assertion that 'The occupation is still ongoing'. The group claimed that 'about 98 percent of Palestinians lived under Palestinian Authority control and had no daily contact with Israelis, soldiers or otherwise'. In reality, the Palestinians were still economically, politically and socially reliant on the Jewish state in 1996, and settlement expansion accelerated across the occupied territories. AIJAC also claims that Ashrawi moderates her message for Western audiences.

29 As quoted in Fisk, 'Interview with Hanan Ashrawi', op. cit.

30 Mike Kelly was also involved in sending reports from Iraq in 2003 detailing alleged abuses by US soldiers in Iraqi gaols. The *SMH* reported on

17 June 2004 that a number of regular reports to Canberra detailed concerns, including from the UN, about US forces mistreating and abusing Iraqi prisoners as far back as June 2003. Kelly's exact role in the saga remains unclear.

31 Sunday, 2 November 2003.

32 Mazzocchi, op. cit.

33 Interview with the author, Sydney, 3 December 2003.

34 Rees continued: 'Of those who were deterred by the controversy, none said "we have to finish our partnership because lobbying by representatives of the Jewish community has caused us to do so". Instead euphemisms were used: "our company is reviewing its sponsorship arrangements", "our company has examined its corporate identity and has to re-position itself". In advance of those excuses/explanations, my advice was that executives of companies were warned "your client base may be eroded because of your support for this year's recipient"'.

35 Geoffrey Brahm Levey & Philip Mendes (eds), *Jews and Australian politics*, Sussex Academic Press, 2004.

36 Tzvi Fleischer, 'The libel against the lobby', *AJN*, 7 November 2003.

37 Wynhausen, op. cit.

38 *World Today*, ABC Radio, 6 November 2003.

39 *SMH*, 8 November 2003.

40 The Sydney Peace Foundation had approached the university in late 2002 and requested permission to use the Great Hall. After the 'tentative booking', the university claimed that there was a clash with another event and allowed the Department of Music to use the space instead. Stuart Rees told Ramsey that a meeting in early 2003 with university management was 'difficult and shameful'. Rees told me it was made perfectly clear that the university feared it would lose the financial support of certain sections of the Jewish community if the Ashrawi event went ahead and preferred to avoid the potential controversy.

41 As quoted in Megan Saunders, 'Jews "damaged" by Ashrawi peace prize protests', *Australian*, 1 November 2003.

42 Colin Rubenstein, 'Ashrawi revisited', *The Review*, December 2003.

43 As quoted in Wynhausen, op. cit.

44 Michael Danby, 'Over the top protest down under', *Forward*, 14 November 2003. Tellingly, Danby did not publish similar views in any major Australian newspaper.

45 ibid.

46 Michael Danby, 'My 30-year track record speaks for itself', *AJN*, 13 August 2004.

47 Colin Rubenstein, 'No appeasement on Ashrawi award', *Forward*, 21 November 2003.

48 *Religion Report*, ABC Radio, 29 October 2003.

49 David Langsam, 'AIJAC's hollow victory', *AJN*, 7 November 2003.

50 Dan Goldberg, 'The tempest', *AJN*, 21 November 2003.

2 How Hanan Ashrawi changed my life (pages 23–38)

1 Robert Fisk, 'Why does John Malkovich want to kill me?', *Independent*, 14 May 2002.

2 Antony Loewenstein, 'Hanan Ashrawi and the price of dissent', *Znet*, 23 October 2003.

3 Judith Butler, 'No, it's not antisemitic', *London Review of Books*, 21 August 2003.

4 'Israeli law limits Arab citizenship', *BBC News Online*, 31 July 2003, viewed April 2006, <news.bbc.co.uk/2/hi/middle_east/3111727.stm>.

5 Sara Roy, 'Living With The Holocaust: The Journey of a Child of Holocaust Survivors', *Journal of Palestine Studies*, vol. XXXII, no. 1, Autumn 2002, issue 125.

6 ibid.

7 Antony Loewenstein, 'Real Sydney people meet Hanan Ashrawi', *SMH Webdiary*, 10 November 2003.

8 Robert Fisk, 'Since when did "Arab" become a dirty word', *Independent*, 4 November 2003.

9 Margo Kingston, *Not happy, John! Defending our democracy*, Penguin Books, Melbourne, 2004.

10 Interview with the author, Sydney, 21 November 2003.

11 Peter Kohn, 'Book accuses AIJAC over Ashrawi affair', *AJN*, 25 June 2004.

12 'Margo Kingston earns wrath of Jewish News', *Crikey*, 28 June 2004.

13 Colin Rubenstein, 'After Ashrawi: in defence of AIJAC's tactics', *AJN*, 2 July 2004.

14 Email to author, 1 July 2004.

15 Antony Loewenstein, 'Ashrawi affair highlighted community's diversity', *AJN*, 9 July 2004.

16 David Southwick, 'How Danby missed his three moments of truth', *AJN*, 6 August 2004.

17 Michael Danby, letter to *AJN*, 23 July 2004.

18 Tony Kushner, 'Wrestling with Zion: an introduction', in Tony Kushner & Alisa Solomon (eds), *Wrestling with Zion*, Grove Press, 2003, pp. 5–6.

3 Journey into Israel (pages 39–66)

1 Ari Shavit, 'Under the Tuscan sun', *Haaretz*, 24 December 2004.

2 Uri Avnery, speech, Germany, 19 March 2005.

3 My departure was no better, with a two-hour interrogation and a demand to drop my pants for a groin inspection.

4 Spiegelman missed out on a place in the Labor primaries by 0.4 per cent in January 2006. He says he will run for preselection again in the future. Mark Franklin, 'Spiegelman pipped at the post', *AJN*, 27 January 2006.

5 Interview with the author, Tel Aviv, 14 February 2005.

6 Guy Spiegelman, 'Why Jewish students are really silent', *Haaretz*, 25 February 2005.

7 ibid.

8 The lives of Palestinians in East Jerusalem have always been made difficult by the Israeli authorities. Amir Cheshin, former Jerusalem mayor Teddy Kollek's adviser on Arab affairs and one of the architects of the city's 1967 policy, revealed the tactics in his book *Separate and unequal: the inside story of Israeli rule in East Jerusalem*, Harvard University Press, 1999:

> [In 1967], Israel's leaders adopted two basic principles in their rule of East Jerusalem. The first was to rapidly increase the Jewish population in East Jerusalem. The second was to hinder growth of the Arab population and to force Arab residents to make their homes elsewhere ... Israel turned urban planning into a tool of the government, to be used to help prevent the expansion of the city's non Jewish population. It was a ruthless policy, if only for the fact that the needs (to say nothing of the rights) of the Palestinian residents were ignored.

As quoted in 'The process of transfer continues: the Jerusalem Municipality plans to demolish 88 houses in Silwan, East Jerusalem', *Israeli Committee Against House Demolitions*, 6 June 2005, viewed April 2006, <www.icahd.org/eng/news.asp?menu=5&submenu=1&item=235>.

9 Most of our interview took place in East Jerusalem, 24 February 2005.

10 Chris McGreal, 'Once mighty Jordan reduced to a trickle', *Guardian*, 9 March 2005.

11 See Palestinian Academic Society for the Study of International Affairs, *Water in Palestine: problems, politics: prospects*, Palestinian Academic Society for the Study of International Affairs, 2003. Fadia contributed a chapter to this report.

12 Interview with the author, Jenin, 18 February 2005.

13 For more information, see <www.cpt.org/gallery/slideshow.php?set_albumName=album03>.

14 A close ally of then acting Israeli Prime Minister Ehud Olmert announced in March 2006 that Hebron would be kept under Jewish

control in any future West Bank withdrawal. *Associated Press*, 6 March 2006.

15 'Hebron: Palestinians storm international mission', *Associated Press*, 8 February 2006.

16 'Israel restricts Gaza access', *BBC News Online*, 9 May 2003, viewed April 2006, <news.bbc.co.uk/2/hi/middle_east/3013473.stm>.

17 Interview with the author, Kibbutz Nirim, 20 & 21 February 2005.

18 The Sharon government agreed in late 2004 to compensate the Gaza settlers in the hundreds of thousands of dollars. *Haaretz* columnist Gideon Levy questioned this rationale: 'To those who are calling for empathy towards these settlers, we must say that they do not deserve empathy since they never showed consideration for the feelings of others'. Gideon Levy, 'Compensate settlers for what?', *Haaretz*, 15 June 2004. The extremity of some settlers was exposed in June 2005 when a handful of right-wing extremists pelted a 16-year old Palestinian in Gaza with large stones and attempted to lynch him. When a doctor approached the youth, one of the attackers screamed, 'If you treat him, we'll kill you'. The settler doctor walked away and ignored the dying boy. The watching media saved the boy until the authorities arrived. 'Nir Hasson', *Haaretz*, 30 June 2005.

19 Interview with the author, Negev, 21 February 2005.

20 Interview with the author, Jerusalem, 23 February 2005.

21 Chris McGreal, 'It's because they feared us, say teenage refusniks gaoled by Israeli army', *Guardian*, 7 January 2004.

22 Molly Moore, 'Elite Israeli troops refuse to serve in the territories', *Washington Post*, 22 December 2003.

23 Also little reported, and a reason given by refusniks for their actions, is the Israeli practice of arresting, imprisoning and torturing Palestinian children. Catherine Cook, Adam Hanieh & Adah Kay, *Stolen youth: the politics of Israel's detention of Palestinian children*, Pluto Press, 2004, reveals that the Israeli forces have arrested over 1900 Palestinian children since September 2000, the vast majority of whom were simply throwing stones at Israeli settlers or the IDF. Children under the age of 18 are routinely detained with no access to lawyers or family visits. In the detention centres, children are interrogated, which can involve beatings with heavy batons, being punched and kicked, and being tied in painful and contorted positions for extended periods of time.

24 Combatants' letter to Ariel Sharon, December 2003.

25 Interview with the author, West Bank, 24 February 2005.

26 Robert Fisk, 'Amira Hass: life under Israeli occupation—by an Israeli', *Independent*, 26 August 2001.

27 Amira Hass, *Drinking the sea at Gaza: days and nights in a land under siege*, Metropolitan Books, 1999.

28 Amira Hass, *Reporting from Ramallah: an Israeli journalist in an occupied land*, Semiotext(e) Active Agents series, Semiotext(e), 2003.

29 Peace Now, led by Etkes, submitted a petition to Israel's High Court in early July 2005, the first such act against an illegal West Bank settlement outpost. By early 2006, the Israeli Supreme Court found that Amona settlement had to be evacuated. In the process of the evacuation, extremist settlers clashed with Israeli troops and caused widespread injuries. Yuval Yoaz, 'Peace Now files first petition against illegal West Bank outpost', *Haaretz*, 3 July 2005.

30 Daniel Dor's *The suppression of guilt*, Pluto Press, 2005, p. 73, reveals an Israeli media in the midst of the second intifada fending off guilt and accentuating victimhood:

> The common denominator [of the Israeli media], the foundational basis, lies in the portrayal of Israel—its government, its military, its people—as an agent without intentions, an innocent society that has been pushed into the operation, just as it was pushed into the entire Intifada, by the sheer force of Palestinian violence, with no agenda of its own except self-defence.

31 Interview with the author, Tel Aviv, 27 February 2005.

32 His *Haaretz* column in late November 2003 titled 'I punched an Arab in the face' caused a stir. It told the story of Staff Sergeant (res.) Liran Ron Furer and his book *Checkpoint syndrome*, which had been virtually ignored in Israel. Furer served in Gaza from 1996 to 1999 and describes how military service turns every soldier into an animal. He catalogues the horrors committed against Palestinians, characterising the occupied territories as a place where anything is permissible. He tells of taking souvenir pictures with bloodied, bound Arabs whom they'd beaten up. One soldier pissed on the head of an Arab because the man smiled at him, and another soldier forced an Arab to stand on four legs and bark like a dog.

> The most disturbing confession involved Furer punching an Arab in the face for no reason. It was a 16-year old mentally retarded boy, and numerous Israeli soldiers beat, kicked and bound him: 'The company commander informed us over the radio that we had to bring him to base. "Good work, tigers", he said teasing us'. Furer told Levy that these were not individual cases:

> We got the message from above that we were to project seriousness and deterrence to the Arabs ... Physical violence

also became normative. We felt free to punish any Palestinian who didn't follow the 'proper code of behaviour' at checkpoints ... During our army service, there wasn't a single incident that made us understand, or made our commanders interfere. No one talked about what was permitted and what was not ... We weren't criminals or especially violent people. We were a group of young boys [and] the checkpoint became a place to test our personal limits. How tough, how callous, how crazy we could be—and we thought of that in a positive sense. No one was ever punished and they just let us continue.

33 A poll released by the Centre for Struggle against Racism in March 2006 found that 68 per cent of Israeli Jews would refuse to live in the same apartment block as an Israeli Arab. The poll also found that many Israelis experience strong discomfort when they hear or see Arabs. Eli Ashkenazi & Jack Khoury, 'Racism had become mainstream', *Haaretz*, 22 March 2006.

34 Tanya Reinhart, *Israel/Palestine: How to end the war of 1948*, Allen & Unwin, 2003, p. 10.

35 Yitzhak Laor, 'In praise of the facts', *Haaretz*, 25 February 2005.

36 ibid.

37 Reuvan Pedatzur, 'More than a million bullets', *Haaretz*, 30 June 2004.

38 Interview with the author, Tel Aviv, 1 March 2005.

39 Tanya Reinhart, 'According to security sources', *Yediot Aharonot*, 24 May 2005.

40 During the 2006 Israeli election campaign, far-right National Jewish Front leader Baruch Marzel called on the IDF to assassinate Avnery because he said the peace activist was a traitor. Nadav Shragai, 'Baruch Marzel: IDF must assassinate left-wing activist Uri Avnery', *Haaretz*, 20 March 2006.

41 Ari Shavit, 'Missing Arafat', *Haaretz*, 11 November 2004.

42 Interview with the author, Tel Aviv, 2 March 2005. He told *Haaretz* in November 2004 that 'I am absolutely convinced that a person like me could have sat with Arafat for a month and emerged with a peace agreement ... We didn't understand that he was a critical element in the wall against [Islamic] fundamentalism'. Shavit, op. cit.

43 After the Hamas win in the 2006 Palestinian elections, Avnery expressed optimism that a peace deal was still possible. The Israeli establishment shunned Hamas but Avnery sees historical parallels in their blindness: 'We have returned to exactly the same point where we were when the PLO refused to recognise Israel and Israel refused

to recognise the PLO, he said'. He believes that the Israeli government must declare itself willing to 'conduct negotiations with the recognised representative of the Palestinian people'. He said the 'terror' against Israeli civilians must stop and a cease-fire be established. 'I don't need a declaration that they [Hamas] recognise the state of Israel', he said. 'Their very willingness to talk with us could be considered recognition.' Tom Segev, '"I don't consider them monsters"', *Haaretz*, 23 February 2006.

44 Former IDF chief Moshe Ya'alon revealed in March 2005 that Israel wanted to 'stop any kind of Palestinian working in Israel by 2008'. 'IDF chief: Palestinian labour to be phased out by 2008', *Associated Press*, 8 March 2005.

45 Tom Segev, 'Absolute evil', *Haaretz*, 28 January 2005.

46 'Ex-deputy Mossad director accuses IDF of losing its morality', *Haaretz*, 8 August 2004.

47 As quoted in 'Clashes mar Mid-East inquiry', *BBC News Online*, 25 March 2001, viewed April 2006, <news.bbc.co.uk/2/hi/middle_east/1241371.stm>.

4 The problem of Zionism (pages 69–96)

1 Norman Finkelstein, *Image and reality of the Israel–Palestine conflict*, Verso, 2001, p. 1.

2 David Remnick, 'The spirit level', *New Yorker*, 8 November 2004.

3 Theodore Herzl, *The Jewish state*, D Nutt, 1896.

4 Yeshayahu Leibovitz, *Yediot Ahronot*, March 1968.

5 Gideon Alon, 'Officer: 20% of soldiers do not view Arab, Jewish lives as equal', *Haaretz*, 7 December 2004. An IDF study concluded that the policy of house demolitions was counter-productive and did nothing to reduce terrorism.

6 Interview with the author, Sydney, 16 August 2004.

7 Palestinian Israeli writer Nur Masalha has proven that Herzl did not entirely ignore the indigenous population and even hoped some would stay and be grateful for Zionism's generosity. Nur Masalha, *Expulsion of the Palestinians: the concept of 'transfer' in Zionist political thought, 1882–1948*, Institute for Palestine Studies, 1992.

8 Ilan Pappe, *A history of modern Palestine: one land, two peoples*, Cambridge University Press, 2003, p. 36.

9 As quoted in 'The Mideast: a century of conflict', *National Public Radio*, 30 September 2002, viewed April 2006, <www.npr.org/news/specials/mideast/history/history1.html>.

10 As quoted in Albert S Lindermann, *Esau's tears*, Cambridge University Press, 2000, p. 125.

11 By 2002, according to the Israeli Ministry of Foreign Affairs, only around 117 000 people remained on kibbutz in Israel.

12 As quoted in Michael Benazon, 'Prophets outcast', *Outlook Magazine*, 2004.

13 Rashid Khalidi, 'Palestinian peasant resistance to Zionism before World War I', in Edward Said & Christopher Hitchens (eds), *Blaming the victims*, Verso, 2001, p. 213.

14 Peter Rodgers, *Herzl's nightmare: one land, two people*, Scribe Publications, 2004, p. 25.

15 As quoted in Ami Isseroff, 'Correspondence related to the British White Paper of 1922', *Mideast Web*, viewed April 2006, <www.mideast-web.org/1922wpcor.htm>.

16 As quoted in Avi Shlaim, *The iron wall: Israel and the Arab world*, Penguin, 2000, p. 10.

17 Khalidi, op. cit., p. 213.

18 Finkelstein, op. cit., p. 88.

19 A book published by Israel's State Archive in 2005 proved that future Prime Minister Yitzhak Rabin had advocated the transfer of Palestinians from the West Bank in 1956 while he was a major general in the IDF. He suggested initiating a war with Jordan and then deporting the Palestinians. 'It would not be a humane move', he said, 'but war in general is not a humane matter'. Amir Oren, 'Book: Rabin backed transfer of Arabs in '56', *Haaretz*, 1 July 2005.

20 As quoted in Edward Said, 'A profile of the Palestinian people', in Edward Said & Christopher Hitchens (eds), *Blaming the victims*, Verso, 2001, p. 239.

21 Bernard Avishai, 'Saving Israel from itself', *Harpers*, January 2005.

22 During the 2006 Israeli elections, *Haaretz* commentator Gideon Levy noted that the major political parties all advocated a similar ideology: 'to get rid of them [Palestinians], one way or another'. Gideon Levy, *Haaretz*, 26 March 2006.

23 Pappe, op. cit., p. 110.

24 David Ben-Gurion, *Letters to Paula*, trans. Aubrey Hodes, Vallentine, Mitchell, 1971, pp. 153–7.

25 Translation of original documents for author by Avigail Abarbanel, Canberra-based writer and psychotherapist.

26 Alan Dershowitz, *The case for Israel*, Wiley, 2003, p. 54.

27 Baruch Kimmerling, 'Israel's culture of martyrdom', *The Nation*, 10 January 2005.

28 ibid.

29 Interview with Tom Segev by Henry Kriesler, University of California Berkeley, 2004.

30 Shlaim, op. cit., p. 24.

31 As cited in Kimmerling, op. cit.

32 Edward Said, 'Introduction', in Edward Said & Christopher Hitchens (eds), *Blaming the victims*, Verso, 2001, p. 1.

33 Pappe, op. cit., p. 130.

34 Kimmerling, op. cit.

35 Another even more murderous campaign, with around 200 killed, occurred in May at Tantura, a small village near Haifa.

36 Rodgers, op. cit., p. 24.

37 Finkelstein, op. cit., p. 58.

38 Finkelstein, op. cit., p. 51.

39 Pappe, op. cit., p. 141.

40 Shlaim, op. cit., p. 33.

41 Ari Shavit, 'Survival of the fittest', *Haaretz*, 16 January 2004.

42 As quoted in Jason Burke, 'From butcher to "lion" to Prime Minister of Israel', *Observer*, 4 February 2001.

43 Seymour Hersh, *The Samson option*, Faber & Faber, 1991, p. 36.

44 Finkelstein, op. cit., p. 22.

45 Hannah Arendt, *Eichmann in Jerusalem: a report on the banality of evil*, Penguin, 1992, pp. 3–12.

46 Kimmerling, op. cit.

47 As quoted in Norman Finkelstein, *The Holocaust industry*, Verso, 2001, p. 21.

48 John Simpson, 'The future of the Jewish settlements', *BBC News Online*, 29 June 2001, viewed April 2006, <news.bbc.co.uk/2/hi/programmes/from_our_own_correspondent/1413738.stm>.

49 Jeremy Bowen, *Six days*, Pocket Books, 2003, p. 323.

50 Tony Judt, 'After victory', *New Republic*, 25 July 2002.

51 As quoted in Noam Chomsky, *Middle East illusions*, Rowman & Littlefield Publishers, 2004, p. 21.

52 Amos Elon, *A blood-dimmed tide*, Penguin, 2000, p. 225.

53 Pappe, op. cit., p. 201.

54 As quoted in Rodgers, op. cit., p. 38.

55 Jeffrey Goldberg, 'Among the settlers', *New Yorker*, 31 May 2004.

56 Avraham Burg, 'The end of Zionism', *Guardian*, 15 September 2003.

57 Shlomo Gazit, *Trapped fools*, Frank Cass Publishers, 2003, p. 333.

58 ibid., p. 338.

59 Bowen, op. cit., p. 330.

60 Bernard Avishai, 'Saving Israel from itself', *Harpers*, January 2005.

61 Said, op. cit., p. 13.

62 David Ignatius, 'Penetrating the terrorist networks', *Washington Post*, 16 September 2001.

63 As quoted in Hersh, op. cit., p. 8.

64 ibid., p. 10.

65 Robert Fisk, *Pity the nation*, Oxford University Press, 2001, p. 388.

66 ibid.

67 In their essay, 'The Israel lobby', *London Review of Books*, 23 March 2006, academics John J Mearsheimer and Stephen M Walt write:

> Since the October War in 1973, Washington has provided Israel with a level of support dwarfing that given to any other state. It has been the largest annual recipient of direct economic and military assistance since 1976, and is the largest recipient in total since World War Two, to the tune of well over US$140 billion (in 2004 dollars). Israel receives about US$3 billion in direct assistance each year, roughly one-fifth of the foreign aid budget, and worth about US$500 a year for every Israeli. This largesse is especially striking since Israel is now a wealthy industrial state with a per capita income roughly equal to that of South Korea or Spain ... Most recipients of aid given for military purposes are required to spend all of it in the US, but Israel is allowed to use roughly 25 percent of its allocation to subsidize its own defense industry. It is the only recipient that does not have to account for how the aid is spent, which makes it virtually impossible to prevent the money from being used for purposes the US opposes, such as building settlements on the West Bank.

68 Glenn Kessler, 'Scowcroft is critical of Bush', *Washington Post*, 16 October 2004.

69 Pappe, op. cit., pp. 196–204.

70 Pappe, op. cit., p. 236.

71 Bill Clinton, *My life*, Hutchinson, 2004, pp. 541–7.

72 ibid., p. 545.

73 ibid.

74 Jeff Halper, 'Frequently asked questions', *Israeli Committee against House Demolitions*, viewed April 2006, <icahd.org/eng/faq.asp?menu=9&submenu=12004>.

75 As quoted in Chomsky, op. cit., p. 215.

76 Hussein Agha & Robert Malley, 'Camp David: the tragedy of errors', *New York Review of Books*, 9 August 2001.

77 Pappe, op. cit., p. 257.

78 Kimmerling, op. cit.

79 As quoted in Elon, op. cit., p. 322.

80 Tanya Reinhart, *Israel/Palestine*, Allen & Unwin, 2002, p. 21.

81 Agha & Malley, op. cit.

82 Reinhart, op. cit., pp. 22–3.

83 Reinhart, op. cit., pp. 42–51.

84 Reinhart, op. cit., p. 60.

85 Clinton, op. cit., pp. 911–16.

86 Reinhart, op. cit., pp. 42–51.

87 Reinhart, op. cit., pp. 27, 51.

88 Jude Wanniski, 'The truth about Camp David', *Aljazeera*, 11 January 2005.

89 As quoted in Eric Rouleau, 'Power to the patriarch', *Le Monde*, 17 November 2004.

90 George W Bush, The White House Rose Garden, June 2002.

91 Christian Zionism is a growing movement of strongly pro-Israel advocates who believe that the establishment of Israel in 1948 was in line with Biblical prophecy and is a necessary precondition for the return of Jesus to rule over the Earth.

92 B'Tselem press release, 26 February 2006.

93 B'Tselem press release, 22 March 2006.

94 'Michael Albert interviews Noam Chomsky, Chomsky on the plan for Palestinians', *Z Magazine*, May/June 2002.

95 Edward Said, 'Israel's dead end', *Al-Ahram*, 20–26 December 2001.

96 Human Rights Watch, 'Israel: don't outlaw family life', 28 July 2003.

97 Meron Rapaport, 'Beilin accuses Sharon government of stealing property', *Haaretz*, 22 January 2005.

98 Akiva Eldar, 'Poll: majority of Palestinians now support two-state solution', *Haaretz*, 18 January 2005.

5 The problem of antisemitism (pages 97–119)

1 Thomas Friedman, 'Campus hypocrisy', *The New York Times*, 16 October 2002.

2 David Frum, 'Marching against war—and Jews', *AEI*, 27 September 2005, viewed April 2006, <www.aei.org/publications/pubID.23254, filter.all/pub_detail.asp>.

3 The circumstances of her 'crimes' remain contentious and her trail was possibly politically motivated. Elaine Cassel, 'The Lynne Stewart case: when representing an accused terrorist can mean the lawyer risks jail, too', *Counterpunch*, 12 October 2002.

4 Amy L Lansky, email to Tikkun, 20 October 2005.

5 Melanie Philips, 'The new anti-Semitism', speech presented to the London Society of Jews and Christians, 29 April 2004.

6 Nick Cohen, 'Anti-Semitism isn't a local side effect of a dirty war over a patch of land smaller than Wales. It's everywhere from Malaysia to Morocco, and it has arrived here', *New Statesman*, 10 October 2005.

7 Lucy Dawidowicz's book, *The war against the Jews 1939-45*, Bantam, 1986, discusses Hitler's desire to eradicate European Jewry.

8 Phyllis Chesler, *The new anti-Semitism: the current crisis and what we must do about it*, Wiley, 2003.

9 'The skinny on "Semitism"', *Forward*, 11 October 2002.

10 Albert S Lindemann, *Esau's tears*, Cambridge University Press, 2000, p. 89.

11 Brian Klug, 'No, anti-Zionism isn't anti-Semitism', *Guardian*, 3 December 2004.

12 Lindemann, op. cit., pp. 97–101.

13 Lindemann, op. cit., p. 207.

14 ibid.

15 Lindemann, op. cit., pp. 104–7.

16 Lindemann, op. cit., pp. 117–18.

17 Deborah Dwork & Robert Jan van Pelt, *Holocaust: a history*, John Murray Publishers, 2002, p. 17.

18 ibid.

19 ibid., pp. 17–18.

20 'Jews', *MSN Encarta*, viewed April 2006, <encarta.msn.com/encyclopedia_761567959/Jews.html>.

21 ADL, *A hoax of hate*, ADL, 2002.

22 'The "Protocols of the Elders of Zion"', *Jewish Virtual Library*, American–Israeli Cooperative Enterprise, viewed April 2006, <www.jewishvirtuallibrary.org/jsource/anti-semitism/prototoc.html>.

23 As quoted in Saul Friedlander, *Nazi Germany and the Jews*, Weidenfeld & Nicolson, 1997, p. 75.

24 Robert S Wistrich, *Hitler and the Holocaust*, Modern Library, 2001, p. 7.

25 ibid., p. 7.

26 ibid., p. 8.

27 George Orwell, 'Anti-semitism in Britain', in *The collected essays, journalism and letters of George Orwell*, ed. Sonia Orwell and Ian Angus, Penguin Books, Harmondsworth, 1970 (1945).

28 'Zionism and racism', *Wikipedia*, Wikimedia Foundation, viewed April 2006, <en.wikipedia.org/wiki/Zionism_and_racism>.

29 Wistrich, op. cit.

30 Peter Novick, *The Holocaust in American life*, First Mariner Books, 2000, p. 8.

31 Norman Finkelstein, *The Holocaust industry*, Verso, 2001, p. 17.

32 ibid., p. 21.

33 ibid., p. 23.

34 Pogroms started in Iraq during World War II because of Nazi manipulation of Iraqi officers. In Algeria, attacks on Jews were caused by their association and connection to the French colonial power.

35 Joseph Massad, 'Semites and anti-Semites, that is the question', *Al-Ahram*, 9–15 December 2004.

36 Marie Woolf, 'The shocking face of anti-Semitism', *Independent*, 16 June 2005.

37 'Anti-semitism on rise in Britain, MP says', *Associated Press*, 18 November 2005. John Mann MP said that the 'liberal and progressive left' was partly to blame for the rise in antisemitism. 'MPs to look at anti-Semitism rise', *Guardian*, 17 November 2005.

38 'Britain's Chief Rabbi: "tsunami of anti-Semitism" sweeping the world', *Associated Press*, 1 January 2006.

39 Geoff Meade, 'Anti-Semitism increasing, study warns', *Scotsman*, 31 March 2004.

40 'Anti-Semitism "on rise in Europe"', *BBC News Online*, 31 March 2004, viewed April 2006, <news.bbc.co.uk/2/hi/europe/3586543.stm>.

41 ibid.

42 Ali Abunimah, 'Arabs, Muslims are not behind European anti-Semitism', *Daily Star*, 16 April 2004.

43 EUMC, *Racist violence in 15 EU member states*, EUMC, April 2005.

44 There was a 20 per cent fall in violent antisemitic attacks around the world in 2005, according to a report issued in April 2006 by the Stephen Roth Institute for the Study of Contemporary Antisemitism and Racism at Tel Aviv University. While France and Canada saw a large drop, there was no change in violent antisemitic attacks in the United Kingdom but a fall in overall antisemitic incidents. Russia and Ukraine saw a steep rise, however. The report claimed the results were influenced by positive, worldwide coverage of the 2005 Gaza withdrawal and relative peace between Israel and the Palestinians. Furthermore, it argued that Western governments have increased their vigilance against antisemitism through education, law-enforcement and legislation. Amiram Barkat, 'Report: anti-Semitic incidents drop for first time since 2000', *Haaretz*, 24 April 2006.

45 A poll released in Sweden in March 2006 revealed contradictory attitudes towards Jews and antisemitism. A majority (59 per cent) rejected antisemitism, but a sizeable minority (36 per cent) were ambivalent. Many felt that Jews exercised a disproportionate influence over the economy, media and foreign policy. Only 3 percent thought

that Israel had 'no right to exist', and 14 per cent believed that 'Israeli policies engender hatred against Jews'. Among Swedish Muslims, anti-semitic attitudes were higher than the average. It seems that while traditional antisemitism is largely absent from Sweden, certain Jewish stereotypes remain among the wider population. Susanna Abramowicz, 'Anti-semitic attitudes in Sweden', *Ynetnews*, 21 March 2006, viewed April 2006, <www.ynetnews.com/articles/0,7340,L-3230392,00.>.

46 According to the American Jewish polemicist Daniel Pipes, 'in its attitudes towards Jews, the Muslim world today resembles Germany of the 1930s'. There is no evidence whatsoever to support this outrageous assertion, despite his claims that 'millions of Jews would perish in another Holocaust'. Daniel Pipes, 'Deadly denial of Muslim anti-Semitism', *New York Post*, 26 October 2003.

47 Abunimah, op. cit.

48 'Viewpoints: Europe and the headscarf', *BBC News Online*, 10 February 2004, viewed April 2006, <news.bbc.co.uk/2/hi/europe/3459963.stm>.

49 Henri Astier, 'French Muslims face job discrimination', *BBC News Online*, 2 November 2005, viewed April 2006, <news.bbc.co.uk/2/hi/europe/4399748.stm>.

50 A Swedish poll released in early 2006 showed negative attitudes towards Muslims were far more serious than those towards Jews. Nearly 25 per cent of Swedes felt there were too many Muslims in Sweden, and 6.7 per cent said Muslims shouldn't be allowed to vote in elections. Abramowicz, op. cit.

51 Abunimah, op. cit.

52 Jeff Jacoby, 'The cancer of anti-Semitism in Europe', *Boston Globe*, 14 March 2004.

53 Bertrand Benoit, 'Anti-Semitism falls in France but hostility to Israel grows', *Financial Times*, 27 April 2004.

54 Emanuele Ottolenghi, 'Europe's "Good Jews"', *Commentary*, December 2005.

55 Yaron Ezrahi, 'Viewpoints: anti-Semitism and Europe', *BBC News Online*, 3 December 2003, viewed April 2006, <news.bbc.co.uk/2/hi/europe/3234264.stm>.

56 ibid.

57 Natan Sharansky, 'Anti-Semitism in 3D', *Jerusalem Post*, 23 February 2004.

58 'New anti-Semitism', *Wikipedia*, viewed April 2006, <en.wikipedia.org/wiki/New_anti-Semitism>.

59 It is clearly antisemitism, he says, when Israel's Magen David Adom, an ambulance service, is refused admission to the International Red Cross. After six decades of exclusion—principally because the

60 Asaf Romirowsky, 'Anti-semitism revisited', *FrontPageMagazine.com*, 28 February 2005, viewed April 2006, <www.frontpagemag.com/Articles/ReadArticle.asp?ID=17158>.

61 Sara Roy, 'Living with the Holocaust', *Palestine Studies*, vol. 32, no. 1, Autumn 2002.

62 600 000 Jews and five million Muslims.

63 Alan Dershowitz, 'Making the case for Israel', *FrontPageMagazine.com*, 1 June 2004, viewed April 2006, <www.frontpagemag.com/Articles/ReadArticle.asp?ID=13590>.

64 Jon Henley, '*Le Monde* editor "defamed Jews"', *Guardian*, 4 June 2005.

65 Tom Gross, 'J'accuse', *Wall Street Journal Europe*, 2 June 2005.

66 ibid.

67 In 2004, France's Interior Minister, Dominique de Villepin, told French daily *Le Monde* that attacks by right-wingers and Arabs on Jews may be related to a rise in Middle East violence. 'French PM: anti-Semitic violence jumps, reasons unclear', *Reuters*, 27 August 2004.

68 Jon Henley, 'Rising tension in France blamed on disaffected Arab youths', *Guardian*, 25 November 2003.

69 John Lichfield and Audrey Jacquet, 'Unsafe for Jews? France is shaken by Sharon's jibe', *Independent*, 20 July 2004.

70 'French protest for murdered Jew', *BBC News Online*, 26 February 2006, viewed April 2006, <news.bbc.co.uk/2/hi/europe/4753348.stm>.

71 Kim Willsher, 'Brutal murder was anti-Semitic crime, says Sarkozy', *Guardian*, 22 February 2006.

72 'French protest for murdered Jew', op. cit.

73 Email interview with Jon Henley, 6 January 2006.

74 Jon Henley, 'A horrifying hypothesis', *Guardian*, 30 July 2004.

75 Jon Henley, 'Attacks on Jews and Muslims soar in France', *Guardian*, 22 March 2005.

76 Matthew Campbell, 'Barbarians of suburbs target French Jews', *Times*, 2 April 2006.

77 Jon Henley, 'France takes on new wave of anti-Semitism in schools', *Guardian*, 1 March 2003.

78 Craig S Smith, 'French Jews tell of a new and threatening wave of anti-Semitism', *New York Times*, 22 March 2003.

79 ibid.

80 Alain Gresh, 'Palestine: the forgotten reality', *Le Monde*, December 2005.

Christian red cross and Muslim red crescent were the only accepted symbols of the organisation—Israel joined the International Red Cross movement in January 2006 under the symbol of a crystal. 'Israel finally joins Red Cross', *Israel Today*, 18 January 2006.

81 Daniel Ben Simon, 'French disconnection', *Haaretz*, 16 December 2005.

82 'France confronts a surge in racism', *SMH*, 21 October 2004.

83 Ben Simon, op. cit.

84 Norman Finkelstein, *Beyond chutzpah: on the misuse of anti-Semitism and the misuse of history*, University of California Press, 2005, p. 22.

85 ibid.

86 Chris Kulawik & Josh Lipsky, 'Hate comes to Columbia', *Columbia Spectator*, 1 March 2006.

87 Phyllis Chesler, 'Are we winning the war on terror?', *FrontPageMagazine.com*, 10 March 2006, viewed April 2006, <www.front-pagemag.com/Articles/ReadArticle.asp?ID=21593>. Isi Leibler shares Chesler's perspective and writes that there should be 'limits' to what can be discussed at universities and conferences. 'Are views which question the right of the state of Israel to exist to be accepted as a legitimate 'alternative' Jewish viewpoint', he asks? Isi Leibler, 'The validation of Jewish anti-Zionism', *Jerusalem Post*, 11 January 2006.

88 George Will, 'The Left's anti-Semitic chic', *Washington Post*, 25 February 2004.

89 Alan Dershowitz, *The case for Israel*, Wiley, 2003, p. 208.

90 Alan Dershowitz, *The case for peace: how the Arab–Israeli conflict can be solved*, Wiley, 2005, p. 198.

91 Alan Dershowitz, 'Making the case for Israel', *FrontPageMagazine.com*, 1 June 2004, viewed April 2006, <www.frontpagemag.com/Articles/ReadArticle.asp?ID=135901>.

92 ibid.

93 Amy Wilentz, 'Just another rant about the Mideast', *LA Times*, 23 September 2005.

94 Finkelstein, *Beyond chutzpah*, op. cit., p. 16.

95 ibid., p. 92.

96 Dershowitz, *The case for peace*, op. cit., p. 212. Dershowitz has charged the renowned linguist with defending a French Holocaust denying academic, Robert Faurisson, and writing an introduction to one of his works. Chomsky has done nothing of the sort; rather he defended Faurisson's right to free speech and was unaware that his writings were being abused by Faurrison. (Chomsky even tried to have his introduction withdrawn when he realised how it was to be used.) Moreover, Chomsky has described the Holocaust as 'the most fantastic outburst of insanity in human history'. Noam Chomsky, 'His right to say it', *The Nation*, 28 February 1981. Faurisson had been barred from the University of Lyon and brought before the French courts for denying the existence of the gas chambers. Around 500 people, including Chomsky, signed

a petition defending Faurisson's civil liberties and this was soon used as an ideological weapon against Chomsky, a chance by his foes to settle old scores. Dershowitz, *The case for peace*, op. cit., pp. 212–15.

97 Dershowitz, *The case for Israel*, op. cit., pp. 167–8.

98 Noam Chomsky, *Fateful triangle*, Pluto Press, 1999.

99 Noam Chomsky, 'Israel, the Holocaust, and anti-Semitism' (excerpt from Noam Chomsky, *Chronicles of dissent: interviews with David Barsamian*, Common Courage, 1992), viewed April 2006, <www.chomsky.info/books/dissent01.htm>.

100 ibid.

101 Interview with the author, Boston, 8 February 2005.

102 Natan Sharansky, op. cit.

103 Jonathan Granger, 'Anti-Semitism up, Jewish group says', *Seven News*, 5 December 2004.

104 Jeremy Jones, 'The hatred files: Antisemitism in Australia 2004', *The Review*, vol. 30, no. 4, April 2005.

105 The 2005 ECAJ report found that antisemitic incidents in Australia had fallen but Jew-hatred in cyberspace was on the rise. Jeremy Jones said that 'threatening email' was now the most common form of anti-semitic abuse in Australia. Peter Kohn, 'Anti-semitic incidents fall, online Jew-hatred increases—report', *AJN*, 9 December 2005.

106 Dawn Cohen, 'An ancient prejudice in the New Age: anti-semitism in alternative Australia', *Overland*, winter, 2004.

107 Jeremy Jones, 'Confronting reality: anti-Semitism in Australia today', *Jewish Political Studies Review*, vol. 16, nos 3–4, fall, 2004.

108 ibid.

109 Tzvi Fleischer, 'Israel in the Australian Media', *Jewish Political Studies Review*, vol. 17, nos 3–4, fall, 2005.

110 Ami Eden, 'Tempers flare at parley on anti-Semitism', *Forward*, 6 February 2004.

111 Brian Klug, 'The myth of the new Anti-Semitism', *The Nation*, 2 February 2004.

112 Geoffrey Robertson QC, 'Foreword' to Jacqueline Rose's *The Question of Zion*, Melbourne University Press, 2005, p. xviii.

113 Ned Curthoys, 'A new anti-Semitism', *Arena*, April/May 2004.

114 Klug, op. cit.

6 The politics of Zionism in the USA (pages 123–43)

1 Edward Said, 'Who's in charge', *Al-Ahram*, 6–12 March 2003.

2 'Israel comes first, says US politician', *Associated Press*, 22 May 2005.

3 Gershon Baskin (co-CEO of the Israel/Palestine Centre for Research and Information), 'Engaging the US President', *Jerusalem Post*, 28 June 2005.

4 As quoted in Nathan Guttman, 'American Jews—still sworn Democrats', *Haaretz*, 2 June 2004.

5 Remarkably, a survey commissioned by the American Jewish Committee found that 59 per cent of American Jews had never visited Israel, principally because of the cost. Thirty-six per cent said they felt 'very close' to Israel' and 41 per cent felt 'somewhat close'. The same poll found 49 per cent would support military action against Iran if they developed nuclear weapons. Shlomo Shamir, 'Survey: 60% of US Jews never visited Israel', *Haaretz*, 21 December 2005. Another poll found that the majority of US Jews are strong supporters of Israel but often avoid supporting it publicly.

6 Mitchell Plitnick, 'Myth and reality: Jewish influence on US Middle East policy', *Jewish Voice for Peace*, 1 June 2005, viewed April 2006, <www.jewishvoiceforpeace.org/publish/article_100.shtml.>.

7 Michael Massing, 'Deal breakers', *American Prospect*, 11 March 2002.

8 ibid.

9 ibid.

10 ibid.

11 Stephen Zunes, 'Why the US supports Israel', *Foreign Policy in Focus*, May 2002.

12 ibid.

13 Larry Kudlow, 'Papa don't breach', *National Review Online*, 29 April 2002, viewed April 2006, <www.nationalreview.com/kudlow/kudlow 042902.asp>.

14 Jeffrey Blankfort, 'Mirror, mirror on the wall, who says they love Israel most of all?', *MELB Congressional Report*, vol. 3, no. 4, summer/fall 1992.

15 Plitnick, op. cit.

16 In December 2005 the US House of Representatives voted in favour of a resolution to chastise the Palestinian Authority for allowing Hamas to participate in the forthcoming elections. The resolution also declared that 'no democracy in the world allows a political party to bear its own arms'—a strange assertion considering that many parties in Iraq openly operate militias—and was part of a concerted effort to undermine international law regarding occupation and human rights, already regularly breached by the USA. Stephen Zunes, 'Democracy and double standards: the Palestinian "exception"', *Foreign Policy in Focus*, 28 December 2005.

17 Nathan Guttman, 'Capitol Hill slow to catch on to new Middle East mood', *Haaretz*, 1 March 2005.

18 Nathan Guttman, 'Lobbying for the pro-Israel candidates', *Haaretz*, 6 July 2004.

19 US politics professor Stephen Zunes has argued that McKinney would have lost even without the influx of 'Jewish money' to her opponent. She was a 'thorn in the side' of the Bush administration and 'challenged the bipartisan consensus of post-9/11 foreign policy'. Stephen Zunes, 'Don't Blame the Jews for Cynthia McKinney's Defeat', *Common Dreams*, 25 August 2002.

20 Tom Tugend, 'Israel tourism drive focuses on Latinos', *Los Angeles Jewish Journal*, 13 May 2005.

21 Uri Avnery, 'With friends like these…', email newsletter, 16 January 2006.

22 Clinton met then Israeli prime minister Binyamin Netanyahu in 1998 and told him that Israel had to withdraw from parts of the West Bank. On the eve of the meeting, Netanyahu met publicly with Jerry Falwell, Christian fundamentalist and friend of the late Israeli prime minister Menachem Begin. Christian evangelists, including Falwell, announced in early 2006 the establishment of a 'Christian AIPAC', an umbrella organisation whereby Christian Zionists could speak in one voice in support of Israel. Their principal aim was to force the US government to 'stop pressuring Israel to give up land for peace'. 'Israel has a Bible mandate for the land', said Pastor John C Hage, founder of Christians United for Israel (CUFI). Ilan Chaim, 'Evangelicals to launch "Christian AIPAC"', *Jerusalem Post*, 2 February 2006. Falwell, a strong opponent of Clinton, claimed later that the meeting was deliberately set up to challenge the President. Craig Unger, 'American "rapture"', *Vanity Fair*, December 2005. A few days before, another friend of Netanyahu's, William Kristol, one of the Jewish neo-conservative leaders, had publicly suggested that a White House sex scandal was about to break. Soon after, the Monica Lewinsky scandal exploded. Uri Avnery adds another twist to the tale: 'Two weeks before the Netanyahu visit, an American Jewish paper had published an ad demanding that the President abstain from pressuring Israel. The ad included a photo of Clinton taken from the back—the very shot of Clinton embracing Monica that was later published all around the world'. Avnery, op. cit. Falwell now boasts that he helped Netanyahu to blackmail Clinton. The President was under intense pressure over the Lewinsky saga and was severely weakened politically. Needless to say, no pressure was put on Israel at that meeting. *Vanity Fair* explained the course of events:

> The next day [after the meeting between Netanyahu and Falwell], Netanyahu met with Clinton at the White House. 'Bibi [Netanyahu] told me later,' Falwell recalls, 'that the next morning Bill Clinton said, 'I know where you were last

night.' The pressure was really on Netanyahu to give away the farm in Israel. It was during the Monica Lewinsky scandal ... Clinton had to save himself, so he terminated the demands [to relinquish West Bank territory] that would have been forthcoming during that meeting, and would have been very bad for Israel.

Unger, op. cit.

23 As quoted in Unger, op. cit.

24 Nicholas D Kristof, 'The Bush and Kerry tilt', *New York Times*, 26 May 2004. Bush and Kerry were so in thrall to the Zionist lobby—this term was ignored by the columnist but these lobbyists were almost certainly the target of his accusations—that Kerry was planting 'his own wet kisses on Mr. Sharon' and Bush's policies were 'so unbalanced that it's now little more than an embrace of the right-wing jingoist whom Mr. Bush unforgettably labelled a "man of peace"'.

25 John Kerry, *Strengthening Israel's security and bolstering the US/Israel special relationship*, position paper, John Kerry for President, July 2004.

26 Nathan Guttman, 'John Kerry position paper outlines support for Israel', *Haaretz*, 2 July 2004.

27 'A committed citizen', *johnkerry.com*, viewed April 2006, <www.johnkerry.com/about/teresa_heinz_kerry/citizen>; Andy Bowers, 'What's a Boston Brahmin?', *Slate*, 1 March 2004, viewed April 2006, <www.slate.com/id/2096401/>.

28 Comments at the annual pro-Zionist ADL leadership conference in May 2004.

29 As quoted in Nathan Guttman, 'Presidential hopeful Kerry woos Jews with Israel anecdotes', *Haaretz*, 4 May 2005.

30 As quoted in Dennis J Kucinich, 'An open letter to Howard Dean', *The Nation*, 3 May 2005.

31 Joshua Frank, 'Howard Dean's blunt message: forget Palestine', *Online Journal*, 30 November 2005, viewed April 2006, <www.online-journal.com/artman/publish/article_282.shtml>.

32 As quoted in E J Kessler, 'Dean plans to visit Israel, political baggage in tow', *Forward*, 8 July 2005.

33 Kessler, op. cit.

34 Hillary Clinton spoke at Princeton University on 18 January 2006.

35 Dan Balz, 'Hillary Clinton crafts centrist stance on war', *Washington Post*, 12 December 2005.

36 Joe Kovacs, 'Sheehan thrashing "war hawk" Hillary', *WorldNetDaily*, 19 October 2005, viewed April 2006, <wnd.com/news/article.asp?ARTICLE_ID=46919>.

37 Maureen Dowd, 'Who's Hormonal? Hillary or Dick?', *New York Times*, 8 February 2006.
38 More than a hundred members of Congress visited Israel in 2005. *JTA*, 15 January 2006.
39 Kristen Lombardi, 'Hillary calls Israel a "beacon" of democracy', *Village Voice*, 11 December 2005. Speaking at Princeton University on 18 January 2006, Clinton warned that a nuclear Iran would be—notice her order of importance—a 'danger to Israel, to its neighbours and beyond'.
40 George W Bush, speech to the American Jewish Committee, 3 May 2001.
41 The *Washington Post* found that Jewish support for the Republicans remained low in 2006, despite Bush's support for Israel, while the Democrats retained the strongest level of support. Two men were blamed: disgraced Republican fundraiser, and Orthodox Jew, Jack Abramoff and former Republican majority leader Tom DeLay, both involved in corruption scandals. Thomas B Edsall, 'Post 9/11 drive by Republicans to attract Jewish voters stalls', *Washington Post*, 6 March 2006. Abramoff funded far-right militias in the West Bank and illegal settlements there. An associate described him to *Newsweek* in 2005 as a 'super-Zionist'. Michael Isikoff, 'Fund-raising: take it to the (West) Bank', *Newsweek*, 4 January 2006.
42 A major conservative Christian advocacy group announced in late 2005 that it would release the voting records of American legislators on Israel in its biennial Christian voting guide. Roberta Combs, president of the Christian Coalition of America, told the *Jerusalem Post* that, 'our heart is with Israel'. Etgar Lefkovits, 'Guide tracks US reps' votes on Israel', *Jerusalem Post*, 27 December 2005.
43 PNAC's website is at <newamericancentury.org/>.
44 PNAC, letter to President Clinton, 26 January 1998, *PNAC*, viewed April 2006, <www.newamericancentury.org/iraqclintonletter.htm>.
45 PNAC wrote to President Bush in 2002 and praised him for his 'strong stance in support of the Israeli government as it engages in the present day campaign to fight terror'. It claimed the USA bore no responsibility for ongoing clashes between Israel and the Palestinians, and urged him to 'accelerate plans for removing Saddam Hussein from power': 'Israel's victory [against terrorism] is an important part of our victory'. PNAC, letter to President Bush, 3 April 2002, *PNAC*, viewed April 2006, <newamericancentury.org/Bushletter-040302.htm>. The letter is signed, among others, by William Kristol, Daniel Pipes, Richard Perle and (former CIA director) James Woolsey.
46 Brian Whitaker, 'Playing skittles with Saddam', *Guardian*, 3 September 2002.

47 The resolution was also adopted in the context of Israel's strong economic and defence cooperation with apartheid South Africa.

48 'Bolton delay offensive to Jewish community, says JINSA', *US Newswire*, 20 May 2005.

49 During his visit to Australia in June 2005, Harris told ABC Radio that although 'he cannot speak for the state of Israel', he believed Bolton would 'make friends for the United States'. 'Bush still fighting to get Bolton approved', *PM*, ABC Radio, 23 June 2005.

50 As quoted in Ori Nir, 'Scandal stymies Israeli effort to pressure Tehran', *Forward*, 29 April 2005.

51 ibid.

52 Soon after the Hamas victory in early 2006, AIPAC was pushing Congress to pass the Palestinian antiterrorist act, HR 4681, essentially halting the vast majority of humanitarian aid to the Palestinians, restricting Palestinian diplomacy in the UN and designating Palestinian territory as a 'terrorist sanctuary'. Such a designation would trigger restrictions on US exports to Palestinian territories. Nathan Guttman, 'AIPAC taking Hamas, Iran issues to Congress', *Jerusalem Post*, 7 March 2006.

53 Peter Slevin, 'Bush backs Israel on West Bank', *Washington Post*, 15 April 2004.

54 *Haaretz* commented in January 2006 that, for the first time in living memory, AIPAC had openly criticised the Bush administration's initial approach towards Iran as 'dangerous' because it hadn't been aggressive enough. Avi Beker, 'American Jews' split personality', *Haaretz*, 1 January 2006.

55 As quoted in Shmuel Rosner & Yossi Melman, 'Cheney: US keeping all options on the table vis-à-vis Iran', *Haaretz*, 8 March 2006.

56 'Rice: US has options on Iran', *Associated Press*, 29 March 2006.

57 John Pilger, 'The next war', *New Statesman*, 10 February 2006.

58 There was controversy during the 2005 AIPAC conference because the Israeli national anthem, 'Hatikva', wasn't sung, only the 'Star Spangled Banner'. Both songs were sung in 2006. Shmuel Rosner, 'AIPAC changes its tune, will sing Hatikva at policy conference', *Haaretz*, 26 February 2006.

59 As quoted in Nathan Guttman, 'AIPAC sends tough message to Iran', *Jerusalem Post*, 5 March 2006.

60 John Bolton, speech at AIPAC policy conference, 27 March 2006, *AIPAC*, viewed April 2006, <www.aipac.org/NER032706_KeyLeaders.htm>.

61 As quoted in Dana Milbank, 'Amid AIPAC's big show, straight talk with a noticeable silence', *Washington Post*, 7 March 2006.

62 Eli Lake, 'How aide at AIPAC became target in US spy case', *New York Sun*, 27 June 2005.

63 The FBI was investigating the activities of Rosen from as early as 1999. Andrew Killgore, 'According to indictment, AIPAC has been under investigation since early 1999', *Washington Report on Middle East Affairs*, November 2005.

64 The Zionist lobby were outraged that the case had even gone to court. Malcolm Hoenlein, executive vice chairman of the Conference of Presidents of Major American Jewish Organisations, said the ruling was 'disturbing'. He argued a whiff of antisemitism could be detected in the government's case. Hilary Leila Krieger, 'Hoenlein: Franklin sentence "disturbing"', *Jerusalem Post*, 23 January 2006. ADL director Abe Foxman went even further and said the verdict could pose a threat to all Jewish lobbyists. Shlomo Shamir, 'US Jewish leaders concerned by Franklin conviction', *Haaretz*, 23 January 2006. The underlying attitude of the Zionist lobby was incredulity that advocating for Israel, no matter how it was done, could be anything other than encouraged by the US government.

65 During the 2006 AIPAC conference, the charges against Rosen were barely discussed, at least officially, according to the *Washington Post*. Milbank, op. cit. As the trial of Rosen and Weissman was approaching in mid-2006, the Jewish community, after being accused of abandoning the men, started openly supporting them and demanding that AIPAC pay their legal costs. Shmuel Rosner, 'Jewish community moves to defend former AIPAC employees', *Haaretz*, 30 January 2006.

66 Lake, op. cit.

67 *New York Times* journalist James Risen revealed in his 2006 book *State of war* that Israel and its intelligence agencies were vital in persuading members of the Bush administration, including Paul Wolfowitz, to dismiss the CIA's advice about Iraq's supposed WMDs. The CIA was sceptical of Israel's intelligence reports that allegedly proved the existence of Saddam's WMD stockpile, because the CIA knew that 'Mossad had very strong—even transparent—biases about the Arab world'. Wolfowitz preferred meeting with Mossad to discuss Saddam, Risen says, because he liked what he was being told. Leonard Fein, 'Knowing what we don't know', *Forward*, 10 February 2006.

68 Steven Rosen's background provides an intriguing insight into the influence of the Zionist lobby on US government policy and its media cheerleaders. It was at Brandeis University that Rosen tutored a young student named Thomas Friedman. Friedman, now a foreign affairs columnist for the *New York Times* and the author of several books, is widely read in the USA and around the world because he is seen to

represent a *Realpolitik* outlook and to promote the USA's noble and benign role in the world. Friedman attended Rosen's Middle East study group, which Rosen dubbed the 'Middle East war policy group', he said, in part because it was an alternative to another group focused on encouraging peace in the region. Rosen became a textbook neo-conservative with a career trajectory similar to those of many in the Bush administration, including a stint persuading the Reagan administration not to negotiate with the PLO. After joining AIPAC, he hired a graduate of the University of Sydney, Martin Indyk, to establish AIPAC's research department. Indyk later became the US ambassador to Israel under Bill Clinton, and is now a member of the board of directors of Frank Lowy's Sydney think tank, the Lowy Institute.

69 Ori Nir, 'Scandal stymies Israeli effort to pressure Tehran', *Forward*, 29 April 2005.

70 Doug Ireland, 'The real AIPAC spy ring story—it was all about Iran', *Znet*, 7 August 2005.

71 As quoted in ibid.

72 Nathan Guttman, 'Focus: the 'dual loyalty' slur returns to haunt US Jews', *Haaretz*, 29 August 2004.

73 James Zogby, 'As AIPAC meets', *Media Monitors Network*, 23 May 2005, viewed April 2005, <usa.mediamonitors.net/content/view/full/15083/>.

74 Juan Cole, 'Feith resigns under pressure of investigations', *Informed Comment*, 28 January 2005, viewed April 2006, <www.juancole.com/2005/01/feith-resigns-under-pressure-of.>.

75 Ze'ev Schiff, 'US-Israel crisis deepens over defense exports to China', *Haaretz*, 27 July 2005.

76 Lake, op. cit.

77 As quoted in John Mearsheimer & Stephen Walt, 'The Israel lobby', *London Review of Books*, 23 March 2006.

78 Hilary Leila Krieger, 'CNN poll: Americans balk at post-disengagement aid to Israel', *Jerusalem Post*, 14 July 2005.

79 *The Nation* and *MSNBC* commentator Eric Alterman compiled a list in 2002 of US journalists and media companies who could be relied upon to defend Israel 'reflexively and without qualification' and included the vast majority of the mainstream media elite, from columnists to media moguls to editors. Alterman even included himself under the category of 'columnists who are likely to criticise both Israel and the Palestinians, but view themselves to be critically supporters of Israel, and ultimately, would support Israeli security over Palestinian rights'. This list included the *Times'* Thomas Friedman, *New Yorker* editor David Remnick and the editorial boards of the *Times* and *Post*.

80 Scott Wilson & Glenn Kessler, 'US funds enter fray in Palestinian elections', *Washington Post*, 22 January 2006.

81 'Underwriting Hamas', *New York Times*, 4 March 2006.

82 Occasionally the Bush administration acts against the wishes of the Zionist lobby. One month before the January 2006 Palestinian elections, and days after the US Congress voted to threaten the Palestinian Authority with withholding aid if Hamas was included in the next government, the USA pressured European donor nations to transfer US$60 million to the Palestinian Authority to pays its salaries. This was done partly in the hope that Fatah would be strengthened in the eyes of Palestinians in the run-up to the poll. Akiva Eldar, 'Congress keeps one eye on the Jewish lobby', *Haaretz*, 18 December 2005.

83 'West Bank withdrawal', *New York Times*, 30 March 2006.

84 In the run-up to the March 2006 Israeli election, after then acting Prime Minister Ehud Olmert announced plans to withdraw some settlements in the West Bank, a number of Christian and Jewish groups formed a new organisation, the United Front for the Land of Israel, to lobby the US and Israeli governments against the plan. Founder of the group, Susan Roth, explained the reasoning: 'Olmert's withdrawal would be a victory for worldwide Islamic terror. It would result in the formation of an al-Qaeda/Islamic Jihad/Iranian-satellite state that would serve as a sanctuary for all kinds of terrorists. The withdrawal would be disastrous for America's war on terror, for Israel and for the Jewish people'. Aaron Klein, 'Americans unite against further pullout', *Ynetnews*, 23 March 2006, viewed April 2006, <www.ynetnews.com/articles/0,7340,L-3231348,00.html>.

85 Rami G Khouri, 'This is why the Islamists are winning', *Daily Star*, 15 March 2006.

86 Ben Stein, 'I don't feel for Felt', *American Spectator*, 3 May 2005.

87 Gary Younge, 'J'accuse', *Guardian*, 10 August 2005.

88 Alex Mindlin, 'Getting published while a spat is hot', *New York Times*, 23 May 2005.

89 As quoted in Marcella Bombardieri, 'Academic fight heads to print', *Boston Globe*, 9 July 2005.

90 Michael Kunzelman, 'Dershowitz in feud over plagiarism allegation', *Associated Press*, 14 July 2005.

91 ibid.

92 Jon Weiner, 'Chutzpah and free speech', *Los Angeles Times*, 11 July 2005.

93 Jon Weiner, 'Giving chutzpah new meaning', *Nation*, 11 July 2005.

94 Gary Younge, 'J'accuse', *Guardian*, 10 August 2005.

95 Kunzelman, op. cit.

96 Neve Gordon, 'Review of Norman Finkelstein's *Beyond chutzpah*', *Znet*, 12 October 2005; Jon Weiner, 'Giving chutzpah new meaning', *Nation*, 23 June 2005.

97 John J Mearsheimer & Stephen M Walt, 'The Israel lobby and US foreign policy', Kennedy School of Government Working Paper no. RWP06-011, March 2006, viewed April 2006, <ssrn.com/abstract= 891198>. An edited version was also published in the *London Review of Books*, 23 March 2006. <http://www.lrb.co.uk/v28/n06/print/ mear01_.html>

98 The findings of a March 2006 Gallop poll indicated that 59 per cent of Americans felt solidarity with Israel and 57 per cent believed the Palestinians should be given no assistance at all. 'Gallop poll: More Americans identity with Israel', *Jerusalem Post*, 14 February 2006.

99 The authors focus on many areas of US foreign policy, but the 2003 Iraq invasion features prominently. Though they are careful not to suggest that securing Israel was the only reason for the invasion, it was certainly a significant factor:

> According to Philip Zelikow, a former member of the president's Foreign Intelligence Advisory Board, the executive director of the 9/11 Commission, and now a counsellor to Condoleezza Rice, the 'real threat' from Iraq was not a threat to the USA. The 'unstated threat' was the 'threat against Israel', Zelikow told an audience at the University of Virginia in September 2002. 'The American government,' he added, 'doesn't want to lean too hard on it rhetorically, because it is not a popular sell.'

100 Eli Lake, 'David Duke claims to be vindicated by a Harvard Dean', *New York Sun*, 20 March 2006.

101 As quoted in ibid.

102 Ori Nir, 'Professor says American publisher turned him down', *Forward*, 24 March 2006.

103 'Mearsheimer and Walt's anti-Israel screed: A relentless assault in scholarly guise', *ADL Analysis*, 24 March 2006.

104 Shmuel Rosner, 'Harvard to remove official seal from anti-AIPAC "working paper"', *Haaretz*, 24 March 2006. The *Australian* informed its readers of Harvard's decision by reprinting a London *Times* article under the headline 'Harvard disowns anti-Jew report'. Richard Beeston, 'Harvard disowns anti-Jew report', *Australian*, 31 March 2006.

105 Mark Mazower, 'When vigilance undermines freedom of speech', *Financial Times*, 3 April 2006.

106 American Civil Liberties Union, 'Free speech', *American Civil Liberties Union*, viewed April 2006, <www.aclu.org/freespeech/index.html>.
107 Michael Lind, 'The Israel lobby', *Prospect*, 1 April 2002.

7 The United Kingdom's climate of dissent (pages 144–56)

1 Ken Livingstone, 'An attack on voters' rights', *Guardian*, 1 March 2006.
2 Bobby Gillespie, 'Here's hoping', *Guardian*, 15 October 2004.
3 Peter Wilby, the former editor of liberal British journal the *New Statesman*, told *Al-Ahram* in 2002 that he didn't 'believe it was anti-Semitic to say that Israel should not exist as a state created some fifty years ago out of what other people regard as their land'. Such brutal honesty is virtually unheard of in the mainstream US and Australian media. Omayma Abdel-Laif, 'The lobby that cried wolf', *Al-Ahram*, 28 March – 3 April 2002.
4 Gerald Kaufman, 'The case for sanctions against Israel', *Guardian*, 12 July 2004.
5 Gerald Kaufman, 'No peace with Sharon', *Guardian*, 7 December 2005.
6 Brian Klug, 'No, anti-Zionism is not anti-Semitism', *Guardian*, 3 December 2003.
7 'Religious populations', Office of National Statistics, October 2004.
8 Mark Curtis, *Web of deceit*, Vintage, 2003, p. 5.
9 Files released to the United Kingdom National Archives in late 2005 indicated that Foreign Office officials were so worried about Margaret Thatcher's pro-Israel sympathies when she became Tory leader in the mid-1970s that they encouraged her to break off contact with local Jewish groups. Diplomats feared that Arab nations would regard her as a 'prisoner of the Zionists'. 'FO concern at Thatcher Jewish links', *This is London*, 29 December 2005.
10 Dean Godson, 'Lessons from Northern Ireland for the Arab–Israeli conflict', *Jerusalem Viewpoints*, no. 523, 1–15 October 2004.
11 In yet more evidence that Blair's government took a one-sided approach to the conflict, it was announced in March 2006 that the Foreign Office had appointed an Israeli government adviser as head of the legal department. Daniel Bethlehem QC had advised Israeli Prime Minister Ariel Sharon in 2002 to block a UN inquiry into the Jenin invasion and defended the Israeli government in 2004 at the International Court of Justice against charges its security wall was unlawful. Ewen MacAskill, 'Israeli adviser switches to top FO job', *Guardian*, 7 March 2006. In a further sign of the United Kingdom's closeness to Israel, the *Guardian* discovered in February 2006 that the Blair government 'is considering weakening laws designed to capture alleged war criminals and torturers who enter Britain, after pressure from the Israeli

government'. This followed a number of failed attempts by British citizens in 2005 to arrest high-ranking Israeli officials for alleged war crimes in the occupied territories. Vikram Dodd, 'UK considers curbing citizens' right to arrest alleged war criminals', *Guardian*, 3 February 2006.

12 Matthew Tempest, 'Diplomats attack Blair's Israel policy', *Guardian*, 26 April 2004.

13 Open letter to the Board of Deputies of British Jews, 30 June 2004.

14 ibid.

15 ibid.

16 As quoted in Hugh Muir, 'The Guardian profile: Ken Livingstone', *Guardian*, 18 February 2005.

17 'What Livingstone told Finegold', *Daily Telegraph*, 15 February 2005.

18 A former London *Times* journalist, Nigel Williamson, revealed in February 2006 that he was also compared to a Nazi by Livingstone.

19 Jewish groups claimed that Livingstone's comments increased anti-semitic abuse. The Community Security Trust (CST) issued a report in February 2006 that found 455 incidents of antisemitism were recorded in 2005, the second highest on record. The definition of antisemitism included hate mail and violent assaults. Jason Bennetto, 'Anti-semitic abuse rises after Harry's Nazi gaffe', *Independent*, 3 February 2006. Robert Wistrich, head of the Vidal Sassoon International Centre for the study of anti-Semitism at the Hebrew University argues that 'Great Britain is today second only to France in serious anti-Semitic incidents among European countries'. In his definition, however, questioning the legitimacy of Israel and Zionism is antisemitic. Robert Wistrich, 'The new British anti-Semitism', *Haaretz*, 16 February 2006.

20 As quoted in Ben Cohen, 'London mayor blasted for comment', *Jewish Week*, 18 February 2005.

21 'Mayor hits back over Nazi claim', *BBC News Online*, 17 November 2005, viewed April 2006, <news.bbc.co.uk/2/hi/uk_news/england/london/4443920.stm>.

22 As quoted in Ben Cohen, 'London mayor blasted for comment', *Jewish Week*, 18 February 2005.

23 Owen Bowcott & Faisal al Yafai, 'Scholar with a streetwise touch defies expectations and stereotypes', *Guardian*, 9 July 2004.

24 Muir, op. cit.

25 Ken Livingstone, 'This is about Israel, not anti-Semitism', *Guardian*, 4 March 2005.

26 Zvi Heifetz, 'I'm ready to meet Ken', *Guardian*, 9 March 2005.

27 Chris Tryhorn, 'Livingstone suspended over "Nazi" jibe', *Guardian*, 24 February 2006.

28 Hugh Muir, 'Allies and critics rally around Livingstone', *Guardian*, 25 February 2006.

29 Ros Taylor, 'Livingstone suspension frozen by judge', *Guardian*, 28 February 2006.

30 Ken Livingstone, 'An attack on voters' rights', *Guardian*, 1 March 2006.

31 ibid.

32 Michael Halpern, letter to the *Guardian*, 2 March 2006.

33 'Mayor blames Middle East policy', *BBC News Online*, 20 July 2005, viewed April 2006, <news.bbc.co.uk/2/hi/uk_news/politics/4698963.stm>.

34 'Sharon slams London mayor's "ignorance' on Hamas, Likud', *Xinhua*, 25 July 2005.

35 ibid.

36 Hagit Kleiman & Yaakov Lappin, 'He always hated Jews and Israelis', *Ynetnews*, 20 July 2005, viewed April 2006, <www.ynetnews.com/articles/0,7340,L-3115255,00>.

37 ibid.

38 Ken Livingstone, 'Three ways to make us all safer', *Guardian*, 4 August 2005.

39 'Timeline: Ken Livingstone vs London Evening Standard', *Guardian*, 24 February 2006.

40 Dershowitz also criticised Sir Iqbal Sacranie, secretary-general of the Muslim Council of Great Britain, for showing solidarity with Livingstone. This was an example, Dershowitz wrote, of a Muslim leader lending support to 'anti-Jewish bigotry'. Alan Dershowitz, 'Why defend bigotry?', *Jerusalem Post*, 13 March 2006.

41 Livingstone provided more ammunition for his critics in March 2006 by telling two Indian-born Jewish billionaire developers that they should 'go back to Iran and try their luck with the Ayatollahs'. London Assembly member Brian Coleman told the *Jerusalem Post* that Livingstone had 'a blind spot when it comes to relations with the Jewish community. He has an antipathy, an antagonism, a personal dislike for the Jewish community'. After Coleman suggested Livingstone's statements were 'anti-Semitic', the mayor denounced him as 'Dr Goebbels'. George Conger, 'Livingstone renews anti-Jewish slurs', *Jerusalem Post*, 23 March 2006.

42 John Pilger, 'Palestinians not alone', *New Statesman*, 3 October 2002.

43 Debbie Berman, 'London and New York rally in massive support for Israel', *Israelinsider*, 7 May 2002.

44 Brian Whitaker, 'Hate mail', *Guardian*, 19 January 2004.

45 Arthur Neslen, 'A Diaspora divided', *Aljazeera*, 9 January 2004.

46 Yasmin Alibhai-Brown, 'We must unite to face the next attack', *Independent*, 24 July 2005.

47 Patrick Hennessy & Melissa Kite, 'Poll reveals 40pc of Muslims want sharia law in UK', *Telegraph*, 19 February 2006.

48 Melanie Phillips, 'An astounding ignorance', 8 January 2006, *Melanie Phillips*, viewed April 2006, <www.melaniephillips.com/diary/archives/001546.html>.

49 Julie Burchill, 'For what we are, not what we do', *Haaretz*, 17 February 2006.

8 Zionism in Australia (pages 157–83)

1 As quoted in Melissa Singer, 'Self-hatred spurs anti-Semitism—Isi Leibler', *AJN*, 12 December 2003.

2 Mark Dapin, 'Man in the middle', *Good Weekend*, 27 November 2004.

3 Danny Ben-Moshe, 'Pro-Israelism as a factor in Australian political attitudes and behaviour', in Geoffrey Brahm Levey & Philip Mendes (eds), *Jews and Australian Politics*, Sussex Academic Press, 2004, p. 131.

4 ibid., pp. 127–42.

5 *Tikkun olam* means 'repairing the world through social action'.

6 John Goldlust, 'Jews in Australia: a demographic profile', in Levey & Mendes, op. cit., p. 26.

7 As quoted in Malcolm J Turnbull, 'Safe haven: records of the Jewish experience in Australia', research guide no. 12, *National Archives of Australia*, 2000, ch. 1, viewed April 2006, <www.naa.gov.au/Publications/research_guides/guides/haven/chapter1.htm>.

8 Chanan Reich, *Australia and Israel: an ambiguous relationship*, Melbourne University Press, 2002, p. 60.

9 Philip Mendes, 'Are anti-Zionism and anti-Semitism one and the same thing?', paper presented to the Anti-Semitism in the Contemporary World Conference, Monash University, 6 February 2005.

10 In the 1970s, Rod Webb (who was later to become Director of Programming at SBS) was Finance Committee chairperson at the Australian Union of Students (AUS) and editor of the Macquarie University newspaper, *Arena*. Webb says that the *Australian* refused to publish paid advertisements by the Friends of Palestine: 'The only supporters of Palestine were the Arab community newspapers, some trade union newspapers, some student newspapers, and the newspapers of some left-wing political parties'. Victorian Labor MP Clyde Holding later displayed contempt for the Palestinian cause, confirming Webb's comments: 'With the decline of that whole heady, awful business, the Vietnam War, a lot of younger radicals were a bit lost for a cause. They

were on the look-out for the next wretched depressed victims of American capitalism—and there were those benighted Palestinians'.

After Webb left Macquarie University, he applied for a job as general manager of the Australian Dance Theatre (ADT) in Adelaide. He received a phone call from ADT chairman (and wine mogul) David Wynn, who asked to meet him. He said Webb seemed perfect for the job, but there was one problem. 'He asked me my attitude towards the PLO', Webb tells me. He said that since the South Australian Premier Don Dunstan was a strong supporter of Israel, and since the ADT relied on state government funding for its existence, they couldn't afford to have someone like Webb seeking funding from Dunstan. 'My response was that I had no special attitude towards the PLO, other than I regarded it as the legitimate representative of the Palestinian people, and that my recent activities—of which he was well aware—were motivated by a view that they had had a raw deal and had every right for their cause to be heard'. Webb didn't get the job but soon found employment as head of the National Film Theatre of Australia. 'A couple of years after my appointment', he says, 'its chairman for that entire period admitted to me that had he known of my politics at the time of appointment, he, too, would have ensured that it didn't happen'. Interview and email correspondence with the author, May 2005.

11 Sol Encel, 'Jews and the Australian Labor Party', in Levey & Mendes, op. cit., p. 59.

12 The 2001 Census found that 213 940 people from Arab countries have settled in Australia, though some estimate the number of Australians of Arab origin to be nearly one million. The Lebanese and Egyptian communities are the largest, and many practice Islam or Christianity.

13 There is scarce data on Palestinians in Australia. *The Atlas of the Australian People: 1991 Census*, Australian Government Publishing Service, 1995, stated that there were 15 000 Palestinians in Australia, though the number is likely to be much higher. The Australian government initially refused to allow individuals to record their country of birth as 'Palestine' on official documents, and also refused to accept Palestinian refugees under any special-entry programs, forcing many to enter Australia from Lebanon and Jordan.

14 'Australians divided on Mideast crisis', *AAP*, 23 March 2006. The polling was conducted by the Labor-aligned lobby group Hawker Britton.

15 As quoted in Lorin Blumenthal, 'Aussies split over support for Israel', *AJN*, 24 March 2006. AIJAC's Colin Rubenstein was encouraged that

only a small number of the people whose sympathies lay with the Palestinians said Israel had no right to exist. The head of the General Palestinian Delegation in Australia, Ali Kazak, said he was surprised the poll didn't reveal more support for the Palestinians: 'All the indications I have are that the majority of Australians support the rights of the Palestinians and the minority support Israel and the occupation of Palestine'. The age and gender breakdown is fascinating. Far more women (90 per cent) than men (78 per cent) thought Israel had the right to exist. Men and women in the 18–29-year age group were the strongest supporters of Israel (89 per cent).

The Jewish community reacted predictably. NSW State Zionist Council president Brian Levitan argued that a lack of support for Israel was probably based on antisemitism. 'When they say they support the Palestinians, what do they mean? They have been offered a state three times and have rejected it.' ECAJ president Grahame Leonard issued the most desperate statement. He said support for the Palestinians was likely to come only from 'far-left groups'. '[The left] is always pro-victim and they see the Palestinians as victims. Often the pro-left circles are pro-victim but this does not necessarily mean that they are anti-Israel. Our own knowledge of Israel suggests that they are victims of their leadership.' Clearly only 'far-left' individuals would support the Palestinian cause.

16 Suzanne D Rutland, 'Who speaks for Australian Jewry?', in Levey & Mendes (eds), op. cit., p. 39.

17 When, in 1987, the AJDS wanted to affiliate with the Melbourne Community Council—a state branch of the ECAJ—they were initially rejected because they refused to agree that all Diaspora leaders should support the current Israeli leadership. They were labelled 'anti-Zionist', and their Jewish credentials were questioned. By September 1993, however, during the period of the Oslo Accords, compromise was reached and they eventually affiliated.

18 Bernard Freedman, 'AIJAC lobby role under the spotlight', *AJN*, 1 April 2005.

19 Suzanne Rutland argues, in *The Jews in Australia*, Cambridge University Press, 2005, that Melbourne is the most vibrant Jewish city in Australia but that Sydney remains less internally divided and more disciplined. After 1945, Melbourne attracted a higher proportion of Polish Jews, while Sydney attracted more Jews from Central Europe, especially Austria, Hungary and Germany. Melbourne's Jews became more community minded and more devoted to Israel. Until relatively recently, Melbourne Jewry raised far more funds for Israel than did Sydney's Jews. South African Jews have recently injected new life into Sydney's Jewry.

20 Despite extensive research, I have not been able to determine who funds AIJAC (though I suspect a number of prominent Australian Jews). The group raises funds through the Jewish community but does not conduct public fundraising. As with Gerard Henderson's conservative Sydney Institute, the source of the funding unquestionably influences the political stance of the organisation.

21 Chanan Reich, senior lecturer in political science at the Yizre'el Valley Academic College in Israel, argues that AIJAC's leaders are convinced when they campaign for Israel and Jewry that they are working 'for values held sacred by most Australians'. The organisation doesn't therefore approve of Jewish dissenting groups such as the AJDS. '[They] regard it as at best led by misguided people', he writes, 'and at worst as self-hating Jews who have collaborated with left-wing, anti-Israel movements'. Chanan Reich, 'Inside AIJAC—an Australian Jewish Lobby Group', in Levey & Mendes (eds), op. cit., p. 212.

22 Michael Cavanagh, 'Most funds went Liberals' way', *AJN*, 13 February 2004.

23 Morgan Mellish, 'Why everybody wants to be with Frank', *Australian Financial Review*, 5 June 2004.

24 Christopher Webb, 'Still chasing a golden lifeline', *Age*, 18 December 2005. Gutnick told the *AJN* in January 2006 that he was not financially supporting Netanyahu in the 2006 Israeli elections. 'Isi Leibler backs Bibi—by 25 000 shekels', *AJN*, 20 January 2006.

25 Dan Goldberg, 'ALP leaders woo Jews', *AJN*, 1 October 2004.

26 The *Business Review Weekly* listed Leibler as worth A\$105 million. 'Rich 200', *Business Review Weekly*, 20 May 2004.

27 As quoted in Greg Sheridan, 'Australia's Prime Minister Howard: a hero in Israel', *Australian*, 17 February 2003.

28 Mark Leibler, letter to *AJN*, 5 December 2003. The same day's paper included a letter from Howard Nathan, a member of the editorial advisory board of AIJAC's *Review* magazine. He wrote that 'some suggestions, even allegations, by some communal leaders that AIJAC is politically aligned are incorrect. For 30 years AIJAC has supported Australian governments of whatever colour so long as they, in turn, have supported Israel'.

29 'The Howard decade', *AJN*, 3 March 2006.

30 Mark Leibler, speech presented Arnold Bloch Leibler's fiftieth anniversary celebrations, Melbourne, 14 April 2003.

31 By 2005, AIJAC was openly calling for action against Iran. 'A limited US-led air strike on key components of the Iranian program' should be an option, wrote Colin Rubenstein in September 2005.

Colin Rubenstein, 'Clock ticks on Iran's nuke threat', *Herald Sun*, 19 September 2005.

32 Sam Lipski, 'Australia's key role in wars affecting Israel', *AJN*, 16 May 2003.

33 The Jewish community has rewarded the Liberal Party handsomely for this support, and the Israeli establishment has noticed. Israeli President Moshe Katsav told an audience in Sydney in March 2005 that the Australian Jewish community was 'one of the most important Jewish communities in the world' and praised the Howard government's stance on terrorism, describing it as an 'example to the free world'.

34 Colin Rubenstein, 'A friend down under', *Jerusalem Post*, 17 October 2004.

35 John Howard, address to Parliament, 27 March 2006, viewed April 2006, <www.pm.gov.au/News/speeches/speech1841.html>.

36 John Howard, address, Howard government tenth anniversary dinner, Great Hall, Parliament House, Canberra, 1 March 2006.

37 Scott Burchill, *SMH Webdiary*, 30 June 2003.

38 Colin Rubenstein, 'Friends down under', *Jerusalem Post*, 25 May 2006.

39 Michael Kapel & David Greason, 'Howard pads up', *Australia/Israel Review*, 1–24 May 1998.

40 John Howard, speech to American Jewish Committee, New York, 30 January 2002. The event was also attended by Australian Jewish billionaire Richard Pratt.

41 'Honouring Prime Minister John Howard in New York City', *AIJAC*, 30 January 2002.

42 As quoted in Dan Goldberg, 'Downer: Australia willing to support Israel at UN, irrespective of others', *AJN*, 9 December 2005.

43 'Australia backs US over Israel barrier', *Associated Press*, 21 July 2004.

44 Alan Ramsey, 'Nobody stands taller than tiny Gloria', *SMH*, 24 July 2004.

45 Telephone interview with the author, 1 November 2004. On John Howard's tenth anniversary in March 2006, the *AJN* interviewed a handful of prominent Australian Jews about his record in office. The vast majority were unanimous in praising his support for Israel and the Jewish community. Isi Leibler said that Howard was 'today unquestionably Israel's greatest supporter in the international arena'. The editorial debated whether Bob Hawke or Howard was the country's greatest pro-Israel Prime Minister and concluded that in a post–September 11 world, Howard was the winner. *AJN*, 3 March 2006.

46 During the 2006 Israeli election campaign, Leibler donated A$7450 to Likud leader Binyamin Netanyahu's campaign. Leibler had been

strongly critical of Sharon's Gaza disengagement plan and disagreed with Israeli withdrawal from occupied territory. 'Isi Leibler backs Bibi', op. cit.

47 Isi Leibler, 'Evil is evil', *Jerusalem Post*, 4 October 2002.

48 As quoted in Andrew Markus, 'Antisemitism and Australian Jewry', in Levey & Mendes, op. cit., p. 116.

49 As quoted in Melissa Singer, 'Self-hatred spurs anti-Semitism—Isi Leibler', *AJN*, 12 December 2003.

50 Bernard Freedman, 'Isi Leibler to question PM on Israel criticism', *AJN*, 21 June 2003.

51 Philip Mendes & Geoffrey Brahm Levey, 'The "Jewish vote" will not be swayed over Labor's Middle East pangs', *Online Opinion*, 30 September 2003.

52 Colin Rubenstein, 'After disengagement', *Review*, September 2005.

53 Colin Rubenstein, 'Israel's political "big-bang"', *Review*, December 2005.

54 Colin Rubenstein, 'End of an era', *Review*, February 2006.

55 Colin Rubenstein, 'Israelis have voted to take control of their own destiny', *Canberra Times*, 31 March 2006.

56 Ted Lapkin, 'Tears of blood still to be shed', *Courier-Mail*, 27 February 2006.

57 As quoted in Larry Schwartz, 'Expats divided on poll but united in weariness of being attacked over Bush', *Age*, 30 October 2004.

58 As quoted in 'Palestine activist debates former Republican adviser', *Green Left Weekly*, 11 August 2004.

59 Israeli human rights group B'Tselem has compiled statistics of fatalities during the second intifada and concludes that the majority killed by the Israelis were children and civilians. A 27 June 2005 press release read: 'Since the beginning of the Intifada (in late September 2000) until 26 June 2005, Israeli security forces have killed at least 1722 Palestinians not taking part in the hostilities, among them 563 minors'.

60 Ted Lapkin, 'Forget peacetime niceties—this is a war', *SMH*, 3 August 2005.

61 Ted Lapkin, 'Hold the apology—freedom is not proof of Habib's innocence', *SMH*, 1 February 2005.

62 D Hurst, letter to the *SMH*, 2 February 2005.

63 Ted Lapkin, 'Clark's vile bedfellows', *Australian*, 22 July 2004.

64 Ted Lapkin, 'The newest face of the oldest hatred', *Perspective*, ABC Radio, 11 April 2005.

65 Paul Heywood-Smith QC, 'Refutation of claim of anti-Semitism', *Perspective*, ABC Radio, 5 May 2005. The Zionist lobby was upset that Heywood-Smith had been given a forum for his 'recognisable anti-

Semitism'. David Knoll, president of the NSW JBD, countered that the ABC had shown gross insensitivity by playing Heywood-Smith's talk on the evening that 'Jewish communities in Australia, and around the world, were commemorating the 60th anniversary of the liberation of the [Nazi] death camps'. He claimed that all of Heywood-Smith's claims were 'demonstrably false' but offered little better than the oft-claimed line: 'Israel, of course, is the only operative democracy in the Middle East'. Knoll was advocating censorship on the public broadcaster. David Knoll, 'Anti-Semitism on Radio National', *Online Opinion*, 17 May 2005.

66 As quoted in Reich, op. cit., p. 201.

67 Rabbi Samuel Tov-Lev, letter to *AJN*, 15 July 2005.

68 'A Zionist debate', *AJN*, 15 July 2005.

69 On the eve of the Israeli election in March 2006, Mark Leibler wrote in the *AJN* that he had known Kadima leader Ehud Olmert for over 25 years—Olmert has been to Australia many times, has relatives here and employs a Melbourne-born foreign policy adviser—though he favoured none of the major parties over another: 'The organisations which I head . . . will work closely, constructively and supportively with the new government . . . irrespective of its political complexion'. Mark Leibler, letter to *AJN*, 10 March 2006.

70 One of Australia's best-known diplomats, Richard Woolcott, recalls a discussion during the Hawke years with then Israeli ambassador to the UN and future Israeli prime minister Binyamin Netanyahu, in which Woolcott proposed a more balanced approach at the UN Security Council. Woolcott was wasting his time, he was told, because Israel had in the USA 'a proxy veto in the Council'. It was 'a surprisingly frank admission', and although the 'Jewish lobby' in Australia wasn't as powerful as in the USA, 'the combination of American and Jewish pressure made it difficult for Australia to move to a more balanced approach'. Richard Woolcott, *The hot seat*, HarperCollins, 2003.

71 Blanche d'Alpuget, *Robert J Hawke*, Schwartz Publishing, 1982. It is an adoring but insightful biography.

72 As quoted in ibid., p. 250.

73 The Iraq war was indirectly linked to Israel, Hawke said, primarily through the American evangelical Right and its dedication to bringing about the Second Coming in Israel. Australia's involvement in the war is motivated by a need 'to have a very strong relationship with this great and powerful country and we're going to do that at all costs'.

74 Interview with the author, Sydney, 21 June 2005.

75 Danby has been accurately described by the *SMH*'s Alan Ramsey as 'the Australian Parliament's most unambiguous and insidious

defender of the Israeli government'. Alan Ramsey, 'ALP fights to find a sense of middle ground', *SMH*, 26 October 2002.

76 ibid. Ramsey rightly highlighted the absurdity of Danby's outrage: the proposed debate would last for all of half an hour. 'That's it—just five minutes each for six MPs in a House of 150 members', he wrote. 'It is a process hardly likely to alter the cause of history.'

77 Mike Seccombe, 'Muzzled, say ALP's critics of Israel', *SMH*, 19 August 2003.

78 Bernard Freedman, 'Labor MP attacks "Jewish lobby"', *AJN*, 19 December 2002.

79 Australia–Israel Parliamentary Friendship Group has contained members of parliament from across the political spectrum. Aden Ridgeway, the second indigenous Australian to be elected to the federal parliament, visited Israel in 1999 as a Democrat member. Michael Danby is Secretary and his closeness with AIJAC allows the group to maintain a predictable line on Israel and recommend such thoughts to the parties. During the 2005 Australian visit of David Harris, American Jewish Committee's Executive Chairman, he commented, after lunching with the group, that, 'it was obvious that there were longstanding friendships between Australian Jewish leaders and elected officials of the major political parties'. Other states have their own Israeli parliamentary friendship groups.

80 *World today*, ABC Radio, 11 November 2002.

81 As quoted in Freedman, op. cit.

82 Telephone interview with the author, 19 April 2005. During our interview, Crean never mentioned any conversations with Arab or Palestinian community leaders about the Irwin controversy, indicating his priorities were appeasing the Zionist lobby on the issue. I asked Crean about the Jewish community's support for the war in Iraq—he was leader in the period before the March 2003 invasion—and he said that Rubenstein didn't pressure him to get the ALP behind a pro-war stance though 'we had a healthy dialogue' and he was very clear on the Zionist leader's support for the effort to topple Saddam 'because of the threat Iraq posed to the state of Israel'.

83 *Lateline*, ABC Television, 1 September 2003.

84 Alan Ramsey, 'Lost, even with a map', *SMH*, 30 August 2003.

85 Julia Irwin, 'Wanted: political currency', *Australian*, 16 July 2003.

86 Bernard Freedman, 'Beazley: Irwin's speech "offensive"', *AJN*, 23 September 2005.

87 As quoted in ibid.

88 *Lateline*, ABC Television, 1 September 2003.

89 Ephraim Nimni (ed.), *The challenges of post-Zionism: Alternatives to Israeli Fundamentalist Policies*, Zed Books, 2003.

90 As quoted in Cameron Stewart, 'Falling out with friends', *Australian*, 5 September 2003.

91 As quoted in ibid.

92 As quoted in Goldberg, op. cit. During the 2004 election campaign, Michael Danby was asked about Cohen's 2002 comments. Danby responded:

> Mr Cohen said there isn't a person who he supports more in Federal Parliament than myself and it's on the basis of what he knows I contribute not only in matters to do with the Middle East, but in the whole gamut of areas ... But the policies of Mark Latham are supporting the security fence, supporting Israel's right to defend itself and explicitly condemning suicide bombing.

As quoted in 'The great debate', *AJN*, 26 September 2004.

93 Barry Cohen, 'Labor pains', *AJN*, 22 October 2004. He named no politicians in his article, yet claimed antisemitism was rife in the party. 'Before the Iraq war', Cohen wrote, 'one of the most senior NSW right-wing MPs told me: "I understand and support Israel's position, but in my group, I'm the only one"'. Cohen later told me he was referring to former leader Mark Latham. 'Soon after', he continued, 'I told a Labor legend: "Anti-Semitism is now rampant in the Labor Party." I expected a vigorous denial. His response confirmed my worst fear: "I know", he said.' Cohen was referring to former ALP national president Barry Jones. Telephone interview with the author, 30 March 2005.

94 Tanya Plibersek, press release, 25 October 2004.

95 *Religion report*, ABC Radio, 3 November 2004.

96 Kevin Rudd, 'Labor has always supported Israel', *Age*, 10 December 2004.

97 As quoted in 'Bites from the "Bomber"', *AJN*, 3 June 2005.

98 Reich, op. cit., p. 205.

99 Dapin, op. cit.

100 Colin Rubenstein, 'Morally evil', *AJN*, 3 March 1995.

101 Dapin, op. cit.

102 When Ariel Sharon lay in a coma in Jerusalem in January 2006, Danby visited the leader, according to the *AJN*, 'in a show of solidarity'. Dan Goldberg, 'Danby among Jewish lawmakers visiting Sharon', *AJN*, 13 January 2006.

103 In August 2005, Michael Danby wrote a letter to the *AJN* and demanded MUP 'drop this whole disgusting project' [*My Israel question*] because it would be 'an attack on the mainstream, Australian, Jewish community'. Danby hadn't read any of this book, merely received my interview questions in late 2004 that he chose to ignore. Michael Danby, letter to the *AJN*, 26 August 2005. A few weeks later—and after mainstream media coverage of the furore—the *AJN* editorialised that it was inappropriate for an MP to call for a book's censure, and the public should wait for the book's release 'before we decide to consign it to the garbage heap of literature'. 'Voices of Reason', *AJN*, 9 September 2005.

104 'Policies: Israel–Palestine', *Australian Greens Online*, viewed April 2006, <greens.org.au/policies/internationalissues/israelpalestine>.

105 Michael Cavanagh, 'Greens' first Jewish senator', *AJN*, 10 September 2004.

106 Peter Staudenmaier, 'Green historian to Webdiary: my work's been abused', *SMH*, 13 November 2003.

9 Public broadcasters under fire (pages 187–209)

1 Robert Fisk, 'I am being vilified for telling the truth about Palestinians', *Independent*, 13 December 2000.

2 Springborg was then an associate professor in politics at Macquarie University. He had questioned the Gulf War and its motives, incurring the wrath of conservative commentators and the Hawke government. He was accused, by AIJAC, of being an 'Iraqi apologist'—primarily because he was a former secretary of the Australia–Iraq Friendship Society—and had previously been critical of Israeli policy. Dr Springborg told a conference at the University of Sydney in February 1991 that Bob Hawke was actively discouraging the study of modern Middle Eastern history—by refusing federal money to universities that pursued it—because of his sympathy towards the Israeli government. Anne Coombs, 'Middle Eastern studies under attack', *Australian Financial Review*, 25 February 1991. He is now director of the London Middle East Institute at the School of Oriental and African Studies at the University of London.

3 Ken Inglis, 'The Gulf War of 1991', *Perspective*, ABC Radio, 18 February 2003; Michael Kapel, 'Notebook', *Australia/Israel Review*, 18 February – 11 March 1998; Geraldine Doogue, 'Power, vulnerability and scapegoats', *Griffith Review*, spring 2003; Committee on Discrimination against Arab Australians & Committee of Arab Australians, *The gulf in Australia: racism, Arab and Muslim Australians*

and the war against Iraq, Committee on Discrimination against Arab Australians, July 1991, viewed April 2006, <journalism.uts.edu.au/archive/vilification/media.htm>.

4 The UN findings were challenged by Human Rights Watch. Human Rights Watch, 'United Nations Jenin Report', press release, 2 August 2002; Peter Cave, 'UN report on Jenin massacre flawed', *PM*, ABC Radio, 4 August 2002.

5 As quoted in 'Bias and misinformation', *Media watch*, ABC Television, 6 May 2002.

6 An Israeli official, as quoted in Fergal Keane, 'Sabra and Shatila: dealing with facts', *BBC New Online*, 17 June 2001, viewed April 2006, <news.bbc.co.uk/2/hi/programmes/panorama/1390979.stm>.

7 Bruce Belsham, 'Why Four Corners was perfectly entitled to accuse Sharon', *Age*, 2 May 2002.

8 As quoted in ibid.

9 'Bias and misinformation', op. cit.

10 'The media and the Middle East', *Review*, June 2002.

11 BBC Reporter Fergal Keane explained his position to *Four corners* producer Bruce Belsham:

> Judge Goldstone called me to say he'd been asked by the Israeli lobby in Australia to issue a statement saying that he had been misled by the program makers. He said the following to me, and is happy to have it quoted: 'I am entirely happy with the way in which my contribution to the program was handled by the BBC. I was not misled by or misinterpreted by the BBC, as any reasonable person who viewed the program could see'.

As quoted in *Age*, 2 May 2002. Keane rejected accusations of bias in the *Jerusalem Post* on 10 July 2001 and stated that '*The Accused* is in the mould of rigorous and balanced BBC journalism, another example of which is a recent documentary which investigated allegations that Palestinian Authority Chairman Yasser Arafat has presided over torture, corruption, and abuse of free speech in the Palestinian territories'.

12 Interview with the author, Sydney, 25 November 2004.

13 'Michael Kroger and bias', *Media watch*, ABC Television, 13 May 2002.

14 Colin Rubenstein, 'The media and the Middle East', *Review*, June 2002.

15 Kroger told ABC Melbourne Radio's Jon Faine in May 2002, 'I think the ABC's treatment of John Howard in the pre and post-election period was not balanced'. *Lateline*, ABC Television, 7 May 2002.

16 Interview with the author, op. cit.

17 Daniel Mandel, 'The ABC of bias', *Review*, June 2002. Mandel is now working for Daniel Pipes's neo-conservative US-based think tank, the Middle East Forum.

18 Amnesty International, *Israel and the occupied territories: state assassinations and other unlawful killings*, Amnesty International, 21 February 2001.

19 'Annan condemns "targeted assassinations" by Israel', CNN, 5 July 2001.

20 Interview with the author, Sydney, 25 November 2004; email correspondence with the author, 2004.

21 AIJAC, SBS-TV and the Middle East, AIJAC, October 2003.

22 *Herald Sun* columnist Andrew Bolt is another constant critic of SBS, accusing the broadcaster of anti-Americanism, 'wicked bigotry' and 'telling lies' about Iraq. See 'SBS: TV for liars', *Herald Sun*, 28 July 2004. The *Australian* also regularly publishes opinion articles condemning alleged anti-US bias at SBS. Barry Hing, a Sydney writer, argued in September 2005 that SBS should be funding documentaries that highlight the positives in Iraq after the fall of Saddam, rather than being 'overwhelmingly negative towards the US'. See Barry Hing, 'More bias on view at the public broadcaster', *Australian*, 26 September 2005.

23 Sol Salbe, *Israel, Palestine and SBS*, AJDS, July 2004.

24 As quoted in Antony Loewenstein, 'Closing down dissent, by AIJAC and SBS', *SMH Webdiary*, 24 September 2004, viewed April 2006, <webdiary.smh.com.au/archives/antony_loewenstein/000275.html# more>.

25 ibid.

26 Israeli human rights group B'Tselem and Bimkom released a report in February 2006 that proved

> settlement expansion was the principal consideration in setting the route in many sections of the separation barrier . . . In exposing the planning aspects of the separation barrier, the report shows how the barrier brings about spatial change and transfer of land ownership. In giving consideration to settlement-expansion plans, Israel has further violated the human rights of the residents of Palestinian towns and villages situated near those settlements.

'B'Tselem and Bimkom in a press conference: separation barrier's route is designed to enable settlement expansion', B'Tselem press release, 21 February 2006, viewed April 2006, <www.btselem.org/english/Press_Releases/20060221.asp>.

27 'The minister's complaint', *Media watch*, ABC Television, 3 November 2003.

28 'ABC a bit biased on Iraq: Alston', *Lateline*, ABC Television, 27 May 2003.

29   'ABC corrects Gaza claims', *AJN*, 24 October 2003.

30   'The man in need of a mirror', *Review*, November 2003.

31   Tim Llewellyn, 'False witnesses', *Guardian*, 16 January 2003.

32   As quoted in 'CanWest bias', *Adbusters.org*, 11 September 2005, <adbusters.org/metas/corpo/canwestwatch/selfcensor.html>.

33   Brian Courtis, review of *Jenin, massacring truth*, *Age*, 10 May 2005.

34   Justin Podur, 'The great war for civilization: Justin Podur interviews Robert Fisk', *Znet*, 7 December 2005, viewed April 2006, <www.zmag.org/content/showarticle.cfm?ItemID=9282>.

35   Brent Cunningham, 'Re-thinking objectivity', *Columbia Journalism Review*, July/August, 2003.

36   Tzvi Fleischer, 'Bad journalism in quest of "higher truth"', *AJN*, 17 February 2006.

37   As quoted in 'Noam Chomsky on failed states: the abuse of power and the assault on democracy', *Democracy Now*, 31 March 2006, viewed April 2006, <www.democracynow.org/article.pl?sid=06/03/31/148254>.

38   Tzvi Fleischer, 'No accountability at public broadcasters', *AJN*, 18 November 2005.

39   Cunningham, ibid.

40   Rupert Murdoch, 'The elusive virus of anti-Semitism', *AJN*, 20 January 2006.

41   Olivia Rousset, 'Israeli soldiers', *Dateline*, SBS Television, 20 October 2004.

42   'New photographs of Abu Ghraib prisoner abuse released', *PM*, ABC Radio, 16 February 2006.

43   Email interview with the author, 22 April 2005.

44   Interview with the author, Sydney, 26 July 2005.

45   Telephone interview with the author, September 2004.

46   Steve Meacham, 'Stronger than fiction', *SMH*, 22 December 2004.

47   Matthew Carney, 'Gaza: the heartland of Hamas', *Dateline*, SBS Television, 2 June 2004.

48   As quoted in Emma Dawson, 'Death of the multicultural broadcaster', *New Matilda*, 8 June 2005.

49   As quoted in Debi Enker, 'Where to now, SBS', *Age*, 27 May 2004.

50   Chalier interview, op. cit. Similar complaints were levelled at the Office of Film and Literature Classification in 2005. Although the office is supposed to represent the Australian community, the *SMH* reported a distinct lack of 'ethnically diverse' members. Alexa Moses, 'Diversity in doubt as censorship looks to fill vacancies', *SMH*, 21 July 2005. At a time when 22 per cent of Australia's residents are born overseas, Howard's Australia is simply not reflecting the changes in the last decades.

51 La Trobe University politics professor Robert Manne wrote in 2003 of a 2001 IPA conference on the ABC that revealed the think tank's real agenda for the national broadcaster: 'If the current attempt to reform the ABC fails', said Michael Warby, the IPA fellow with special responsibility for the media, 'if the collective wins yet again, if yet another attempt to impose accountability for management is defeated by the ABC collective, then it must be smashed and replaced as the principal public broadcaster. This will be the only alternative left'. Robert Manne, 'Greedy right aims for ABC', *Age*, 2 June 2003.

52 'Janet Albrechtsen's view', *Media watch*, ABC Television, 9 September 2002.

53 As quoted in 'Albrechtsen's ABC appointment sparks controversy', *SMH*, 24 February 2005.

54 As quoted in Margaret Simons, 'Fear and loathing at the ABC', *Monthly*, May 2005.

55 'Koval denies ABC confidentiality breach', *AAP*, 24 March 2006.

56 *Lateline*, ABC Television, 23 July 2004.

57 *Facts, figures, fantasies*, Friends of the ABC, September 2003.

58 Media, Entertainment and Arts Alliance, *Press freedom report 2001–2005*, MEAA, 6 May 2005.

59 According to its website, Freedom House is a 'non-profit, nonpartisan organization [and] a clear voice for democracy and freedom around the world'.

60 'Donald McDonald and press freedom', *Crikey*, 12 May 2005.

10 The other side of the story (pages 210–34)

1 'Death gives peace a chance', *Australian*, 12 November 2004.

2 'Jenin war crimes investigation needed', Human Rights Watch press release, 3 May 2002, viewed April 2006, <www.humanrightswatch.org/press/2002/05/jeninmap0503.htm>.

3 Paul McGeough, *Age*, 18 April 2002. Israel kept the media out of Jenin, allowing rumours to take over, and Israel's Foreign Minister Shimon Peres even called the incursion a 'massacre'.

4 Gedaliah Afterman & Ben Fishman, 'Untruth and consequences', *Review*, July 2002.

5 Greg Philo & Mike Berry, *Bad news from Israel*, Pluto Press, 2004. The aim of the study was to determine how mainstream television coverage of the conflict affected the feelings of 'average' viewers towards the Israelis and Palestinians. Viewers were asked questions about the occupation, settlers and violence perpetuated by both sides. It was discovered that the vast majority had little or no understanding of what the conflict was about.

6 Greg Philo, 'What you get in 20 seconds', *Guardian*, 14 July 2004.

7 Cohen has appeared on just about all the leading US media outlets, including CNN, NPR, *Today* and *Larry King live*.

8 Journalists find 'calm' when only Palestinians die, FAIR, August 22 2003

9 *CBD turns to NPR as latest 'bias' target*, FAIR, 17 May 2005.

10 Alison Weir, *New York Times minimises Palestinian deaths*, If Americans Knew, 25 April 2005.

11 If Americans Knew is a non-profit organisation that aims, according to its website, to 'inform and educate the American public on issues of major significance that are unreported, underreported, or misreported in the American media'. Their primary focus is the Israel–Palestine conflict.

12 As quoted in Scott McConnell, 'The weekly standard's war', *American Conservative*, 21 November 2005.

13 The major News Limited publications in Australia are the *Australian*, Melbourne *Herald Sun*, Sydney *Daily Telegraph*, Adelaide *Advertiser*, Hobart *Mercury*, Brisbane *Courier-Mail* and the extremely popular website news.com.au.

14 In terms of covering the Middle East, the outstanding figures include Tony Walker, stationed in Cairo in the 1980s and early 1990s, and a biographer of Arafat who was often criticized by Zionist groups in Australia. He has worked for the *Australian Financial Times* and the *Age* as foreign affairs and defence correspondent. Walker is currently the political editor of the *Australian Financial Review*. His writings on the 2003 Iraq war won him a Walkley in 2003. Fairfax editor-in-chief Paul McGeough is another courageous journalist. His writings on the Israel–Palestine conflict—some collected in *Manhattan to Baghdad*, Allen & Unwin, 2003—are a testament to his determination to stray from the official briefings and deep into the West Bank and Gaza. Other distinguished correspondents include many ABC reporters and Michael Ware, a former News Limited journalist who now works for *Time* magazine.

15 The ABC stationed three journalists in Israel in early 2003, 'like the first Gulf war a probable target for Saddam'. 'ABC positions itself for best coverage', ABC press release, 18 March 2003.

16 Richard Carleton, 'The great divide', *60 minutes*, Nine Network, 17 October 2004.

17 Telephone interview with the author, 19 November 2004.

18 Email interview with author, 21 March 2005.

19 Daniel Okrent, 'The hottest button: how the *Times* covers Israel and Palestine', *New York Times*, 24 April 2005.

20 'Palestinian Authority: annual report 2004', *Reporters without Borders*, viewed April 2006, <www.rsf.org/article.php3?id_article=9933>.

21 Interview with author, Sydney, 27 January 2005.

22 Peter Manning, *Dog whistle politics and journalism*, Australian Centre for Independent Journalism, 2004.

23 Dunn died in 2005 and was generally popular with the Jewish community. Tzvi Fleischer, editor of AIJAC's *Review*, wrote in 2005 that Dunn 'was generally fair in presenting the views of both sides [in the conflict]'. Tzvi Fleischer, 'Israel in the Australian media', *Jewish Political Studies Review*, vol. 17, nos 3–4, fall, 2005.

24 Daniel Okrent, 'The war of words', *New York Times*, 6 March 2005. Okrent offered this definition of 'terrorism': 'An act of political violence committed against purely civilian targets is terrorism; attacks on military targets are not'.

25 Tzvi Fleischer, 'Yasser's yes men and media blind spots', *AJN*, 26 November 2004.

26 Victor Kattan, 'BBC reporting doesn't tell whole story', *Arab Media Watch*, 5 April 2005, viewed April 2006, <www.arabmediawatch.com/modules. php?name=News&file=article&sid=2703 - 41k ->.

27 Robert Fisk, 'CNN caves in to Israel over its references to illegal settlement', *Independent*, 3 September 2001.

28 A 2002 FAIR report explained the difference in language used when referring to Palestinians and Israelis. 'In US Media, Palestinians Attack, Israel Retaliates', *FAIR*, 4 April 2002, viewed April 2006, <www.fair.org/activism/network-retaliation.html>.

29 As quoted in Denise Leith, *Bearing witness*, Random House, 2004.

30 Chris McGreal, 'BBC says sorry to Israel', *Guardian*, 12 March 2005.

31 Telephone interview with the author, 11 April 2006.

32 Terry Lane, 'I surrender', *Generation*, September 1992.

33 Mark Franklin, 'More clarity for journos after Israel visit', *AJN*, 6 January 2006.

34 Melissa Singer, 'Winning the propaganda war', *AJN*, 29 April 2005.

35 'About us', *HonestReporting*, viewed April 2006, <www.honestreporting.com/a/About_us.asp>.

36 'Moral absurdity downunder', *HonestReporting*, 24 August 2001, viewed April 2006, <www.honestreporting.com/articles/45884734/critiques/Moral_Absurdity_Downunder.asp>.

37 Media Study Group, 'The Age newspaper study', *Media Study Group*, 5 November 2003, viewed April 2006, <www.mediastudygroup.com>. The articles analysed were published between June and August 2003.

38 As quoted in Peter Kohn, 'Age Middle East coverage "overwhelmingly one-sided"', *AJN*, 28 November 2003.

39 Fairfax journalist Mark Forbes (currently Indonesian correspondent but then the *Age*'s reporter in Canberra) told me that the report's

authors had been to federal Labor MP Michael Danby's office and he had approved of their findings.

40 Telephone interview with the author, March 2004.

41 As quoted in Alan Sipress, 'Israeli media lays blame on "macho" Netanyahu', *Australian*, 28 September 1996.

42 Telephone interview with the author, 27 January 2005.

43 Don Wycliff, 'Secrecy's corrosive effect in terrorism case', *Chicago Tribune*, 2 February 2006.

44 Amira Hass, 'Using the Holocaust to ward off criticism', *Haaretz*, 16 March 2005.

45 Interview with the author, Boston, 8 February 2005.

46 Edward Said, 'Dignity and solidarity', *Al-Ahram*, 26 June – 2 July 2003.

47 Howard told his comments to Melbourne's 3AW radio on 11 November 2004.

48 As quoted in Peter Kerr, 'We expected more from Howard, say Palestinians', *SMH*, 22 November 2004.

49 'Palestinians criticise Howard funeral snub', *ABC News Online*, 11 November 2004, viewed April 2004, <www.abc.net.au/news/newsitems/200411/s1241542.htm>.

50 'Arafat's death', *West Australian*, 12 November 2004.

51 Greg Sheridan, 'Powerful symbol but weak leader', *Australian*, 12 November 2004.

52 Leanne Piggott, 'The two Yasser Arafats', *Australian*, 12 November 2004.

53 'Arafat's end offers a new start for peace', *Australian*, 13–14 November, 2004.

54 Ed O'Loughlin, 'Palestinians mourn passing of an era', *SMH*, 12 November 2004.

55 Sheridan, op. cit.

56 Ted Lapkin, 'Israel's right to exist at core of conflict', *Australian Financial Review*, 15 November 2004.

57 Life and peace after Arafat, *SMH*, 12 November 2004.

58 'Chance to get back on road to peace', *Age*, 13 November 2004.

59 Taimor Hazou, 'Quashing myths of Arafat legend', *Herald Sun*, 17 November 2004.

60 Andrew Bolt, 'A Palestinian sickness', *Herald Sun*, 19 November 2004.

61 Dennis Ross, *The missing peace*, Farrer, Straus, Giroux, 2004, p. 3.

62 Robert Malley & Hussein Agha, 'Camp David: the tragedy of errors', *New York Review of Books*, 9 August 2001.

63 As quoted in Tanya Reinhart, 'The peace that kills', 6 December 2000, viewed April 2006, <www.tau.ac.il/~reinhart/political/PeaceThatKills.html>.

64 Tanya Reinhart, *Israel/Palestine*, Allen & Unwin, 2003, p. 14.

65 Robert Malley, 'Fictions About the Failure at Camp David', *The New York Times*, 10 July 2001.

66 Reinhart, *Israel/Palestine*, op. cit., p. 44.

67 Reinhart, *Israel/Palestine*, op. cit., p. 35.

68 Ze'ev Schiff, 'Beilin's final agreement', *Haaretz*, 23 February 1996.

69 Reinhart, *Israel/Palestine*, op. cit., p. 35.

70 Robert Fisk, 'How to shut up your critics with a single word', *Independent*, 21 October 2002.

71 Robert Fisk, 'The erosion of free speech', *Independent*, 11 March 2006.

Conclusion: Where to next? (pages 235–53)

1 Edward Said, 'What has Israel done', *Al-Ahram*, 18–24 April 2002.

2 Telephone interview with the author, 27 January 2005. Dafner is head of Kadima in Melbourne (the Yiddish club, not the Israeli political party) and is an SBS broadcaster.

3 Alan Dershowitz, 'Spielberg's fictions', *Jerusalem Post*, 22 January 2006.

4 Charles Krauthammer, 'Munich, the travesty', *Washington Post*, 13 January 2006. Krauthammer also lashed out at George Clooney's *Syriana*, an 'anti-American film' and one that 'Osama bin Laden could not have scripted ... with more conviction'. Charles Krauthammer, 'Oscars for Osama', 3 March 2006.

5 'Spielberg: "fundamentalists" in Jewish community angry with me', *Haaretz*, 30 January 2006.

6 Tony Kushner, 'Defending "Munich" to my mishpocheh', *Los Angeles Times*, 22 January 2006.

7 Neal Ascherson, 'A master and myths of Munich', *Observer*, 15 January 2006.

8 Amiram Barkat, 'Just exactly who or what is anti-Semitic', *Haaretz*, 15 March 2006.

9 Professor Robert Wistrich, a Hebrew University historian, believes the complete opposite to Lerman, and claims that left-wing British academics are becoming 'obsessive' over their preoccupation with Israel and Jews. He calls this a wave of 'British anti-Semitism ... [that] is less new than it seems'. Daphna Berman, 'Historian: anti-Semitism is on the rise among leftist UK academics', *Haaretz*, 11 March 2006.

10 Daphna Baram, 'Who really sets Jews against Jews', *Jerusalem Post*, 1 March 2006.

11 Ruth Sinai, 'NII: one-quarter of Israelis live below poverty line', *Haaretz*, 24 January 2006.

12 Roee Nahmias, 'Study: half of Arab population poor', *Ynetnews*, 19 February 2006, viewed April 2006, <www.ynetnews.com/articles/0,7340,L-3218260,00.html>.

13 Gershom Gorenberg, 'Israel's tragedy foretold', *New York Times*, 10 March 2006. Documents from Israel's Ministry of Justice, presented to the High Court in March 2006, reveal that both Labor and Likud worked closely together with settlers' associations and land dealers in the early 1990s with the explicit purpose of obtaining West Bank land. Akiva Eldar, 'Documents reveal Labor–Likud plans for West Bank', *Haaretz*, 8 March 2006.

14 Interview with the author, Tel Aviv, 14 February 2005.

15 Tom Segev, *Elvis in Jerusalem*, Metropolitan Books, 2002, p. 7.

16 As quoted in ibid.

17 In the wake of the Hamas victory in early 2006, the UN released a report that criticised Israel's so-called 'security measures' since the election and their detrimental effect on the Palestinians. Jerusalem's withholding of customs and VAT funds owed to the Palestinian Authority was limiting the authority's ability to provide essential services. Akiva Eldar, 'UN: Israel's tightened security exacting heavy humanitarian toll', *Haaretz*, 28 February 2006.

18 Amira Hass, 'Israel cuts off eastern West Bank from rest of West Bank', *Haaretz*, 13 February 2006.

19 'After weeks of Israeli closure, Gaza Strip is completely out of bread', International Middle East Media Center, 16 March 2006.

20 Gideon Levy, 'As the Hamas team laughs', *Haaretz*, 19 February 2006.

21 Israeli human rights group B'Tselem released a report in January 2006 stating that one-third of the Jewish population did not know the route of the 'separation barrier'. Encouragingly, more than one-third supported changing the route of the wall so that it ran directly along the 'Green Line'. 'About one-third of the Israeli public does not know the fence's route', B'Tselem press release, 31 January 2006.

22 Aluf Benn, 'Improve the image', *Haaretz*, 16 February 2006. A few days later, Livni told a conference in Israel that the country's legitimacy was starting to wane internationally and could only be restored by establishing a Palestinian state. She feared world pressure to establish a bi-national state. It should be noted that she expressed no concern for the rights of the Palestinians or any interest in ending the occupation, merely observing that Israel needed to work on its PR. 'Conflict hurts Israel's legitimacy, minister says', *Reuters*, 23 January 2006.

23 A senior assistant to the Tel Aviv state prosecutor wrote to a Jerusalem court in February 2006 that Israeli human rights groups, such as B'Tselem, 'besmirch the state of Israel and its security forces, and harm its reputation around the world'. Furthermore, some groups do 'not devote themselves to "defending human rights" … but to defending the rights of Palestinians only'. In her view, wrote Israeli journalist Tom

Segev, 'either the Palestinians do not fall under the category of persons entitled to human rights, or they are not human beings'. Tom Segev, 'Patriotism sans borders', *Haaretz*, 10 March 2006.

24 After my appointment in late 2005 to the board of Macquarie University's Centre for Middle East and North African Studies, AIJAC complained—along with federal Labor MP Michael Danby—that my appointment was inappropriate because I had been critical of Israel and tended, like 'academic Middle East studies in Australia', to 'overwhelmingly blame all regional problems on Western imperialism and racism, real or imagined'. Tzvi Fleischer, 'Scribblings', *Review*, February 2006.

25 Colin Rubenstein, 'Friends down under', *Jerusalem Post*, 25 May 2003.

26 The US ambassador to Baghdad, Zalmay Khalilzad, said in March 2006 that the Iraq war had opened a 'Pandora's Box' of sectarian strife and had caused the rise of religious extremists who 'would make Taliban Afghanistan look like child's play'. Julian Borger & Ewen MacAskill, 'US envoy to Iraq: "We have opened the Pandora's box"', *Guardian*, 8 March 2006.

27 'Israel "may rue Saddam overthrow"', *BBC News online*, 9 February 2006, viewed April 2006, <news.bbc.co.uk/2/hi/middle_east/4696038.stm>. In the same speech, Yuval Diskin admitted that Israel's security services show more leniency towards Jewish terror suspects than towards Israeli Arab or Palestinian suspects.

28 Flynt Leverett, former senior director for Middle East affairs at the National Security Council, says that Iran offered in May 2003 to open talks with the USA on a variety of issues, including the nuclear matter. 'The Iranians acknowledged that WMD and support for terror were serious causes of concern for us, and they were willing to negotiate', he says. The Bush administration turned them down. Gregory Beals, 'US accused of blowing chance for Iran deal', *SMH*, 22 February 2006. Arguably the greatest beneficiary of the Iraq war has been Iran, with increased regional dominance and a central Shiite government in Baghdad closely aligned with the Islamic state. Megan K Stack & Borzou Daragahi, 'Iran was on edge, now it's on top', *Los Angeles Times*, 17 February 2006.

29 In February 2006, the head of the Iranian Jewish community bravely wrote to Ahmadinejad and protested against his statements on the Holocaust, saying the Iranian Jewish community was concerned. 'Iranian Jewish leader protests Ahmadinejad remarks', *Jerusalem Post*, 12 February 2006. The European Jewish Congress filed a complaint in the International Criminal Court (ICC) in the Hague in early 2006 against Ahmadinejad for incitement to genocide. Amiram Barkat,

'Jewish group wants Ahmedinejad tried in ICC', *Haaretz*, 19 February 2006. Iran's foreign minister claimed his President had been misunderstood. 'How is it possible to remove a country from the map?', asked Manouchehr Mottaki. 'He [Ahmadinejad] is talking about the regime. We do not legally recognise this regime.' 'Iranian FM denies wanting to "wipe Israel off the map"', *Reuters*, 21 February 2006.

30 Stefan Smith, 'Former Iranian president attacks Ahmadinejad over Holocaust', *AFP*, 1 March 2006.

31 'The gathering clouds in Tehran', *AJN*, 17 February 2006.

32 Larry Derfner, 'We can live with a nuclear Iran', *AJN*, 23 December 2005.

33 'Report: Israeli forces said searching for Iranian nuclear sites', *Haaretz*, 3 March 2006.

34 Nathan Guttman, 'AIPAC sends tough message to Iran', *Jerusalem Post*, 6 March 2006.

35 Yitzhak Benhorin, 'Israel warns of "evil axis" world war', *Ynetnews*, 21 February 2006, viewed April 2006, <www.ynetnews.com/articles/0,7340,L-3219516,00.html>.

36 Former IDF chief of staff Moshe Yaalon told a conservative US think tank in March 2006 that Israel had a military option against Iran and would work alongside US and European forces. He claimed such an attack would set Iran's nuclear program back by years, though Iran would likely retaliate against any strike with Shihab missiles, missiles from Lebanon and rocket attacks from the occupied territories. Yaalon claimed Iran 'would have nuclear technology within a year and a half, and will have the bomb within three to five years'. Yitzhak Benhorin, 'Yaalon denies revealing Israel military secrets', *Ynetnews*, 10 March 2006, viewed April 2006, <www.ynetnews.com/articles/0,7340,L-3226267,00.html>.

37 Meirion Jones, 'Britain's dirty secret', *New Statesman*, 13 March 2006.

38 Herb Keinon, 'J'lem mum on Straw's pledge to tackle Israel's nukes next', *Jerusalem Post*, 13 March 2006.

39 Isi Leibler, 'Let's rethink how we fight Jew hatred', *Jerusalem Post*, 24 October 2004.

40 Beth Duff-Brown, 'Groups condemn "Israeli apartheid week"', *Associated Press*, 31 January 2005.

41 The environment in which such intimidation occurs needs to be understood. Daniel Pipes and Martin Kramer of the pro-US think tank Middle East Forum run a website, Campus Watch, the primary aim of which is to criticise any academics who have shown 'hatred of Israel'. One professor was even placed on the list because he had supported Palestinian academic Edward Said. Pipes has said he wants students

to inform on professors who are guilty of 'campus anti-Semitism'. Reports of their 'unpatriotic bias' are published on the website, and students are encouraged to 'debunk' the abuse of academic freedom.

42 Juan Cole, 'The new McCarthyism', *Salon.com*, 23 April 2005, viewed April 2006, <dir.salon.com/story/opinion/feature/2005/04/22/mccarthy/index.html>.

43 The American House of Representatives has even toyed with introducing an advisory board to 'oversee' area studies at universities, enforcing a kind of academic bill of rights with eight guiding principles.

44 Alisa Solomon, 'When academic freedom is kicked out of class', *Forward*, 4 March 2005.

45 Matthew Thompson, 'A degree of racism', *SMH*, 28 August 2004.

46 Joshua Parker, 'The uni cycle', *Review*, August 2004.

47 Alan Dershowitz, 'Israel-hatred on campus', *Israel Insider*, 9 March 2004.

48 Natan Sharansky, 'Tour of US schools reveals why Zionism is flunking on campus', *Forward*, 24 October 2004.

49 Sara Taylor, 'Member of Israeli Parliament speaks on campus', *Daily Bruin Online*, 12 January 2004, viewed April 2006, <www.dailybruin.ucla.edu/news/articles.asp?id=31161>.

50 David Horowitz, 'The first terrorist people', *FrontPageMagazine.com*, 26 January 2006, viewed April 2006, <www.frontpagemag.com/Articles/ReadArticle.asp?ID=21056>.

51 Michael Tarazi, 'Why not two peoples, one state?', *New York Times*, 5 October 2004. Tarazi continues (and the paper received massive complaints from the Zionist lobby for simply printing the article): 'They [the Palestinians] are increasingly questioning the most commonly accepted solution to the Palestinian–Israeli conflict—"two states living side by side in peace and security", in the words of President George W Bush—and are being forced to consider a one-state solution'. Tarazi argues that 'most Israelis recoil at the thought of giving Palestinians equal rights, understandably fearing that a possible Palestinian majority will treat Jews the way Jews have treated Palestinians'. He wants a state 'in which citizens of all faiths and ethnicities live together as equals'. Besides, he says, 'it is simply a recognition that Israel and the occupied Palestinian territories already function as a single state. They share the same aquifers, the same highway network, the same electricity grid and the same international borders'. 'The only question', he concludes, 'is how long it will take, and how much all sides will have to suffer, before Israeli Jews can view Palestinian Christians and Muslims not as demographic threats but as fellow citizens'.

52 Amiram Barkat, 'Haaretz probe: Jews no long a majority in pre-pullout Israel', *Haaretz*, 11 June 2005.

53 Khalid Amayreh, 'Palestinians say peace with Israel is no longer within the realm of possibility', *Aljazeera*, 7 August 2005.

54 Tony Judt, 'Israel: the alternative', *New York Review of Books*, 23 October 2003.

55 Israeli journalist Ari Shavit has spent years interviewing and observing Sharon, and soon after his incapacitation concluded that the Israeli leader 'felt a profound uncertainty about the Jews' ability to maintain sovereignty, and to hold on to the land and to preserve it. He spoke about the Arabs with great envy—they, he said, knew much better how to keep their honour and their land'. Ari Shavit, 'The General', *New Yorker*, 23 January & 30 January, 2006.

56 Polling data suggest that the large support for Hamas was partly the result of dissatisfaction with the ruling Fatah party and the failure of the 'peace process' with Israel. A few days after the Hamas win, a poll in a Palestinian Authority newspaper stated that three-quarters of people who voted for Hamas opposed calls for the destruction of the Jewish state and 84 per cent supported a peace deal with Israel. '75% of Hamas voters oppose destruction of Israel', *Jerusalem Post*, 31 January 2006.

57 Donald Macintyre, 'Olmert to redraw Israel's borders "within four years"', *Independent*, 10 March 2006.

58 Days after the Hamas victory, Likud Chairman Binyamin Netanyahu compared it to the rise of the Nazis in Germany in the 1930s. Lilach Weissman, *Haaretz*, 29 January 2006. Similarly outlandish statements were repeated by many leading Israeli politicians in the run-up to the 28 March election.

59 Harvey Morris, 'US tells moderates to stay out of Hamas Cabinet', *Financial Times*, 10 March 2006.

60 The *New York Times* reported in February 2006 that the USA and Israel 'are discussing ways to destabilise the Palestinian government so that newly elected Hamas officials will fail and elections will be called again'. Steven Erlanger, 'US and Israel are said to talk of Hamas ouster', *New York Times*, 13 February 2006.

61 Prominent US Zionist lobbyists have campaigned strongly against Hamas, claiming the party poses an existential threat to Israel. It is accepted, however, that negotiations in some form between the parties are all but inevitable. Ori Nir, 'Clash seen over hard line on Islamists', *Forward*, 3 March 2006. Australian Minister for Foreign Affairs Alexander Downer has at least supported the continuation of financial support to the Palestinian people. Alexander Downer, 'The clear lesson for Hamas: with electoral victory comes responsibility', *SMH*, 2 March 2006.

62 Khalid Mish'al, 'We will not sell out people or principles for foreign aid', *Guardian*, 31 January 2006.

63 Ilan Pappe, 'To boldly go', *Guardian*, 20 April 2005.

64 Tanya Reinhart, 'Why us?', *Yediot Aharonot*, 4 May 2005.

65 Isi Leibler, 'Professors of hate', *Jerusalem Post*, 5 May 2005.

66 'A state of denial: an interview with Ilan Pappe', *News from Nowhere*, September 2002.

67 Email interview with author, 30 March 2005.

68 'Britain's nutty professors', *AJN*, 3 June 2005.

69 Ruth Wajnryb, 'The pariah state', *AJN*, 6 May 2005.

70 Some of the United Kingdom's leading architects announced in February 2006 that they were considering an economic boycott of Israel's construction industry in a protest against the occupation and security wall. Oliver Duff, Rob Sharp & Eric Silver, 'Architects threaten to boycott Israel over "apartheid" barrier', *Independent*, 10 February 2006. Only a few weeks later, one of those involved, leading British architect Richard Rogers, backtracked from his initial brave stance. He had been commissioned to redevelop some areas in New York State, and a handful of local politicians complained about his pro-Palestinian stance, threatening to withdraw the contract. Within a short time, Rogers issued a statement that praised Israel's wall and said that the Middle East conflict is between 'a country that is a terrorist state and a country that's a democratic state. I'm all for the democratic state'. So much for principles. Clearly even expressing sympathy for the Palestinian cause can be detrimental to one's career. 'An American inquisition', *Nation*, 3 April 2006.

71 'World Council of Churches gives nod to Israeli divestment proposal', Episcopal News Service, 21 February 2005.

72 Amos Harel, 'Fearing arrest, IDF officer cancels studies in UK', *Haaretz*, 26 February 2006.

73 Amiram Barkat, 'Alan Dershowitz volunteers to defend IDF officers abroad', *Haaretz*, 8 March 2006.

74 Amos Harel, 'Top IDF brass outraged by officer's UK travel ban', *Haaretz*, 3 March 2006.

75 Amos Harel, 'IDF officers: we have less freedom than terrorists', *Haaretz*, 3 March 2006.

76 Andrew Friedman, 'Lawsuits PR opportunity for Israel', *Ynenewst*, 27 February 2006, viewed April 2006, <www.ynetnews.com/articles/0,7340,L-3221542,00.html>.

77 'Renounce terror: PM urges Hamas', *Reuters*, 27 January 2006.

78 'Hamas win disastrous: Beazley', *Herald Sun*, 27 January 2006.

79 'The Hamas dilemma', *SMH*, 6 March 2006.

80 Ed O'Loughlin, 'Under the gun in Gaza', *SMH*, 4 February 2006.

81 Rami Khouri, 'On democracy, Arabs mistrust the American messenger', *Daily Star*, 4 February 2006.

82 Manne was voted Australia's leading public intellectual in a 2005 *SMH* survey. Michael Visontay, 'Australia's top 100 public intellectuals', *SMH*, 12 March 2005.

83 Robert Manne, *Left, right, left*, Black Inc., 2005. Dr Clinton Fernandes, historian and author of *Reluctant saviour*, Scribe, 2004—a compelling look at Australia's belated 'liberation' of East Timor—wrote in *Overland* in September 2005 that during his years as editor of conservative magazine *Quadrant*, Manne was a constant apologist for the Indonesian invasion. He practically ignored the genocide in Timor— the worst slaughter relative to population since the Holocaust—and ignored the fact that it could have been stopped by withdrawing Western support to the Indonesian military. Instead, he continues, 'many self-described public intellectuals in Australia and the US said little about it, preferring instead to denounce Pol Pot in Cambodia, where they had no prospect of terminating the atrocities of the Khmer Rouge'. Fernandes convincingly argues that Manne refused to struggle against 'crimes in which his government was complicit' and listed any number of articles in *Quadrant* that defended the Indonesian occupation. His collection of political essays from 1977 to 2005, *Left right left*, essentially ignores East Timor.

84 Robert Manne, 'When the tug of Jewish loyalty meets the brutality of Israel', *SMH*, 6 December 2004. Applied linguist Ruth Wajnryb responds in the *AJN* by claiming that Manne has a 'base case of Chomskyitis' and questions his belief that 'Israel has, as a matter of policy, pursued a permanent occupation role'. The occupation is excusable, she argues, because of 'Israel's long-time commitment to a two-state solution'. Ruth Wajnryb, 'Robert Manne's bad case of Chomskyitis', *AJN*, 14 January 2005.

85 Telephone interview with the author, 6 April 2005.

86 Telephone interview with the author, 27 January 2005.

87 Telephone interview with the author, 28 November 2003.

88 Ami Eden, 'Playing the Holocaust card', *New York Times*, 29 January 2005.

89 A study by a geographer at the University of New South Wales found that more than one in three Australians had no knowledge about Islam. Debra Jopson, 'Ignorance rules our knowledge of Islam', *SMH*, 20 March 2006. Peter Manning, former head of ABC news, now Adjunct Professor of Journalism at University of Technology Sydney, says that the Australian media are 'tainted by racism' towards Arab people and portray them as 'tricky, sleazy, sexual and untrustworthy'. Ian Munro, 'Portrayal of Muslims "tainted by racism"', *Age*, 18 March 2006.

90 Telephone interview with the author, 1 February 2005.

91 Afif Safieh, 'I never compare the Palestinian Nakba to the Holocaust', *Independent*, 8 August 2005.

92 Interview with the author, Sydney, 25 May 2005.

Epilogue: The legacy of the 2006 elections (pages 254–9)

1 Abraham Rabinovich, 'A "wily apparatchik" rides Sharon's trust to victory', *Australian*, 31 March 2006.

2 Gideon Levy wrote in *Haaretz* that Sharon's Kadima Party, led by Ehud Olmert, had convinced young people that 'indifference' was a valid political position. 'Nothing can get adults to take to the streets anymore', Levy wrote, 'neither the cruelty of the occupation nor the injustices of poverty'. Gideon Levy, 'Kadima's children', 5 March 2006.

3 One reason for Kadima's relative success was articulated by a young Israeli: 'Until the disengagement from Gaza', said Dalit Nemirovsky,

> I could not forgive Ariel Sharon for his past mistakes—for Sabra and Chatila, for his refusal to negotiate with the Palestinians, for his belief in a Greater Israel. But he showed that he was strong enough to change his mind. He recognised that he was wrong and did something to correct his mistakes. He earned my respect. We don't belong there [the West Bank] and we should get out.

Lisa Goldman, 'Sharon earned my respect', *Guardian*, 23 March 2006.

4 Lieberman receives strong support from the roughly one million Russian speakers in Israel; he is virulently anti-Arab and believes in the redrawing of Israel's borders to exclude its Arab citizens. Conal Urquhart, 'Anti-Arab hardliners find favour with Israel's immigrants', *Guardian*, 29 March 2006. Soon after the election, an Arab member of the Knesset accused Lieberman of being anti-Semitic: '[He] incites against citizens of the state because they are Arabs, because of the colour of their skin. He spews venom. If anyone else would say against the Jews what Lieberman says, he would be branded an antisemite'. Ilan Marciano, 'Arab MK: Lieberman anti-Semitic', *Ynetnews*, 24 April 2006, viewed April 2006, <www.ynetnews.com/articles/0,7340,L-3243167,00.html>.

5 Gideon Levy, 'One racist nation', *Haaretz*, 26 March 2006.

6 Many Israelis saw the election differently, believing that social issues and growing poverty were central themes, the usual strengths of the Labor Party. Allyn Fisher-Ilan, 'Israeli vote campaign highlights growing poverty', *Reuters*, 22 March 2006. Israel's defence burden is three times higher than the Western average, and this is directly influencing

the growing gap between rich and poor. Hadas Manor, 'Israel's defense burden 3 times higher than Western average', *Globes*, 30 March 2006.

7 *Haaretz* journalist Amira Hass writes that Israel's occupation is in fact deepening:

> Gazan natives are not permitted to be in the West Bank. Palestinians, including residents of Jericho, are not permitted to be in the Jordan Valley (except for those with official addresses there). It is prohibited to drive in a private car through the Abu Dis checkpoint (which divides the northern and southern parts of the West Bank). It is forbidden to enter Nablus by car. It is forbidden for Palestinians residing in East Jerusalem to enter West Bank cities (except for Ramallah). Citizens of Arab states married to Palestinians are prohibited from entering the West Bank.

Amira Hass, 'The uber-wardens', *Haaretz*, 12 April 2006.

8 Gideon Levy, 'One racist nation', *Haaretz*, 26 March 2006.

9 'A small step towards peace', *Guardian*, 28 March 2006.

10 Mazal Mualem & Aluf Benn, 'Kamida says convergence will begin before November 2008', *Haaretz*, 9 April 2006. Olmert told the *Wall Street Journal* in April 2006 that his 'convergence' plan—to withdraw 70 000 settlers from the West Bank—would cost up to US$10 billion and would take 18 months. He signalled the need for US financial assistance. Yitzhak Benhorin, 'Olmert: convergence to cost USD10 billion', *Ynetnews*, 12 April 2006, viewed April 2006, <www.ynetnews.com/articles/0,7340,L-3239420,00.html>. *Haaretz* commentator Aluf Benn warned Israel to stop always asking the USA for financial assistance and to start asking, 'what the Americans get out of it'. Aluf Benn, 'Enough handouts', *Haaretz*, 14 April 2006.

11 Romesh Ratnesar, 'Israel should not be at the forefront of a war against Iran', *Time*, 9 April 2006.

12 Roee Nahmias, 'Most Israelis, Palestinians want peace talks', *Ynetnews*, 26 March 2006, viewed April 2006, <www.ynetnews.com/articles/0,7340,L-3202488,00.html>.

13 'Envoy: US supports road map but understands unilateral move', *Haaretz*, 12 April 2006.

14 The US and European Union cut aid to the Palestinian government in early 2006, but Russia continued to provide aid. 'Report: Russia to give PA aid', *Associated Press*, 18 April 2006.

15 'Haniyeh: Palestinians won't be cowed', *Associated Press*, 14 April 2006.

16 *Haaretz* reported that Bush told Olmert he believed in Sharon's 'vision' and hoped the new Israeli Prime Minister would follow in his foot

steps. Aluf Benn, 'Bush congratulates Olmert, invites him to White House', *Haaretz*, 29 March 2006.

17 Ratnesar, op. cit.

18 'Rice: US might back unilateral withdrawal from the West Bank', *Associated Press*, 30 March 2006.

19 As quoted in 'Envoy: US supports road map but understands unilateral move', *Haaretz*, 12 April 2006.

20 Gedaliah Afterman, 'Howard hints at Israel trip', *AJN*, 7 April 2006.

21 Zionist organisations lined up to praise Olmert. AIJAC's Mark Leibler wrote to the Israeli Prime Minister expressing his 'full confidence' that he would be 'a worthy successor to Ariel Sharon'. 'Community leaders congratulate Olmert', *AJN*, 7 April 2006.

22 'Olmert's achievements', *Times*, 29 March 2006.

23 'Israel's retreat from Judea', *SMH*, 30 March 2006.

24 'Israel's odd election', *Australian*, 28 March 2006.

25 'Olmert's mandate', *AJN*, 31 March 2006.

26 Colin Rubenstein, '"Convergence" in Israel', *Review*, April 2006.

27 Ali Waked, 'Hamas blames Israel for bombing', *Ynetnews*, 18 April 2006, viewed April 2006, <www.ynetnews.com/articles/0,7340,L-3241209,00.html>.

28 After the suicide attack, the *SMH* editorialised that Hamas was 'failing the test' of responsible government and deserved financial isolation. 'Hamas failing the test', *SMH*, 19 April 2006. The *New York Times* agreed, arguing that 'Hamas's support for terrorism encourages Mr Olmert's strategy of unilateral separation from the Palestinian people'. 'The face of Hamas', *New York Times*, 19 April 2006.

29 Robert Fisk, 'Another brick in the wall', *Independent*, 3 April 2006.

30 'Diet instead of wisdom', *Haaretz*, 20 March 2006.

31 Danny Rubenstein, 'On the way down', *Haaretz*, 10 April 2006.

32 Gideon Levy commented that in the months since the Gaza withdrawal, Israel had deliberately maintained a stranglehold over the Palestinians living there: 'They live in prison. Their daily routine includes humiliation that is no less terrible than malnutrition'. Gideon Levy, 'There is no hunger in Gaza', *Haaretz*, 9 April 2006.

33 Israel's largest bank, Bank Hapoalim, severed ties with the Palestinians in early April 2006, further weakening the Hamas government. Harvey Morris, 'Israel's largest bank severs ties with Palestine', *Financial Times*, 5 April 2006.

34 Ismail Haniyeh, 'A just peace or no peace', *Guardian*, 31 March 2006.

35 Chris McGreal, 'Abbas: our sons will fight for a just deal', *Guardian*, 8 April 2006.

36 Conal Urquhart, 'Hamas in call to end suicide bombings', *Observer*, 9 April 2006. After a suicide bombing in Tel Aviv in mid-April 2006, carried out by Islamic Jihad, the Israeli government blamed Hamas. *Haaretz* commentator Ze'ev Schiff recommended a 'forceful' response in Gaza and the West Bank. Ze'ev Schiff, 'Sharp blow calls for sharp response', *Haaretz*, 19 April 2006.

37 Ze'ev Schiff, 'Hamas government offers Israel "quiet for quiet"', *Haaretz*, 7 April 2006.

38 'We'll study any Israeli talks offer: Hamas PM', *AFP*, 5 April 2006.

39 The Hamas culture minister told the *Guardian* that he was against belly-dancing in public, liked the film *Titanic*, wanted to ban casinos and alcohol, but doesn't 'want our people to become like the Taliban'. Chris McGreal, 'Bellydancing out, cinema in, says Hamas', *Guardian*, 6 April 2006.

40 Itamar Eichner, 'PA minister: no room for Israel on land', *Ynetnews*, 3 April 2006, viewed April 2006, <www.ynetnews.com/articles/ 0,7340,L-3235497,00.html>.

41 A day after being sworn in as a member of the Palestinian Cabinet, Zahar claimed the USA was committing 'big crimes' against Islamic and Arab countries. The statement earned a rebuke from US ambassador to the UN John Bolton, who said that 'casual slander is an inauspicious way to begin'. 'US Ambassador Bolton: Palestinian foreign minister off to bad start', *Associated Press*, 31 March 2006.

42 Hamas's mixed messages continued months after its electoral win when its political leader Khaled Mashaal told a conference in Tehran that Palestinians would never recognise Israel. Roee Nahmias, 'Mashaal: we'll never recognise Israel', *Ynetnews*, 15 April 2006. Arab states urged Hamas to recognise Israel within pre-1967 borders. 'Arab states advise Hamas to adopt Arab peace initiative', *Reuters*, 16 April 2006.

43 Amira Hass, 'Convergence to a border of convenience', *Haaretz*, 5 April 2006.

44 Major General Yitzhak 'Haki' Harel, a senior member of the IDF General Staff, revealed the attitude of the Israeli establishment towards the Palestinians in an interview with the *Jerusalem Post* in April 2006. He warned that Israel might launch a ground invasion of Gaza, told Palestinians living there to 'work in Egypt and live off the Arab countries', and said Israel was on the verge of another conflict with the Palestinians. Yaakov Katz, 'S'ecurity and defence: "We are at war"', *Jerusalem Post*, 13 April 2006.

45 'Jon Elmer interviews Hanan Ashrawi', *Progressive*, April 2006.

46 Afterman, op. cit.

ABBREVIATIONS

ABA	Australian Broadcasting Authority
ABC	Australian Broadcasting Corporation
ADC	Anti-Defamation Commission
ADL	Anti-Defamation League (US)
ADT	Australian Dance Theatre
AEI	American Enterprise Institute
AIJAC	Australia/Israel and Jewish Affairs Council
AIPAC	American Israel Public Affairs Committee
AIR	*Australia/Israel Review*
AJDS	Australian Jewish Democratic Society
AJN	*Australian Jewish News*
ALP	Australian Labor Party
AUJS	Australasian Union of Jewish Students
AUS	Australian Union of Students
AUT	Association of University Teachers (UK)
CAMERA	Committee for Accuracy in Middle East Reporting in America
CE	Common Era
CIA	Central Intelligence Agency (US)
CNN	Cable News Network
CRIF	Conseil Représentatif des Institutions Juives de France
ECAJ	Executive Council of Australian Jewry
EU	European Union
EUMC	European Union Monitoring Center
FAIR	Fairness and Accuracy in Reporting
FOI	Freedom of information
ICC	International Criminal Court
IDF	Israeli Defense Force
IPA	Institute of Public Affairs
IRA	Irish Republican Army
JAO	Jews Against the Occupation
JINSA	Jewish Institute for National Security Affairs (US)
NPR	National Public Radio (US)
NSW JBD	New South Wales Jewish Board of Deputies
PLO	Palestinian Liberation Organisation
PNAC	Project for the New American Century
SBS	Special Broadcasting Service
SMH	*Sydney Morning Herald*

TIPH	Temporary International Presence in Hebron
UN	United Nations
USA	United States of America
WCC	World Council of Churches
WMDs	Weapons of mass destruction
ZFA	Zionist Federation of Australia

GLOSSARY OF TERMS

Balfour Declaration On 2 November 1917, the British Foreign Secretary promised the establishment of a Jewish state in the land of Palestine that would not negatively affect the indigenous population.

Fatah The political wing of the PLO.

Goy/goyim Non-Jews.

Green Line The 1967 borders between Israel and the land it occupied in the 1967 war (the Golan Heights, Gaza Strip and West Bank).

Hamas (Arabic acronym for Movement of the Islamic Resistance) Militant Islamic group formed in 1988 during the first intifada, initially with Israeli assistance, as an attempted buffer against the PLO. The group has been engaged in a terror campaign against Israel, as well as providing social services to the Palestinian people. The group won power in the January 2006 Palestinian election.

Hizbollah (Arabic for 'Party of God') This Shiite militant group, strongly supported by Iran and Syria, was founded in 1988 in resistance to Israel.

Intifada (Arabic for 'shaking off') The Palestinian uprising against the Israeli occupation in 1987 and 2000.

Irgun Founded in 1937 by Jews determined to establish a Jewish state in Palestine, this group conducted terrorist actions against the British, including the infamous 1946 King David Hotel bombing and attacks against Palestinians. Future Israeli Prime Minister Menachem Begin became its leader in 1941.

Islamic Jihad Militant Islamic organisation dedicated to violent resistance to the Israeli occupation. The group has used suicide bombers in this struggle and continues to do so.

Knesset (Hebrew for 'assembly') The Israeli parliament.

Labor The founding 'social-democratic' political party of Israel, which was led by David Ben-Gurion.

Likud Founded in 1973, this parliamentary party represents right-wing elements in Israel. It first won power in 1977 (with Menachem Begin as leader).

Mossad (Hebrew for 'institute') The Israeli secret service.

Muqata Yasser Arafat's presidential compound in Ramallah.

Nakba Phrase used by Palestinians to describe the 1948 war and the loss and expulsion of their people.

Palestinian Authority The official title of the legislative body that runs Palestinian affairs in the occupied territories. Its President was Yasser Arafat until his death in 2004. Mahmoud Abbas is his successor.

Palestinian Liberation Organisation (PLO) Founded in 1964 as a body designed to represent Palestinians, it was led by Yasser Arafat and become dedicated to establishing Palestinian independence and statehood.

Refusniks (also known as *Yesh Gvul*) Israeli soldiers who refused to serve in the 1982 Lebanon war. The movement now includes Israeli soldiers who refuse to serve in the occupied territories.

Shoah The Jewish Holocaust.

Stern Gang Founded in 1939, this Zionist terror group was dedicated to the establishment of a Jewish homeland in Palestine.

GLOSSARY OF NAMES

Mahmoud Abbas (Abu Mazin) A member of Fatah, he served as the Palestinian Prime Minister in March–October 2003 and was elected President of the Palestinian Authority in January 2005.

Yasser Arafat Founder of the Fatah movement, leader of the PLO until his death in 2004 and winner of the Nobel Peace Prize in 1994.

Hanan Ashrawi A leading Palestinian, Christian politician, she served in Yasser Arafat's cabinet, though resigned over corruption, and resides on the Palestinian Legislative Council. She was a player in the 1990s peace talks with Israel.

Ehud Barak Israeli Prime Minister 1999–2001, former Mossad operative and key participant in the 2000 Camp David talks.

Menachem Begin First Likud Israeli Prime Minister, 1977–83, and a former head of the Zionist terror group the Irgun.

David Ben-Gurion Founder of the state of Israel and Prime Minister in 1948–53 and 1955–63.

George W Bush The US President since 2001, he called Ariel Sharon a 'man of peace' in 2002 and supported the annexation of vast areas in the West Bank for Jewish homes.

George Bush Senior US President 1989–93, he 'liberated' Kuwait from Iraq in 1991.

Jimmy Carter US President 1977–81, he helped secure the Camp David peace accord between Egypt and Israel in 1978.

Bill Clinton US President 1993–2001, he was involved in the 1993 Oslo Peace Accords and the 2000 Camp David talks.

Moshe Dayan Israeli Minister of Defense during the 1967 war, Foreign Minister in 1977–79 and a significant participant in the peace deal between Egypt and Israel.

Theodore Herzl Austrian journalist who founded the Zionist movement at the end of the nineteenth century.

Binyamin Netanyahu Israeli Prime Minister 1996–99, former ambassador to the United Nations and Finance Minister during the Sharon years.

Ehud Olmert Israeli Prime Minister since January 2006, leader of the Kadima Party and former mayor of Jerusalem.

Shimon Peres Acting Prime Minister after the 1995 assassination of Yitzhak Rabin, he was awarded the 1994 Nobel Peace Prize for his role in the Oslo Accords.

Yitzhak Rabin Israeli Prime Minister 1974–77 and 1992–95, before being assassinated in 1995 by a Jewish extremist because of his peace initiatives with the Palestinians.

Yitzhak Shamir Israeli Prime Minister 1983–84 and 1986–92, and member of the Zionist terror group Irgun.

Ariel Sharon Israeli Prime Minister 2001–05, former Israeli commando, founder of Likud and Minister of Agriculture, Housing and Defence until he was found to be indirectly responsible for the 1982 Sabra and Shatilla massacres in Beirut. He is also known as the grandfather of the settler movement.

BIBLIOGRAPHY

Books

The following books provided essential information during the writing of this book and are useful for further reading on the Israel–Palestine conflict:

Ali, Tariq, *The clash of fundamentalisms*, Verso, 2003.

Ali, Tariq & David Barsamian, *Speaking of empire and resistance*, Scribe, 2005.

Amiry, Suad, *Sharon and my mother-in-law*, Granta, 2005.

Arendt, Hannah, *Eichmann in Jerusalem*, Penguin, 1992.

Baram, Daphna, *Disenchantment: the Guardian and Israel*, Guardian Books, 2004.

Barghouti, Mourid, *I saw Ramallah*, Bloomsbury, 2004.

Ben-Ami, Shlomo, *Scars of war, wounds of peace*, Oxford University Press, 2006.

Ben-Menashe, Ari, *Profits of war*, Sheridan Square Press, 1992.

Bowen, Jeremy, *Six Days*, Pocket Books, 2003.

Carey, Roane & Jonathan Shainin (eds), *The other Israel*, The New Press, 2002.

Chomsky, Noam, *The fateful triangle*, Pluto Press, 1999.

Chomsky, Noam, *Middle East illusions*, Rowman & Littlefield, 2004.

Clinton, Bill, *My life*, Hutchinson, 2004.

Cockburn, Alexander & Jeffrey St Clair (eds), *The politics of anti-Semitism*, AK Press, 2003.

Cook, Catherine, Adam Hanieh & Adah Kay, *Stolen youth*, Pluto Press, 2004.

Cooley, John K, *An alliance against Babylon*, Pluto Press, 2005.

Curtis, Mark, *Web of deceit*, Vintage, 2003.

Dor, Daniel, *The suppression of guilt*, Pluto Press, 2005.

Dwork, Deborah & Robert Jan van Pelt, *Holocaust: a history*, John Murray Publishers, 2002.

Ellis, Mark H, *Out of the ashes*, Pluto Press, 2002.

Elon, Amos, *A blood-dimmed tide*, Penguin, 2000.

Finkelstein, Norman G, *Beyond chutzpah*, University of California Press, 2005.

Finkelstein, Norman G, *Image and reality of the Israel–Palestine conflict*, Verso, 2001.

Finkelstein, Norman G, *The Holocaust industry*, Verso, 2001.

Fisk, Robert, *The great war for civilisation*, 4th Estate, 2005.

Fisk, Robert, *Pity the nation*, Oxford University Press, 2001.

Friedlander, Saul, *Nazi Germany and the Jews*, Weidenfeld & Nicolson, 1997.

Gazit, Shlomo, *Trapped fools*, Frank Cass, 2003.

Hass, Amira, *Drinking the sea at Gaza*, Owl Books, 1999.

Hass, Amira, *Reporting from Ramallah*, Semiotext(e), 2003.

Hersh, Seymour, *The Samson option*, Faber & Faber, 1991.

Hirst, David, *The gun and the olive branch*, Nation Books, 2003.

Kidron, Peretz (ed.), *Refusenik!* Zed Books, 2004.

Kimmerling, Baruch, *Politicide*, Verso, 2003.

Kingston, Margo, *Not happy, John!*, Penguin, 2004.

Kushner, Tony & Alisa Solomon (eds), *Wrestling with Zion*, Grove Press, 2003.

Leith, Denise, *Bearing witness*, Random House, 2004.

Levey, Geoffrey Brahm & Philip Mendes (eds), *Jews and Australian politics*, Sussex Academic Press, 2004.

Lindermann, Albert S, *Esau's tears*, Cambridge University Press, 2000.

McGeough, Paul, *Manhattan to Baghdad*, Allen & Unwin, 2003.

Nimni, Ephraim (ed.), *The challenge of post-Zionism*, Zed Books, 2003.

Novick, Peter, *The holocaust in American life*, Houghton Mifflin, 2000.

Pappe, Ilan, *A history of modern Palestine*, Cambridge University Press, 2004.

Philo, Greg & Mike Berry, *Bad news from Israel*, Pluto Press, 2004.

Pilger, John, *Tell me no lies*, Jonathan Cape, 2004.

Reich, Chanan, *Australia and Israel: an ambiguous relationship*, Melbourne University Press, 2002.

Reinhart, Tanya, *Israel/Palestine*, Allen & Unwin, 2002.

Rodgers, Peter, *Herzl's nightmare*, Scribe, 2004.

Rose, Jacqueline, *The question of Zion*, Melbourne University Press, 2005.

Rutland, Suzanne D, *The Jews in Australia*, Cambridge University Press, 2005.

Said, Edward, *From Oslo to Iraq and the roadmap*, Bloomsbury, 2004.

Said, Edward, *Power, politics and culture*, Bloomsbury, 2004.

Said, Edward & Christopher Hitchens (eds), *Blaming the victims*, Verso, 2001.

Segev, Tom, *Elvis in Jerusalem*, Metropolitan Books, 2002.

Shlaim, Avi, *The iron wall*, Penguin, 2001.

Terry, Janice J, *US foreign policy in the Middle East*, Pluto Press, 2005.

Wistrich, Robert S, *Hitler and the Holocaust*, Modern Library Edition, 2001.

Zertal, Idith, *Israel's Holocaust and the politics of nationhood*, Cambridge University Press, 2005.

Websites

The following websites provide up-to-date information on the Israel–Palestine conflict:

electronicintifada.net/new.shtml

Information on Israel's occupation of the Palestinian territories.

english.aljazeera.net/HomePage

Middle East news from an Arabic perspective.

www.bitterlemons.org/

Weekly newsletter discussing the major issues related to Israel–Palestine.

www.breakingthesilence.org.il/index_en.asp

    Israeli soldiers tell stories of their activities in the occupied territories.

www.btselem.org/English/index.asp

    Leading Israeli human rights group.

www.counterpunch.com/

    Leading US magazine, publishing alternative views of the conflict.

www.haaretz.com/

    Liberal Israeli daily.

www.icahd.org/eng/

    Israeli Committee Against House Demolitions.

www.jao.org.au/

    Sydney-based Jews Against the Occupation.

www.jpost.com/

    Conservative Israeli daily.

www.miftah.org/

    Hanan Ashrawi–founded Palestinian human rights group.

www.normanfinkelstein.com/

    Dissenting US historian.

www.palsolidarity.org/main/

    Pro-Palestinian International Solidarity Movement.

www.rhr.israel.net/

    Rabbis for Human Rights.

www.robert-fisk.com/

    Unofficial site of the *Independent*'s Middle East correspondent.

www.stoptorture.org.il/eng/

    The Public Committee against Torture in Israel.

www.tikkun.org/

    Progressive US Jewish group.

www.ynetnews.com

    Israeli daily *Yediot Ahronot*.

www.zmag.org/weluser.htm

    Leading US magazine, featuring alternative views of the conflict.

zope.gush-shalom.org/home/en

    Leading Israeli peace group.

INDEX

Abbas, Mahmoud, 95
Abbott, Tony, 10–11
Abington, Edward, 129
Absentee Property Law (1950), 96
Abu-Dis, 232
Abu Ghraib prison, 204
Abu-Harthieh, Mohammed, 43
Academic Friends of Israel, 153
Adams, Phillip, 117, 191
Age, 223, 230
Agha, Hussein, 231
Ahmadinejad, Mahmoud, 106, 136, 239
Albrechtsen, Janet, 207
Alhadeff, Vic, 20
al-Husseini, Haj Amin, 76
Ali, Ameer, 167
Alibhai-Brown, Yasmin, 155
Almog, Doron, 246–7
Alston, Richard, 197
American Civil Liberties Union, 143
American Enterprise Institute (AEI), 97
American Israel Public Affairs
    Committee (AIPAC), 124, 134–8
    annual conference (2005), 125
    funding of, 126–7
    influence of, 124–5
    Iran scandal, 136–8
    lobbing of members of US
      Congress, 126–7
    workshops for students, 241
Annan, Kofi, 191, 214
Anti-Defamation Commission (ADC),
    198–9
Anti-Defamation League (ADL), 108
antisemitism, 71
    and anti-Zionism, 114, 145–6, 236
    in Australia, 117–18, 242
    contemporary cases, 106–10
    in Europe, 101–2, 106–7
    far-right perpetrators, 107
    in France, 110–13
    in Germany, 102–3
    history of, 99–103
    legitimate criticism conflated with,
      119
    by or against Muslims, 105–6
    opinions of Jewish intellectuals and
      leaders, 108
    personal experiences of, 109
    in postwar period, 103–6
    Protocols of the Elders of Zion, 102
    publication suppressed, 140
    shaming the critics, 118–19

'3D' test, 109
    in UK, 104, 106
    'vague motivations', 107
anti-war movement, 97–9
anti-Zionism, 24, 28–9, 54, 171, 236;
    Zionism
apartheid in South Africa, 60
Arab-American Institute, 224
Arab Liberation Army, 77
Arab states, support from Soviet Union,
    86
Arabs
    dislike of, 29
    negative image of, 252
    portrayal in media, 251–2
    racist discussions of, 143
Arafat, Yasser, 7–8, 62, 228
    Camp David summit, 92–3, 230–1
    death of, 40, 95, 128, 227–30, 233
    liaison with US government, 86
    Oslo Accords, 90, 231
    PLO, 83
    on suicide bombing, 91
Armitage, Richard, 133
Arnold Bloch Leibler, 162, 163
Ashrawi, Hanan
    defence of Palestinian cause, 7
    on Israel–Palestine solution, 258–9
    Sydney Peace Prize, 3–22, 35–6
    views on death of Arafat, 7
    views on Israeli occupation of
      territories, 6–7
Asper, Izzy, 200
Association of University Teachers (AUT,
    British), 245–6
Atkins, Dennis, 220
Atlantic Monthly, 143
Australasian Union of Jewish Students
    (AUJS), 242
Australia
    antisemitism in, 117–18
    attacks on Jews, 117
    close identification with Israel, 157,
      256
    early Jewish settlement, 158
    financial support for Jewish causes,
      162
    Jewish students in, 242
    Muslim population, 160
    political environment in, 156
    post-war Jewish immigration, 158
    pro-Israeli stance in UN, 166–7
    support for Palestine or Israel, 160
    Zionist lobby in, 5, 160–2, 157–83
Australia–Israel Parliamentary
    Friendship Group, 176